I0124217

THE
FORBIDDEN
KNOWLEDGE OF
ENOCH

Second Edition

THE
FORBIDDEN
KNOWLEDGE OF
ENOCH

Second Edition

R.J. VON-BRUENING

R.J. VON-BRUENING PUBLISHING

THE FORBIDDEN KNOWLEDGE OF ENOCH - Second Edition
Copyright © 2025 by R.J. von-Bruening. All rights reserved.

No part of this publication may be reproduced, stored in or introduced into a retrieval system, or transmitted, in any form, or by any means (electronic, mechanical, photocopying, recording, printing or otherwise) without prior written permission of the copyright owner and author, except as provided by USA copyright law.

Scripture quotations are taken from the Holy Bible, King James Version, Cambridge, 1769. Used by permission. All rights reserved.

Book design by R.J. von-Bruening, Copyright © 2025. All rights reserved.
Cover design by Joel Uber, owned by R.J. von-Bruening
Illustrations by R.J. VON-BRUENING Publishing
Interior design by R.J. von-Bruening.

ISBN-13: 978-1-7329096-7-0
   1. Curiosities and Wonders.
   2. World History.

First Edition - 2013, Published by Tate Publishing and Enterprises, LLC.
ISBN: 978-1-62854-459-6

Table of Contents

The Mirror

The mirror never sees its own refection,
Always thinking it is all.
Never looking behind the veil,
Not trying at all.

Secrets & Mysteries of the Forbidden knowledge;
Once lost, now known.

How the Light of the world,
Shines through my eyes.

From Heaven to Earth,
The exile and birth.

Angels to Demons,
With Heaven to Hell.

The Fallen, The Lost,
The Empire, Long gone.

The shadows move always,
When not looking at all.

Forgotten stories, left untold,
Of the magnificent armies of old.

The Battles, the Blood
The Glory, the Gore.

R.J. VON-BRUENING

Great Heroes and Fools,
Forgotten by all.

Above and Beyond,
Behind and Within.

The war rages on,
Souls from within.

The Kingdom, The Towers,
The Paradise Lost.

The terrible cost that was paid,
On that one ancient day.

Was all that was lost,
And the debacle it was.

How nothing was hidden,
And the truth is so clear.

But, always remember: The Mirror...

For it will never see its own refection,
Always thinking it is all.
It will never look behind the veil,
It will never try at all.

Introduction

Welcome to the Second Edition of The Forbidden Knowledge of Enoch. A book that has taken almost a decade to get back into print. I would like to take a few moments to explain this long process to those who have read the first edition. For those who have not read the first edition you may think of this as a little history of this book.

Soon after the first edition was published, the publisher went out of business. Which began an interesting journey for The Forbidden Knowledge of Enoch. A journey that had actually started before the book was even published.

This journey began shortly after signing the contract. The publisher began make numerous demands for changes to the manuscript. I being completely new to the book business happily did what they asked without much question. I was just so excited to be working with a publisher for my very first book, I did not ask enough questions.

What I did not realize at the time was that the publisher was actually changing what I had originally written. This was primarily done through the back and forth we were doing for the editing. What I was not aware of at the time was they were discarding what I had written or radically changed it during this editing process. They put a limit on the number of images I could have in the book. This resulted in removal of twenty-eight pictures and the related text for these pictures. Additionally, there were copyright issues with some of the remaining pictures that the publisher never resolved as they promised. These two items alone resulted in poorly edited and disjointed book that was difficult to follow while containing numerous mistakes. It simply was not the book I wrote and I was very disappointed in it.

If that was not bad enough, in less than two years after getting the first edition published, the publisher abruptly went bankrupt and completely out of business. This began a long struggle over ownership, copyrights, and trying to get my files returned to me. Once this was accomplished, I have to admit I was so burnt out that I had no desire to have anything to do with the book business.

After a few years, I returned to The Forbidden Knowledge of Enoch with the full intent of fixing all the problems with it. But, after realizing that I did not have a file of the printed book that could be edited and I would have to return to the original manuscript to fix it. At the time, it seemed like such a daunting task that I decided to just completely rewrite the entire thing. This resulted in my books "Unlocking the Dream Vision: The secret history of creation" and "The Exodus & Beyond: Book II of Unlocking the Dream Vision."

Since the publication of those books, I have not had any reason to even think about republishing The Forbidden Knowledge of Enoch. Simply because I think those books are better at presenting the idea of the hidden story contained within the esoteric symbolism than the first edition.

Remarkably, the thing that changed my mind was a strange uptick of interest in the book on social media that began about eighteen months before the publication of this second edition. This uptick was not only strange but it was massive when compared to any past interest for The Forbidden Knowledge of Enoch. During this time, I have also received numerous requests from people wanting to know where they could get a copy or if was ever going to published again.

This new interest is what made me finally change my mind and begin the process of fixing The Forbidden Knowledge of Enoch and getting it back in print.

There have been a number of important changes made to this edition when compared to the first edition. One of the biggest changes is that the twenty-eight images that had to be removed for the first edition have been included. This also includes all the text that was removed. This alone makes a huge difference for conveying a few different ideas that came across as confusing in the first edition. There have also been numerous corrections made throughout the entire book that make it easier to understand. I think this is especially true for those who have little to no knowledge about the esoteric symbolism. I also think these changes have made the entire book a more enjoyable read overall. I do hope you enjoy this new and improved version of The Forbidden Knowledge of Enoch.

Chapter 1

The Riddle of the 'something'

*There are only two mistakes one can make along the road to truth; not going all
the way, and not starting.*
~ Buddha ~

A s far back as I can remember in my life, I have always had the same
nagging feeling with the same thoughts; that something about the world
wasn't quite right. Even though I have never known exactly what that
"something" was. There are many other people who have had this very same
feeling and thought in our modern world. It is something that many can very
easily relate to. I think it is one of the reasons why so many people in the world
believe in conspiracy theories along with crazy religions that make some of the
most outlandish claims.

It is this general feeling that "something" is clearly wrong with almost
everything we have been taught about our world over the years by the major
institutions of society. This is also one of the major driving forces behind most
of the suspicions that people have about the world around them. But there is one
major problem with all of it, there really doesn't seem to be any one thing that
ties it all together in a way that allows people to actually understand what is
really going on around them.

This lack of a "unifying factor" is the primary reason why there has been so
much confusion and misunderstanding on what is "really" going on in the world.
I think this unknown factor has its origin in the fact that the "picture" of the
world, as it is presented to us by society, is composed of many different elements,
which are normally broken into subjects.

5

These subjects are then taught and reinforced by all the different institutions of society, as religion, politics, economics, history, science, philosophy, and others, in and by themselves. I have noticed that it is very seldom that any of these subjects are allowed to cross-over in any meaningful manner. If this is allowed to happen, problems develop. This because the average person can quickly see and understand that each of these subjects do not really "fit together" in the way we have all been taught to believe by society.

I think, I may have found this missing "unifying factor" that so many of us have been looking for. But, before I can begin presenting this idea, I must explain a couple of important things about this book and how it is presented. For it is written in a rather unique way when compared to almost any other book you have ever read. This is because it tells a story in a way you normally wouldn't tell it; in a very messy backwards kind of way. That may seem confusing or even strange at the moment. But it will be become clearer to you as you read it. In time, you will come to understand why it has to be told in this rather odd way. This is one of many aspects that you may not understand for large part of the text and is not explained until much later.

Since this story must be basically told backwards, there are many times that the text will seem to wander around or drop off with nothing more than questions or possibilities. The reason for this is because you must be aware of certain ideas, concepts, and possibilities, before you can understand their meaning, origin, and reasoning behind them. To put it very simply, you must understand the meaning of the effect, before you can understand the reason for the cause. This goes against our everyday thinking, in that cause comes before effect and you can only understand the effect, if you understand the cause, and that the meaning of either is normally unimportant. I know, a little confusing at the moment, but you will understand later on what I truly mean and why I address it now.

Because of this reason, I have presented this possible missing "unifying factor" as a thought experiment, starting with questions and speciation about the popular pop-culture Ancient Astronaut Theory in order to build a hypothetical frame-work to help tell this story. Again, that might seem a bit strange here at the beginning, especially with a book titled "The Forbidden Knowledge of Enoch," but you will understand much later in the book on why I had to start this journey in the way that I have. Now, with that said, I will begin this thought experiment and speciation with the following six questions. This is so we can begin our journey into the known and the unknown, with the hope of finding the truth to the Forbidden Knowledge of Enoch and hopefully provide an answer to the riddle of the something:

1) Is there "really" anything to this whole "Ancient Astronaut Theory" as currently presented by the popular media in books and TV shows?

2) Are the ancient religious stories that we are all so familiar with, really talking about some type of advance extra-terrestrial alien civilization that came to earth thousands and thousands of years ago?

3) Were our ancestors too primitive to understand who these individuals where? Thereby misinterpreted them as gods?

4) Is this contact where all the ancient religious stories, legends, and myths come from?

5) Has modern science misinterpreted the evidence?

6) Is there evidence to support any side in this argument?

With these questions now in mind, I will now begin with the current understanding of the Ancient Astronauts Theory along with some of the ideas and concepts that are claimed to support it. With the hope of providing some answers to the above questions and the many more that will come.

We begin this idea with something that everybody agrees on, that at some point in the deep, dark, misty depths of pre-history, something extraordinary happened that led to the creation and development of humanity.

This is the point where science, religion and the ancient astronaut supporters start taking their different paths, and for the rest of us, the confusion begins. Once again, I believe I may have found a pathway through this mass of confusion. This path appears to have quite a bit of probable evidence to provide some starting points on actually proving this idea one way or another. But, before we can get started, I must clarify a few things on how this "thought experiment" is set-up along with the general concepts that it is based on.

The first part of this thought experiment or hypothesis, is loosely based upon the work and claims made by many writers such as Zecharia Sitchin, Erich von Daniken, David Icke, David H. Childress, Peter Kolosimo and many others including the Ancient Aliens documentary television series that ran for many years on the History Channel.

The perspective of this thought experiment and story in general has evolved through my research over the years into the mysteries of our own history and forgotten past that has many parallels with the Ancient Astronaut Theory. Additionally, there are a number of other elements that I will be including at the beginning such as numbers and vague references to other stories without going into any detail or referring to any particular or specific source work. I wish to clarify the reasons for this lack of citation and reference.

The first and foremost reason is because that as far as I can personally tell, almost every individual, (supported and debunker) all appear to base their claims on the exact same set of source documentation and "evidence." This common source documentation is remarkably small when looked at as a whole.

The sources that I find that are most commonly cited are the Bible, both Old and New testaments, the Egyptian book of the dead, the Epic of Gilgamesh, the Vedas of India, a few surviving Mesoamerica stories, like the Popol-Vuh of the Maya, plus a few other fragments that happened to survive the destruction by the conquistadors, and the Book of Enoch. There is also a very heavy reliance on ancient Greek, Egyptian, and Sumerian mythology.

There are also a number of rather odd and obscure artifacts that appear to show weird and peculiar things that many have interpreted as some type of representation of "God-like" or "Alien-like" beings. Many have argued that our ancestors mistook these beings as "gods" because of their advanced technology. There are a number of other fragmented stories that are vaguely referred to by the supporters of the ancient astronaut theory. Which, if you spend a small bit of time researching this you will quickly discover that the stories are so fragmented that can be interpreted and skewed in many different directions, entirely based on the perspective of the storyteller.

This small amount of source material can be easily found on the internet, downloaded for free, and read in less than a few weeks with little effort in research and study. There are literally less than 1,000 pages of source material. When reviewed as a whole, this number begins to go down rather quickly when you look at just the material and stories that the ancient astronaut theorists cite; moreover, this allows anyone to go and read this material first hand.

If you do this, I think you will find the same thing that I did, that much of the so called "evidence" is rather lacking to say the least and very vague at the very best. With most of it depending on your own personal viewpoints, thoughts, and what you personally believe is or isn't evidence on this subject.

Over the years I have personally found that there are some rather good arguments for both sides of the subject, but that none of them seem to really settle the issue either way. This makes it incredibly difficult for anyone to say who has the better argument.

Over the years I have noticed that one of the major components missing in the whole ancient astronaut theory is that there isn't any consistency to the "whole" story. What I mean is that even though there are some very good and plausible arguments presented for specific items or stories, there doesn't appear to be any consistent "timeline" of any of the events that are claimed to have happened. I have found, as have many others, that each supporter of the ancient astronaut theory has a different idea of when these supposed events took place. Some say within the last few thousand years, others say possibly as far back as 450,000 years ago to everywhere in between.

This lack of a consistent timeline for these events makes it very difficult to quote any one person or work. They are all over the place and really don't make much sense outside of their common argument that some type of alien or aliens came to Earth thousands of years ago. So, I just grabbed a little bit of everything, including my own personal knowledge of ancient stories that I have heard or read about over the years. I have then used this information and have tried to put together something that might be close to what is generally claimed by the ancient astronaut theory.

As for the numbers I will be using, here at the very beginning. These are based on my basic understanding of the general ancient astronaut theory and should be viewed only as a rough estimation. The information is so fragmented and covers so many different traditions that it is impossible to pin down any hard numbers that could be spoken of with any absolute confidence.

There does appear to be a consistency in the ancient stories and traditions that the number of "gods" or "aliens" was rather small. These individuals never seem to number more than about a thousand, to around twenty-five-hundred. The stories also say they follow a chain-of-command structure. Staying within the Judeo-Christian tradition this chain of command follows a simple three-layer structure at the beginning consisting of "God" or "Lord" at the top then the Arch-Angels and then finally the Angels, with humans following at the end. This is very similar to many other ancient traditions and the ideas of a hierarchy of higher, major and lesser gods. This is the basic idea of leadership I will be beginning with.

You the reader are free to add and subtract any point you wish for your own personal viewpoint. Nothing that I will be presenting in the beginning here is absolute fact and is fully open to debate. It is not meant to be offensive to anyone. It is only to provide a common base-line for me to work within and to present an intriguing idea that may just explain strange things, like ancient astronauts and few other remarkable items.

Chapter 2

The "Gods" come to earth.

Let us be silent, that we may hear the whispers of the gods.
~ Ralph Waldo Emerson~

O ver the years it has been argued by many people that thousands upon thousands of years ago in the deep mists of pre-history before mankind walked the earth. That a highly advanced and very powerful group of "beings" came to Earth and established a type of outpost or possibly a colony? This colony was for the purpose of food production and natural resource extraction. It has been claimed that many of the ancient stories from around the world seem to indicate that this "Group" was rather small in number with possibly a three-tier organizational structure.

Within the ancient traditions along with the various claims that I am aware of. These sources give me the impression that this "organizational structure" of these mysterious being seem to consist of three levels in the beginning.

The first level seems to be made up of what is normally thought of as the "High gods" that came before all the others. There are a number of mythologies that hint that these "First ones" could be a type of ruling Council or even a governmental body of the gods themselves. It is traditional believed that these "First Ones" consist of a very small number of individuals normally between 9 to 12 individuals.

The second level consists of what is sometimes traditionally known as the "minor gods" that seem to number around 300 or so individuals. In a number of ancient traditions these "minor gods" appear to fill some type of administration role. Within the Judeo-Christian tradition, these "minor gods" would be the powerful Arch-Angels.

The third level is the traditional "lesser gods" that numerous mythologies remember as the divine servants commonly sent to communicate the wishes of the "gods" with humanity. Within the Biblical tradition this group is remembered as the "Watchers" or "Fallen Angels." Traditionally they are believed to have numbered up to a maximum of about 600, with 200 being the more common number remembered. In some of the most ancient traditions these "Watchers" appear to either command the general labor force or is part of the general labor force providing the necessary resources for the other gods.

These "Higher gods" or First-gods are normally remembered as being so powerful that the only way to describe them was as being like a force of nature. One of the best examples that I can think of is the legendary "First Gods" of ancient Greek mythology. Like the Greeks, there are a number of other myths that remember these First-gods as a rather uncaring lot with little to no concern given to any that stood in their way.

The focus of many of the ancient stories appear to be how these First-gods created the "Minor gods" for the production of material for the First-gods and failure meant death. It is believed that this arrangement went on for an unknown period of time, quite possibly tens of thousands of years. At some point over this long period of time, the conditions began to deteriorate and the "minor gods" began to resist the tyrannical and oppressive rule of First-gods.

This oppression became so great that these Minor-gods refused to provide the necessary labor for the production of the food and material that was needed by the other gods. The ancient stories seem to indicate that at this point the Minor gods with the help of the "Lesser-gods" destroyed their tools and then protested against the First gods. It is hinted at within the stories that possible warfare or even full rebellion had broken out and this was when the original group of the First-gods and the Minor-gods broke into two sides.

This situation became so dire that a Grand Council of all the gods had to be created to intervene on the behalf of all. This great Council of the gods, discovers that the grievances of the Minor-gods are just and the crimes of the First-gods are great. So great that the original arrangement could not be reestablished but a solution had to be found. For the great gods of heaven needed someone to provide the necessary labor for the production of the food and materials.

The stories indicate that the solution to the problem was the creation of "Man." Man would provide the labor that was needed. Man would tend the crops in the fields and the animals. Man would toil in the mines and dig the canals. Man would provide the service that was needed for all the gods. In addition, to

12

man providing the labor, he would also be made in their image, so he would be pleasing to their eye and easy to look upon. Additionally, to help smooth over any hard feelings; the Minor-gods and the Lesser-gods" would become the ones to look over and guide this new race of mankind or humanity. This is the point that these Lessor-gods become thought of and remembered as the "Watchers."

A large number of people have proposed and believe that these Watchers are also the Fallen Angels that are spoken of in the Judeo-Christian tradition and vaguely remembered in the Bible. What many people do not realize is that the origin of this idea of the Watchers and the Fallen Angels being the same has its origin in the ancient Book of Enoch. In fact, the Book of Enoch provides most of the ideas and the actual story of the tradition of the "*Fall of the Angels from grace.*"

I am going to go with the idea that this is a valid and reasonable assumption; that the "*Fallen Angels*" spoken of in the Biblical tradition and the "*Watchers*" that the Book of Enoch describes are in fact one and the same. I also think it is reasonable to assume that all the ancient stories and traditions that speak of any type of lower level being that was below other gods or a God are all related. Not only are they related, but they are possibly giving different details about the same set of events.

Now, with this general scenario in mind, I would like to begin playing devil's advocate with what will at first appear to be a very radical and controversial interpretation of the ancient creation stories that are all so familiar to us. My starting point will be with the creation of man along rather traditional religious thinking. I will begin by constructing this hypothetical scenario within the framework of a largely forgotten story that is contained within the Book of Enoch. Specifically, the story that is contained in "The Book of Dream Visions, Chapters 85 to 90, of the Book of Enoch. From there, I will move out and try to tie it all together with various other mythologies, legends, ancient creation stories and modern science.

The reason I am choosing the particular part of the Book of Enoch is because it is one of the most fascinating and intriguing stories I have ever read. In addition, over the years I have noticed that the Book of Enoch seems to always come up in one way or another when talking about this idea.

Once again, this is the book that most of the elements about the Watchers and the Fall from grace of the Angels originate from. This is rather well known by many, but the element that isn't well known or even spoken about is this "Dream Vision" of Enoch. Remarkably, this could possibly be one of the most important stories of all time that is virtually unknown to the average person. Also, I believe the ones that have read it over the years have misinterpreted what they were reading.

This Dream-Vision of Enoch contained deep within of the Book of Enoch has been traditionally interpreted as an allegorical and symbolic account of the history of Israel that uses animals to represent human beings and groups of humans and human beings to represent angels or a higher state of existence. I am going to diverge greatly from that traditional interpretation.

We start when Enoch begins telling his son Methuselah of his dream:

"I saw in a vision on my bed, and behold a bull came forth from the earth, and that bull was white; and after it came forth a heifer, and along with this (latter) came forth two bulls, one of them black and the other red. And that black bull gored the red one and pursued him over the earth, and thereupon I could no longer see that red bull."
(Book of Enoch 85: 1-5)

It is agreed by all that this is describing the ever-famous story of Adam & Eve as well as the Cain & Abel story that is so familiar. Traditionally, the colors of the bulls are viewed in a symbolic fashion with white representing purity, red for blood, black for sin. But I wish to look at this from a new perspective that the colors of the above bulls are not symbolic and could actually be racial characteristics along with the shocking revelation that Cain & Abel where not the sons of Adam & Eve. Also, I would like to put forward that these may not be individuals, but different groups based along what we call racial lines.

So, that the above verses the "white bull" may not represent one man named Adam but that it may be a group of white skinned males. The "black bull" is Cain and is a group of black skinned males with the "red bull" represents Abel and may be a group red-skinned males that were killed by the Cain group. There is also the possibility that is Able group might have been a group whose numbers were decimated and were scattered to the point that they were no longer a factor in the story. The "heifer" clearly represents Eve and as we will learn, appears to be a genetically neutral group of females that is able to pass on the primary characteristics of the fathers. This idea also makes me wonder if the nineteenth century idea of classifying humanity into three racial groups consisting of Caucasian, Negroid, and Mongoloid might come from this story. The verses also suggest that the heifer was genetical neutral so she would pass on more of the father's traits, which in this case appears to their skin coloring. This seems to parallel modern humans. Why this is important is unknown, but later on, we will see why this idea might be important and may answer a long-standing mystery in the process.

If we continue to speculate along these lines. I think it could be argued that it appears that the heifer or Eve could to be what is described by modern science as "Mitochondria Eve" [1] which is believed to be the first small group of closely related females that all humans appear to be descended from. It is estimated that Mitochondria Eve lived around 200,000 years ago. Which could mean that this creation scenario of man may have taken place at approximately 200,000 B.C. which according to the text resulted in the establishment of two main racial groups:

"But that black bull grew and that heifer went with him, and I saw that many oxen proceeded from him which resembled and followed him. And that cow, that first one, went from the presence of that first bull in order to seek that red one, but found him not, and lamented with a great lamentation over him and sought him. And I looked till that first bull came to her and quieted her, and from that time onward she cried no more. And after that she bore another white bull, and after him she bore many bulls and black cows. And I saw in my sleep that white bull likewise grow and become a great white bull, and from him proceeded many white bulls, and they resembled him. And they began to beget many white bulls, which resembled them, one following the other, (even) many."
(Book of Enoch 85: 6-10)

If any of this is true, then it also brings up a very important idea. Because for one female to be able to have enough children to establish a viable reproducing population, her lifespan would have to be much greater than today, again, unless it is a group we are speculating about. In addition to that line of reasoning, it appears that many of the ancient stories, especially the Bible, speak of very long lifetimes for the first humans. Staying with the biblical tradition, these life spans are said to be between 300 to 900 plus years.

Could any of that be true? Modern science says no, but I have not found any scientific evidence that early humans could not or did not really live that long. I am not saying that the evidence doesn't exist, all I am saying I have never seen or found it. Since I don't know one way or another, I am going make the assumption that these long life-spans are either true or that it is possible for these "years" are actually speaking of generations. Which for example, that the 980 years of Adam spoken of in the Book of Genesis could be 98 or 980 generations of Adam, either way, a very long amount of time.

Before we go any farther, I would like to pause and do a general recap this basic idea and help establish a time-line based on this idea of a Mitochondria-eve of humanity existing around 200,000 B.C. along with the idea that this is the actual beginning of humanity. I would also like to add the idea that these first humans were originally created by some unknown type of advanced species that our ancestors called and worshipped as God or gods. Which is very similar to the more modern idea that this mysterious species may have been some type of extra-terrestrial aliens. At the moment, it makes no difference if you choose to believe if these mysterious beings were actual gods or extra-terrestrial aliens. Since there is much controversy over their identities and in order to help cut down on the confusion from this point forward, I will now refer to this group as the "Main-Group."

In this scenario, this mysterious Main-Group creates mankind as a slave race to provide the necessary labor to sustain this group and is organized exactly the same way modern humanity has organized slave-labor or concentration camps that appear to be broken along racial lines, possibly for type of identification.

Using World War II concentration and slave camps as an example from history. It is possible that some number of the individuals in the group that is traditionally known as "Adam" were used as "kappa." Kappa is term for a few special individuals that were chosen to control the other slaves or prisoners that were given some type of reward, like better living conditions, or better food for their help. These individuals tend to be the most violent prisoners with little to no personal ties to the groups they are overseeing. This is done in order to keep the requirements for man-power of the guards low in the camps.

If this line of thinking is correct and early humanity was organized along these lines. Then the Minor-gods and Lesser-gods, who later become the ones known as "Angels" and then "The Watchers," aka "Those Who Watch," which are consistently mentioned by the ancient astronaut theorists. They are also spoken of by most of the Judeo-Christian traditions. This Angels or Watchers are actually the guards of this slave-labor-camp. This would help explain why the Angels became known as the Watchers. It was because that is exactly what a prison guard does, they watch the prisoners or slaves. These Watchers will become important very soon.

We now have early humans providing the labor, the Lesser gods or Angels now known as "The Watchers" are overseeing, guarding, and interacting with this human slave-labor. Which I will now refer to as the "Fallen-Group" instead of Watcher group as you might think, you will understand later why I did this. Then finally, the others that I referred to as the Higher and Minor gods or Main-Group is some type of administration arm of this operation.

This basic arrangement appears to have been stable for a very long period of time, perhaps for tens of thousands of years. Over this very long amount of time, it is agreed within all of the ancient and modern stories that at some ancient point in time a forbidden type of intimate relationship developed between a small unknown number of these Watchers or Fallen-Group and the human females they were guarding.

During this time, it appears that these relationships developed to the point that these Watchers started having some ethical problem with this arrangement. This ethical or moral problem leads to one of them deciding to do something about it. This individual Watcher, decides to plan, organize, and then implement an uprising or rebellion with a number of his fellow Watchers in order to free the human slaves that they have developed intimate relationships and possibly even families with.

Remarkably, this event has been recorded in every tradition, culture, religion, myth & legend that has existed from that point in time until our present day. I want to present this event as one of, if not the most important event in all of human history. This uprising, rebellion, or coup, of the ones known as the Watchers is the one singular event of when we, the human race, defined a large number of our beliefs and individual thought. Now, before you think I have "lost my marbles", please allow me to explain before you pass judgment.

Every single ancient culture has this story in some form. It has been told in many different ways, by many different peoples. So, let us stop for a moment and consider the implications of this scenario with the proposal that these stories are talking about the same event. There are three components that I have found to be consistent across all different ancient traditions and cultures.

The first is that a god or great father-like figure convinces and organizes his fellow gods to rise against older gods. The second is that the older gods are often depicted as a type of darkness or chaos and sometimes as a force or embodiment of nature that defeats them in an epic "War in Heaven." The third factor is this great war in heaven then brings knowledge and freedom to an enslaved humanity. This knowledge is most often described as some form of light representing a type of enlightenment or awakening. This knowledge or enlightenment is always brought to humanity by the leader of the uprising. This is why this individual becomes known and the "Bringer of the light" or the "Light Bearer." In many cultures this individual is remembered as a "being of light" this is difficult if not impossible to look directly upon.

For example: In Greek mythology, Zeus the Father-God and leader of his fellow Olympians or Watchers rise up against Zeus's father Kronos the older god and the other Titans. Who are typically the embodiment of some type of a force

17

of nature. It is said that Zeus defeated them in a spectacular battle and then imprisoned them.

Once the older gods are defeated, these new gods then turn their attention to humanity by taking human women as wives. Normally, in much of Greek mythology it is only Zeus and many times he is describe as turning himself into a bull. After he seduces some helpless maiden and then nine months later her giving birth to half-god and half-human children.

This is just one of many examples of the same basic story in every tradition from around the world be it Mesopotamia, Egyptian, Babylonian, Native American, or even the Western Judeo-Christian tradition. This individual High-God, Sky-God, Father-God, God of Gods, goes by many names, Zeus, Wooden, An, Ahura Mazda, Marduk, Yahweh, Jehovah, Allah and literally hundreds and hundreds of other names. But in reality, they are all talking about the same individual and the monumental event of the gods coming to Earth.

I think all of these stories are all talking about this event in some way. I also think that at this particular moment in time these gods or Watchers along with the vast majority of humans that they freed believed this entire situation as a very good thing. So good in fact, that it literally became the foundation for all of human society.

This rebellion of the "Watchers" is the event that the scholars, theologians, historians, and the common man have been debating for thousands of years. Whose creation story is the correct one, which is most complete, and/or acceptable? It is very important to keep in mind throughout this book that any creation story that contains the following elements is talking about this rebellion: Father God or Supreme God figure, Creation of the world but not man, with this normally being done through a "Bringer of light" that brought some form of enlightenment and knowledge for the world to early humans. The ever-famous verses one through five of Genesis, Chapter 1, is a good example of what I am try to explain of stories containing the above elements:

"In the beginning God created the heaven and the earth. And the earth was without form, and void; and darkness was upon the face of the deep. And the Spirit of God moved upon the face of the waters. And God said, Let there be light: and there was light. And God saw the light, that it was good: and God divided the light from the darkness. And God called the light Day, and the darkness he called Night. And the evening and the morning were the first day."
(Genesis 1: 1-5, KJV)

As you are no doubt aware, there are many other examples in almost every single tradition that contains these elements of a "Light" and that it was a "Good" thing. This is also related to the event that has been recorded and past down in the Western Judeo-Christian tradition as the fall of Lucifer and his fellow angels along with the corruption of humanity that resulted in the great deluge or flood.

For many, this might be kind of a big leap of how these verses from Genesis that are clearly discussing the creation of the world by God, be related to the whole "Fall of the Angels" story? At first it may be confusing and sound a little bit odd to be thinking that the creation verses from Genesis could also be speaking of the event that we know as the fall of Lucifer and his fellow Angels. How could this dichotomy of the creation story in Genesis also be speaking of the fall of the Angels? Is this idea even possible?

Not only is it possible, but as we go along, you will find that it is highly probable that this idea is correct. This will become clearer to you as I develop this hypothetical situation and thought experiment to provide you with additional information, ideas and possibilities that seem beyond belief. I will now return to the Book of Enoch to expand upon this idea in greater detail.

This rebellion or "The Fall of the Angels" that many of us know of so well is the major focus of the Book of Enoch. It is also the basis of the ancient astronaut theory in general. It should be noted that the Book of Enoch is the source for the vast majority of the Judeo-Christian tradition related to Angels and their fall from grace. This is a major reason of why I chose this text to work within.

This rebellion in heaven resulted in the original group fragmenting into two warring factions, with one I called the Main-Group being defeated and most likely imprisoned with the triumphant faction or Fallen Group ruling Earth.

From chapter 83 in the Book of Enoch there appears to be a description of the final battle of this rebellion and the probable destruction of a large ship that our ancestors called the "Heaven." The following verses speak of this "Heaven" crashing to earth and causing a great destruction that resulted in a large explosion that created an equally large crater.

"...I saw in a vision how the heaven collapsed and was borne off and fell to the earth. And when it fell to the earth, I saw how the earth was swallowed up in a great abyss, and mountains were suspended on mountains, and hills sank down on hills, and high trees were rent from their stems, and hurled down and sunk in the abyss. And thereupon a word fell into my mouth, and I lifted up (my voice) to cry aloud, and said: 'The earth is destroyed.'"
(Book of Enoch 83: 2-6)

After this destruction of when the "heaven collapsed" these Watchers come to earth and take human wives and live among mankind as gods. Within the Judeo-Christian tradition, this event will later become known as the great rebellion between God and Lucifer that results in the Fall of the Angels and the corruption of mankind. It is also the same story of Zeus and his fellow Olympians fighting and defeating the Titans before coming to Earth. This basic story can be found in every ancient tradition. This is one of the first clues that all of these ancient stories are all talking about this event of a great War in Heaven between the gods.

If we take a moment and look at an earlier part in the Book of Enoch from Chapter six. We will find that it gives some of the details on the "deal" that led to this rebellion of the Watchers. It also provides the name of the location for this arrangement and the only full list of names of the primary leaders of this group that I am aware of, outside of Greek and Egyptian mythology. I find these names interesting; I am unsure if these names are correct in any way or even important to the overall story, but they do help in establishing the idea that these might be actual individuals and real events that are occurring.

This text also seems to help set the general Judeo-Christian feel about it with it being where a large part of the concept and tradition of Fallen Angels and the origin of the devil are based on. This is open for debate for many people, but the similarities between these two stories in Enoch and Genesis 6 seem to be more than mere chance. I think it should be noted that they are at least related in some way; if for no other reason than that they both come from the same tradition.

"And it came to pass when the children of men had multiplied that in those days were born unto them beautiful and comely daughters. And the angels, the children of the heaven, saw and lusted after them, and said to one another: 'Come, let us choose us wives from among the children of men and beget us children.' And Semjaza, who was their leader, said unto them: 'I fear ye will not indeed agree to do this deed, and I alone shall have to pay the penalty of a great sin.' And they all answered him and said: 'Let us all swear an oath, and all bind ourselves by mutual imprecations not to abandon this plan but to do this thing.' Then sware they all together and bound themselves by mutual imprecations upon it. And they were in all two hundred; who descended in the days of Jared on the summit of Mount Hermon, and they called it Mount Hermon, because they had sworn and bound themselves by mutual imprecations upon it. And these are the names of their leaders: Samjazaz, their leader, Arakiba, Rameel, Kokabiel, Tamiel, Ramiel, Danel,

Ezeqeel, Baraqijal, Asael, Armaros, Batarel, Ananel, Zaqiel, Samsapeel, Satarel, Turel, Jomjael, Sariel. These are their chiefs of tens."
(Book of Enoch 6: 1-8)

These verses from the Book of Enoch are very similar to the controversial passage from Genesis, Chapter 6 that seem to be describing the same events; The fall of the angels and the wickedness of man.

"And it came to pass, when men began to multiply on the face of the earth, and daughters were born unto them, That the sons of God saw the daughters of men that they were fair; and they took them wives of all which they chose. And the LORD said, My spirit shall not always strive with man, for that he also is flesh: yet his days shall be an hundred and twenty years. There were giants in the earth in those days; and also after that, when the sons of God came in unto the daughters of men, and they bare children to them, the same became mighty men which were of old, men of renown. And GOD saw that the wickedness of man was great in the earth, and that every imagination of the thoughts of his heart was only evil continually."
(Genesis 6: 1-5, KJV)

After the above events, the Book of Enoch goes on to describe what these individuals' taught mankind. Which for this hypothetical situation, is civilization and technology which is most likely more advanced than our own today with all the complexity that it entails. I find this to have a similar connotation with its relation to Greek and Egyptian mythologies and what they describe as the type of knowledge the "gods" brought to them.

"And Azazel taught men to make swords, and knives, and shields, and breastplates, and made known to them the metals (of the earth) and the art of working them, and bracelets, and ornaments, and the use of antimony, and the beautifying of the eyelids, and all kinds of costly stones, and all colouring tinctures. And there arose much godlessness, and they committed fornication, and they were led astray, and became corrupt in all their ways. Semjaza taught enchantments, and rootcuttings, Armaros the resolving of enchantments, Baraqijal (taught) astrology, Kokabel the constellations, Ezeqeel the knowledge of the clouds, (Araqiel the signs of the earth, Shamsiel the signs of the sun), and Sariel the course of the moon. And as men perished, they cried, and their cry went up to heaven.
(Book of Enoch 8: 1-4)

21

We need to pause for a moment to take a closer look at two small sections from the lines above, "*and they were led astray*," and "*And as men perished, they cried, and their cry went up to heaven.*" This is describing what will become a very familiar theme throughout history; that the initial good conditions and ideals of a new civilization will deteriorate and break down over time. This will eventually lead to violence and possible open warfare.

I agree with the Biblical tradition that the primary reason for this break-down in this society is because of the offspring of this unholy union of the Watchers and human women. These bastard children of the Fallen Angels will become the ones that are remembered in many different traditions as "*Giants*" and the great "*men of renown*" spoken of in Genesis 6, and many heroes that were said to be half-god and half-man. These are also the ones known as the Nephilim in the Biblical tradition. In time they will become the basis for the idea of demons that are the dammed sprits of these unholy offspring that are killed before and during the great flood.

Within chapter seven of the Book of Enoch it gives an indication of the chaos and horror that was caused by these Giants or Nephilim. It speaks of how they turned against men and "*devoured mankind*" along with what could be describing possible genetic engineering with other animals. These verses could be providing additional details to the story contained within chapter six of Genesis in the Bible.

"And all the others together with them took unto themselves wives, and each chose for himself one, and they began to go in unto them and to defile themselves with them, and they taught them charms and enchantments, and the cutting of roots, and made them acquainted with plants. And they became pregnant, and they bare great giants [Nephilim], whose height was three thousand ells: Who consumed all the acquisitions of men. And when men could no longer sustain them, the giants [Nephilim] turned against them and devoured mankind. And they began to sin against birds, and beasts, and reptiles, and fish, and to devour one another's flesh, and drink the blood. Then the earth laid accusation against the lawless ones."
(Book of Enoch 7: 1-6)

If we then return back to the allegorical and symbolic account in the Dream-Vision contained in the Book of Enoch that I started with in order to continue this story. These verses contain even more information on the situation and the events occurring at this point. I will refer to this event as "The Fall of the Watchers" from now on, for no other reason than that I like the sound of it.

"And again, I saw with mine eyes as I slept, and I saw the heaven above, and behold a star fell from heaven, and it arose and eat and pastured amongst those oxen. And after that I saw the large and the black oxen, and behold they all changed their stalls and pastures and their cattle, and began to live with each other. And again, I saw in the vision, and looked towards the heaven, and behold I saw many stars descend and cast themselves down from heaven to that first star, and they became bulls amongst those cattle and pastured with them [amongst them]. And I looked at them and saw, and behold they all let out their privy members, like horses, and began to cover the cows of the oxen, and they all became pregnant and bare elephants, camels, and asses. And all the oxen feared them and were affrighted at them, and began to bite with their teeth and to devour, and to gore with their horns. And they began, moreover, to devour those oxen; and behold all the children of the earth began to tremble and quake before them and to flee from them."
(Book of Enoch 86: 1-6)

We will now return to building on where my original scenario began within the Dream Vision. As you can see, this passage is very similar to other stories relating to The Fall and I would like to take a moment and take a closer look at the part about how Enoch, "...*behold a star fell from heaven.*"

In the Western Judeo-Christian tradition this fallen star is Lucifer, a being of light that corrupted mankind with knowledge. In Greek mythology, this is Zeus coming down to earth, then changing himself into a bull to seduce a human female or any other story that has this theme, star, light, mating with humans. There are also similar stories in the many of the esoteric schools of thought and occult religions that are supposed to be at the center of a number of secret societies and their symbolism. This esoteric and occult belief may have something to do with all of this, but what could it be?

This symbolism of the bull that is contained within this story in the Dream Vision of Enoch along with all the Greek stories that are related to bull symbolism seems to be more than just a coincidence to me. Especially when they all seem to have some type of reference to the night sky and the stars. Remarkably this whole idea of the bull is still with us today contained within the constellation Taurus. Could this be some type of clue? What is the connection between the bull of mythology and the constellation we call Taurus the Bull? Could there be more here than we thought?

We need to return back to the hypothetical situation and its radical interpretation of this story to hopefully find some answers. The leader of the Fallen-Group, Zeus, Lucifer, Satan, Light-bearer, Bringer of light, Alien, etc., comes down from "heaven." When this event happens, it looks like a falling star. I am going to speculate that its brightness was very similar or equal to the planet Venus for two reasons. The first is due to the many references to Venus or a star similar to Venus in many different ancient traditions. The second is that I think it is a type of astronomical reference to what was actually happening in the night sky at this point in time.

The event of this leader of the Fallen Group of this rebellion coming to Earth must have looked like a falling star with a similar brightness of Venus. This is a good description of what a modern-day spacecraft looks like when it is reentering the atmosphere. This type of event would have been seen over a large area and possibly witnessed by almost everybody alive at the time. This could be why this event is remembered in so many ancient and modern traditions. It appears to have left a large long-lasting impression on all who saw it.

After this arrival of this star that fell from heaven the text talks of how the large and black oxen changed their way of life and began to live together and soon after many other stars descended from heaven, became large black bulls, and mated with the cattle.

This appears to be speaking of the leader coming to Earth first and paving the way so to speak for his fellow Watchers who aided in the uprising and who also had possible relationships with human woman, who soon followed him to Earth in order to establish their new lives as gods. This also gives us the information on which group this Fallen Group came too. Keeping with the earlier racial idea, this is the group known in the Judeo-Christian tradition as Cain.

The story also gives the indication that these "stars" could change their appearance as needed for the situation at hand. This raises a number of questions on how this could be accomplished and what level of technology that would be required. This is also similar to other traditions that have the idea of the gods or God, being able to change their shape or appearance at will.

I will not be expanding on any of those questions on how they could have changed their appearance or the technology required at this point in time, it is not the point of this book. I will leave it to you the reader to speculate on the actual details.

There is the possibility that these individuals might not have set out to be gods but that the circumstances may have been similar as seen numerous books, movies, and videos of science fiction stories. That the real reason for the rebellion was nothing more than that they didn't like what the powers-that-be were doing to the local population and rose-up and did something about it. They began to have an ethical problem with the oppression and exploitation that was occurring and the inmate sexual relationships came later as these two groups lived together after the rebellion.

Then over time because of their technology and knowledge they became to viewed and treated as gods. Especially, if they were immortal: either naturally or through the use of technology. This might be a good point to stop and establish whether or not these individuals are immortal or not. In this scenario, I am going to keep the traditional idea that they are in fact immortal or have an immensely long lifespan either naturally or through the use of technology.

If it is through technology that they have long life spans, what type of technology could they have been using? In keeping with the mythology and the stories contained within the Book of Enoch and the Bible, the technology is normally described as a "tree of life" whose fruit or nectar provide life to all that eat or drink of it. This sounds like some type of age retardant drug that is taken orally on a regular basis and is produced by a piece of technology that looks like a tree is some way to somebody who doesn't understand what he is looking at.

Either way, these individuals established a society and civilization based around this event. Most likely there are a number of people that aren't really happy with the new situation. These being the ones that were allied and working with the old Main-Group, that all the stories indicate were defeated and imprisoned. As from earlier, using my idea is that this group was the ones remembered as Adam and were symbolically remembered as the white bulls. Could this be where all this animosity and hatred that exists between whites and blacks today comes from? I do not know, but it is an intriguing thought.

All the ancient stories also seem to indicate that children that were born to the gods and their human wives, the primary leader of the gods son or sons would be the most important. In Greek mythology these powerful sons of the gods include the Hercules & Perseus stories we have learned about in school. In Norse mythology Thor and Loki are good examples. Also, like the text in the Book of Enoch and the Bible, these half-god, half-man children, these "Nephilim" started the problems in this new little civilization. They appear to break into factions and start killing or possibly even eating humans mating with everything or possibly some type of genetic engineering. I am thinking this might be the action taken against the former allies of the Main-Group. In short, you have the Main-Group with the group of Adam or the white bulls resisting or fighting against the Fallen-Group and the black bulls.

This Fallen-Group is led by members of the Nephilim with the foot soldiers being the black humans of the line of Cain. It is possible that this version of the story with the Book of Enoch along with the Bible is from the viewpoint of the Main-Group and Adam side.

I am hoping that you are starting to get the idea that there are two warring camps now and these two-camps could be the reason we basically have two main versions of this same story. With each having their own ideologies, viewpoints, and mythology on this situation. This is also the reason why I originally broke them into two groups, the Main-Group and the Fallen-Group.

After this possible resistance is defeated it maybe they have nothing better to do but to fight amongst themselves or possibly, which is the idea I like, it was just "open-season" on anybody that was connected to the Main-Group. In this case, the ones known as Adam, who were white, would not have a real good view of this action. From the other side's point of view, they most likely viewed as if they were doing something good by getting rid of people who helped the gods that enslaved them. I think you can begin to get the idea of how this could be the root of the animosity and hatred that still exists today between many white people and black people of today. It could be based on how these two-camps might be looking at and remembering these ancient events. It also gives us our first glimpse of how this ancient story starts to become intertwined with itself.

Traditionally, this violence and wickedness leads to and is a major factor in the event we know as "The Deluge" or "The Great Flood." This flood, that is recorded in what appears to be every single tradition on the planet, much like the story of the Fall of the Angels in all it many versions. But this is not the traditional idea that most likely jumped into your head, I think it could really be a story of the return of the Main-Group that was defeated thousands of years earlier in the great rebellion and of them reasserting control over Earth. Defeating the Fallen-Group, their human allies remembered as the line of Cain that was led by the Nephilim. I would also like to add the idea that since the time of the Fall of the Angels, a civilization had been created. A civilization that possessed advanced technology with enough resources and manpower that it was able to supply a large enough military that they could not be easily defeated with a frontal assault without proper planning and preparation. Which would have also included the need to have the support of the local population.

This probably first started with covert operations that rebuilt support with any survivors of their old allies, the group of Adam. These cover operations would be proceeded by guerrilla style tactics with the aim of possibly getting the Nephilim to break into factions and fight each other. Once open warfare had broken out then invasion could happen. This is the event that is recorded as the great flood and possibly being the final battle or the largest one that changed the tide of war. The idea I want to get across is that this is all part of a series of events that describe the invasion, conquest, and reestablishment of the old order on

Earth. This becomes recorded and remembered as the as the great world-wide flood.

> *"And again, I saw how they began to gore each other and to devour each other, and the earth began to cry aloud. And I raised mine eyes again to heaven, and I saw in the vision, and behold there came forth from heaven beings who were like white men: and four went forth from that place and three with them. And those three that had last come forth grasped me by my hand and took me up, away from the generations of the earth, and raised me up to a lofty place, and showed me a tower raised high above the earth, and all the hills were lower. And one said unto me: 'Remain here till thou seest everything that befalls those elephants, camels, and asses, and the stars and the oxen, and all of them.'"*
> (Book of Enoch 87: 1-4)

These events appear to be speaking of a war led by *"beings who were like white men."* They also appear to take the author of the story, Enoch, up and *"away from the generations of the earth to a lofty place and showed me [him] a tower raise high above the earth."* For the moment, I only wish to make you the reader aware of this person, being *"taken up,"* and seeing a *"tower."*

It is important that you remember this description and imagine it through your own eyes. Later, this will become clear once I will give a more complete reason for what I am going to say next. This and a few other references of what appears to be the author of Enoch, being *"taken up"* in some way; are actually all one event seen from the viewpoint from almost the end of the story. For right now, just make a mental note so to speak, because it will be needed for later.

As for the *"beings that looked like white men"* that are spoken of, I think they are the individual leaders of smaller groupings of the Main-Group. If this is a military operation, then these "beings," who are also be known as the four Arch-Angels, Michael, Gabriel, Uriel and Raphael in the Biblical tradition, are most likely the lead officer of each military unit or operation. Without any greater detail, it is very difficult to say what level of technology was being used. If any of the ancient stories can be believed, I think it would be safe to say that some type of weapons of mass destruction was used and that this would require at least the same level of technology we have today. As you can now see, this idea is starting to seem a little bit like what the ancient astronaut supporters claim. Could we have missed something?

These events of a possible war, led up to one of the most interesting stories of the flood I have ever read with a level of detail that seems to be lacking in other versions that I am aware of. But at this point of the story, read it with the idea that this *"enclosure"* that is spoken of is really that: a large enclosure of some type. This enclosure could be the area that the Fallen Watchers ruled over and could be where the idea of the *"Lost Paradise"* comes from. Because, from the point of view of the Fallen Watchers and their allies: it would be like losing a paradise if you lost your entire civilization. As with any military operation these events most likely killed not only the enemy but possibly many of the group of Adam also.

"And one of those four went to that white bull and instructed him in a secret, without his being terrified: he was born a bull and became a man, and built for himself a great vessel and dwelt thereon; and three bulls dwelt with him in that vessel and they were covered in. And again I raised mine eyes towards heaven and saw a lofty roof, with seven water torrents thereon, and those torrents flowed with much water into an enclosure. And I saw again, and behold fountains were opened on the surface of that great enclosure, and that water began to swell and rise upon the surface, and I saw that enclosure till all its surface was covered with water. And the water, the darkness, and mist increased upon it; and as I looked at the height of that water, that water had risen above the height of that enclosure, and was streaming over that enclosure, and it stood upon the earth. And all the cattle of that enclosure were gathered together until I saw how they sank and were swallowed up and perished in that water. But that vessel floated on the water, while all the oxen and elephants and camels and asses sank to the bottom with all the animals, so that I could no longer see them, and they were not able to escape, (but) perished and sank into the depths. And again I saw in the vision till those water torrents were removed from that high roof, and the chasms of the earth were leveled up and other abysses were opened. Then the water began to run down into these, till the earth became visible; but that vessel settled on the earth, and the darkness retired and light appeared."
(Book of Enoch 89: 1-9)

After this destruction of all the animals and once the waters had been removed from the enclosure, we are told of the imprisonment of the *"fallen stars."* This imprisonment of the fallen stars part of the story, much like Enoch being taken away from the generations of the earth, I think is from a much later part of the story, which I will address in later chapters. But for now, just keep the idea that something "really bad" happened to these fallen stars.

And I saw one of those four who had come forth first, and he seized that first star which had fallen from the heaven, and bound it hand and foot and cast it into an abyss: now that abyss was narrow and deep, and horrible and dark. And one of them drew a sword, and gave it to those elephants and camels and asses: then they began to smite each other, and the whole earth quaked because of them. And as I was beholding in the vision, lo, one of those four who had come forth stoned. (them) from heaven, and gathered and took all the great stars whose privy members were like those of horses, and bound them all hand and foot, and cast them in an abyss of the earth.
(Book of Enoch 88: 1-3)

We have now reached the point where I would like to pause and begin my "thought experiment." Which is the reason for this radical and rather strange interpretation of the story of the Creation of Man, the Fall of the Angels and the Great Flood based on the Book of Enoch and the mysterious Dream Vision it holds.

Chapter 3

The beginning of an idea

Wisdom begins in wonder
~Socrates~

E verybody seems to agree that something prolific took place in the past that led to these stories. Regardless, of your own personal beliefs, feelings, or ideas about the stories relating to and known as; the Creation of Man, the Fall of the Watchers, and the Great Flood, something must have happened all those many eons ago to lead people to remember these stories no matter how you view it.

The big question is, and has always been; What actually happened? What really happened in the ancient past that led to all these different but similar stories from all these different cultures and traditions that are so clearly separated not only by thousands of miles but also thousands of years in time. to be remembered and recorded as the Creation of Man, the Fall of the Watchers, and the Great Flood?"

Many people over thousands of years have spent their whole lives wondering and working on this question in some shape or form.

Entire religions and civilizations have been built around these stories being literally true including many in our own world of today. There is no question that people have very strong feelings, beliefs, and opinions on these stories and will defend them with the greatest of passion and conviction. Despite the consequences to the bitter end. But the truth be told, there does not seem to be much in the way of actual evidence to support any one viewpoint. In fact, outside of the fact that we have these stories, it is very difficult say much of anything

31

with much confidence. As I have read these stories over the years, it appears to me that they are all speaking and recording the same series of events. This has always made me wonder, like many others, if any of these stories could actually be true?

Because in my mind I keep thinking: That if there was some event or events in the ancient past that were so big and so important that it affected enough people on the planet. So much so, that every single culture would remember and recorded it in their stories, mythology, and legends. Wouldn't it leave all kinds of "evidence" behind?

Shouldn't this be rather easy to "prove" these stories one way or the other rather simply? For example, if we take the Great Flood recorded in the Bible. All you just have to do is look for the evidence of a world-wide flood, if you find it, then a great flood must have happened, if you don't, then unfortunately, it did not happen and you have to start over with a new idea.

This where the problem lies, we don't seem to have any actual "evidence" that anything like a great world-wide flood happening at any time in the past few million years. However, there seems to be all kinds of evidence indicating that large local flooding, possibly like when the black sea was formed at the end of the last ice age, could have led to the flood stories that we have today. Which is a great idea, but once again, it still cannot and does not explain how all the different cultures on the planet seem to remember and tell the same story of a great flood long ago. Like so many others through the ages, this has always puzzled me and made me wonder what really happen all those years ago and is there any way to prove it?

After spending countless nights reading and researching the subject. I came to the same conclusions and the same unanswered questions like everybody else has before me. So, in my failure, I decided an entirely new approach was necessary that had to be based on a new set of assumptions. With the first being that something must have been missed by everybody.

But what had been missed? Not only that, but how could I of all people find it with my given knowledge on the subject and my limited resources? Because to be perfectly honest; although I have a strong technical background rooted in the sciences and have a great love of history. I am only an amateur researcher a hobbyist if you will. I do also have a strong if odd background in occult knowledge, secret societies, esoteric thought, along with being an amateur astronomer with a rather odd interest in the mythology of ancient cultures. What hope would I of all people have in figuring out anything new when so many thousands upon thousands if not millions of others that have come before me have also failed?

32

After some giving it all some good thought, I decided to give it a shot. Because I am only an amateur researcher and the only thing I have to lose, is my time, besides, I might learn something new in the process.

In order to get started, I decided I had to just completely start over from scratch. Starting with a fresh look at all the available information on ancient cultures, sites, myths, legends and symbols that I could get my hands on. Once that was done, I then started treating it all as nothing more than raw data that may or may not be true or even related to what I was seeking.

This is the same approach that most of us use every single day to help filter out the noise of our modern world where we are bombarded with never ending steam of information from hundreds of different outlets with an equal number of viewpoints with all of them normally speaking about the same subject. By treating it all as little more than raw data, you can filter out much of the noise rather easily by looking for common terms that cut across all the different sources. For example, the same names, references, concepts, themes or ideas that are spoken of in some form across the different sources. They similar or common terms could quite possibly be pieces of the truth and hopefully a clue to what must have been missed.

As I began to go through the dusty old books and read the ancient stories on their worn pages. I started to notice that there seemed to be common set of names, references, concepts, themes, and symbols that began to pop up. No matter where I looked or what approach I took; these same references to names, concepts, and symbols kept coming up in the information. Some of these mysterious references I was rather familiar with but there were others I had never heard of before. One of the first common items I noticed was almost universal references to the night sky, especially in the most ancient of stories.

The most ancient stories of humanity all have some reference to the night sky. This normally represented through either a star or stars coming down to Earth and of something happening in the sky related to this event. Another common element in the stories is that there are a large number of references to bulls and the Taurus region of the night sky. This includes the ever-famous Pleiades star cluster along with the numerous stories coming from ancient Greece about this cluster of stars. With one of the best examples being the story the 7 sisters and the missing sister Atlantid. There also appears that a large number of the most mysterious ancient monolithic sites are aligned with the Orion and Taurus constellations along with the Pleiades grouping of stars.

These references to the stars of the Orion and Taurus constellations leads me to believe that these stars where very important to our ancestors across a number of different cultures. I am by no means the first to notice this or the first to point it out. But I do think that this is the part of the sky we need to be looking at. Our ancestors went to a lot of trouble to design, align, and build a number of very large buildings pointing to this part of the night sky for some strange and mysterious reason. I, like so many others, would like to know why this grouping of stars was so important to our ancestors?

Then, I began to notice that all the ancient stories regardless the tradition or culture all seemed to be speaking of the exact same set of events. With the only real difference being small details like names or places in stories clearly related to the Creation of Man, the Fall of the Watchers, and the Great Flood as remembered within the Judeo-Christian tradition.

As I thought more about the stars. I have come to the conclusion that whatever the missing piece is. It must have something to do with the stars in the constellations of Orion and Taurus with some connection to the Pleiades grouping of stars. The added fact that these stars are only visible during the months of winter must also be related somehow to these stories of the Creation of Man, the Fall of the Watchers, and the Great Flood. But what could it be?

With those ideas in mind, I would like to move back into my thought experiment. Before we go any farther, I must state that what I am about to propose will at first seem to be one of the craziest and possibly one of the most radical ideas you have ever heard in your life related to these ancient stories. Due to the radical nature of this idea, I must ask you to please withhold judgment until you have read the whole scenario and see the connections I am making. Once you the reader have done that, I think you will wonder "How could anybody miss this? Because it all seems so obvious once it is all pointed out"

With that said, it is now time to go down the rabbit hole and see what we can find. But be forewarned that it is, and isn't, what you think it is.

To begin with, I think these events that are remembered as the Creation of Man, the Fall of Lucifer and his fellow Watchers, and the Great Flood that we have today. All might possibly be real events that took place in time. In addition, I think I may have figured out a way to accurately date these with an independent method with evidence that has been right in front of our faces the whole time.

I will start with the event that is known as the Fall of the Watchers or "The Fall" and then work my way out from there.

If this event of the gods or Watchers coming to Earth after a great war in heaven, bringing freedom, knowledge, and civilization to an enslaved mankind really happened. Then I think it is safe to assume that this would be viewed as the greatest event of all time. It would have been so monumental that their entire civilization and society would change and be based upon or heavily influenced by this event.

This event would be so important that it would be remembered by being marked, celebrated, and it would in time become the single most important thing to this civilization and society. It would be recorded in mythology, song, it would be recorded in writing, and there would be massive yearly celebrations. It would literally be like, from a traditional America perspective, New Years Eve, St. Valentine Day, St. Patrick's Day, Easter, Memorial Day, Fourth of July, Veterans Day, Halloween, Thanksgiving and Christmas, all rolled up into one grand day with all of the meaning and emotion that each one of the days have for people. I think the early development of the Catholic Church is a perfect example of this idea.

The early development of the Catholic Church had rather unassuming beginnings. It started with one man of humble origins with a simple message and a small handful of followers. Remarkably, this early sect did not disappear once its leader Jesus had been crucified but it survived against the odds and within a few centuries it had evolved into a large complex bureaucratic hierarchy. This institution slowly grew into an organization that not only ultimately challenged but in time replaced the Roman Empire. This huge organization with all its structured dogma, rhetoric, celebration, ritual, scripture, churches, buildings, meanings and symbolism are all based on the one singular event in history that was believed to have happened by Christians. The resurrection of the Christ three days after the crucifixion, thereby leading the way to salvation of life after death for the dedicated and true believer.

After the crucified and Jesus' resurrection, the early Christians started to repeat his message. But more importantly, they started to meet on a regular basis to peach and teach this message of salvation. These meetings also paved the way for the dedicated to teach and recreate the message and events of the Jesus' life leading up to his crucifixion. An example of this is how the last supper became the basic idea for the sacraments of the Mass or how the events leading up to the crucifixion become the Passion story of Christ along with being the basis for many of our holidays and traditions that we celebrate today in the Western world.

This incredibly complex system of traditions, meanings, celebration and ritual that make up the whole idea of Christianity can be summed up in one simple thing, a symbol, a Cross or Crucifix. The idea that the Crucifix represents Christianity is universal, even unbelievers recognize it. It is a very powerful symbol with its own mythology with numerous legends that has given this symbol a life of its own. Despite the fact that is far removed from its simple origin as a form of execution.

Keeping this idea in mind of how a very simple symbol can come to represent so much. I think it is reasonable to assume that this civilization and society would have some type of symbol that represented the event of The Fall of the Watchers.

I think it would be just like today or any other time in history and that the true believers would prominently display their most important symbols. They would have it in their homes, they would wear it as jewelry, they would use it in artwork, it would be very important to them. I think it would be so important that the people who believed in it would do almost anything to protect and preserve it for future generations even if the original civilization that created it was destroyed and forgotten. Although the original civilization that created was gone, the idea and meaning would still be known to a few and live on in the shadows. Once again, the early Catholic Church and its development in pagan Rome is again a good example of this.

I think this might be the missing piece I am looking for, a symbol. It would be just as important as the story but much easier to preserve and pass on. I also think it must be a simple symbol too. A symbol that anybody could make very easily just like the Christian cross. But what symbol? What shape? Where to look?

If we take this idea of a symbol that must be based upon a simple shape and combined it with the rest of the idea. Because I know that the stars of the constellations of Orion and Taurus, including the Pleiades grouping of stars in the winter night sky were very important to our ancient ancestors. So, there must be a connection between these stars and this idea of a symbol, but what is that connection?

Could the shape be based on some grouping of the stars in that part of the night sky? But, once again, what shape? For that matter, which stars? Looking at the area of the night sky, I do not think the shape could be a bull like the constellation Taurus or a hunter like Orion; the shapes are much too complex to be made easily by the average person. The other problem is that I do not see any simple shapes made up by any of the stars in this region of the night sky.

Even if you use astronomy software that shows the night sky as it was thousands of years ago. I still do not see any pattern of stars that make up any simple shape that could be the basis of a symbol. The only interesting thing that I found was that it appears that around 11,000 B.C. ($\pm$ 3,000 years) the Pleiades star cluster appear to have had seven stars instead of the six that are visible today. But that really is not anything new. It has been known for hundreds of years that Pleiades cluster goes back many thousands of years in human culture possibly even to the very beginning.

Although this idea seems promising. The astronomy software makes it look like this idea might be a dead-end. Just another idea that there should be an ancient symbol from this time legendary time of he Fall of the Watchers that is based on a possible grouping of stars in the region of the constellations Orion and Taurus.

With seemingly coming to a dead end and not sure really what to do next with this whole idea of a symbol based on the stars found the stars of the Orion and Taurus constellations. I decided to just start looking at any and all symbols in general, both ancient and modern. Then I would try and decipher their true meanings, or possible meanings. This in and by itself was a fascinating journey into a world that many know very little about.

Chapter 4

Symbols – An idea takes shape

The grave and the image are equally links with the irrecoverable and symbols for the unimaginable.
~C.S. Lewis, A Grief Observed~

As I started this fascinating journey into the symbolism. I began by looking at all the symbols that surround us in our modern world while searching for understand to their true meanings and origins. I was surprised to find how the symbols surround us, bind us, and are the very means in which we transmit our culture, our traditions, and our thoughts history.

Most of the symbols that surround us are simple straight forward and rather mundane. They are so very common that we do not even think about them. These symbols tend to be the everyday normal letters, numbers, and simple shapes we use every single day of our lives.

Other symbols are much more complex in their structure and their meaning. But they still tend to be very common with many people viewing them as rather mundane in our modern world. It is not unusual for these symbols to have multiple meanings that can change rather quickly in time or mean different things to different people. These symbols include advertisements, company logos and artwork, political artwork, pictures of national leaders, among other examples. This type of symbolism normally tries to invoke some type of emotional response when seen. It is also used to try and influence people's thinking or behavior.

Then there are a small number of symbols that seem to be nothing but mystery surrounded in secrets that are only spoken of in hushed whispers. Symbols that are rumored to be ancient in origin that hold great power, but only to those who understand their ancient secrets. These symbols of mystery are surprisingly still very common and familiar to us all. As with the more mundane symbols, they are so common that most people do not even notice them or give them a second thought if they do happen to take notice of them.

These symbols of mystery literally appear on every single item that is manufactured, built, advertised, displayed, sold or seen today. It makes no difference if it is public or private ownership, government or religious, traditional or modern. It was and is still very surprising and rather shocking to me once I noticed and started looking at these symbols. There appears to be great artistic liberty given to the individuals that produce this work and it can be presented in most any way, as long as the basic shape is adhered too.

These symbols of mystery that I am speaking of are so very familiar to us all. In fact, they are so familiar this might come as quite a shock to many once they are pointed out and then begin to notice the symbolism for themselves. It should be noted there are many more symbols of mystery than the fourteen that I will be examining here. All of these symbols have very specific stories and traditions associated with them that I will only briefly touch upon. This is because of the incredibly large amount of existing material that has already been written and produced on this subject and about each of these symbols.

I highly recommend that you do your own research on the following symbols and any other ones that you personally notice. It can be a really interesting journey into a world of secret societies, their mysteries, and the different schools of esoteric thought with their occult like religious beliefs they follow. It is a mysterious ancient world that most people believe had disappeared long ago. A time of wonder, mystery, and what some would say magic. The symbols of mystery that I wish to focus on are as follows:

The Flaming torch.
The Caduceus consisting of two serpents coiling around a staff with wings.
The winged-sun-disk or solar-disk.
Two stone columns, typically with one broken in half.
Three stone columns, with the center one higher or larger than the other two.
The Lightning bolt.
The Phoenix.
The Owl.
The sun.
The moon, normally shown as a crescent.
Five-pointed star, normally presented as a pentagram, sometimes inverted.

Six-pointed star or Hexagram, familiar to most as the star of David.
The pyramid or triangle with the all-seeing-eye.

These thirteen symbols, along with a few others, are literally on everything around us in our modern world. You can find them in one shape or form on every single item in your house, on every advertisement, on the cover of every book, in every company logo, every picture, and every single piece of media or artwork.

If you take a few minutes and look around you. You will find that all the products in your home will have some version of the above symbols of mystery. At first you might not see it, but you will if you keep looking.

Two of the easiest examples to begin with is the pyramid or triangle shape being hidden as a capital "A" or as a pyramid shape in a company logos or product advertisement. The second one is the all-seeing-eye, which is normally paired with either the sun or the winged disk with rays of light coming from it. Both of these symbols are very easy to spot in company logos or any number of other products, especially the ones from the largest companies.

These symbols seem to be incredibly important to the wealthiest and most powerful men and women on the on the planet. They must be; they are literally put on everything. I have also noticed that these same wealthy people seem to spend a rather large amount of time, resources and money to debunk, discredit and confuse any discussion or serious look at this subject of the symbolism. They also seem to attack the whole ancient astronaut idea or that any of the ancient stories could be true history in some way.

This makes me wonder if one of these symbols of mystery could be what I am looking for? Could one of them be the missing piece? Where did these symbols come from? Why do they seem so important to the elites of the world? What do they believe? Are they really "occult" symbols? With so many questions and with so few answers in sight could this be the right path to what I am looking for?

These questions led to spending a great deal of time researching the above symbols and learning a great deal about the subject of the occult knowledge and esoteric thought. I also found a great number of conspiracy theories relating to Freemasonry and a few other esoteric groups. Freemasonry as a whole appears to be centered on the beliefs and practices of Hermetic thought, with esoteric thought that draws upon Rosicrucianism with an influence from Gnosticism. Many of their ideas appear to be found in the more modern Hermetic Order of the Golden Dawn.

I found that the whole subject of Freemasonry, Rosicrucianism, and other secret societies to be filled with almost nothing but misinformation with never ending claims of hoaxes, conspiracies, secrets and lies. Because of this, I must state, that I personally believe that most of this misinformation actually comes from the membership of these various groups themselves. It appears to me and many others that they are playing both sides against the middle and are hiding in plain sight.

Regardless of what your personal beliefs or feelings on the matter, all these symbols point to and eventually lead back to Freemasonry, Rosicrucianism, Gnosticism, the occult, and the general conspiracy claim that the upper leadership of these groups, especially Freemasonry, ultimately worshippers and serve the Fallen Angel popularly known as "Lucifer." This conspiracy also claims they have a sinister plan of taking over the world to impose a New-World-Order of masters and slaves. Now, personally, I do not know if any of that is really true or not. I do know that many of these claims are pretty far out there, to say the least and some of them are downright crazy. But, to tell the truth, these symbols always lead back to these groups and these rather crazy claims.

As I have researched this subject, it has led me to the conclusion that the group that is generally accepted and known as Freemasonry and their Lodges have a basic underlining theme that is loosely based on some type of ancient mystery religion. This mystery religion appears to be based in the secrets of Hermetic thought, Gnosticism, Rosicrucianism, with a mix of the supposed teachings and beliefs behind the more modern Hermetic Order of the Golden Dawn. It has elements of the occult religious idea of a great and powerful God of Light that came to Earth with secret knowledge which is only for a small select group. It also has a very strong Greek, Mesopotamian, with a heavy Egyptian influence, with many rites rooted in these ancient cultures.

The whole subject of Freemasonry, Gnosticism, Rosicrucianism and Hermetic Order of the Golden Dawn and the esoteric or occult belief of a great God of Light that was the Bringer of Light in the form of knowledge and enlightenment is hard to study and research. The primary reason is because the entire idea is based on secrets in stories that are not really ever told to the general public, written about or discussed with anybody who is not a member. The few pieces of information that are available to the general public are not much help with it all only seeming to confuse the matter more.

As I researched this subject, I found references to Helena Blavatsky and her followers of the Theosophical movement. There are also references to the ever-famous Aleister Crowley and the Hermetic Order of the Golden Dawn. A group claimed to be founded by a Mr. William Robert Woodman, a Mr. William Wynn

Westcott, Mr. Samuel Liddell and Mr. MacGregor Mathers in 1887. It is also claimed that these founding members where members of Freemasonry and members of secretive Societas Rosicruciana it Anglia (S.R.I.A.). It is said that Westcott was the initial driving force behind the establishment of the Golden Dawn and it is through him how this group is related to Freemasonry. You will also find books like "Morals and Dogma" by famous Freemason Albert Pike or books like "Pawns in the Game" by William Guy Carr that speak of how elites worship Lucifer worship and grand conspiracies to control the world with secret knowledge from lost civilizations.

You will also find strange references to stories of Atlantis and other ancient lost civilizations. These stories have references to the thirteen symbols of mystery mentioned before. There are other vague, largely forgotten stories that speak of "Gods of Light" coming to Earth long ago.

There are odd rumors and hints that the "real" story is found somewhere in the Bible and the Book of Enoch. These tend to have vague references to names contained within both books and the Fall of the Watchers. There are whispers of gruesome acts related to the evil Moloch spoken of in the Bible. There are also whispers of demons and forgotten gods mixed in with more familiar stories about ancient Greek gods like Apollo or Zeus taking human wives by force. All of these strange stories, rumors and whispers have numerous vague references to mysterious and powerful magical or divine artifacts that have equally strange rituals and otherworldly powers associated with.

The entire thing is pretty macabre, but, in the end, the whole thing will just lead you right back to Freemasonry and similar groups with an endless line of conspiracy theories that only leads to more questions that only go in one big never-ending circle.

Faced with this problem, I decided that the only thing I could do was to focus on the symbols themselves and any concepts that might to be related to them. I also decided to keep an eye on Freemasonry and the other secret societies and what these groups writes about the subject of the symbolism. Since it is rather clear they seem to be connected somehow. I am not really sure at this point where this will lead, but there seems to some type of connection between these symbols of mystery and what I am looking for.

As time went along and I researched these symbols. I began to notice there are multiple stories, ideas, concepts, and meanings about each symbol. Most of these stories are rooted in the classical Western tradition with a heavy Judeo-Christian influence with an esoteric and occult flavor to the belief. It is a confusing mess of stories and ideas spanning up to more than a dozen different traditions and cultures, reaching across thousands of years.

Over time as I examined this material looking for common themes, names, and references. I began noticing that a small number of names, symbols, and mythological stories maintained a rather repetitive theme.

This theme focuses on various stories spread across a dozen cultures that speak of of forbidden knowledge, lost empires, forgotten battles, and legendary wars between the gods of heaven. These stories also hint at a great betrayal and cowardice that led to the ruin of everything. There are names of the Fallen Watchers found in the Book of Enoch and the symbolism of the Bible along with other ancient texts that are all related in some strange way to Greek, Egyptian, Mesopotamian, and even Native American and Eastern mythology.

All of this leads me to think that it is possible that the Book of Enoch, especially the Dream Vision, is providing the general outline of the story along with some details of certain events and the Bible providing many of the details the story. Additionally, the Greek, Egyptian, Mesopotamian, Native America, and Eastern mythology also help to provide some of the details. This is why I started this hypothetical scenario, this thought experiment, with the story contained in the Book of Enoch. It is because almost everything I have found out about these symbols of mystery seems to point back to the Book of Enoch and the story of the Dream Vision. Our next step is to start exploring the thirteen symbols of mystery we looked at before.

The first symbols we will begin with is the Flaming Torch. This was a symbol I was already familiar with and one of the easier ones to understand. The Flaming Torch has two main stories associated with it. One is directly from Greek mythology while the other one is from the Western tradition that has been influenced by Greek mythology and thought. The first one is the story of Prometheus and his stealing of fire from the gods and giving to humanity. This also includes his punishment from Zeus for this transgression. The second is the idea that the Flaming Torch represents the gods or even God bringing enlightenment to humanity, a light out of the darkness so to speak. Both of these stories are talking about the same thing, the event that I have been referring to as the Fall of the Watchers.

The second symbol, the Caduceus, which is two serpents coiling around a staff with wings. This is also a rather very familiar symbol to most. The Caduceus is commonly mistakenly used as a symbol of medicine and medical practice, especially in North America. This improper use has caused widespread confusion with the traditional medical symbol, the rod of Asclepius, which has only a single serpent coiled around it with no wings.

The Caduceus is actually the "Herald's Staff" that is carried by heralds or messengers of the gods. The messenger god Hermes of Greek mythology with

Hermes, also known as Mercury in Roman mythology are by far the most famous examples of this Herald's Staff and the gods that carried it.

A story that many may not be familiar with is the story in Greek mythology of Iris, the messenger goddess of Hera. She said have been the personification of the rainbow that linked the mighty gods of Mount Olympus to humanity just as the sun unites the Earth with heaven. She was believed to travel with the speed of the wind from one end of the world to the other and into the depths of the sea and the underworld.

In Roman iconography the Caduceus was often depicted as being carried in the left hand of Mercury, not only the messenger of the gods, but also the guide of the dead and the protector of merchants, shepherds, gamblers, liars and thieves and representing writing and eloquence. These stories and ideas are also related to The Fall of the Watchers and the interaction between the gods and humans.

The third symbol is the Winged Sun-Disk. This is also a rather easy one to understand that has many stories associated with it. The Winged Sun-Disk is a symbol that has been associated with divinity, royalty and the power to rule because of its connection to gods that stretched across all the ancient cultures of the old would, including, but not limited to Egypt, Mesopotamia, Anatolia, Persia, Asia Minor and so many more. This symbol has also been found in the records of ancient cultures of South America and Australia.

One of the primary ideas I noticed about this symbol was the idea of some god, like Ahura Mazdā from the Zoroastrianism tradition of Persia or of the sun god Shamash or even Ashur in Assyrian iconography shown flying in his winged disk above his armies of human warriors conquering any that opposed them. The other common idea related to the Winged Sun-Disk are references to the sun and its divine nature. It also viewed as being God-like and the source of light that it brings all the gifts to humanity while also giving kings the power to rule. These are more references to the Fall of the Watchers and the bringing of light or enlightenment of a divine nature to humanity in a divine nature while also imparting the power to rule other humans.

The fourth symbol is the Two-Stone-Columns. There are many stories associated with the Two-Stone-Columns. The first and possibly best-known story is that they are they represent the Two Columns that stood in front of the First Temple of King Solomon. These are said to have been two copper, brass, and bronze pillars which stood in the porch of the first Temple in Jerusalem named as Boaz and Jachin.

Within Freemasonry it is believed that they represent wisdom and strength. In the broader esoteric tradition, they are believed to represent the sacred masculine and feminine. Many followers of various different esoteric and occult beliefs believe that when one of the columns is shown broken in half that this represents the rape of the sacred feminine by the Fallen Angel, Lucifer. Again, the same ideas of the Fall of the Watchers. I think we are starting to see a pattern here.

The fifth symbol, the rather uncommon Three Stone Columns. This symbol has many esoteric elements that are very similar to the symbol of the Two-Stone-Columns. These columns are thought to represent Wisdom, Strength and Beauty.

The idea surrounding these Three-Stone-Columns is very similar too and again rooted in the tradition of the First Temple of King Solomon. The Third Column adds the concept of Beauty. The other more occult idea is that the Third Column represents the blending of the sacred masculine and feminine into one perfect being in order to become God-like. This is also normally related the idea of the Bringer of Light that came to Earth and enlightened mankind with divine knowledge.

It is not uncommon within esoteric thought these Three-Stone-Columns are also a symbolic representation of the powerful Trident carried by the sea god Poseidon. It is also related to the Trident-like weapon of the Hindu god Shiva the Destroyer. In Christian tradition and iconography, the Trident is well known as the weapon and staff of the Devil. Here again, we keep encountering the same ideas. What is going on here?

The sixth symbol is the Lightning-Bolt. In Western Tradition, the mighty Lightning Bolt is always associated with Greek god Zeus. Most are familiar with the stories of how he used his mighty thunder bolts to defeat the fearsome Titans. The Lightning Bolt is also commonly thought of as some type of weapon of righteousness that Lord God uses to strike down the unrighteous or the unbelievers that displeased him.

It does seem strange that the Lightning Bolt or Thunder Bolt is always divine weapon of the Supreme god in every single ancient religion and culture we know of. It appears to be a universal idea. This symbol is not directly connected to the Fall of the Watchers, but it is a clear reference to one of the most powerful weapons of the gods that was used during many of the events we are exploring.

The seventh symbol, the legendary Phoenix. This symbol is one of the most ancient symbols connected to the idea of resurrection in some form. Within Egyptian mythology the Phoenix is a magical bird that lives for 100 years and dies in a burst of flame only to be reborn out of its own ashes to live once again.

There are also vague esoteric references and hints that the Phoenix represents the eventual rebirth or resurrection of the Lost Empire of the Fallen Watchers that is said to have existed before the Great Flood. Once again, more ideas that seem connected to the Fall of the Watchers. It is beginning seem like all of the

THE FORBIDDEN KNOWLEDGE OF ENOCH

stories or ideas related to these symbols are connect to do with the idea of the Fall of the Watchers. The mystery only deepens when one realizes that all of these symbols are commonly used by the largest companies and most all of governments on the planet. This realization has to give one pause and make you wonder what is going on here? Why are these symbols so important?

The eighth symbol is the wise Owl. This symbol, like the other seven also has a dual meaning. The first is positive and commonly known. The second is darker, hidden, and so sinister that most would only describe it as evil.

The first meaning of the Owl is the one most are familiar with, the general idea that the Owl represents knowledge and wisdom. It is also an ancient symbol that has always been closely associated to the gods and divine wisdom. It is not uncommon for the Owl to be a messenger from the gods to humanity.

The other viler meaning of this symbol is well known in Christian and occult circles for being connected to and sometimes being used as a representation of the ancient evil god commonly known as Moloch. It is believed that Moloch was a god that was worshipped by the Phoenicians. It is also claimed that Moloch or a Moloch-like god was also worshipped by the Canaanites. What makes Moloch unique is the great number of associations of this god with a particular kind of propitiatory child sacrifice of being burned alive by their own parents. This was said that the reason this horrible act would be done to gain personal power, material wealth, and the protection of Moloch.

Interestingly, in some of the more obscure esoteric writings of various groups. Moloch is believed to be the son of Azazel the Fallen Watcher that taught mankind the art of war and some nameless human woman. Which would make him originally a Nephilim. Although, I think it should be noted there does not appear to any actual historical evidence to support any of this. But this does not stop these groups from claiming he was the grand General of a vast unholy army that was known for its brutal and cruel treatment of those they conquered, especially of the mothers of the conquered. They claim it was from the cruel practice of Moloch taking the children from their mothers of those he had conquered and then having them burned alive before their mother's eyes before raping and then killing the mothers once their children had burned to ash.

As you can see, eight out of eight of these symbols have something to do with the same stories and ideas of the Fall of the Watchers. What about the other five symbols? Are the symbols of the Sun, the Moon, the Five and Six-pointed-stars also connected to this idea? What about the All-Seeing-Eye and the pyramid? Do they have anything to do with the same story?

The symbolism of the Five and Six-pointed-stars appear to be related to the idea that they are somehow representing when God of Light or Lucifer came to earth. Because it is describe as looking like a star falling from heaven. It is also believed that this Fallen Star was about the same brightness as Venus as I mention earlier. They also a number of occult and pagan stories that all seem to be interpreting this same event of some type of God of Light that came to earth long ago with it appearing to be a like falling star to those that witnessed it.

As for the last few symbols of mystery, the Sun, the Moon, the All-Seeing-Eye and Pyramid. I could not find anything that would fit as nicely as the other symbols. Could it be these symbols are from an older tradition? That could be true, but, as time went along, I could not find any good connections between these symbols and this idea.

The more I researched, the I seemed to find. As I began hitting dead ends, I began trying to think of new ideas. One idea that came to mind was if the sun and moon were seen as an annular eclipse. This a solar eclipse where the moon does not quite cover the whole disk of the sun. This has the effect of making the sun and moon like a giant eye looking down from heavens. Although I like this idea, I have no clue where, if anywhere, this idea might fit in. The idea also does not seem to fit when symbolism of the pyramid is added in.

The few esoteric references I could find all seem to point back to ancient Egypt in some fashion with vague whispers about a possible secret cult of Osiris and the Giza Plateau. There are also strange references about the Phoenix, the concept of resurrection, and Jesus Christ, but no details or real evidence to back any of it up. It is at this point in my research that it all started to became very murky, confusing, and with very little of any of it making any sense at all.

This is where it stopped, the All-Seeing-Eye, the Pyramid, the Moon, the Sun. No matter where I turned, no matter where I went, no matter who I talked to, no matter what, I just came back to a whole bunch of conspiracy theories and even more confusion about it all.

Like all the ones that came before me, that is where the idea stopped and has stayed for quite some time, years in fact. No new ideas, no new clues, and no idea where to look next. Not only that, but the real truth was the fact that I was at a complete lost to what I was really looking for. It was all starting to look like a big waste of time on my part and little more than a lost cause. So, as time went along, it slowly moved to the back burner while moved on to other hobbies and projects.

Remarkably, it was through my hobby of being an amateur astronomer and trying to learn how to take digital images of astronomical objects with my telescope that led to a breakthrough that completely changed the way I was thinking about and approaching this entire subject.

Chapter 5

Breakthrough?

From Heaven to Earth, The exile and birth
~The Mirror, R. J. von-Bruening~

I shall adopt new views as fast as they shall appear to be true views.
~Abraham Lincoln~

As I said at the end of the last chapter. It was my hobby of amateur astronomy that provided the breakthrough I needed to start putting the pieces together in way I never imagined before. It is also the idea that led me to think that this legendary Fall of the Watchers may have actually had happened. Not only did this event occur but I realized that it could also be dated. Additionally, there is evidence to support this idea. I think most will it find it rather surprising that this evidence is all around us and very familiar to us all.

One amazing aspect of this idea is that once I saw the connection the rest of the pieces just sort of fell into place on their own with next to no effort. This was when I knew I had to be on to something real. At first it seemed too crazy to be true. But after some more research while putting all of my skills and knowledge to their absolute limit. I think I may have found the piece that ties everything together in such a simple and elegant way. I think by the end you will find it as hard to deny that this is not the missing piece, we have all been searching for.

This breakthrough was quite by accident. I was working on something completely different than ancient religions stories and the possible connections to modern idea of ancient astronauts. It began with me kind of a geek and just playing around with my hobby of amateur astronomy. The strange part is that I was not actually doing any astronomy with a telescope. But I was casually cruising the internet for astronomy related websites, general information, and software. I was not really looking for anything in particular, I just looking for anything that might catch-my-eye or seemed interesting and was related to astronomy.

In doing this, I happened to run across an astronomy freeware program that simulated an imaginary space ship flight through space centered on Earth. What was remarkable about this program was that you could set the variables and it would display what some of the local star fields and some of more common constellations would really look like if you could take a space ship trip to some of the close-by stars that would take hundreds if not thousands of years to complete.

The data for the program was based on the Hipparcos satellite scientific mission of the European Space Agency or ESA. The satellite was launched in 1989 and operated between 1989 and 1993. I spent a few days playing around with it, seeing what it could do, setting up little space flights to and from earth to different stars and then just watching it play out. It did not take long before I ran through all the flight simulations that this little program could do.

After I started getting bored with the flight simulations. I began to realize the significance of what this little program could do. This program could be set-up to display the proper motion and parallax of the stars and display it in real time from a perspective of standing on earth over a period of about 100,000 years from the year 1991. Once again, with all of it being based upon the Hipparcos satellite data.

Just as with the flight simulations. I played around with putting all kinds of different dates and times and then watched the movement of the stars as the program ran. As I was starting to run a simulation back though time, I was interrupted and had to walk away from my computer for a few minutes without setting a stop date for the simulation.

When I returned a few minutes later. I noticed that the simulation did not stop at 100,000 BC as I had expected it to. In fact, it was still running backward in time and displaying the movement of the stars in real time. I then noticed the dates that were being calculated and they went far beyond 100,000 years ago. I was surprised to see that this little freeware went beyond 100,000 years for the movement of the stars in the night sky. This was unlike any other astronomy software I had seen I had seen before and it was free.

Once I discovered that this little freeware program could do this. I once again started playing around with it. I began by looking at the few different constellations that are in the program and running the simulation out for hundreds of thousands of years both past and future.

It was while I was doing this that the breakthrough happened, all by pure chance. I set the program to center on the Orion and Taurus constellations and just started the program running backward though time. As the years slowly ticked by, I watched the screen as the little stars moved around on screen. I watched how after thousands of years the Orion constellation slowly started falling apart as the brightest stars like Betelgeuse, Rigel, and the belt stars slowly moved away from one another though time. I also noticed that as time went farther back the Orion constellation looked more like hunter than it does today. I also noticed that the Taurus constellation wasn't quite as distorted as Orion with it retaining much of its modern shape. It seems that it these stars have always looked somewhat like a bull.

As the small counter on the screen was slowly turning backward clicking off the years one by one and the stars moved around the screen. I did not see anything new or that seemed unusual in any manner. I did not see any simple shapes, no patterns, or anything else that seemed out of the ordinary, just little stars randomly moving around on a computer screen.

This was the unchanging pattern as the little counter was ticking away the years. First it was 10,000 years, then 50,000 years, and soon after it hit 100,000 years. Just as quickly. the counter approached 125,000 years, then it passed 150,000 years ago.

Then, soon after the counter ticked pass the 150,000-year mark, then boom, it happened. Something that just stopped me in my tracks. Something that would change everything about my understanding of these ancient stories of the Fall of the Watchers. What I saw displayed on my computer screen was a set of the brightest stars in the Orion and Taurus region of the night sky that were arranged into a very particular pattern that made a very distinctive shape that made an easily recognizable symbol.

As soon as I saw it, I instantly recognized the shape and I could identify the symbol that was based upon it. I also then quickly realized that if a certain astronomical phenomenon occurred at the same time, it would give an almost perfect match to the symbol that I recognized. It appeared that I had found the missing piece I looking for. I had found the symbol and it was right in front of my face the whole time, without me ever realizing what I was looking at.

This particular shape that these particular stars made at a particular moment in time are so very familiar to every single person on the planet. It is literally on everything you see around you; we are assaulted daily by it on every single product or item you can buy. In fact, you have most likely seen this symbol a dozen or so times today without even realizing it. You are most likely looking at one of the oldest representations on the planet. A symbol, which represents, celebrates, and remembers the monumental event of the Watchers rising up against the old order that brought freedom and civilization to an enslaved humanity.

What is this particular symbol that am I speaking of? It is the same symbol that is on the back of every single U.S. one-dollar bill. It is the Unfinished Pyramid with the All-Seeing-Eye floating above it. This was the shape I saw displayed on my computer screen. I saw the three brightest stars in that region of the winter sky, Betelgeuse, Aldebaran and Rigel making a great triangle in the sky. It was an almost perfect copy and match to the Great Pyramid, it had the same shape, the same dimensions, it also appeared to have the same ratios to pi and possibly more important, it had the same odd 52-degree angle that everybody has wondered about.

This angle of 52 degrees is one of the oddest features of the Great Pyramid and has been commented on by thousands of different people over the centuries. This is because from a construction and engineering viewpoint this angle makes absolutely no sense. Not only does it not make any sense, but no one has ever come up with a good argument on why the builders of the Great Pyramid picked this odd angle. Simple common sense tells you that a 45-degree angle would be much more practical and vastly easier to work with than the actual 52-degree angle we see on this building.

This realization that this angle could be based upon an ancient alignment of certain stars at the time of the Fall of the Watchers could possibly explain the reason why this angle was used. For my personally, this is much more than a simple coincidence.

Additionally, if you were to have annular eclipse of the sun and moon that passed through this set of stars around sunset or sunrise at the right time of the year. It would look like a great big eyeball looking down upon the Earth appearing very similar to the image on the back of the One-Dollar bill.

If that was not enough of a shock; the date that the program showed was even more startling, it displayed 172,000 BC as a date. Once I got over the shock of what I had seen, I started running the program forwards and backwards from around this date. This triangle pattern appeared between approximately 180,000 BC and 155,000 BC with 175,000 BC to 165,000 BC being the closest match to the actual shape and dimensions of the great pyramid.

This date of 175,000 BC to 165,000 BC is startling and beyond belief. I found it just as shocking as you must hearing it for the first time. It is date that next to impossible to accept, it is just too far back in time based on what we know. Just as you are right now, I did not want to believe it either. My first thought was that there was no way this could be right. There had to be some problem with the program, after all, it is freeware and not originally designed to do what I was using it for.

Not wanting to believe it, I decided the best thing to do was to work it all out by hand. I sat down with my star charts and catalogs and working out the calculations by hand. When I started, I was very confident that I would prove the program was wrong and the dates of 175,000 BC to 165,000 BC was nothing more than wishful thinking and I had not found anything new.

So, I began the slow work of looking up star locations, proper motion and parallax, while trying to account for other changes in the earth's orbit over time like precession and obliquity. As I did the work and started actually plotting the positions of these stars over time, I quickly noticed, that I was coming up with very similar pattern with remarkably similar dates.

Although my calculations have a great degree of uncertainty and the dates I provide here are based on an average of those estimations. But, as we go along, I will provide some additional reasons on why this average date may be the correct one. Amazingly, no matter what I did, I kept coming up with dates around 155,000 BC give or take 15,000 years. To make matters worse, I could not find any mistakes even with all the uncertainty in my calculations.

The more I researched and ran the numbers the more it seemed those dates fit. I then went back and re-ran the program forwards and backward around this time measuring everything I could with the limited abilities of the program. While doing this, I started noticing that there were two other well-known stars moving around in the same area of the sky, Pollux and Bellatrix. When I included them into the simulation and much to my surprise, I found another shape with a pattern that was as unmistakable as the triangle shape was before. This is when everything started falling into place and this epiphany began to take shape in my mind.

The basic idea that formed in my mind is this; what I am calling Fall of the Watchers took place sometime around 155,000 BC, give or take about 15,000 years. This was a time when the three brightest stars in the western winter sky, Betelgeuse, Aldebaran, and Rigel made an almost perfect copy and match of the Great Pyramid.

This could be the reason why the Great Pyramid was built. It was originally a great monument to the astounding and almost unbelievable, monumental, and mind-blowing event of a great Lord of Light came to Earth. An event that looked like looking like a Falling-Star. A Fallen-Star that brought freedom, enlightenment, and civilization to humanity. For untold millennium by all the ancient cultures of the world this event was remembered as a great day. It is only thousands of years later that within the Western Judeo-Christian tradition this monumental event is transformed in the rebellion against God and the Fall of Lucifer and his fellow Angels.

If this idea is true, then this would mean that the Great Pyramid was the first monument built to celebrate and commemorate this almost unbelievable event. This grand building was carefully aligned to these three bright stars. Additionally, the construction of this great building must have started soon after this great event. Due to the fact that these stars no longer line-up within about a 10,000-year period based my estimations.

If we pause for a moment to imagine in our minds what it would be like to go back in time and see the Great Pyramid all those thousands upon thousands of years ago. What I think you would see, if you were standing at the entrance of the causeway that led from the River Nile to the Temple that once stood in front of the Great Pyramid looking toward the western sky. Just after sunset or just before sunrise around the time of the winter solstice with the pyramid between you and the horizon. You would see a monumental impressive visual sight of this overwhelmingly massive pyramid shaped mountain of white limestone on the ground. With the exact same triangle shape matching it in the night sky right above it. If you were to add in the already impressive colors that normally accompany sunsets or sunrises, you would have a spectacular sight by anybody's standards. It would be extremely powerful sight to anybody that saw it.

Additionally, if at any time during this alignment an annular eclipse happened to occur at the same time just after sunrise or just before sunset while this celebration of this event occurred. Then you would have this incredible view in the sky with what would have looked like a giant eyeball set at the apex of the Great Pyramid looking down upon the world. This type of event would be even more impressive if by chance the other two bright stars Rigel and Aldebaran were visible during such an event. Although this does provide a possible answer to the symbolism of the All-Seeing-Eye, at a much later point we will explore another possibility that may provide a much more realistic idea of what the All-Seeing-Eye might actually represent.

Now, I know this idea seems crazy at first. But, if you think about it for a few minutes, you quickly realize, that this crazy idea is testable. If anything about this idea is correct, then everything about the Great Pyramid will line up with these three stars perfectly at around these times. This should allow you to pin down the actual and true construction date for this building, independently, by the stars themselves.

Not just the layout of the building, but the various shafts that originate from the Kings and Queens chambers should point to stars that would have only been visible at this long distant date. The northern shafts still appear to point towards the north celestial pole. If this thinking is correct, then it should be unmistakable to even the untrained eye. If it is incorrect, then nothing will line up and it will be back to drawing board with this idea going down in flames and thrown into the dustbin of history.

Additionally, and remarkably, noticed another star pattern when I added the star Pollux into the mix. As I went beyond 155,000 BC, to my amazement, a new pattern began to take shape as the stars moved through time. Starting at approximately 200,000 BC, the four stars Betelgeuse, Aldebaran, Rigel and Pollux lined-up to made a diamond shape. This diamond shape is made up of two triangles with stars Betelgeuse and Aldebaran as the base of the triangles with the star Rigel being at one apex and the star Pollux being at the other. If this line of thinking is correct, it does not take much realize that this basic configuration could be the origin of the six-pointed-star or Star of David symbol. I think this double triangle shape of these stars and symbol of the Star of David cannot be discounted out of hand.

I think this is much more than just a mere coincidence that these shapes are so close together. I also noticed that if you follow the movement of these stars as a group over a long period of time you will notice their shape slowly changes. This slow change in shape over time is what I think is one of the most important parts of this thought experiment. Because if you follow these stars over time starting around 210,000 BC you will see that the shape goes from a four-star diamond shape of two triangles to the familiar Great Pyramid shape at around 175,000 BC. The pyramid shape only comes into play when the star Pollux does not line up.

If we keep moving through time following these same stars. We will find that around 72,000 BC these stars make a new triangle shape with Pollux moving out of the picture. The stars Rigel and Aldebaran again make the base of the triangle with Betelgeuse at the apex. But, unlike the Great Pyramid, this triangle shape is much flatter than before. This flatter shape in fact appears to match the shape of the Pyramid of the Sun located at Teotihuacan in Mexico.

Remarkably, the Pyramid of the Sun is similar to the Great Pyramid in the sense that it appears to have been based upon the same pattern of stars but at a much later date. We see the same shape, the same ratios to pi, and we see the same odd matching angle of 43.5 degrees that is observed in the Pyramid of the Sun. Which appears to match the angle between these stars at around 72,000 BC. As with the Great Pyramid, this could explain a great number of mysteries related to not only these, but many other ancient monuments that have peculiar angles or mysterious layouts.

This way of thinking led me to a new idea. That you should be able to trace this civilization though time based on these stars. Because every time they built a great monument for some important event, the architecture, the site layout, and the angles would reflect the changes in the night sky based on these same stars. This would then allow you to actually date the time period of when these massive buildings were built. For example, whenever there was a large political change or societal upheaval. The new rulers would take over the existing system and then impose themselves upon it, just like we do today. They would then build new monuments and buildings to reinforce their power with the architecture reflecting this change, thereby allowing us to trace this change through time. If we trace these changes through time, we will discover that this idea is not as crazy as it first might have seemed.

Starting around 200,000 BC, we can easily see the diamond shape made by the stars Betelgeuse, Aldebaran, Rigel and Pollux. Again, it does not take much imagination to see the possible beginnings of the Six-Pointed-Star or the Star of David symbol. It should be noted that the location of the belt stars of Orion in this picture are not in the correct position. They are shown only for reference purposes.

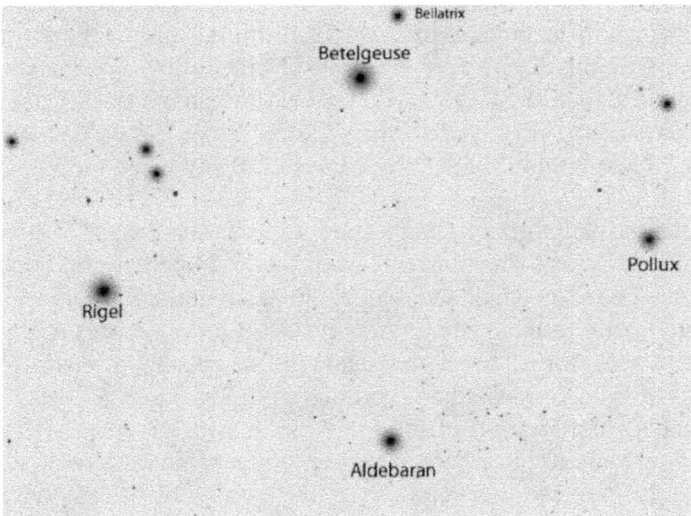

View of the Betelgeuse, Rigel, Pollux and Aldebaran 210,000 BC. Facing west with the stars just above the horizon after sunset. (Fig.1) [1]

Based upon the oldest stories from the earliest civilizations I think this was a time of slavery. A time when there was only one group of gods in charge. There does not appear that there were no monuments built during this time period, for there was no reason for them, just a possible symbol based on the pattern of stars in night sky that were somehow related to the gods and their mighty power.

After thousands of years, the mysterious group I have called the Watchers begins to establish their power. At around 155,000 BC (+ 15,000 years) these Fallen-Watchers need to establish their power and control over the human population. Just like we do today, they just take the existing symbol and change it slightly by removing one star. This is most likely because at this time it had moved and no longer made a nice clean diamond shape. This moment of the stars is what changes this simple diamond shape into the triangle that will become the basis of shape of the Great Pyramid we all know so well today.

The next image will give you a good idea of how the Great Pyramid and the night sky might have looked at this ancient time. Unlike before, the familiar belt stars of Orion and the star Bellatrix are very close to what their actual positions would have been.

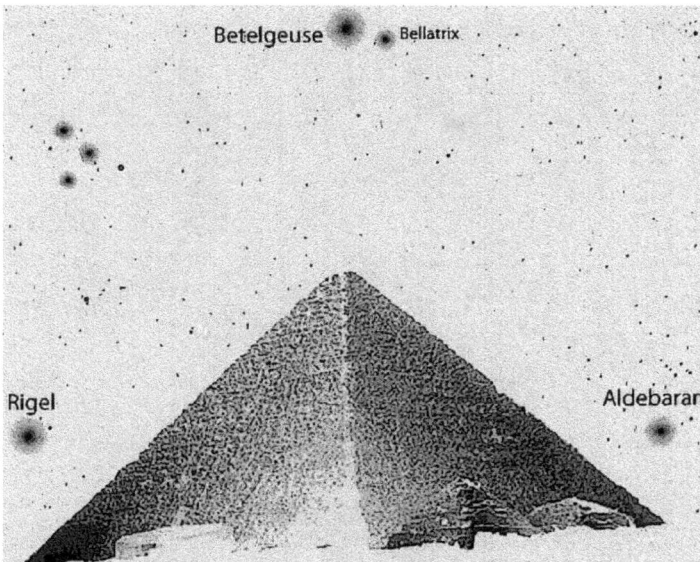

The Great Pyramid, 155,000 BC. (+ 15,000 years) Not to scale. (Fig.2) [2]

As this society develops over time and increases in population and complexity. I think the Great Pyramid is constructed to honor the great event of the great Lord of Light coming to Earth and freeing humanity from slavery. I think it is fair to say the Great Pyramid was most likely a project that was used to keep the newly freed population busy by using their existing skills and infrastructure.

I base this on idea or concept that some form of mining was taking place as reported in many ancient traditions. This would also give the reason to why the Great Pyramid was constructed in the first place, it was to commemorate and remember this great of event of the Lord of Light coming to Earth before the stars moved too far out of place.

After tens of thousands of years have passed, around 72,000 BC, the Main-Group returns and reestablishes their control and power over the Earth. This is reflected by bringing back the fourth star Pollux into the symbolism made up by the stars of the night sky. Once this Main-Group had reestablished their power, they began building new monuments to their greatness. The architecture of this new building would reflect this change in the night sky. Because the new buildings would be aligned with this old grouping of the same bright stars.

This new phase of construction would not only include the establishment of new sites and monuments, but they would also take over the existing sites that the Fallen-Watchers had established. This was done by incorporating the new alignments into the new monuments showing their power.

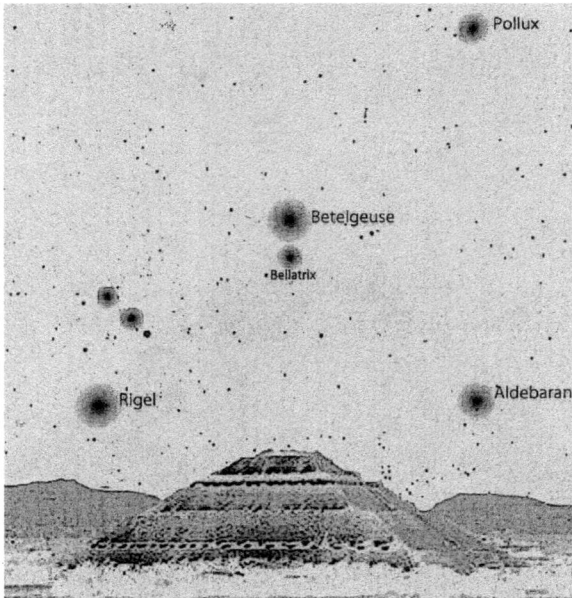

Pyramid of the Sun in Teotihuacan, Mexico at approximately 70,000 BC. (Fig.3) [3]

This is why there is the change in the shape of the general pyramid design that we can see is reflected in the Pyramid of the Sun in Teotihuacan, Mexico. The following image shows what the Pyramid of the Sun with the configuration of the four brightest stars in the night sky may have looked like about 72,000 years ago. I wish to point out that the star Bellatrix and the Orion belts stars may play a possible role in the alignments.

This change of the positions of the stars would explain the anomaly observed and recorded over the years that the pyramids of Menkaure and Khafre on the Giza plateau appear to have been built at a later date than the Great Pyramid. Also, the pyramids of Menkaure and Khafre have a slightly different building style than the Great Pyramid. Most notable is that both pyramids have a much simpler internal structure without the chambers and shafts that are found within the Great Pyramid.

If this scenario is correct, then this simpler internal design of would make sense. Because these pyramids were built to reflect a political change that incorporated the old ideas and symbolism. While at the same time, these pyramids were also used to show how the Main-Group was now superseding the existing power structure, especially when it came to the night sky.

I think this is why the other two pyramids were added to the Giza Plateau. It was done to reflect the political power change that took place among the gods. Once these new pyramids were constructed the apex of each pyramid would line up with the stars Rigel, Betelgeuse, Aldebaran, and possibly Pollux.

As we explored earlier, would mean if you were looking west from the Nile, the star Rigel would line up with the Pyramid of Menkaure, Betelgeuse would line up with the Great Pyramid, and Aldebaran would line up with the Pyramid of Khafre. There is also a possible alignment with the star Pollux lining up the pyramid of Khafre.

The final image in this series of images of the Giza Plateau will give you a much better idea of how the Pyramids of the ancient Giza Plateau and the night sky may have looked to the local population around 70,000 BC. I do think it would have been a rather impressive sight to anyone who had seen it in real life. I also believe it would have made a large emotional impact on the people who come to see this once a year. The bright star on the right-middle side is the star Cygnus, I included to show that it might have been related to these alignments.

This allows us to realize that the reason we are seeing the same basic architecture and style that is separated by great amount of time. It is because we are seeing the same continuous civilization over tens of thousands of years. Not only are we watching one continuous civilization over thousands of years, but we are also seeing the big political and social changes reflected in the architecture. This change is due to the changing alignments of the brightest stars of Rigel, Betelgeuse, Aldebaran, and possibly Pollux.

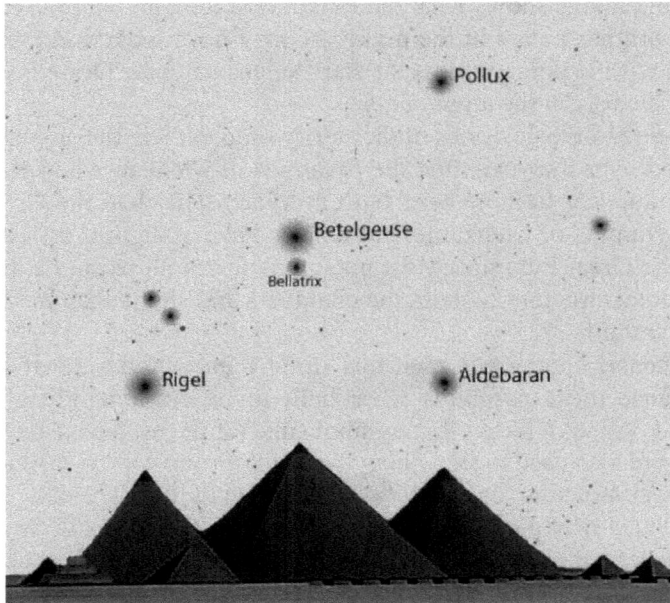

Giza Plateau, 70,000 BC. (+8,000 yr). (Fig.4) [4]

Although it first started with a simple diamond shape, over time, it slowly changed. At the time of the Fall of the Watchers the stars had moved into the nice clean shape of a triangle with a side angle of 52 degrees as seen the Great Pyramid. Then thousands of years later when the Main-Group had reestablished their power the stars had moved into a flatter triangle seen reflected in the design of the Pyramid of the Sun at Teotihuacan.

Then later, once these stars had moved so far from their original positions that their original simple shapes disintegrated. The newer buildings and designs of various building complexes would have been based on these individual stars. But since the original shape had disappeared long ago, the new lay out of the individual buildings would look out of place when compared to the older ones due to this change in alignment.

This also seems to be the time the Pleiades grouping of stars begins to become important. It could be when the general pyramid shape finally falls apart in the night sky, the ancients start using the Pleiades grouping of stars. As with today, I think this was simply because they are in the same part of the night sky as the other stars we have looked at and the also stand out when compared to the other stars in the area. This would mean that the Pleiades cluster could provide another set of stars to use as a way to date these events. In a later chapter, I will explore this idea in greater detail along with some very interesting artifacts that support this idea about the Pleiades cluster.

This idea, that the Great Pyramid of the Giza Plateau could be over a hundred thousand years old. Not to mention that other similar sites around the world could be tens of thousands of years older than we have ever believed before is most likely more than most can take. To be perfectly honest, I am not sure I really believe any of this myself. Because if it is true in any way, it would have major implications in our way of understanding and thinking about our origins, our genesis.

Since these dates go so far back in time and are so radical, I decided I had better reexamine the whole idea and carefully look for mistakes or other problems. In addition, I do not really want to be like all the other so-called theorists and just come up with an idea with some vague references that do not seem to fit what we know or not be able to back it up with something more than just a few possible star alignments or fragments of some ancient stories.

Chapter 6

Returning to Enoch

And all the days of Enoch were three hundred sixty and five years: And Enoch
walked with God: and he was not; for God took him.
~Genesis 5:23, 24~

W e will now return to the original hypothetical scenario or thought
experiment with keeping the ideas of the last few chapters in mind.
We will start by trying to establish a timeline with the idea that the
Fall of the Watchers occurred around 165,000 BC while trying to use our current
scientific understanding of the last few hundred thousand years of human
existence to aid us. I will also be taking a very literal interpretation of the Dream
Vision contained within the Book of Enoch. Additionally, this interpretation will
be relying heavily on my personal understanding of the esoteric symbolism and
some of the occult beliefs behind them.

Our story begins around 250,000 BC or even possibly earlier. Where a small
technologically advanced group of unknown individuals came to Earth. Once
here, they quickly established a colony or outpost for the purpose of food
production and natural resource extraction. Then, slowly, over an unknown
amount of time, the conditions begin to deteriorate to the point of where a strike
or rebellion occurred among the class that performed the necessary labor for
creation to function. Although the details of this rebellion are vague, it was bad
enough that it led to the creation of a slave race that would provide the necessary
labor. The creation of this slave-race was the result of genetic engineering that
took an existing species already here on Earth and making them slightly more
intelligent. With this occurring at approximately 225,000 BC.

In this scenario, I am going propose that this new Slave-race was not only Man that is spoken of in the ancient stories. But, more importantly, I am also going to propose that it was the species known to us today as Homo Neanderthalensis or Neanderthal man. This is due to the fact that Neanderthal is the only species found in the fossil record dating from this ancient time. Another reason is that in my mind, based on the way Neanderthal was built, he is kind of a perfect match for the idea of creating a humanlike species that was going to be used for heavy manual labor.

If we take a moment and think about how Neanderthal was physically built and different from ourselves. We will find that he is a very good fit to Bull described the Dream Vision in the Book of Enoch. If we do this, I think you will also easily see and understand how Neanderthal could be described as a "Bull" when compared to later versions of known modern humans. Specifically Cro-Magnon Man, our most direct ancestor who is also known as Homo Sapiens and ourselves Homo Sapiens-Sapiens. Additionally, as we go along, we will see that this idea is also in line with the Mitochondrial Eve idea that was mentioned earlier.

Physically, Neanderthals were very robustly built and were very strong and powerful, especially compared to ourselves. They had a body that was generally heavy and solid with a strong musculature for its size. The average Neanderthal was stronger than the strongest humans alive today. This robustly built body normally had longer collar bones and wider shoulders that sat atop a barrel-shaped rib cage which was much larger than a modern human. They had larger kneecaps with the thigh bones being thick and bowed. They also had proportionally shorter legs with a longer torso and a longer pelvic area than modern humans. In addition to the physical differences, Neanderthal also had a larger cranial or skull capacity of modern humans.

These physical differences are why I think Neanderthal had an almost perfect body design for heavy back breaking labor. At least physically, Neanderthal appears to be built to be the perfect slave. These differences also make it easy to imagine how Neanderthal could be described as being like a Bull when compared to us.

The next idea I would also like to propose is that what we find in the fossil record; is not showing us individuals that live in small family that live in small tribal society that shelter in caves. But could in fact be showing us the remains of individuals that could be escaped slaves or exiles from this slave-race society. That might be quite a leap for most, but it would explain many of the injuries, trauma and arthritis observed in the remains found in Neanderthal remains today.

If we take a moment and think about this, we will discover this outrageous idea is not so outrageous after all.

It has been remarked by many experts over the years that Neanderthal showed a high frequency of fractures and injuries that is comparable to that of modern-day rodeo professionals and other professions that have frequent contact with large combative animals. Remarkably, this pattern of injury can also be just as easily explained by slave-labor. I also spend quite a bit of time trying to find any studies that compared the pattern of injury found in Neanderthal remains to those victims of more modern-day slavery that was used for heavy manual labor and found none. So, it makes it rather difficult to dismiss either way when the comparison does not appear to have ever been done in the first place.

Now, although the data does not exist, but if we take a moment to explore this idea. I believe it is rather easy to come up with a number of examples of what could have been going on at this time that allows us to get a better idea of may be happening with Neanderthal. The America Civil War might be one of the best examples from more recent history.

If Neanderthal lived in a slave-based society as I am putting forward in this scenario. Then what we find in the fossil record could actually be individuals that had been escaped or exiled slaves. These would have been people that would have had great trouble living off the land. It is easy to think they would have had little to no knowledge on how to survive without the support of society.

If we look at the time period of before and during the America Civil war when slaves escaped from the south trying to go north in the bid for freedom and a new life. While in process trying to live off the land, hiding, avoiding capture, not knowing who was friend or foe. For their own survival these individuals tried very hard no to draw any attention to themselves or to any others with them. I think this simplified scenario can give you a good general idea of what these Neanderthals could have been experiencing.

The main thing to keep in mind in using this example. Is that while these modern-day slaves had a direction and a place to run to, it is likely that Neanderthal on the other hand, would have had no "North" to escape too. He would have just the vast endless wilderness in which to disappear. They would have always had the never-ending fear of capture and the return to a life of slavery with the possibility of being executed.

I think it is highly probable that these individuals would have banded together in small groups hiding in caves while trying to stay out of sight leaving little to no trace behind. Which is very much like what we find today in the fossil record when it comes to Neanderthal. This would also help explain the degenerative diseases that are clearly found in individuals with nutritional deficiencies that appear to be common in the remains of the older Neanderthal population.

So, as you can now understand, this outrageous idea is not so outrageous as it first sounded. Because it does fit our current understanding of Neanderthal. Although the idea it does fit the current evidence, it is missing many other pieces. In order to help fill in some of the missing pieces to this puzzle we need to take this idea of Neanderthal slavery and return to the idea of the Fall of the Watchers.

This general situation of Neanderthal being used as a slave went on for thousands of countless years until the ones recorded in the Book of Enoch as the Watchers rebelled and freed mankind. This rebellion and the freeing of humanity is the event I have been referring to as The Fall of the Watchers. As many are already aware, this event of the Fall of the Watchers then leads to the events that are later remembered as the Great Flood.

After this Fall of the Watchers, it would have been necessary for the new rulers to have to set-up a whole new society that was not based upon slavery. It would also have to use the existing skills and infrastructure of the local population. This then brings us back to the building of the Great Pyramid on the Giza Plateau which in my mind would be the perfect project that would fit the bill. It would take hundreds if not thousands of years to build. But, more importantly, it would keep the freed slaves busy for a very long period of time. A period of time that would be long enough to allow for the establishment of an entirely new society and belief system that was not based upon slavery.

This idea goes a long way in explaining how many of the great stones many have been moved. For Neanderthal is much stronger than modern humans. He was short, strong, and built like a bull. By luck or design he was very well built for moving large masses around with nothing more than brute strength. Also, given the time period we are talking about here, I have to wonder if any of the large animals from this time could have been used in the construction of any of these ancient monuments? Along with Neanderthal, it would help explain how the largest blocks could have been moved without modern technology.

Eventually, once this grand construction project was completed. More individuals would be available for food production or other tasks and population would in time increase. This population increase would make it necessary for immigration to new lands for resources and living space. Based on the fossil record, it appears that this started occurring around 150,000 BC. This is when we begin seeing Neanderthal moving north across the Eurasian landmass into Europe where he is firmly established by 125,000 BC.

We also have to remember that during this time there are very long periods of time when not much of anything happens outside of day-to-day life. The endless days of working the fields, taking care of family, making and trading items needed by others occupy most of their time. But there was also the never ending need to gather crops, animals, and raw materials to sacrifice to the gods. What little is known point to the idea that during these times existence was a nice but rather boring and routine. If, by chance there were any problems among any groups over land or resources the gods just intervene and put an end to it.

With all the ideas we have covered in mind, I will now return to my hypothetical scenario where I left, at the time of the Great Flood when the Main-Group had returned. I will begin with the previous text from the Book of Enoch found in Chapter 88, 1.

"And I saw one of those four who had come forth first, and he seized that first star which had fallen from the heaven, and bound it hand and foot and cast it into an abyss: now that abyss was narrow and deep, and horrible and dark."
(Book of Enoch 88: 1)

In this scenario, I think this verse of the imprisonment of the *'fallen stars'* that is clearly spoken of here did not occur at this point of the story. I prefer to use the more traditional viewpoint that these fallen stars were not imprisoned at this point in time. They were just denied access too or use of their divine powers or technology. They were in a matter cast down from heave or exiled to Earth.

I think this is the point where the idea of that the fallen stars only real power is the power of temptation. The temptation of the forbidden knowledge of the divine and the secrets it contained. This was the forbidden knowledge of freedom with all the technology and power that come from it. This was an ideal that had to be destroyed by the ones returning for it does not bode very well for a slave society to have any ideas of freedom within the slaves themselves.

I think this was a major factor in this invasion and re-conquest of Earth. The civilization that had been created by the Fallen-Group and their offspring had developed to the point that that slavery could not be imposed again easily. This is also the beginning of the idea of the "Lost Paradise" that is so fondly remembered in many different traditions. I think this could be the reason why it was decided that most everybody alive at the time would be killed in a Great Flood.

This resulted in gods flooding the original enclosure that was built to hold the slaves Although they save a few of their old allies, the group remembered as Adam. This was done by instruction them to construct an ark to survive the coming flood of this enclosure. This raises the questions of this enclosure and of its location. This also raises the additional question; can this event be dated?

First, I will address a possible location of this enclosure. Which I suspect, based on the many different flood stories from countless traditions, this enclosure would have to be some type of large low-lying valley that could be flooded and then drained or pumped out. Which looking an any detailed map of the world, the Mediterranean basin would be a good match.

The Mediterranean basin could fit the descriptions given in the ancient stories of a large area that could contain a number of human communities. It would go a long way in explaining the strange reports and claims made over the years of ancient ruins under the Mediterranean Sea that nobody can explain. I think it would be an ideal central location not only in size but it would also be relatively easy to contain and control a sizable population with a small number of guards. Just like the Watchers described by Enoch. What I think could have happened might be much like when the Black Sea was formed as the last of the ice melted from the last Ice Age.

This would mean that the Mediterranean basin was a large low-lying valley with few possible fresh water lakes at the lowest points being fed by the river systems that still exist today. These river systems could be the original rivers spoken of in many different ancient traditions. For example, the four rivers that come together to form one river in the Garden of Eden as described in the Book of Genesis in the Bible. I suspect this might be the reason nobody has ever found them because they are not only looking in the wrong place, but also the wrong time.

As for a possible date for this Great Flood. I have always thought that the Toba super-eruption that occurred approximately 72,000 BC give or take 2,000 years. It is a very good fit for the idea of a world-wide catastrophe that would have decimated most of the human population. The Toba super-eruption is recognized as one the Earth's largest known volcanic eruptions. It is believed to have plunged the planet into a 6-to-10-year volcanic winter and with possibly an additional 1,000-year cooling episode. This change in climate resulted in the world's human population being reduced to as few as 1,000 or less breeding pairs of humans.[1] This created a bottleneck in our human evolution that has been proposed to have caused modern races to differentiate abruptly approximately 50,000 to 70,000 years ago. These dates also are very close the alignments of the stars Rigel, Betelgeuse, Aldebaran and Pollux that I proposed earlier.

During this event, this enclosure, which was the Mediterranean basin was flooded by opening up the Straits of Gibraltar thereby letting the Atlantic Ocean flood in. This would have been a catastrophic event to anyone that was living in the area. If this was witnessed from a high vantage point above the valley or the side. I surmise that it would look similar to what is described as the Great Flood in the Bible. This in turn this would mean that the mighty Ark did not settle upon Mount Ararat in modern day Turkey. But it would have settled on one of the mountains that now make up the many islands of the Mediterranean Sea.

Returning to the Dream Vision where the four that looked like white men went to that *"white bull and instructed him in a secret."* All agree is referring to the story of Noah and who is later raised up to some type of higher state. This account of the Great Flood gives a slightly different description of the story that is found in the Bible. But I suspect in may be more accurate than the traditional story of who was on the Ark. Which was not a bunch of animals, but a few chosen Bulls or Neanderthals in which to create a species that would be easier to control. This would help breed out the idea of freedom and hopefully allow the reestablishment of the same type of slave society as before. These three bulls are remembered as the three sons of Noah that are spoken of in the Bible. With that text appearing to provide additional details to this story.

> *"And one of those four went to that white bull and instructed him in a secret, without his being terrified: he was born a bull and became a man, and built for himself a great vessel and dwelt thereon; and three bulls dwelt with him in that vessel and they were covered in."*
> (Book of Enoch 89: 1, 2)

After the Great Flood we are told the waters receded and the Ark came to rest upon land. The story appears again to break along mysterious racial lines. A white, red and a black bull are again described as before in the creation of bulls earlier. I cannot help but wonder if this is connected in some way to some of the racism we still have today? Is it something that is left over from a long-forgotten conflict between different groups of individuals that we have next to nothing in common with? Could we possibly trace these groups based on the information contained in the Bible? So many questions with so much confusion with few answers in sight.

> *"But that white bull which had become a man came out of that vessel, and the three bulls with him, and one of those three was white like that bull, and one of them was red as blood, and one black: and that white bull departed from them."*
> (Book of Enoch 89: 9)

The next part of the text of the Dream Vision seems to speak of possible genetic engineering and the creation of new species. I am going to make the assumption that Neanderthal is the genetic matrix that these new species are created within and that the sheep that is spoken of is the one we know as Cro-Magnon-Man. Who starts to leave traces of themselves in the fossil record at about 40,000 or so years ago.

Much like Neanderthal, Cro-Magnon-Man were robustly built and powerful. Their bodies were generally heavy, solid, and with a strong musculature. The forehead was straight with slight brow ridges and a tall forehead.[2] Cro-Magnons were the first humans of the genus Homo to have a prominent chin. The brain capacity was about 1,600 cc on average, which is about 100 cubic centimeters larger than the average for modern day humans.[3]

Cro-Magnon were anatomically modern, straight limbed and tall compared to the contemporary Neanderthals. They are thought to have been about 5'5" to 5'7" (166cm to 171cm) tall. [4] They also differ from modern day humans in having a more robust physique and a slightly larger cranial capacity.[5] The Cro-Magnons had long, fairly low skulls, with a wide face, a prominent nose, similar to features seen in modern Europeans. A very distinct trait is the rectangular orbits of the eye sockets.

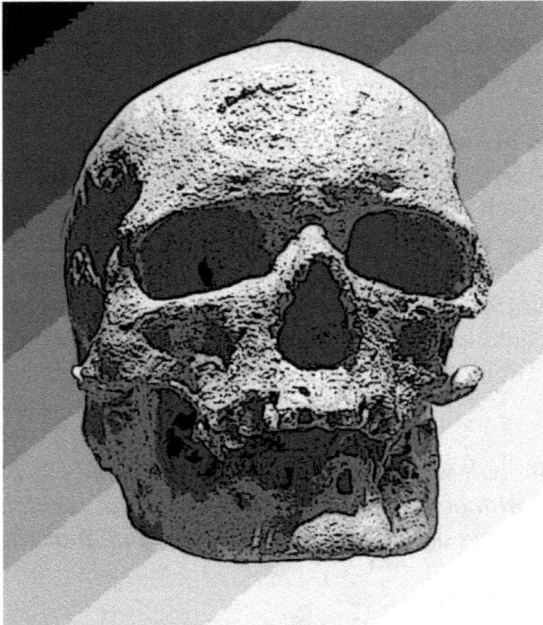

The original "Old man of Cro-Magnon," Musee de I'Homme, Paris. (Fig.1) [6]

I would like to put forward the idea that this is also the time period where most all the ancient stories that speak about monsters and people that were said to be half-human and half-animal come from. I would also like to put forward the idea that this is the time where the term Son of Man comes from in the Judeo-Christian tradition. With the general idea being that if Neanderthal is remembered as the Man or the First Men, then Cro-Magnon who was born of this Man then he becomes the Son of Man. This would also mean that the possible time period for these events occurring was between 70,000 BC to around 39,000 BC with the sheep or Cro-Magnon-Man being born around 41,000 years ago.

"And they began to bring forth beasts of the field and birds, so that there arose different genera: lions, tigers, wolves, dogs, hyenas, wild boars, foxes, squirrels, swine, falcons, vultures, kites, eagles, and ravens; and among them was born a white bull. And they began to bite one another; but that white bull which was born amongst them begat a wild ass and a white bull with it, and the wild asses multiplied. But that bull which was born from him begat a black wild boar and a white sheep; and the former begat many boars, but that sheep begat twelve sheep."
(Book of Enoch 89: 10-13)

There appears to be up to possibly seventeen different genetic groups created including the sheep. This is in addition to the Main-Group, the original Bulls or Neanderthal, the Nephilim and the members of the Fallen-Group each of who are also associated with a different animal type.

There is another idea I would like to propose. Because it appears that these different genera of animals spoken of in the Dream Vision could be the animals spoken of in the Biblical story of the Great Flood of Noah. It would go a long way in explaining many mysteries surrounding this most ancient of stories and who created these beings and how any of the followers of the Fallen-Group could have survived the destruction of the Great Flood. They could have been some of the animals remembered in the story. I will leave it to you to decide if this could be a possibility worth concerning for greater thought or time.

I am going to speculate that each of these groups had the traits of or possibly looked like the animal described in the text due to their mannerism or dress. That the ones called lions had lion like traits, possibly powerful & graceful like a lion or possibly they actually looked like lions. Maybe much like what we see in ancient statues and carvings, with the Sphinx being the best example of a creature that has the body of a lion and the head of a man.

This then raises the idea that these lions or possibly the Sphinx ruled in this area known to us as ancient Egypt. That would also mean that the other animal references from other cultures and traditions are possibly speaking of the same events. If true, then you might be able to trace the distributions of these groups though the various monuments like the Sphinx. This might allow you to be able to figure out what areas they ruled or lived in.

There also appears to be some type of conflict between these different groups with the text stating "*and they began to bite one another.*" I think this could be referring to some of the ancient Greek stories that speak of conflict between the different gods, monsters, strange creatures and their followers.

This brings us to the last line of verse thirteen which speaks of a white bull begetting "*a black wild boar and a white sheep.*" This line just jumps out at me, because it reminds me of the story that is contained in the Epic of Gilgamesh along with many questions. Could this be the time that is spoken of in the Epic of Gilgamesh? Could the "*black wild boar*" be Enkidu spoken of in the Epic? Is this the wild man that was created by the gods as Gilgamesh's equal to distract him from oppressing the citizens of the city-state of Uruk?

Could the Epic of Gilgamesh actually be a detailed account of this ancient time? Could all the other stories and carvings of strange beasts and battles with monsters and demi-gods be real in some fashion? Could all of the ancient stories and traditions be talking about the same things? Have we all been looking at this in the wrong way? Also, is this what all the esoteric religions are trying to get at through the symbolism? Is this how it all starts tying together through ancient mythology? Strange as it sounds, it is starting to appear that way.

Traditionally, within the Dream Vision, the twelve sheep have been viewed as the same twelve tribes of Israel that are contained within the Bible. This is one of the primary reasons put forward by scholars that this text is talking about Israel and is just the Biblical story in a symbolic form.

This is most likely correct, but I think we need to expand upon this idea a little bit. In the aspect that these sheep should be thought of as representing the different tribes of Man. Which in the Biblical story is the twelve tribes of Israel.

On an interesting side note, the traditional idea of the twelve tribes of Israel is incorrect, because the Bible very clearly states that there were originally thirteen tribes of Israel, not twelve as many believe. The tribes of Israel in the Bible are: Reuben, Simeon, Judah, Zebulun, Issachar, Dan, Naphtali, Gad, Asher, Benjamin, Ephraim, Manasseh, and Levi. Which is thirteen, not twelve. They reason everyone thinks there were twelve tribes is because the tribe of Levi was given no territorial allotment of land except for a small number of cities located within the territories of the other tribes.

This lack of a territorial allotment of land for the tribe of Levi is the reason everybody, including Biblical scholars and experts included, thinks there are only twelve tribes of Israel. The reason everybody forgets about the tribe of Levi is because of the ancient tradition of the division of people based on the apportionment of land. If you had no land, you had no resources, which meant you had no economic power or political power because you could not raise or pay of the necessary manpower that was required in ancient societies. Additionally, in these ancient societies it was common for the elites to view someone without economic or political power as always being possibly dangerous to those that do. As a landless person, you would quickly have been viewed as a common person or people and thereby not recorded like all the other faceless souls that make up most of society as the lower classes. Although the tribe of Levi was vastly different from the common person because they were the priests, they still owned no land and are thereby normally forgotten about.

Getting back to our scenario. It is with these sheep or twelve tribes of man made up of Cro-Magnon-Man are then moved around by the Main-Group. This Main-Group as I have been calling them, enters the story as the *Lord of the sheep,* who is always being spoken of in the singular.

"And when those twelve sheep had grown, they gave up one of them to the asses, and those asses again gave up that sheep to the wolves, and that sheep grew up among the wolves. And the Lord brought the eleven sheep to live with it and to pasture with it among the wolves: and they multiplied and became many flocks of sheep."
(Book of Enoch 89: 13-15)

Strangely, outside of the Bible, there does not appear to any other cultures that remember this part of the story. I am personally unaware of any similar stories speaking of these events story. But I think the next set of verses give some hint to something the wolves did that later led to a gruesome ritual that is still remembered today. Although it may not be clear to you, they also give a hint to the time line of events and how they unfolded.

"And the wolves began to fear them, and they oppressed them until they destroyed their little ones and they cast their young into a river of much water: but those sheep began to cry aloud on account of their little ones and to complain unto their Lord."
(Book of Enoch 89: 15-16)

The first line of these verses provides the important clue to understanding that the wolves are the ancient Egyptians and this is a slightly different account. It is also our first clue to what might actually be going on here.

The verses speak of how the wolves *"destroyed their little ones."* This is a very telling piece of information for anyone that has studied occult knowledge or esoteric thought. This term has traditionally been interpreted as meaning some type of human sacrifice of children.

Traditionally, within Western religious circles and esoteric thought there is only one historically affiliated individual in the western tradition that is associated with child sacrifice, Moloch. Moloch, who is also known as Molech in the Bible is claimed to be a god that was worshipped by the Phoenicians and figures heavily in the Bible. It is also claimed that most of the ancient cultures of Middle East, including the Ammonite, Hebrew, Canaanite, among others worshipped Moloch and performed rituals of child sacrifice to them. These rituals to the god Moloch have traditionally been understood to be the ceremonial sacrifice of children by their own parents.

It is claimed that this horrible sacrifice would take place in front of a large brass or bronze idol of the god Moloch. This large idol would normally have the head of a bull and the body of a man. This figure would be seated, cross legged, with its hands and arms out-stretched over a cone shaped pit. In this pit, a large fire would be built and kept burning for a number of days, until a fair number of hot coals had been created. After this pit of fire had been prepared. It is said a mysterious and gruesome ceremony would be under taken that would result in parents tying up their very own children and then throwing them on the out-stretched hands of the idol. As they watched their child burned alive quickly turning to ash, they pray and ask for rewards in this world from Moloch.

This is the ritual and ceremony that is recorded in the Bible and meant by the term *"passing through the fire"* or *"passing children through fire."* As well as being documented in Scripture. It is also recorded in other traditions that had practices of rendering an infant immortal by *"passing them through the fire."* The early Greek myth of Thetis or the myth of Demeter as the nurse of Demophon are examples of this ritual.

Within the esoteric thought and occult traditions there are a number of different ideas and concepts related to Moloch. But, remarkably, for all the claims and Moloch's fame along with the Biblical references, there is actually very little evidence supporting any of the many claims made about Moloch or the rituals said to be made in his honor. Additionally, although there is really no evidence supporting what I am about to state there are two ideas about Moloch that stand out to me.

The first of these is the idea that Moloch was originally a prince of hell or even a possible son of Lucifer the Fallen Angel. He is said to have led a great army against the returning Angels before the Great Flood. It is also said that he died just before the Great Flood fighting the Arch-Angels of Heaven. Then at some later point in time through some mysterious process he was reborn as a god and has since become a symbol for the Lost Paradise of the Fallen Watchers and their followers.

In another idea, he is once again originally a Nephilim or possibly even a Giant. But, unlike the other idea, he did not die in battle but that he survived the Great Flood. After the Great Flood he becomes one of the many that were damned to walk the Earth as lost souls and demons. It is hinted at that he is related in some fashion to the wolves spoken of in the Dream Vision. He is thought of being a possible leader of the wolves or maybe a god they worshipped at some point in the ancient past. It is believed that he hated mankind and blamed them for the loss of the paradise that the Fallen Watchers had built. He also hated humanity because they were the favorite of the hated Lord-God.

This I find very interesting that there seems to be esoteric and occult beliefs that appear to be based directly on the Dream Vision that is in the Book of Enoch that are also clearly rooted in the Biblical tradition. These stories seem to me to be at the core of the idea of worshipping the Fallen Watchers and their hybrid offspring as some type of god, normally viewed as evil in some manner.

Interestingly enough, these ancient ideas seem to be related to ceremonies that are claimed to happen in elite circles. One of the most famous of these is the claim of an idol being worshipped by the elites that meet at Bohemian Grove in Monte Rio California. It has been witnessed that in front of a large owl-like idol the elite members of Bohemian Grove perform a ceremony known as the "Cremation of Care." Which is a reenactment of a child sacrifice to an unknown god, which many believe is Moloch, in the hope for Earthly power and the return of the Lost Paradise of the Fallen Watchers.

Although this sounds outrageous, there is ample evidence supporting these claims. Which raises many questions of why are some of the most powerful people on the planet involved in performing a reenactment of a ritual of child sacrifice? A ritual that appears to be based on an ancient and rather sinister religion that requires the sacrifice of helpless children for Earthly gain?

The very fact that anyone is seriously performing rituals based on the ancient idea of child sacrifice. Should make any sane person stop and think, if only for a moment, why would anybody be doing anything even closely related to child sacrifice? Even if it is all just a "reenactment" why would some of the most powerful men on the planet be doing this? This alone makes me wonder if there could be much more to this idea of the Fall of the Watchers and these more outrageous esoteric stories and ideas? I am beginning to believe so.

The next few verses speak of how one of the sheep or Cro-Magnon-Man somehow escapes the wolves to the wild asses who then give up that sheep to the wolves. We are told after these events this Cro-Magnon-Man laments to the Lord of the sheep which then comes and speaks with him.

> *"And a sheep which had been saved from the wolves fled and escaped to the wild asses; and I saw the sheep how they lamented and cried, and besought their Lord with all their might, till that Lord of the sheep descended at the voice of the sheep from a lofty abode, and came to them and pastured them. And He called that sheep which had escaped the wolves, and spake [spoke]with it concerning the wolves that it should admonish them not to touch the sheep."*
> (Book of Enoch 89: 16-18)

As you can see, this is very similar to the Moses and Exodus story contained within the Bible. The pieces that are missing from the Dream Vision are the details related to when Moses escapes Egypt into the desert and eventually meets the Lord-God as the burning bush. This is one of the reasons people have confused these stories, just like the twelve tribes. These events are not only talking about Pharaoh and ancient Egypt but also about early man and his dealings with people being influenced by surviving Nephilim and even a possible second slavery for man.

Which, after speaking with the Lord or Main-Group, the sheep or Cro-Magnon-Man returns to the wolves who are possibly under Nephilim influence to tell them to stop their oppression. As you can guess, this did not go over too well and results in more oppression.

> *"And the sheep went to the wolves according to the word of the Lord, and another sheep met it and went with it, and the two went and entered together into the assembly of those wolves, and spake [spoke] with them and admonished them not to touch the sheep from henceforth. And thereupon I saw the wolves, and how they oppressed the sheep exceedingly with all their power; and the sheep cried aloud."*
> (Book of Enoch 89: 18-20)

This leads to the Main-Group or Lord coming and smiting the wolves and leading the Cro-Magnon-Men to safety by dazzling and blinding the wolves.

This seems to be suggesting that some type of advanced weaponry was being used. Possibly something that looked like lightning? Could it have been a type of ship? Was this a military operation? The truth be told, it could have been any of these and so much more.

In this developing scenario I think it was more of a military operation to free this group of humans from the wolves. I also think it is possible that the Nephilim with the help of members of the defeated Fallen-Group are moving around somewhere in the back ground providing aid or advice. This operation results in the wolves being blinded. Although this blinding may have been physical it also seems to be symbolically related to ignorance. Which in turn gives the indication that many of the wolves, including the sheep, did not have any understanding of the circumstances or the actual motives behind the actions of the "gods."

"And the Lord came to the sheep and they began to smite those wolves: and the wolves began to make lamentation; but the sheep became quiet and forthwith ceased to cry out. And I saw the sheep till they departed from amongst the wolves; but the eyes of the wolves were blinded, and those wolves departed in pursuit of the sheep with all their power. And the Lord of the sheep went with them, as their leader, and all His sheep followed Him: and His face was dazzling and glorious and terrible to behold."
(Book of Enoch 89: 20-23)

This version of the story is so very similar to the Biblical Exodus story of Moses and the Egyptians. That I cannot help but wonder if the ancient people that eventually became known as Jewish people of today might have high-jacked this story while adding their own names and places making it their own? Could this be why there appears to be small discrepancies between the two stories? Could we have all been missing something? Have we been looking at this ancient story the wrong way? If any of these ideas or concepts about this timeline are correct, then all of these things could possibly be true.

After the liberation of the humans from the wolves and even possibly some surviving Nephilim they are led to a sea of water that is divided providing a path to safety for them. Once again, this is similar to the Exodus story, but, unlike the Exodus story it the Lord and not Moses leading them. As with the Bible, we are told the army that was pursuing them was then destroyed when the waters crashed back in on them drowning them.

This seems to be telling us that the biblical story could be providing possible details to this more general story in the Dream Vision. Additionally, could the ones we remember as Moses and Pharaoh in the Exodus story actually be Cro-

Magnon Humans from 28,000 to 38,000 years ago and not the more traditional 3,000 to 4,000 years ago? Could these small differences between the Bible account the Dream Vision of Enoch, among other traditions actually be what was added by others over the centuries in an effort to make it theirs? I think it is something to give serious thought too.

"But the wolves began to pursue those sheep till they reached a sea of water. And that sea was divided, and the water stood on this side and on that before their face, and their Lord led them and placed Himself between them and the wolves. And as those wolves did not yet see the sheep, they proceeded into the midst of that sea, and the wolves followed the sheep, and [those wolves] ran after them into that sea. And when they saw the Lord of the sheep, they turned to flee before His face, but that sea gathered itself together, and became as it had been created, and the water swelled and rose till it covered those wolves. And I saw till all the wolves who pursued those sheep perished and were drowned."
(Book of Enoch 89: 23-27)

These events then lead them to being led into a wilderness that had no water, no food, but that their eyes were opened and they began to see and understand.

"But the sheep escaped from that water and went forth into a wilderness, where there was no water and no grass; and they began to open their eyes and to see; and I saw the Lord of the sheep pasturing them and giving them water and grass, and that sheep going and leading them."
(Book of Enoch 89: 28-29)

Once again, this is so very similar to the Exodus story that is contained within the Bible. I think the idea of *"pasturing them and giving them water and grass"* is given in greater detail in the Bible. This part of the story is the story of the Lord-God providing water and food for the Israelites after their escape from Egypt while in the wilderness. Which, if this possibly timeline is correct, then the real reason we have never found any actual evidence of the great Exodus of Egypt and Moses outside of the biblical story is because we are looking at the wrong time period and at the wrong people.

Before we move on, I wish to pause for a few moments and go over a few of the major points we have covered in order to put a clearer picture in your mind of the idea that is in my head.

At this point we now have possibly a dozen, up to two dozen different groups of humans. Most of these groups are broken into two main camps that I have called the Main-Group and the Fallen Watchers or Fallen-Group. As with tradition, neither side can stand the other and view each with disdain and hatred while viewing themselves as the ones being the good rightful rulers of this world. We also have a number of ancient stories, mythology, and traditions about the same type of events that seem to have taken place at different times with different individuals.

My point is, we now see and understand that have two Creation of Man stories, two War-in-Heaven stories, two Lords of Light coming to humanity stories, two stories of individuals that were half-human and half god stories. We also have two stories of being led out of darkness into the light along with an unknown number of stories of sex, violence, battles and war spread across almost 150,000 years. With realizing that of this is being seen and recorded by all these different groups which then comes down to us though two main traditions, the monotheistic tradition and the esoteric and occult traditions.

This is why it has been so confusing to everybody. It is because we have not only missed, but we have also forgotten how the story goes together and how big it really is. This is why all the stories seem related and talking about the same events, it is because they are. They are just looking at it from one of the countless different viewpoints about the same events. Then add in thousands of years of mixing of stories and you end up with one huge confused mess that makes no sense while seeming to all be connected over an almost unbelievable span of time.

Chapter 7

Exodus

Thou shalt not bow down thyself to them: for I, the Lord thy God, am a jealous
God, visiting the iniquity of the fathers upon the children unto the third and
fourth generation of them that hate me;
~Exodus 20:5~

The next verses of text continue with what appears to be the Exodus story
of the biblical tradition. With the Main-Group or Lord appearing before
the people causing them to become terrified of his presence and before
"His" face. As with the Biblical story, this leads the sheep or Cro-Magnon-Men
to choosing a leader to speak to this Lord on their behalf.

*"And that sheep ascended to the summit of that lofty rock, and the Lord of
the sheep sent it to them. And after that I saw the Lord of the sheep who stood
before them, and His appearance was great and terrible and majestic, and
all those sheep saw Him and were afraid before His face. And they all feared
and trembled because of Him, and they cried to that sheep with them [which
was amongst them]: 'We are not able to stand before our Lord or to behold
Him.' And that sheep which led them again ascended to the summit of that
rock,"*
(Book of Enoch 89: 30-32)

This story along with the biblical story seems to be where the stories of a
Moses-like-figure that ascends a mountain to speak to with his Lord-God on
behalf of the people originate from. These verses also bring to mind the Epic of

Gilgamesh and the story on tablet nine of Gilgamesh's journey to a far and distant land in search of immortality from the legendary Utnapishtim, one of the few survivors of the Great Flood and had been granted immortality by the gods. The Epic mentions Gilgamesh crossing a mountain pass and battling lions and taking their skins. Could this be referring to Egypt in some fashion or maybe the Sphinx?

He then journeys to the twin peaks of Mount Mashu located in a great cedar land at the ends of the earth. It has been theorized that this "Cedar Land" could possibly be the great forest that once covered Lebanon and western parts of Syria. With the pass he moves through being the one that lies between the parallel Lebanon and Anti-Lebanon mountain ranges. It is claimed in the Epic that the entrance to the land where Utnapishtim lived was guarded by two terrible scorpion-like-men and that no man had ever crossed beyond that point. The story also tells us of how after these guards stop and question Gilgamesh, they recognize his semi-divine nature and allow him to pass. He then travels through the mountains along what the Epic calls the Road of the Sun, which he follows until he arrives at a beautiful garden paradise full of jewel-laden trees.

There are actually a rather large number of cylinder seals and other artifacts that scholars believe show a number of different scenes from the Epic of Gilgamesh. Many of them appear to show Gilgamesh battling a lion with the wild-man Enkidu battling a bull. This is one thing about these ancient cylinder seals that everybody agrees on both expert and laymen alike.

A great number of these ancient cylinder seals show a star with eight-rays or points radiating out from it. This symbol of the eight-pointed star has been traditionally viewed as some type of representation of a god or being divine-like. This ancient star symbolism is very similar to the six-sided star symbol that is so common in our own modern-day.

These ideas raise so many questions. Could this symbolism be related somehow? Could this star symbolism be representing some type of a ship that so many people claim is evidence for Ancient Astronauts? Is this ship where the idea of the star symbolism comes from? Could these stories be related and speaking about the same events from different points of view? Could the Epic of Gilgamesh actually be some type of detailed account of the some of the events in the Book of Enoch? Could you figure out where the garden paradise full of jewel-laden trees was located at? As we go farther along with this thought experiment and if the idea of the alignments is correct, we might be able to start answering some of these questions and so much more.

THE FORBIDDEN KNOWLEDGE OF ENOCH

Illustration of the Eight-Ray-Solar-Disk or Solar Disk Symbol. (Fig1) [1]

Continuing on with the verses of the Dream Vision. The sheep begin to become *"blinded and wander from the way which he had showed them."* This line is one of the reasons, why I suspect *"blinded"* may also be related to ignorance or not understanding what was really going on. This makes me wonder, if the real reason that the "sheep" become "blinded" is because of remnants of the Fallen Watchers are corrupting them somehow?

There could be some type of ongoing hot and cold political going on with both sides trying to avoid an open shooting war. This situation would get worse over time with a constant struggle between the two groups over the labor force they both needed. It could also be an indication that the Lord-God or Main-Group was not having direct contact with the population on a regular basis. What little contact that did occur was mainly though some type of intermediary middle man. This could be where the idea of the gods or God choosing only one individual to have contact with and then working though that person to control society as seen in the Exodus story.

"but the sheep began to be blinded and to wander from the way which he had showed them, but that sheep not thereof. And the Lord of the sheep was wrathful exceedingly against them, and that sheep discovered it, and went down from the summit of the rock, and came to the sheep, and found the

greatest part of them blinded and fallen away. And when they saw it they feared and trembled at its presence, and desired to return to their folds. And that sheep took other sheep with it, and came to those sheep which had fallen away, and began to slay them; and the sheep feared its presence, and thus that sheep brought back those sheep that had fallen away, and they returned to their folds."
(Book of Enoch 89: 32-36)

This violence that is used against the sheep to return them to their folds. Appears to indicate that whatever way that was shown to these early Cro-Magnon humans was not well received. Again, this could be due to them being corrupted by remnants of the Fallen Watchers.

This violence also seems to show us that this Main-Group seems to rule though fear and intimidation. If this is true, this could be an indication to why the Fallen Watcher rebelled in the first place so long ago. Additionally, it could also mean that the Fallen Watcher might not be quite as demonic as most think. This could be a description of a civil war or power struggle within the groups themselves. But, without knowing the specific details it is difficult to say what is going on with any confidence. Although, it is clear that something very significant happened all those thousands of years ago. Something so significant it was remembered in all the different ancient stories and myths.

The next set of verses speaks of how that sheep which had brought back the others to their folds was raised up in some way above the other sheep and turned into a man or higher state of being. That man then "*built a house for the Lord of the sheep*" and placed all the sheep in that house. Soon after this, that sheep that had come and met the first one from earlier in the story and who that went with the other sheep to talk to the wolves dies.

"And I saw in this vision till that sheep became a man and built a house for the Lord of the sheep, and placed all the sheep in that house. And I saw till this sheep which had met that sheep which led them fell asleep: and I saw till all the great sheep perished and little ones arose in their place, and they came to a pasture, and approached a stream of water. Then that sheep, their leader which had become a man, withdrew from them and fell asleep, and all the sheep sought it and cried over it with a great crying."
(Book of Enoch 89: 36-39)

These verses might be a better fit for the Epic of Gilgamesh than the idea I presented before. Could the sheep that had met that first sheep one be the one we

84

remember as Enkidu? Could this be related to the beginning of Gilgamesh's quest for immorality where he eventually meets Utnapishtim? It does seem that Gilgamesh's quest for immortality after Enkidu death would be a better fit for these verses. Could this be describing the time between the death of the sheep that had met the first one and the eventual death of the first one?

These questions lead to even more questions. Such as could this sheep that became a man or raised to a higher state of being actually be Gilgamesh the great hero and leader of men? Could the "house" that is spoken of be the first city of an empire or kingdom that existed and ruled over by Gilgamesh? Could all the ancient legends that speak of some semi-divine leader of men be speaking of the same events? With finally, could we figure out when and where this all might have happened? Although it might seem impossible to answer these questions. We might be able to figure out a few details on the location of these events and possibly the time in which they occurred by returning to the Epic of Gilgamesh.

As we saw earlier, the Epic speaks of Gilgamesh going on a quest from Mesopotamia to what may be Egypt, them moving north from the Nile River valley to the Cedar Land. The Epic does state that Gilgamesh was the King of Uruk and modern science does substantiate that Gilgamesh was a real person and the ruler of the ancient city of Uruk in Mesopotamia.

Using the Epic as our guide, we can trace Gilgamesh's path from Uruk to Egypt, where he most likely followed the ancient coast line heading west until he came to the ancient land of Egypt. From there he traveled northward to the forests and valleys of Lebanon and Syria. Where we are told that he takes the "Road of the Sun" to the grand garden paradise with the jewel-laden trees and meets Utnapishtim. This would place this paradise of jewel-laden trees somewhere in western Turkey.

This part of the Epic is also clue to a possible location of the legendary Ark of Noah within the biblical tradition. It also provides us a reason why nobody has ever found anything related to Noah's Ark and the Great Flood in general. It is simply because everyone is looking in the wrong place. Because this ancient story seems to be telling us that the correct location of Noah's Ark should be somewhere around the area of Aegean Sea. If true, then this would mean that Noah's Ark most likely came to rest on one of the many mountains of the Aegean Sea, which are now islands today. If my idea of the Mediterranean basin is the location of the great enclosure that was flooded is correct. Then the Epic of Gilgamesh appears to also indicate that this is the area where we need to be looking at.

As for the possible time period for these incredible events. In this timeline I am building, I think these events occurred sometime between 34,000 BC to

28,000 BC. This is also the time just before and after we see Cro-Magnon-Man begin migrating out of Southern and Eastern European areas into the Middle East and the eastern Africa regions in the fossil record. The next part of the text could to be speaking of this migration of Cro-Magnon-Man.

We are told that after the death of the first sheep that became "*a man and that led them.*" It describes them crossing a stream of water that they had come to before the death of that first sheep or leader. Could this be referring to one of the many river-systems that exists or once existed between Africa and the Middle East? The text also speaks of how the eventually came to a pleasant and glorious land. Could this be where the idea of a "promised-land" comes from? Could this pleasant land be area around the ancient city of Uruk? Could it be possible that the stream of water spoken of in the Dream Vision could be the river Euphrates in modern day Iraq? If the Epic of Gilgamesh is actually talking about the same events as this story in the Book of Enoch, we may be able to actually locate evidence for some of these ancient stories.

The text then speaks of how two leaders arise and take the place of those leaders that had passed from this world. I think this part might be referring to all the ancient stories that speak of two-brothers which are commonly known as being twin-brothers in the ancient stories. There are many different myths and ancient stories about two-twin brothers. Almost all of them seem to have the same general theme of the brothers constantly struggling with each other while bringing order out of the chaos of the world.

Within the ancient cultures of North and South America, Vedic India, or even the mythologies of Castor and Pollux or Atlas and Gadeiros of Greek fame. The brothers are always ridding the world of terrible monsters. They are also known for ridding their people of disease while they create order out of the prevalent chaos in the world. In some of the mythologies the monsters are presented as a type of primordial enemy of gods that seek to exterminate all life in order to make the world unfit for humans.

Could these be stories speaking about fighting the last of the Nephilim and the Fallen Watchers? Could all these stories of twin-brothers be talking about two leaders doing everything they could to hold a fragile and loosely tied together group of twelve different tribes of man together after their great leader had died? The Dream Vison does seem to indicate that something like this may have been going on.

"And I saw till they left off crying for that sheep and crossed that stream of water, and there arose the two sheep as leaders in the place of those which had led them and fallen asleep (lit. 'had fallen asleep and led them'). And I

saw till the sheep came to a goodly place, and a pleasant and glorious land, and I saw till those sheep were satisfied; and that house stood amongst them in the pleasant land. And sometimes their eyes were opened, and sometimes blinded, till another sheep arose and led them and brought them all back, and their eyes were opened."
(Book of Enoch 89: 39-41)

This "house" that is spoken of, appears to a special type of new building like a temple or monument. I also think that this new building would have been most likely been aligned with the original stars we have explored. If this thought experiment is current, then there might be a way to figure out its location.

These verses also seem to be telling us that the Main-Group or Lord of the sheep does not seem to always be around leading or instructing these people. This would help to explain why the sheep become "blinded" and lose their way, or as many traditions say, they come under the influence of the Fallen Watchers and their bastard offspring the last surviving Nephilim along with their allies.

The text implies a large amount of time passes and a new leader arises long after the death of the twin-brothers. This new leader reunites the different groups that had been blinded. This leader quickly leaves the story with this line in the text being the only mention of him that I am aware of. I do not know who he could be or if he was important in anyway besides holding this group together. He may have been pushed out of power because of what comes next, some type of war among the animals between the dogs, foxes, wild boars and the sheep.

The text seems to indicate that the dogs, foxes and the wild boars were winning the war by devouring the sheep, until the Main-Group raised-up another sheep to be a ram or leader. This ram then begins attacking the dogs, foxes, and wild boars until he destroys them. The text hints that this was done is pincer like attack that wipes out the other side's forces.

"And the dogs and the foxes and the wild boars began to devour those sheep till the Lord of the sheep raised up [another sheep] a ram from their midst, which led them. And that ram began to butt on either side those dogs, foxes, and wild boars till he had destroyed them all."
(Book of Enoch 89: 42-44)

The next set of verses talks of how this leader becomes unseemly, behaves badly, and abuses his power. This might be where it all began with the idea of how power and glory can corrupt even the best of men and greatest of leaders.

"And that sheep whose eyes were opened saw that ram, which was amongst the sheep, till it forsook its glory and began to butt those sheep, and trampled upon them, and behaved itself unseemly."
(Book of Enoch 89: 44-45)

These ideas, when taken with the next part of the text and as strange it might sound. They could possibly be related to the events that are spoken of in the ancient Greek stories of Dionysus and his dealings with King Lycurgus of Thrace. A man who is driven insane by Dionysus because he bans the worship and the cult of Dionysus in the city state of Thrace.

There is also this reference again about the dogs oppressing the sheep. I cannot help but wonder if these terms might have something to do with all the references about dogs in the ancient mythology? Could the dogs of Orion the hunter, Canis Minor and Canis Major be related in some way?

"And the Lord of the sheep sent the lamb to another lamb and raised it to being a ram and leader of the sheep instead of that ram which had forsaken its glory. And it went to it and spake to it alone, and raised it to being a ram, and made it the prince and leader of the sheep; but during all these things those dogs oppressed the sheep."
(Book of Enoch 89: 45-47)

Could this have something to do with Orion the hunter or any of the other legendry hunter myths? The next two verses seem to hint that it could be referring to these other ancient hunter stories through the symbolism of the dogs.

"And the first ram pursued that second ram, and that second ram arose and fled before it; and I saw till those dogs pulled down the first ram. And that second ram arose and led the [little] sheep. And those sheep grew and multiplied; but all the dogs, and foxes, and wild boars feared and fled before it, and that ram butted and killed the wild beasts, and those wild beasts had no longer any power among the sheep and robbed them no more of ought."
(Book of Enoch 89: 47-49)

This could be speaking of Orion, Nimrod, Gilgamesh or any of the other great hunter-like figures that kill the "wild beasts." It is confusing which of the stories could be related to these verses. But I am sure that there is some type of relation between them all. It could be that all the stories about great hunters remembered in so many traditions could be speaking of this time and maybe one or more of these leaders. This could also be the time that the Osiris stories of Egypt originate from. They just seem to have all become so intertwined that at the moment I do not see how to unravel them from one other.

This new leader of men that reunites the people then raised an army that was used to crush the enemy of the "wild beasts." This could be the first empire of man and all these different stories are all talking about the events leading up the creation of this empire.

Could this also be the beginning of the story and the idea of Atlantis and how it was the center of a worldwide sea-fairing trading empire? Could it be related to the other myths that speak of ancient lost civilizations? The next set of verses I find to be very interesting and may be more important than the Fall of the Watcher was and is more relevant to the world of today.

The reason I think that this text speaking of a tower and could be related to the stories of Atlantis that speak of some type of tower that was the at the center of the island or city and was also the location of the ruling god or point of contact between this god and humans.

"And that ram begat many sheep and fell asleep. And that house became great and broad, and it was built for those sheep: and a tower lofty and great was built on the house for the Lord of the sheep, and that house was low but the tower was elevated and lofty, and the Lord of the sheep stood on that tower and they offered a full table before Him."
(Book of Enoch 89: 49-50)

In Plato's myth of Atlantis, the god Poseidon fell in love with the beautiful Cleito and carved his beloved, a great palace and high tower out of the large high mountain located at the center of the island. The myth also says that Poseidon then enclosed the grand palace and tower with three circular moats to protect his love, and to connect it the city and the sea.

In the Biblical tradition this tower is the Tower of Babel that was said have been built by Nimrod the great-grandson of Noah. In the Book of Genesis, it is said that he was the first monarch and that *"he began to be a mighty one in the earth"* and *"He was a mighty hunter before the LORD."* [2,3]

This also appears to be a clue that ties many of these ancient stories together and gives an indication that they are all speaking of the same individual and the mysterious events that surround him. Who this individual exactly was or what his real name was; are things we may never know with any certainty. However, it is clear that this individual made an incredible impact on his society and was highly regarded by the people around him. So highly regarded that he was remembered in so many different traditions, cultures, and myths that are separated by not only time but also by great distance.

Traditionally, it is believed that the building of the tower led to Nimrod's reputation as a king that was rebellious against God. According to the biblical story and tradition, the generations following the Great Flood, there was a united humanity that spoke a single language. These people are said to have migrated from the east to settle in the land of Shinar. This is where these people resolved to build a city with a high tower. A tower *"whose top may reach unto heaven; and let us make us a name, lest we be scattered abroad upon the face of the whole earth."* [4]

In Aztec mythology there is the similar story of "Xelhua" the 'Architect' who was said to be one of the seven giants that escaped and survived the Great Flood by ascending the great mountain of Tlaloc in the terrestrial paradise. It is said that afterwards he built the Great Pyramid of Cholula. The account is recorded by a Dominican monk and found in chapter 6 of the Mexican Ophiolatreia.

In the Ophiolatreia we are told that *"When the waters subsided, one of the giants, called Xelhua, surnamed the 'Architect,'"* went to Cholula. Here is built an artificial hill in the form of a pyramid. A pyramid that was to a memorial of the Tlaloc which had served for an asylum to himself and his six brethren. He ordered bricks to be made in the province of Tlalmanalco at the foot of the Sierra of Cecotl. In order to convey them to Cholula he placed a line of men from Tlalmanalco to Cholula who passed them from hand to hand. The gods beheld with wrath an edifice the top of which was to reach the clouds. Irritated at the daring attempt of Xelhua, they hurled fire on the pyramid. Numbers of the workmen perished. The work was discontinued, and the monument was afterwards dedicated to Quetzalcoatl. [5]

There are a number of common themes that run through all of these tower stories and traditions. One of the most common that is nearly a universal idea is that this legendary tower reached to heaven. It is also very common to hear that some type of offering was always given to the god that stood upon it. Sometimes this offering was accepted while at other times it was rejected, but there is always this idea of an offering.

I think this 'offering' that is spoken of is nothing more than food and material that was demanded by the gods for their protection. This is just a slick way of tricking early humans into being slaves without them knowing it by the gods. This would be an effective manipulation tactic to control and exploit a more primitive society. Especially, with that added bonus that you would not need the use of a large military force. In this case, you would only have to make them fear you because you might unleash your wrath and smite them for their disobedience. Many traditions speak of this godly wrath being a heavenly or divine power that takes the form of lightning or thunder bolts that cause great destruction and death to those who defied the will of the gods. In others this wrath takes the form of natural disaster like an earthquake or a great and terrible storm that is focused on the transgressors. In addition to this wrathful power of the gods. The stories speak of how the gods always handpick the leaders of men and give them some form of divine power in order to receive their commands and do their bidding. I think this divine power that allows these leaders to communicate with the gods must be some type of technology.

At this point, I would like to put forward the idea that this society and civilization could be the foundation for the ancient and almost forgotten empire of Atlantis. I think it would be reasonable to think that the vast majority of the population of this civilization was kept at a rather primitive level of society and technology. Only the gods or certain humans picked by the gods had access to advanced technology or knowledge. I would also like to raise the idea that these events could have occurred at some point after 28,000 BC.

The reason for this logic is because this is when the fossil record begins to show us that Cro-Magnon man had moved over much of the worlds' surface. Based on recent finds it is very possible this included North and South America. This would fit into most of the ideas and concepts of a lost civilization that spanned the world in antiquity. I think it could also be a close match to what is described as the generations of Noah in the Bible and how they moved across the world and were divided into different groups.

As for a location of this capital city and tower, I can only guess at its true location. A quick internet search of Alantis and you will discover that just about every single location on the planet has been proposed. I have found over the years that the account given by Plato is the only one that gives any description of this capital city.

Within Plato's account, he gave a rather good description of the size of the island and this is the clue that so many miss. He described the island of Atlantis as being comprised mostly of mountains on the northern portions of the island that encompassed a great plain of an oblong shape in the south. He also gave the dimensions of the island as three thousand stadia by two thousand stadia across the center, which is about 345 miles (555 km) by about 230 miles (370 km). If you look on the map for any island that even comes close to this size is the modern island nation of Cuba, especially if we remember the ocean levels would have been much lower than today. The idea that Atlantis could be somewhere in the area of Cuba or the many Caribbean islands is not a new idea by any means. But I do think it fits into the other ancient mythologies is related somehow.

This possible clue could be that Plato's account is just one small piece of a much larger picture. Because if you look at all the known ancient sites located in North and South America. You will notice that large amount of them appear to be located within an arc with Cuba at the center. It could be that the Atlantis myth comes from a forgotten civilization that was the hub of an ancient empire centered on a great city located on the island of Cuba. Is it possible that l many of the sites and events that are remembered mythology are mistakenly focused on the wrong place?

The reason I present this idea is because as I examine the ancient sites in the Americas. I find one that could also perfectly fit these stories of a great city being destroyed by the gods the ancient ruins of Puma Pumku. These ruins show the evidence of a great destruction on a scale that can only be compared to that of our own day. The quality of the stone work at Puma Pumku is some of the finest in all of human history with many pieces weighting up to 200 tons apiece.

One of the most unique aspects of this mysterious site is the fact that whatever grand building stood there was literality blown into a million little pieces with most of it spread over a rather large area. Only the very largest pieces of stone survived this catastrophic destruction of whatever building stood on the site. Much of the ruins are little more than rubble. But the largest stones appears as if they were thrown around and turned upside-down by some great explosion leaving the scattered ruins we see today. This could be a clue that Puma Pumku was the location of a tower that stood upon a great building that was destroyed by the fire of the gods that is remembered in many traditions.

There is another possibility to the location of this tower that may sound a little strange at first at first. But it could explain a few of the mysteries and the lingering questions about some of the stories contained in the Biblical tradition. It could also help explain the lack of archaeological evidence concerning the Exodus and the Temple of King Solomon in Jerusalem, commonly known as the First Temple. It might provide a clearer understanding of some of the circumstances surrounding these stories.

I think, this "house that became great and broad" which had tower build upon it that "lofty and great" that Enoch speaks of is speaking of what is recorded in the Bible as King Solomon's Temple and Citadel. Which means that the leaders that are described in the Dream Vision of Enoch are most likely the individuals that the Bible remembers as King David and his son King Solomon.

If this thought experiment is pointed in the right direction. Then all of this would provide the real reason why we have not found any real archaeological evidence for the original Temple of King Solomon or King Solomon or for so many other ancient mysteries. It is because these events took place tens of thousands of years earlier than we have been traditional taught. Possibly as much as 20,000 years earlier, if any of these ideas I am presenting are correct.

This raises the possibility that this could all be tested and that there might be actual evidence of these events. I think that since Jerusalem has always been the traditional location for King Solomon's Temple while it has also been associated with other holy men and historical events. That this could be a possible location for the tower. If any of this is true, then all we would have to do is excavate to deeper levels that date this far back in time. If any of these events actually happened then the evidence would be found at these older levels. But only if you know what time period you actually need to look at.

This could also help explain what the original founding members of the Order of the Knights Templar were doing at the Temple Mount about 900 years ago. It also gives us a possible idea to what they could have found under the Temple Mount. They are the only ones that I am aware of in history that could have dug deep enough to actually have found something from this ancient age along with a long-lost civilization. It is even possible that they may have found some type of advanced technology. Now, we need to return to the Dream Vision of Enoch, but please keep all of these ideas and possibilities in mind as we will return to this subject of the tower a little later in the text.

The next set of verses revisits the same old theme started before with the sheep beginning to error again and going their many ways while they "*forsook*" their house. I think this could be telling us about a corrupting influence by the Fallen-Watchers and their allies. This seems to be hinting that they and their allies have been working in the back ground trying to undermine the Main-Group because they want or need the same labor, resources, and technology.

This is very similar to the events and conditions that we have today in our own modern world and the blatant corruption of society by what many claim is an unseen force pulling the strings. This force appears to a very small group of individuals that has used treachery, murder, betrayal, greed and an almost unbelievable lust for power with a longing for glory while trying to reestablish their Lost Paradise and what they believe is their proper rule over the Earth. This little conspiracy theory is something else to keep in mind for we will explore this in more detail a bit later in the story.

The Main-Group or the Lord of the sheep tries to intervene by choosing some of the Cro-Magnon-Men or sheep to go and speak to the others with the hope of them returning from their corrupt ways. These wayward people who could be under the influence the Fallen Watchers attack and slay the ones sent from the Main-Group.

The next few lines also help provide a clue to a number of ancient accounts that speak of an individual being taken up into the heavens and then returning years later occasionally it is hundreds of years later. Although it will not make much sense at the moment, this individual, the sheep that was not slain by the others could be the original witness and author we know of as Enoch. If sheep that was saved and "*brought up to me*" that is spoken of is actually the one we call Enoch, then it would explain how this version of the story was witnessed and recorded.

"And again, I saw those sheep that they again erred and went many ways, and forsook that their house, and the Lord of the sheep called some from amongst the sheep and sent them to the sheep, but the sheep began to slay them. And one of them was saved and was not slain, and it sped away and cried aloud over the sheep; and they sought to slay it, but the Lord of the sheep saved it from the sheep, and brought it up to me, and caused it to dwell there. And many other sheep He sent to those sheep to testify unto them and lament over them."
(Book of Enoch 89: 51-53)

There appears to be an ancient Akkadian cylinder seal showing this event of an individual being "saved" from being slain by the other sheep. This cylinder seal shows two large figures wearing odd head gear on either side of an individual being taking up. The one on the right appears to be fighting and stabbing a bull-like figure in the back with a sword. This bull could be symbolically representing Neanderthal who could be the First Men. The one on the left above the lion figure with wings or Griffin may be the one saving the individual. This probably the reason he is shown above the others, because he is flying somehow. My guess is that Griffin is some type of technological advanced ship that came to represent the leader or the Lord of the sheep that is spoken of by Enoch.

The griffin figure has what appears to be a man walking behind him. Could this man be one of the sheep that is trying to slay the others that were sent to them by the Lord of the sheep? Does this ancient cylinder seal image show the alliance between some of the groups that are spoken of in Enoch? Are these the lions and the other sheep with quite possibly the Lord of the sheep that is shown here?

If you look at the last few symbols that are on this seal with the above idea in mind, the object on the right could be the tower that is spoken of. This idea may seem strange, but you will understand a little later. For now, I wish to bring to your attention is the two symbols of the crescent moon and the star above the head of the man on the left. These two symbols are something to keep in mind as they relate back to the moon and star symbols I spoke of earlier. It is very difficult to see in this image if the star-like symbol above the crescent moon has six or eight rays coming out of it. As we go along, you will notice it is very similar to other images we will explore.

An impression from an Akkadian cylinder seal. Inscription Translation: Irra, priest. (2,400 BC – 2,200 BC) (Fig.2) [6]

The next image is very similar to the first one and is rather striking in its appearance. It appears to show the same scene without the details of the bull, the man, or the griffin figure. But it does show the two god-like figures in a slightly different manner. On this cylinder seal they are shown as having wings and they are shown as having on more traditional-like clothing. This image also differs by showing a Winged-Sun-Disk" or Solar-Disk above the individual being taken up and saved.

There are numerous other cylinder seals that appear to show the same scene but with additional elements and symbols that we will explore in a later chapter. At the moment I only wish to point out is the almost unbelievable fact that these cylinder seals are according to experts separated by almost 1,500 years in time and by an unknown number of different cultures. Yet they all contain the very same symbols and events. This is clearly an important story to have been recorded and preserved over such a long period of time.

These events eventually led the sheep to falling away entirely from the Main-Group and his "house and tower." This leads to the Main-Group attacking all of the Cro-Magnon humans regardless of whom they were or who they were allied with.

Neo-Assyrian cylinder seal of the 9thC BC (late)-8thC BC (probably) Inscription
Translation: (Seal) of Nabu-shar-usur, son of the priest, of Adad. (Fig.3) [7]

The text speaks of how their eyes were "*blinded*" once again, and that "*much slaughter*" was wrought upon the tribes of man or herds of sheep by the Main-Group. I think that some of the sheep must have fought back because of the statement of how they "*invited that slaughter;*" this does not sound like a group that is very fearful of their enemy.

> "*And after that I saw that when they forsook the house of the Lord and His tower they fell away entirely, and their eyes were blinded; and I saw the Lord of the sheep how He wrought much slaughter amongst them in their herds until those sheep invited that slaughter and betrayed His place.*"
(Book of Enoch 89: 54)

This war results in the Main-Group unleashing all the other groups upon the tribes of man. Starting with what appears to be the lions, tigers, wolves, hyenas leading the way with all of them possibly under the leadership of the foxes. Not knowing who or what these animals or groups really where, it is almost impossible to "really" understand anything, outside of the idea that the sheep or Cro-Magnon humans were attacked by basically everybody else on the planet under the control of the Main-Group or Lord of the sheep. After these corrupted

Cro-Magnon humans have been defeated, they are then turned over for either slavery or what appears to be execution with complete extermination not out of the question.

> *"And He gave them over into the hands of the lions and tigers, and wolves and hyenas, and into the hand of the foxes, and to all the wild beasts, and those wild beasts began to tear in pieces those sheep. And I saw that He forsook that their house and their tower and gave them all into the hand of the lions, to tear and devour them, into the hand of all the wild beasts."*
> (Book of Enoch 89: 55-56)

The Main-Group then abandoned the tower and the city to the wild beasts. They also allowed the other animals to loot, pillage and burn the sheep or Cro-Magnon humans. In turn, the witness, who must be the one we call Enoch. Begins appealing to the Main-Group for mercy in regard to the Cro-Magnon humans being devoured by the wild beasts, but, alas to no avail. The Main-Group remains "unmoved" and then He "rejoiced" that the Cro-Magnon humans were devoured, swallowed, and robbed.

> *"And I began to cry aloud with all my power, and to appeal to the Lord of the sheep, and to represent to Him in regard to the sheep that they were devoured by all the wild beasts. But He remained unmoved, though He saw it, and rejoiced that they were devoured and swallowed and robbed, and left them to be devoured in the hand of all the beasts."*
> (Book of Enoch 89: 57-58)

The next set of verses in the Dream Vision are some of the most interesting, confusing, and quite possibly the most important to our own modern world. These verses speak of how the Main-Group calls "seventy shepherds" and their "companions" so they might "pasture" the remaining sheep.

There has been quite a bit of debate over the centuries about whom or what these "seventy shepherds" represent. It has been argued that they could be various religious leaders in Jerusalem from the time of Josiah believed to be around 620 BC. Others believe these shepherds have something to do with the stories and legends of Nimrod and the number of languages that mankind spoke after the destruction of the tower that reached up to heaven. It has also been proposed that this could even be related to Atlantis and these seventy shepherds are the kings that ruled over the final days of that long-lost empire. It is also believed that the greatest of these kings later became the twelve great gods of

Olympus and the numerous lessor gods of ancient Greece after the island of Atlantis sank into the sea on that ancient fateful day.

In keeping with the original scenario. I think these are most likely a new group of Watcher-like beings that are assigned to punish the wayward Cro-Magnon humans that have turned against the Main-Group because they have been corrupted by the Fallen-Group and Nephilim. The text seems to indicate that these new Watchers were ordered to destroy a certain number of Cro-Magnon humans in general. This is clearly describing some type of extermination program and a large-scale collective punishment of the population.

This extermination program could explain where the idea of human sacrifice has its origin in so many ancient cultures. They could just be recreating this manic destruction of humanity that happened so long ago when the gods or as we now know, these shepherds were exterminating humans in this ancient war. I also think that the Americas might be the location for these events because the practice of this gruesome ritual was so wide spread among the native tribes not so long ago.

Remarkably, there does appear to be an ancient cylinder seal that is showing this extermination program. This cylinder seal has the same symbols of the eight-pointed star and the crescent moon as we touched upon before. There is a slight difference in that the crescent moon has what appears to be a circle above it along with a similar eight-pointed star on it. This is very similar to the All-Seeing-Eye and is clearly associated with the gods in some way. Could this be another clue as to its origin? How is it related to the pyramid shape from before? Is there something more to these ancient cylinder seals? What do these symbols actually represent? Could they represent the "gods" themselves?

With the idea that these symbols represent the gods or divine beings. This could mean that the "disk" above the moon symbol also be a representation of the "ship" that these beings used? If it is a ship, could it be what our ancestors remembered and called the Heaven? Could the word "Heaven" be the actual name of this object? What are these symbols showing us? Again, there are so many questions and I am sure there must be a connection between them all.

Returning to the cylinder seal, the main focus of the scene appears to be some type of human sacrifice at an altar by larger beings. If this is showing the extermination of the sheep in Enoch, then it is possible the larger figures are the "shepherds" that Enoch speaks of.

"And He called seventy shepherds, and cast those sheep to them that they might pasture them, and He spake to the shepherds and their companions:

'Let each individual of you pasture the sheep henceforward, and everything that I shall command you that do ye. And I will deliver them over unto you duly numbered, and tell you which of them are to be destroyed and then destroy ye.'"
(Book of Enoch 89: 59-60)

Goddess, Suppliant Goddess, Priest, and Worshiper Carrying Kid Before Sun God with Goddess and Goat Behind; in the field: Star Demonic Mask, Bull, Human Head, Star and Crescent Cylinder seal and impression. Mesopotamia, First Dynasty of Babylon: (ca. 1894–1595 B.C.) (Fig.4) [9]

In the next set of verses, the Main-Group calls another individual and speaks to him. The Lord of the sheep orders him to observe and record everything these new Watchers or shepherds unleash against the Cro-Magnon-Man humans. It seems that the Main-Group is aware of or actually knows that these shepherds will not do as they are commanded. I think this is because they must also be corrupted by the Fallen-Watchers or could be allied with them. This individual is then told that he is only to observe and record everything so that there will be a testimony against the shepherds and not to interfere. Who this individual that is recording these events is unknown. I can find no other reference of a similar figure in any other tradition or mythology currently available.

"And He gave over unto them those sheep. And He called another and spake unto him: 'Observe and mark everything that the shepherds will do to those sheep; for they will destroy more of them than I have commanded them. And every excess and the destruction which will be wrought through the shepherds, record (namely) how many they destroy according to my

99

command, and how many according to their own caprice: record against every individual shepherd all the destruction he effects. And read out before me by number how many they destroy, and how many they deliver over for destruction, that I may have this as a testimony against them, and know every deed of the shepherds, that I may comprehend and see what they do, whether or not they abide by my command which I have commanded them. But they shall not know it, and thou shalt not declare it to them, nor admonish them, but only record against each individual all the destruction which the shepherds' effect each in his time and lay it all before me."
(Book of Enoch 89: 60-64)

These new Watchers start their work and begin to slay and destroy more than they were commanded too, along with the help of the lions, tigers, and the wild boars who ate and devoured the greater part of the Cro-Magnon humans. It is at this point that the original tower built upon that house is burnt and destroyed. The house is also demolished by the ongoing warfare and extermination program.

The idea that the tower was burnt and destroyed possibly by fire from the sky; seems to be nearly universal in every single ancient tradition and culture much like the idea of the offering. The destruction of the tower is normally done by the gods and not a singular god. Even within the Bible, the text speaks it is plural and speaks of us. This destruction of the tower is accomplished by raining fire or some other divine destruction from the heavens. Unlike the Great Flood, this destruction of the tower is normally because of mankind's arrogance or outright disrespect of the gods or their power.

"Go to, let us go down, and there confound their language, that they may not understand one another's speech."
(Book of Genesis 11: 7)

These ancient stories all appear to be all speaking of and remembering the very same event or a set of very similar events. An event the resulted in the gods destroying a great tower by raining fire from the sky that terrified all that saw it. In many versions the surrounding city is also destroyed with a great loss of life.

"And I saw till those shepherds pastured in their season, and they began to slay and to destroy more than they were bidden, and they delivered those sheep into the hand of the lions. And the lions and tigers eat and devoured the greater part of those sheep, and the wild boars eat along with them; and

they burnt that tower and demolished that house. And I became exceedingly sorrowful over that tower because that house of the sheep was demolished, and afterwards I was unable to see if those sheep entered that house.
(Book of Enoch 89: 65-67)

We are then told that the new Watchers and their associates delivered a certain number of the Cro-Magnon-Man humans to the wild beasts to be devoured. As predicted, these new Watchers destroy more than they were ordered too. This destruction or what appears to an extermination program and genocide of Cro-Magnon-Man is so great that it begins to move the witness that is observing these events. He is so taken by what he sees he begins "*to weep and lament on account of those sheep.*"

"And the shepherds and their associates delivered over those sheep to all the wild beasts, to devour them, and each one of them received in his time a definite number: it was written by the other in a book how many each one of them destroyed of them. And each one slew and destroyed many more than was prescribed; and I began to weep and lament on account of those sheep."
(Book of Enoch 89: 68-69)

These events are all witnessed and recorded in a "book" that is read before the Main-Group by the one that was instructed to observe the shepherds. This book is then taken by Him and He "*reads it and sealed it*" and then "*laid it down.*"

Could this "book" that is spoken of be related to the idea of a "Book of Life" that is spoken of in the Bible's book of Revelation? Could this book be some type of technology? Could this be some type of video recording that is being recorded, played, and then saved on a removable medium? Who are the good guys and who are the bad guys in all of this? Is this an ongoing war of extermination and genocide like World War II? Why are they destroying the Cro-Magnon-Man humans? What could have been so horrible that the Lord of the sheep felt it was necessary to destroy all the sheep? At the moment, without more information, it is really difficult to say what is truly going on. Outside of what appears to be wide spread death and destruction on an epic scale, a Biblical scale.

"And thus in the vision I saw that one who wrote, how he wrote down every one that was destroyed by those shepherds, day by day, and carried up and laid down and showed actually the whole book to the Lord of the sheep (even) everything that they had done, and all that each one of them had made I away

with, and all that they had given over to destruction. And the book was read before the Lord of the sheep, and He took the book from his hand and read it and sealed it and laid it down."
(Book of Enoch 89: 70-71)

The next set of verses in the text of the Dream Vision raises even more questions than before. It also points out something that everyone seems to have missed. The nest verses of the text speak of how a second tower was built after the first was destroyed. This idea that more than one tower was built will prove to be very important in understanding the origin and ultimate meaning behind many of the symbols that surround us today. It will also provide the basic foundation to understanding many of the elements of the symbols and how they all fit together and tell a forbidden story of history.

"And forthwith I saw how the shepherds pastured for twelve hours, and behold three of those sheep turned back and came and entered and began to build up all that had fallen down of that house; but the wild boars tried to hinder them, but they were not able. And they began again to build as before, and they reared up that tower, and it was named the high tower; and they began again to place a table before the tower, but all the bread on it was polluted and not pure."
(Book of Enoch 89: 72-73)

Chapter 8

The Tower

And they said, Go to, let us build us a city and a tower. Whose top may reach unto heaven; and let us make us a name, lest we be scattered abroad upon the face of the whole earth.
~Genesis 11:4~

T he Dream Vision of Enoch speaks of how *"three of those sheep"* turned back and entered the house and began to rebuild it and the tower that stood upon it. We are also told that the tower was named *"the high tower"* and a table was placed before that tower. Then we are told that bread was placed upon that table but that *"bread was polluted and not pure."*

This story clearly states that there were at least two towers built not one as traditionally believed. One was built for the Main-Group or Lord God with their help or guidance and for their benefit. The other was built after the first one was destroyed. The story hints at that this was possibly an attempt to appease the gods in the hope the death and destruction would cease. This second tower fails in its task and is destroyed like the first one. If the ancient stories can be believed. Then it is possible that this second tower could be the one remembered as the one that was destroyed by fire coming from the heavens. Although it is equally possible that both of these towers were destroyed in a similar manner and remembered as a single event. The important idea here is this idea that there was more than one tower. This naturally raises a number of different possibilities and questions.

I think there is a vital clue that may help not only help reconstruct what happened but will provide a clearer picture of the situation. All we have to do is combine everything I have presented up to this point with the all the ancient monolithic monument sites that are large enough to support a tower as described in the story. If we do this, we can put part of this long-forgotten story and lost history back together.

Expanding upon the ideas presented in the last chapter about the lost city of Atlantis being the capital and center of a large empire that may have stretched around the globe. I think this world-wide-empire was based upon a network of towers that were used exactly as described in the ancient stories as places where people brought offerings to the gods. What many will find remarkable is the Biblical story of the Temple and Citadel of King Solomon is one the most complete and detailed descriptions of this type of event.

This network of towers was used by the Main-Group to receive offerings or resources from humans. It was also an overwhelming visible reminder of the power of the gods or God that stood upon it that would be seen daily. Additionally, it appears that each tower was placed in a central location in relationship to the surrounding population and needed resources. This network of towers also appears to be closely connected to the countless pyramids and pyramid-like structures around the world. As you will see, I have reason to believe that all the problems that led to the war and eventual downfall of this empire was caused by religious and political trouble at one of these towers, specifically the Temple and Citadel of King Solomon. The Bible gives a very detailed account of this building along with the troubling events that surrounded it.

What many will find remarkable, is that I have found a series of ancient Mesopotamian and Sumerian cylinder seals, along with a few other ancient artifacts. That when they are combined with the Biblical story and tradition, the Dream Vision of Enoch in the Book of Enoch and this overall idea I have presented up to this point. They appear to tell this story of the towers in pictures.

As you will see, these ancient cylinder seals have the most astonishing set of images that seem to tell a large part of this story of two-towers that were at the center of this conflict. They also provide many key elements in understanding how all of this fits together in one consistent story line.

The first image I will present contains a winged figure standing in the center with one foot on what looks like a lion with its right hand holding a rope connecting them together, like a dog leash. This is clearly some type of god-like being that has vanquished or conquered a human group or foe that is symbolically represented by a lion. This could be some type of indication of which groups could have been involved and where this event may have occurred at with the idea I spoke of earlier with the lions and sphinxes being related to ancient Egypt.

This imprint, made from a cylinder seal found in Mesopotamia during the Akkad Period (circa. 2,334-2,154 BC) Oriental Institute, University of Chicago. (Fig.1) [1]

Although it is difficult to see, there is also what appears to be an image of a large "Star" between the two figures in the center. This style of Star is found on many different ancient artifacts from around the world. This symbol appears to be related to one of these two groups that I have been calling the Main-Group and Fallen-Watchers. I am beginning to think that this could be a representation of the Main-Group or Lord-God of the Biblical tradition.

I also have to wonder if this could be a representation of what our ancestors called the "Heaven" and if this was what it actually what it looked like when seen from the ground? If that line of thinking is correct then this Heaven would have had to been a very large object that was in a rather low Earth orbit to be seen like this from the ground. Could this possibly be some type of large technologically advanced ship that is used by these beings and this is how it was seen by our ancestors when they were present? This idea may seem odd right now but it will make more sense as we look at a few more ancient artifacts.

The next cylinder seal image in this series is one that has been made rather famous by the late Zecharia Sitchin in his book 'The 12th Planet' from his 'Earth Chronicles' series of books. He put forward the idea that the Star that is seen between the two figures is actually our Sun with the eleven surrounding objects being the moon and the planets of the solar system. Mr. Zecharia Sitchin claimed in his interpretation that the objects surrounding the Sun in the image are our moon and the planets of our solar system. He also claimed our ancient ancestors knew about the lay-out of the solar-system. He also proposed that there are actually ten planets orbiting the sun and not nine or eleven, if you count the moon. Please keep in mind that he passed away before Pluto lost its place as a planet.

This was basically the foundation of his whole idea of a race of ancient aliens he called the Anunnaki. Which he claimed were a race of extra-terrestrials that came from a planet in an orbit that took it beyond Neptune that he called Nibiru. He claimed that this hypothetical twelfth planet of Nibiru was in a highly elliptical 3,600-year orbit around the sun. He also and attributes the creation of the ancient Sumerian culture to these Anunnaki. His books have sold millions of copies worldwide and have been translated into more than 25 languages.

Outside of his followers, I can find no scholar or expert on ancient Mesopotamia that agrees with his interpretation of these objects. To the best of my knowledge, all the scholars and experts pretty much all agree that these objects are not the planets of our solar system but are actually the Pleiades star cluster. A number of images that I will be presenting as we go along will support this scholarly conclusion. That the objects that Mr. Zecharia Sitchin claims are the planets of our solar system are actually a representation of the Pleiades star cluster and the Star that is seen in the center is not the sun but actually a symbol that is related to the gods or divine beings in some fashion.[2]

This star on this cylinder seal is slightly different than the previous one. With it only has six-rays or points emanating from it. This could be related to the six-sided star symbol of today. This symbol again, appears to represents the ones I am calling the Main-Group which has traditional been remembered as the Lord-God of the Bible.

This Star symbol is always shown in the sky no matter which culture or tradition you find it in. This leads me to believe that it could actually be what our ancestors called the 'Heaven' and that it was really a large ship or object in a low Earth orbit. If this is true, then we might be able to tease a few bits of information from this cylinder seal. We might even be able to get a rough idea of its size and possibly its orbit if this is an actuate recreation of the Pleiades star cluster and this object's relationship to it.

Focusing on to the eleven objects that surround the central star and assuming that idea that they are an actuate recreation of the Pleiades cluster is correct. This could be a clue to when these events took place. It could also be a clue to why the Pleiades were so important to our ancestors. They were related to certain important events that involved the gods and their interaction with our ancient ancestors.

If we could figure out when the Pleiades star cluster contained eleven stars in this configuration, we be able to figure out the approximate date of these events. Since the Pleiades cluster only contains six stars visible to the naked eye today.

and it is known for a fact that it takes thousands of years for the stars to move and change positions.

Cylinder seal VA-243 in the Berlin Near Eastern Museum (Fig.2) [3]

This allows us to understand that this is showing us that these events took place thousands of years earlier than anybody ever thought or even dreamed of. Based on simple knowledge of astronomy it is clear that any artifact showing the Pleiades cluster in this type of configuration with more than six or possibly seven visible stars had to take place prior to 10,000 BC. As we go along, I will present you with a number of other cylinder seals that will support this conclusion by showing the Pleiades cluster changing over time.

Returning to the image on the cylinder seal and the seated figure on the right. This figure is holding some type of strange looking Staff. What this staff is and what it represents has been debated over for years. Some say it is nothing more than a staff that represented kingship or had a religious purpose. Others have proposed that it could be a type of technology that looked like a Staff that came from the gods. I find it interesting that most have missed that this Staff looks to be very similar to the Caduceus in its basic design. So similar that I have to wonder, could this be showing us the origin of this symbol and the idea behind it? Is this why it is always connected to the gods?

Taking moment to think about this Staff and the idea of symbols. Could this be where the Caduceus or Herald's Staff that is so common in Greek and Roman iconography and spoken of in their mythologies comes from? This Staff which is clearly shown on this cylinder seal it is easy to imagine how it could be thought of as two serpents coiling around a staff with wings which is always associated with the gods. Since this Herald's Staff has always been associated with the gods. Could these individuals seen on this cylinder seal actually be the gods themselves? Is this how they actually looked to our ancient ancestors? As we examine other cylinder seals, I think you will agree that these individuals are the gods themselves and this is how they roughly looked like to our ancestors.

At first it may seem to be quite a stretch that this cylinder seal that dates from almost 1,200 to 1,500 years earlier and from a completely different culture could be showing the same Caduceus or Herald's Staff of the ancient Greeks and Romans. But it is well known that these cultures were not connected in any meaningful way, yet here we see the same type of Staff being recorded. This appears to tie a number of different cultures together in way that just does not make any sense with our current thinking of history. It also appears to be related to the story of the Dream Vision in the Book of Enoch and also connected to the Bible. All very mysterious, but I think it can be said with confidence that the idea of a Staff of the gods like the Caduceus goes back to the oldest known civilizations. It is also clear that was so important to our ancient ancestors that it was passed down through the generations to our own modern day.

Moving back to the cylinder seal and the other two figures on the left side that appear to be holding hands. They have what appears to be some type of strange looking object beneath them along a similar style as the staff. This may be advanced technology that came from the gods. With keeping in mind of the towers. I think this could be the possible related to the lay-out or foundation work for the original tower that appears in so many of the ancient traditions.

The next cylinder seal we will look at, appears to show the same staff as above but from a different culture. On this cylinder seal this staff appears that it is being brought to a similar looking figure seated on different type of throne. The style and similar scenes between these two-cylinder seals, gives the impression that scene comes before the previous cylinder seal.

An Akkadian green serpentine cylinder seal, circa. 2,334-2,154 BC. (Fig.3) [4]

This cylinder seal also shows a smaller individual holding what appears to be some type of animal standing behind all the other larger figures. This could this be some type of offering to the gods by one of the local humans? Again, are these cylinder seals be showing us what these gods actually looked like and their size in comparison our ancient ancestors?

I think these cylinder seals are actually showing the difference between us lowly humans and the gods. I also think the experts have been misinterpreting these seals and images as a whole. Traditionally, scholars have put forward the argument to explain these images is that they are showing these individuals as larger than life or that they are greater than the average human. They also claim that there is such a heavy use of arcane symbolism whose true meaning may never be known to us because we are just too far removed and forgotten too much that their true meaning may never be known. But as you can see for yourself it is clear that the creators of this artwork viewed these beings being larger than humans in many different ways and that they are the primary characters in these scenes.

The next cylinder seal we will look at appears to show the same scenes as the two previous cylinder seals but combined into one image. One main difference is this image is the object being held between the two gods on the left side is depicted as a container on top and what looks like a scorpion below it. What exactly this object is unknown and is clearly open to debate. But, when we compared to the first cylinder seal, I think it is safe to say this is showing us some type of technology that could be related to the construction of the tower.

Akkadian cylinder seal. Dated to between 2,250 BC to 2,500 BC. (Fig.4) [5]

Although that idea might seem strange, but when I look at this object and think of building a tower. My imagination is instantly filled with ideas of large construction equipment and other related heavy equipment. When I try and think of what type of modern-day heavy equipment could possibly look like these objects and is needed to build a large building. Only two come to mind, a drilling rig of some type or a large mobile pile-driver. Either one of these modern-day pieces of construction equipment could easily be misinterpreted by people that did not understand what they were looking at. I can understand how the business-end of this type of equipment could be looked at being like a scorpion or thought to act like one. This is all open to debate, primarily due to the lack of detail in these images. But, when taken as a whole with the additional cylinder seals I will be presenting, you will come to understand that this idea will not sound as unlikely as it does at the moment.

This modern impression of a cylinder seal from Tell Billa, which shows two cultic scenes involving a boat ride and a procession toward a temple. This artifact is still missing from the Iraqi National Museum collection. The artifact dates to around 3,000 B.C. (Fig.5) [6]

If these images are showing the possible lay-out or foundation work for the tower. Although what is more likely at this point in the story is the lay-out of the "house" that becomes "great and broad." Then this next cylinder seal could be showing some of the construction of this house that was great and broad. This would fit the many different traditions in that imply that the great temple of in this case the tower that was built upon that house was actually built by humans but was done under the guidance of the gods.

The cylinder seal I wish to present to you is the one that could be showing the actual construction of the tower upon the house along with the different parties that were involved. It includes many elements and symbols that appear to fit almost perfectly into what is recorded and remembered in many of the ancient stories and traditions.

We can see that there are three large figures that are very similar to the large beings seen on the other cylinder seals. There is also a smaller figure on the lower right-hand side of the image that appears to be a King. The two large figures on each side of the image are most likely the leaders of the different groups of gods spoken of in so many ancient traditions. Each one seems to be associated with the symbols of the Crescent Moon on the left and the eight-pointed Star on the right. There is a Winged-Sun-Disk between them these two figures and over the third figure. If the earlier idea of the multiple pointed Star representing the Main-Group is correct then the crescent moon must represent the Fallen-Watchers. These two symbols can then be used to trace these groups through time on the artifacts. This conclusion will become clearer and self-evident as we explore other artifacts.

Cylinder seal showing the construction of the Tower. Berlin Museum. (Fig.6) [7]

On the top left- and right-hand sides you can see the Pleiades star cluster that shows a total of ten stars and not eleven like we saw on the cylinder seal VA-243 made famous by the late Mr. Zecharia Sitchin. You will notice that the configuration of the Pleiades star cluster on this cylinder seal is also different and shows that the stars have moved since the events shown the first cylinder seal. This appears to be evidence that these events took place over thousands of years. Which seems to disprove the claims and timeline presented by modern-day scholars and archeologists. We will look at some additional cylinder seals that will support this conclusion shortly.

The third figure in the center is pointing at what is undeniably a tower. You will also notice it has a strange wavy line between its head and the building. This clearly represents some type of connections between this figure and the tower. It could possibly represent some type of mental interface with the tower or even some type of construction technique. It could also represent how the information to build the tower was given to the local population of humans so the tower could be constructed. I do have to wonder if this is connected to the Caduceus we saw earlier?

The final item I wish to examine before moving on to the next cylinder seals is the tower and the small two step pyramid-like structure it sits upon. This small structure could be the house that the Dream Vision of Enoch speaks about. As you know, this type of multi-step building is very common throughout all the ancient cultures and traditions around the world. If this type of building was truly used as a foundation for the tower. This would help explain why multi-step buildings were important and why they are so common. Based upon this idea, this would mean that the step pyramid monuments found around the world could be the foundations for these towers of the gods.

Ishtar image and a worshipper below a canopy flanked by winged genies (Fig.7) [8]

These next two-cylinder seals are showing us a similar scene. In the first one we can see an individual kneeing before what the scholars say is the god Ishtar in what appears to be some type of structure with two winged beings on each side. This could be showing the choosing of a leader by the gods. But, in light of the story of the Dream Vision, I think this could be related to God or his Angels coming to the one we remember as Enoch. This could be showing us when the "Lord of the sheep called some from amongst the sheep and sent them to the sheep," Book of Enoch, 89: 52. Hopefully this idea will become clearer to you as we go deeper into this entire idea. The second cylinder seal shows the same scene but with additional information showing us that the different god-like beings are standing on some type of strange winged animal instead of having wings as seen on the first one.

Neo-Assyrian - 8thC BC - Inscription Translation: Seal of Ahu-lamur. (Fig.8) [9]

The next cylinder seal we will look at is similar to the two I presented earlier showing Enoch being saved and taken away from the generations of the earth. This one has a different symbolic representation of the tower in a slightly different style than before. On this seal the tower looks much more like a large tree with an equally large bird upon it. This change in the style of how the tower is shown is a very important factor in understanding how you can trace this story across all the different cultures and traditions of the world. As we examine more cylinder seals and couple of other artifacts, this difference in how the tower is shown will become much more apparent to you.

There are also a number of animal figures that appear to be similar to the animals that are described in the Dream Vision of Enoch. This image also includes the Pleiades star cluster in the upper center of the image. As you will notice, this representation of the Pleiades is also slightly different than the two previous images that we have seen. On this cylinder seal we can see that there are eight stars in two parallel lines of four instead of the ten and eleven seen earlier.

Akkadian - 2400BC-2200BC - Dark green serpentine cylinder seal, possibly showing the ascent to heaven of Etana (Fig.9) [10]

This obvious change in the number of stars in the Pleiades star cluster and their position clearly indicate that a long period of time has elapsed between the images. In fact, so much in time has passed that the stars themselves have moved and radically changed position. As you can see, these artifacts appear to be recording the actual movement of the individual stars of Pleiades cluster over an almost unbelievable amount of time. Once again, this should provide a way to date these events to within a few hundred years and give us better indication to which time period we should be looking at for evidence.

The next cylinder seal we will look at returns us to the tower. It seems to show a change in the structure of the tower and could be another phase of the construction of this monument. This image appears to show that a modification or improvement to the existing spear-like structure we saw earlier has taken place.

This image also contains the same similar god-like beings along with the symbols of the Star and the Crescent Moon, but with one major difference. This one also contains the winged-sun-disk that clearly shows a bearded man inside a Winged-Disk above the tower. This gives the impression that this Winged-Sun-Disk is actually some type of flying craft that is clearly connected to the gods. Given the description in the Dream Vision this could be the Lord of the sheep that once stood upon that great and mighty tower.

This image also contains two half-man, half-animal beings standing on each side of the tower. Could these be the "black wild boar" that Enoch speaks of? Again, could this be what Enkidu really looked like?

Cylinder seal and modern impression: bull-men flanking deity above sacred tree; winged deity holding horned animal heads. Date: ca. mid-8th–7th century B.C. (Fig.10)
[11]

These half-man half-animal figures are very common and appear across numerous artifacts and cultures. They must have been important to many of these events, but unfortunately, who exactly these people where are still a complete mystery. Outside of the familiar figures of the Greek god Pan or Enkidu of Sumerian fame along with a few legends there does not appear to be any surviving information about these people or who or what they actually were. For now, they must stay in the realm of mystery and legend. Although these people are a mystery, according to the Dream Vision they appear to the same group that Enoch calls the 'black-wild-boar.'

Moving on to the next cylinder seal. This seal appears to show the next phase of the construction of the tower. This image clearly shows some type of outer-structure being lower into place by the individual in the Winged-Sun-Disk. These two images of the winged-sun-disk and the individual sitting in it appear to be showing the exact same type of craft. These two-cylinder seal make it very hard to deny that this Winged-Sun-Disk represents some type of flying craft.

The image also shows two bird-men with wings standing on each side of the other two figures. These winged figures appear to be a type of bird-like creature with a human body with the wings and head of an eagle. In relation to the Dream Vision of Enoch, could this actually be one of the 'birds of heaven' that are spoken of? Are these cylinder seals actually showing us what the wild-black-boar and some of the birds of heaven spoken of in the Dream Vision might have looked like? There are many who would say no, but that may be too quick of an answer. As we keep looking and exploring this idea you just might agree in the end that we are actually seeing some of these legendry beings on these artifacts.

Seal of chalcedony, 9th Century BC. (Fig.11) [12]

Returning to the cylinder seal and if we take a closer look at the tower in the center. We will see that this tower has a number of mechanical looking structures sticking out of it. The tower in the previous image also has very similar looking structures sticking out of the main structure. When you look at the two human looking individuals standing on each side, you can see they are holding on to some type of line with small little horse-shoe-like shaped objects at the ends coming out of the Winged-Sun-Disk above the tower. These small horse-shoe shaped objects bring to mind some type of tie-down mechanism for anchoring a flexible-like outer structure. This would mean that the small structures emanating from the central structure are a type of internal support system that seems very similar to modern day tower and tall building construction techniques.

This image is clearly showing us that this tower was covered by a flexible outer surface that was lowered into place by the Winged-Sun-Disk. This covering appears to have been supported by the internal support system that emanates from the central structure of the tower. In is now next to impossible to deny that these cylinder seals are showing us different phases of construction along with the parties involved.

The next cylinder seal is rather self-explanatory when compared to the other we have just examined. It is not very hard to see that it is a scene of the completed tower and "the Lord of the sheep stood upon that tower and they offered a full table before Him."

Cylinder sea and impression Mesopotamia, Neo-Babylonian period (ca.1000–539 B.C.) (Fig.12) [13]

We can also see two individuals that appear to be wearing fish-like suits on each side of the tower. These individuals have been seen on numerous other artifacts and have been traditional related to a god known as Dagon or Dagan. Dagon was equated with Enlil due to their shared role as the "fathers of gods" in ancient Mesopotamia. It is believed by many that this god came from the waters to teach mankind about civilization, reading, writing, math, and good government. These fish-men have also been connected to the Lord-God of the Biblical tradition.

The next image we will look at is one that has been used by the Ancient Astronaut supporters. According to Scholars the object in the center is a symbolic representation of the Tree of Life that is spoken about in many ancient traditions. While the Ancient Astronaut supporters argue that it is a symbolic representation of human DNA and proof of their idea that extraterrestrials came to earth and messed with our DNA. They also argue that the Winged-Sun-Disk seen here is a representation of an alien ship.

As we now know because of the previous cylinder seals, along with more to come, both the Scholars and the Ancient Astronaut supporters are incorrect. This not a symbolic representation of either the Tree of Life or human DNA, it is fact a highly stylized symbolic representation of one of these towers that the gods stood upon. Once you realize that these objects are actually towers and not the Tree of Life or human DNA that all the Scholars and Ancient Astronaut supporters have always said they are, everything changes.

117

Currently found in the British Museum (Fig.13) [14]

Once you realize these symbols represent a tower. You can realize that it is always shown in the same basic way as highly stylized symbolic tower with a symbol for the gods that stood upon it. This basic image of the tower and the god above it as we have seen; can be found in every single ancient culture and tradition around the world. This understanding allows you to follow this story around the world and through all the different cultures.

As for the Winged-Sun-Disk. I am beginning to think it might really be some type of ship that was used by these beings that our ancestors called gods. I am also thinking that the earlier images of these beings we have seen on the cylinder seals might be what they really looked like or at least how they looked to our ancestors. While keeping in mind that our ancestors might not of had any clue who or what these beings where or that their magical or divine power came from advanced technology.

The next cylinder seal impression we will look at is a rather famous one. It has appeared in numerous books and a large number of scholarly papers over the years. All of my research seems to indicate that all the experts agree that this is a scene from the Epic of Gilgamesh when he is battling the lions that are spoken of in the story.

King Standing on Sphinxes and Holding a Lion in Each Hand: Palm Tree with Winged Sun Disk Above. Persia, Achaemenid period. (ca.550–330 B.C.) (Fig.14) [15]

This cylinder seal impression takes on a completely new meaning when looked at with the ideas we have been exploring in mind. It is now easy to see that the Tree of Life and the Winged-Sun-Disk that is floating over it are actually a highly stylized symbolic representation of a tower and the glory of the god that stood on it. This is also a good example of how this basic stylized representation of the tower is shown and should provide you an idea of what to look for in other artifacts.

It is starting to seem like this network of towers provided the infrastructure and support for the Main-Group which allows them to establish their empire around the world. I think this is the most logical explanation for how this story is remembered around the world by everybody.

The next cylinder seal I wish to show you is one I think, shows the outcome of this empire being established around the world. A meeting between the two major parties. I also think this could represent some type of agreement between them.

This meeting and possible agreement between the Main Group and the Fallen Watchers leads to them working together. The reason I think this is because there are many artifacts that show the symbols of the Star and the Crescent Moon joined together. I think this is showing us a time when there was an alliance between the two parties. This alliance is also the beginning of what went wrong all those years ago.

Cylinder seal Date: 9th-8th century B.C (Fig.15) [16]

The reason I say this is because over the years as I have studied stories about the tower and related mythologies. They commonly imply that there was a great betrayal at the center of everything that went wrong all those thousands of years ago. This betrayal has always been a mystery to everybody and many different ideas have been proposed over the years on what it was and who it involved. Many state that this betrayal was what led to the destruction of the towers.

This mysterious betrayal may be able to be finally explained by this alliance. There is a cylinder seal that seems to show this betrayal that led to the end of everything. This cylinder seal may show one of the most important forgotten episodes of history. When viewed in light of understanding that we are seeing a tower and not a tree, you can quickly realize what this seal is actually showing us. The betrayal was, the Fallen-Watchers stealing the knowledge and technology from the original tower for themselves.

A cylinder seal located in the Museum at The Hague. (Fig.16) [17]

These events then lead to the Fallen-Watchers corrupting the first tower and taking control of it. If the idea that there was a network of towers. I think it would be reasonable to suspect that the Fallen-Group may have taken many of them over and not just one. I think it is also reasonable to think these events played out in a similar fashion around the world as part of a larger strategy to gain power. This would help explain why so many different traditions from around the world has a similar story.

The next cylinder seal shows another meeting between the two parties. If this idea is correct, then this meeting may have taken place after the tower had fallen away. It clearly shows the symbolism of both the Crescent Moon symbol of the Fallen-Watchers and the six-pointed Star of the Main-Group. It also shows two different towers with each one appearing to be associated with each group.

Cylinder seal Date: ca. 9th–8th century B.C. (Fig.17) [18]

This cylinder seal also includes the common feature seen on many other cylinder seals. It is the animal that the god-like figure with the strange objects on its shoulders is standing upon. This could actually be an animal or symbolically represents an animal powered mode of transportation. But, within this thought experiment, I think it is something more than that. I think this is symbolically showing us a technology that was like an animal but was not understood by the artist making this cylinder seal. In the sense that our ancient ancestors might view a modern-day vehicle as some type of animal.

The next item of great importance on this seal is the fact that it shows the Pleiades star cluster with only seven stars. When compared to the earlier seal we have seen with eight stars in the Pleiades with Enoch being saved and taken up from the generations of earth. This allows us to realize that those events must have taken place prior to this scene. This is more support that these seals are showing us that these events actually took place over a period of many thousands of years and thousands of years before what modern experts claim.

The next cylinder seal contains the same beings, symbols, towers and Pleiades grouping of stars as before. This cylinder seal is clearly related to the other cylinder seals and it appears to be showing the same scene as the previous image. This seal also gives a good example of the different styles that are used to represent each element of the scene in a symbolic manner.

Ancient cylinder seal. Meeting between the "gods" (Fig.18) [19]

According to the Dream Vision of Enoch, this meeting or meetings appears to fail in whatever its attempt was. This then leads to the first tower to fall away entirely. There are a number of cylinder seals that seem to show this change in the political control of the tower. This change is shown through the image of the tower and that the upper part of the tower changes from a spear-like shape to a Crescent Moon shape.

Although it is impossible to know it this was an actual physical change to the tower or just symbolic change, but it clearly showing us that some type of political change is happening in relationship to the ongoing situation. It is also possible that control of the tower may have changed hands a couple of different times with the Fallen-Watchers finally taking control until the tower is destroyed. When you over-lay the story of the Dream Vision with these cylinder seals, they seem to provide a background to understanding that these events are part of a great war between the gods. A war that the Dream Vision of Enoch, the Bible, and many other traditions from around the world speak of.

The next cylinder seal shows us this change in tower. It also shows how these god-like figures are shown with wings instead of strange objects protruding from their shoulders. Once again, we see the Griffin-like animal in the center. We can also see the Pleiades cluster of stars a just seven stars in a line.

Assyrian cylinder seal (Fig.19) [20]

The next cylinder seal gives us a better view of this meeting between the different parties. Once again, this a good example of how the same scene is show in different artistic styles but still contain all the same symbolic elements.

Cylinder seal. Date: ca. 1,000–900 B.C. (Fig.20) [21]

It is at this point that I would like to pause and back up a little to take a closer look at the events of Enoch being saved and taken from the generations of the earth. I would also like to closer look at some of the symbols we have seen. The reason we need to do this, is because there are a few artifacts that tie a number of these different symbols together. Although it might not make much sense at the moment, these symbols are also directly related to our modern-day world. In addition, there are a couple of ideas and concepts that you need to be made aware of at this point to help you better understand some of the meaning behind all the symbols and how to read them.

As we have seen, there are a large number of these cylinder seals along with numerous ancient artifacts that have the same three primary symbols associated with them. Two of these three symbols; the Crescent Moon and the eight or six-pointed Star we have already touched upon with some detail. Also, I think it is rather clear that they represent each one of these two groups that are at the center of this story. With the star, representing the Main-Group, or Lord of the sheep, and the Crescent Moon symbol, representing the ones I have been calling the Fallen-Watchers. So far, the third symbol, the Winged-Sun-Disk, or Solar-Disk has only been looked at with the vague idea that it is an advanced ship and quite possibly the Heaven that is remembered within tradition. I have not looked at the common representations of how this symbol looked at on how it fits into the symbols of today. In the next image we can see a much clearer image of these three symbols as they are commonly seen on the ancient artifacts.

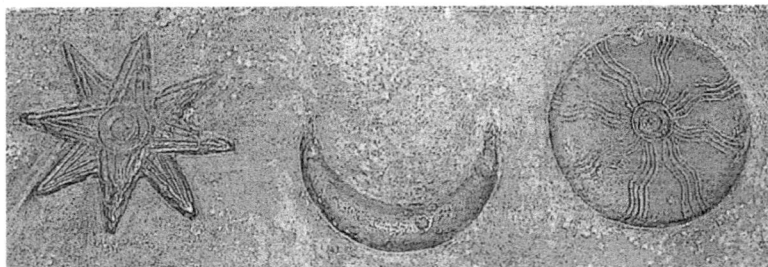

Close-up of the eight-pointed-Star, Crescent Moon, and the Solar-Disk symbolism. (Fig.21) [22]

The experts all agreed that the Winged-Sun-Disk and this Solar-Disk as seen in the last image are actually symbolically representing the same object. The problem has always been the same with this symbol and that is the question of what this object really was. To avoid going into a never-ending tangent on this debate, for this thought experiment I am going to assume that this is actually a symbolic representation of the ship or craft that these gods used as their primary means of transportation.

There is another cylinder seal that shows a scene that gives the overwhelming impression that this was a real physical object that was built by the gods. Many have argued that it shows one of these craft having maintenance performed on it or possibly built. I suspect that the large god-like figure on the right is the leader of the Main-Group or Lord of the sheep. There are a few other seals and artifacts that we will look at shortly that support this idea. Also, please make note of the object this individual is holding we will see it again.

Ancient Sumerian Stele. (Fig.22) [23]

It is very hard to deny that this is artifact is showing us one of these solar-disks up close and that it was most likely a real physical object. I think it can be said that regardless of the argument this is clearly a symbol and object that is directly associated with the gods themselves. It is also rather easy at this point to understand how these three symbols are related to each other. It is also rather easy to understand how they could be related to the Caduceus. But, at the moment, it is rather difficult to see the connection back to the symbol of the Pyramid and the All-Seeing-Eye. To understand this piece of the puzzle we must look closer at and understand the event of Enoch being saved and taken from the generations of the earth.

Unless you understand the basic story of why Enoch was saved and taken up into heaven away from the generations of the earth, you will never understand how any of this actually ties together into one understandable story. Additionally, the true meaning of the symbols will forever be a mystery to those who seek to understand them if you do not know about this event. This is the event that changed everything. To understand this event, you must understand that it was the pivotal turning point that led to this great and destructive war of the legendary towers. This is the event that brings the symbols together into one place and imparts their primary meaning into them.

I know all of this can sound very confusing, but please, let me explain with a quick recap.

The Dream Vision of Enoch tells of how the sheep go their many ways and turn their back on the Lord of the sheep. This leads to the sheep forsaking the house and tower of the Lord of the sheep. This causes the Lord of the sheep to call some of the sheep to him and send them as emissaries to the ones that had fallen away.

The next set of events that are described in the Dream Vision are the most important. Because it tells us of how all the emissaries but one, are slain. The one that is not killed and manages to escape was saved by the Lord of the sheep. This killing of the emissaries of the Main-Group by the Fallen-Watchers and their allies is the event that sets off this war. This is the reason why it is so important; it was the first shot in this war and it was witnessed by a large number of individuals. It is when the Fallen-Watchers and their allies rebelled against and attacked the Main-Group.

Remarkably, there is an ancient artifact that clearly shows everything that I am trying to say along with all the symbols together in one picture. It also allows us to help fill in some of the missing pieces for the location of these events.

This artifact has been interpreted by scholars as being an anthropomorphized version of the goddess Tanit. The reason for this interpretation is because this stele was used by the Carthaginians as grave marker that was set up over burial Urns that contained the cremated bodies of babies, small children and animals which had been sacrificed to the goddess Tanit and her consort Baal Hammon. Interestingly enough, even though the script and the artifact are clearly Carthaginian origin it is almost identical to that of Canaanite inscriptions, symbolism and belief. This connection has also been used as a connection to our own modern world with the idea of the occult practice and worship of Moloch along with the practice of child sacrifice.

In light of everything we have covered up to this point, you should be able to see symbolic connections between the Dream Vision of Enoch and the cylinder seals and other artifacts. You should also begin realizing and understanding that the traditional interpretation of this artifact and so many others have to be incorrect. Because we can now see that this artifact is not showing us the goddess Tanit, but it is actually showing us Enoch being saved and taken up to heaven away from the generations of the earth. Which according to tradition and the Bible was done by the Lord-God Himself: "*And all the days of Enoch were three hundred and sixty and five years. And Enoch walked with God: and he was not; for God took him."* Book of Genesis 5: 23-24.

This stela comes from a religious precinct known as the Tophet in the ruins of Carthage. (Fig.23) [24]

You can now easily see with your own eyes not only all the symbols but you can also begin to actually understand what you are looking at. But only if you know this story of the Dream Vision of Enoch. You can now see and understand the symbolism of the Solar-Disk, the Star, the Crescent Moon, the Pyramid, a temple with the Caducei on each side, and most important of all you can see Enoch being taken away from the generations of the earth.

This artifact provides us with the missing pieces of the story. When Enoch escapes from being slayed by the other sheep. He flees to a temple in Egypt and uses the Caducei to contact the Lord of the sheep. Just before the sheep get to him. Which based on this artifact is presumably close to the Great Pyramid. Shortly after he contacts the Lord of the sheep he is saved and taken away.

Which, once again, the Bible and tradition says this was done by the Lord-God Himself. Based on the ancient artifacts it is clear that it had a great impact on all who saw it and they recorded it. Given the fact that it also started a great war only added to its importance.

This then allows us to begin to see how easily these symbols slowly evolved into the symbols we know so well today of the Pyramid with the All-Seeing-Eye. This is one of the two main events that this modern-day symbol represents. The first event was the Fall of Lucifer and his fellow Watchers came to free humanity from slavery. This was the time of the great Bringer of Light coming down to earth to impart divine knowledge. The other event is the beginning of this almost forgotten war against the Main-Group and their allies.

This is the reason why every single explanation you have every heard about these symbols is so vague, or never sounds quite right, it is because they are wrong. We will return to this subject in a later chapter and explore this in greater detail, but this artifact reinforces everything I have proposed up to this point concerning these symbols and their true meaning. It is next to impossible to deny when you can see it with your very own eyes.

Now that we have this understanding, we need to return to the story of the towers as told by the cylinder seals to see if we can find more information on what happens next. We pick up the story when the tower comes under the control of the Fallen-Watchers and their allies we saw on the previous cylinder seals. We also saw that after a meeting between the parties leads to changes made to the towers.

Cylinder seal Date: ca. 1,000 to 700 B.C. (Fig.24) [25]

This next cylinder seal clearly shows that the tower is undergoing some type of change, possibly preparing for war. Once again, we do not know if this is an actual physical change to the tower or something more symbolic. The symbolism of this cylinder seal gives the impression that the Fallen-Watchers may have access to their own Winged-Sun-Disk. It is also possible that this is another piece that has been overlooked. That maybe these groups are fighting over not only control of the towers, but also the technology and ability to build them?

The next cylinder seal shows a scene that is clearly related to this war. This ancient cylinder seal known as the "War Seal" has always been a mystery to the experts on what it actually shows. Experts believe it is showing some type of scene that is related to a war but outside of that they claim the symbolism does not make any sense as a whole. You will quickly understand why all the experts and scholars have not been able to interpret this cylinder seal or any of the others correctly. It is because they either do not know this story or they do, they do not want the general public to know it. With that said, this seal when looked at, starting on the right side with the Pleiades star cluster and then moving left, you can understand the scene and what the experts cannot.

Neo-Assyrian, the War Seal – 800 BC-750 BC (Fig.25) [26]

As we have already learned, at the time when the Pleiades star cluster had this configuration of seven stars. The Fallen-Watchers were in control of some of the towers. They then at some point launches a attack against the Main-Group and their allies. This seal has a rather interesting feature that we have not seen on the others which is the symbolism of the trident. The trident that is seen and spoken about in many different ancient cultures and traditions. It is always described as a great weapon of the gods; the only difference between the stories about this legendry weapon is which god actually had it and who it was used against. In this image it appears to be under the control of the Fallen-Watchers. I think it should be noted that it is possible that both sides each had their own trident weapon.

129

The next cylinder seal shows another scene in this ongoing saga of war. By this point you should be beginning to understand the symbolism on the seals and its connection the story of the Dream Vision of Enoch. You should understand that on this cylinder seal we are seeing a tower being attacked by the "beasts of the field" and the "birds of heaven". We can also understand that these animals are symbolically representing people and groups of people. In the next chapter we will examine more of the Dream Vision that will give you a better understanding of why these birds of heaven and the beasts of the field shown allied together.

Antelopes attacked by birds, signs of Cypro-Minoan script, cylinder seal and its impression. Hematite, Late Bronze II (maybe 14th century BC). From tomb 1 at Sinda in Cyprus. (Fig.26) [27]

As this war unfolds, I think the Main-Group loses control of a number of towers with it being possible that they may have lost all of them. I also think that the Pleiades star cluster shows that the events of this war took place over a very large amount of time. When you combined this idea with the rest of the western Judeo-Christian tradition along the stories in the Bible. It is easy to see that there was much more going on than just a great military campaign. I get the impression that there was also a great campaign on both sides for the hearts-and-minds of the general population. This may be a clue as to why these events appear to play out so slowly over such a large amount of time quite possibly thousands of years. There could have been limits on how they could actually fight each other and the resources they used.

One of these possible limits on their actions could have been the simple fact that both sides were doing everything they could to keep all the humans believing they were the all-powerful gods. In my mind this would place great limits on how they could fight this war. This was simply because if either side actually told the humans what was going on or showed too much the whole sweet deal would fall apart. I think it is also reasonable to assume that the overall general population was kept rather small and self-limiting to help the gods keep control of the lowly little humans.

There is one other possible limit on their actions and is based on my own general impression of all the stories about the gods or God I have ever heard about in my life. As I have read and researched the ancient stories about the gods and the God of the Bible. I have always had the impression and general idea that all of these gods are a rather lazy bunch and they really do not personally do very much at all. This general laziness of the gods has always led me to think that the gods very seldom actually did any of the real fighting and were dependent on their followers to do most of their dirty work. This would vastly limit how and when they could fight simply because after a large battle it may take decades for the population to recover and be able to fight again.

With these ideas in mind, I would like to present the following three-cylinder seals. These cylinder seals are easier to understand that there must have been times of peace and rebuilding between the parties during this war. Two of these seals show the Pleiades star cluster in the similar seven-star configuration as seen on the previous seal. This again supports, that all these events are occurring around the same time.

These cylinder seals also show two towers together with each with a slightly different design. This difference in design may be an important clue on to what their function may have been. When looked at with the idea that a great war going on. It is very difficult not to think of a modern-day missile system. It is possible that these seals are showing us meetings where one side is threatening the other.

Cylinder seal, Date: ca. 1,000–900 B.C. (Fig.27) [28]

Neo-Assyrian – Dated to around the 9th century BC (Fig.28) [29]

Neo-Assyrian – Dated to 729BC-700BC (Fig.29) [30]

As you can see, these meetings lead to the first real visible change in the towers and provide the next major part of the story.

The symbols on the next cylinder seal we will look at are clearly related to the Main-Group. Although it may seem strange when you first look at it. This cylinder seal is a good example of the gaps that exist with the cylinder seals. This cylinder seal shows the same god-like figures doing something to a tower. It appears as if it is being set on the back of an animal. This strange animal has always been interpreted by the experts as a dragon and connected to the ancient god Marduk in some way.

This scene takes on new meaning when looked at with all the information and ideas I have presented. I think this is clearly showing that the Main-Group had to make major changes in how they were fighting this war. They could have been starting to lose the war which forced them to change tactics. This seal could be an indication that the Main-Group had lost control of all the towers and this is the reason for the change.

This cylinder seal seems to be showing us that they took the military capabilities of the towers and placed them on a mobile platform. This appears to be accomplished by the other two tower-like structures on either side of the tower. The other structures appear to be some type of cable-crane system that was used to lift this tower into place on the mobile platform. The two structures also appear to be connected by a line that arcs over the tower and just brings to my mind the idea of a crane system being used to lift large masses. Although it might be difficult to see, if you look closely at the crane-like structure to the right. You will see the second tower that matches the previous cylinder seals showing two different tower-like structures. This may be an indication of what is really going on. Which are the weapon systems of the towers was being loaded onto a platform in order to move it around as needed.

Plate XXXIII, seal d (Fig.30) [31]

The image also contains the Pleiades star cluster of seven stars as before. You will notice the stars are in a slightly different configuration than before. This configuration gives you a much better idea of how these stars were actually moving in the night sky. Additionally, it is more evidence that these ancient cylinder seals are really recording the real historical movements of these stars' tens of thousands of years ago.

133

Cylinder seal from the Berlin Museum of Ancient Near East in Frankfort, Germany.

We need to pause for a moment and take a look at this cylinder seal with the idea of the symbols in mind. As you have seen, many of the symbols are directly rooted in the story of the Dream Vision of Enoch and told on the cylinder seals. With those ideas in mind, it is rather easy to see that this seal is possibly showing us the origin of the idea and concept behind the symbol of the Three-Columns. With third tower actually representing this idea about the construction of a mobile weapons platform. I also cannot help but think this had to be a major turning point in this war.

Before we explore this, I wish to present you with a cylinder seal that has also been quite a mystery to scholars about what it might be showing us. In light of this story and the previous cylinder seal, it is easy to see and understand that this seal is showing us the same crane-system that was used to construct this platform as we just saw. This seal does not show any symbolism about which side this structure belonged too. It could also be a clue that both sides had access to similar equipment.

Cylinder seal from the Uruk Period, ca. 3,300BC – 3,000BC. (Fig.31) [32]

Returning back to the strange animal that is having the towers placed upon its back. Although this animal may seem confusing and strange at first. But, with our new knowledge we can very easily figure out what we are looking at. In order to do this, we must return into the Book of Enoch and the Bible to get an idea of the identity of this animal. Both the Book of Enoch and the Bible speak of two very powerful but mysterious creatures that were created and under the control of the Lord-God of Bible. One was the great and terrifying monster known as Behemoth who lived on the land and the equally frightening sea-monster remembered as Leviathan.

Looking at the cylinder seal, I think we are seeing the construction of the great beast of the land that is remembered as Behemoth. That statement might seem strange at first and you might not understand at this point of how I am making this connection between this ancient cylinder seal and that legendry monster that was in service of the Lord-God of the Bible. We need to pause for a few moments so I can explain this strange connection.

Surprisingly enough, there are numerous different stories, myths, and legends within the Judeo-Christian tradition about these two great monsters. Although there are great differences in the many stories about these monsters. They all do have some common elements that never seems to change regardless of the story. They all agree that both of these monsters are created and controlled by the Lord-God of the Bible. They also agree that mighty Behemoth was great and terrible monster of the land and that Leviathan was a terrifying monster of the sea. It is also agreed that chapters 40 and 41 of the Book of Job in the Bible gives the best description of Behemoth and Leviathan. Although the information about Behemoth is rather vague when compared to Leviathan.

The primary difference between all the different stories about these monsters tend to be about what happened to them. I think this is due to the fact that the neither the Bible nor any other book of the Biblical tradition says what happened to them. In some of the stories these monsters were killed or died long ago. In other stories is said they will return at the end of time and serve the righteous in the final battles against darkness. While in other more modern stories they are somehow transformed into demons that serve the Lord of Darkness. All of which seem to support the idea that most are just trying to fill in the blanks and the truth is that we will never know what may have happened to these legendary beasts.

Although there is great mystery surrounding these great beasts. When you combined these stories with the Dream Vision of Enoch along with the cylinder seals. You can begin to understand how all these seemly unrelated things are actually connected together. But, in order see how it really fits together we must take a closer look at some more cylinder seals and their connection to this terrifying sea monster known as Leviathan.

The sea monster Leviathan has a great number of stories surrounding it with chapter 41 of the Book of Job giving a very detailed description of this creature. I recommend that you should take a few minutes and go and read this chapter from the Book of Job. If you do this, will quickly realize that the Book of Job is describing a large metal object that sounds very similar to a modern-day submarine in its construction. The primary difference between this description of Leviathan and a modern-day submarine is the fact that Leviathan is said to have been able to raise its front section out of the water. If we return to the cylinder seals with this description of Leviathan in mind along with everything we have learned about the symbolism, you might be surprised by what we find.

135

The first cylinder seal we will examine clearly shows a boat or ship on the water. It also has the same familiar god-like figures from before. There is no doubt that this is showing a boat of some type that is carrying a god. You can also see other one of these god-like figures that appears to be part of the boat itself. Which based on the idea that Leviathan could raise up its front section out of the water, I think this is showing us Leviathan and the god that was in control of it. It is also showing us a connection between the idea of who this god was and how this god was connected to the sea in some manner.

Akkadian seal impression showing Mesopotamian sun god in a boat with human torso; from Tell Asmar, Iraq. (Fig.32) [33]

The next cylinder seal contains a very similar scene to this one but provides vastly more information with its symbolism. It shows both the Star and the Crescent Moon symbols that identify the two different groups. It also shows Leviathan slightly different with a head that closely matches the description in the Book of Job.

Unlike the previous seal, the figure in the center of the image and the focus of the scene is holding a Trident-like object in his hand. This object is very similar to the one we saw earlier on the War Seal. Legend, myth, and history always presents this as a great weapon. Based upon the symbolism we see on this cylinder seal. Then this seal is showing us that the Main-Group was attacking the Fallen-Watchers using Leviathan with all of these events happening at sea. It also gives the impression that the figure holding the trident is the leader that is in control of the mighty Leviathan. This would mean that this is a possible image of the one that is remembered as the Lord-God within the Biblical traditions.

Battle of Marduk and Tiamat, Neo-Assyrian Cylinder Seal, 900 - 750 BCE (Fig.33) [34]

The last cylinder seal in this series is very similar to the previous one. Although it does not appear to show the eight-pointed Star just the Crescent Moon symbol. Unlike the first cylinder seals we just looked at. This seal has the Pleiades star cluster on it and it shows the same configuration as other cylinder seals we have seen. This tells us that these events were taking place around the same time.

Neo-Babylonian cylinder seal, c. 7th - 6th Century BC. Depicting two standing robed figures facing one another, one holding a trident, a reclining goat behind with another robed figure further to right. (Fig.34) [35]

When we compared this to the seal showing the construction of Behemoth along the other cylinder seal. It is clear that this event must have taken place before the construction of Behemoth. Once again, that may seem a bit confusing at the moment, but I will be presenting another cylinder seal supporting this conclusion shortly. This gives us the idea that Leviathan had have been built first. If it was built first, then it is reasonable to think that it could have been used by the Main-Group long before the outbreak of war. To me, I think this provides us with a clue to how the idea of Atlantis being a worldwide sea fairing empire also begins to tie back into this all and Leviathan.

These cylinder seals appear to be showing us the great a legendry sea monster Leviathan and the Lord-God that controlled it. I think Leviathan is pretty easy to imagine what it could have actually looked like when these cylinder seals are combined with the description in the Book of Job. Which is of a large metal sea going vessel that is very similar in size and shape to a modern-day nuclear submarine. Once again, the primary difference being that with Leviathan its front section that could raise and lower like a giant head. The description given by Job seems to indicate that all the weapon systems were contained in this front head section. It also gives the idea that it really looked like a great terrible sea monster to all those that saw it. The cylinder seals and other related artifacts also give the impression that this was an actual description of this monster. I also cannot help but think that the Main-Group went out of their way to make Leviathan really look like a monster to help fool our ancestors.

Now, if these cylinder seals are actually showing us Leviathan, then there should be more cylinder seals showing us Behemoth than the one we have already seen. Remarkably there is a cylinder seal that shows us the completed animal with the towers placed upon its back. With our new understanding of the symbolism, it is very easy to recognize that this creature must be the one remembered as Behemoth.

If this cylinder seal is showing us Behemoth and the others are showing us Leviathan is there anything that might give us a better idea of what we are looking at here on this cylinder seal? Unfortunately, there just does not appear to any good descriptions about Behemoth like we have with Leviathan. There are only vague references to some great monster that looked like some dragon with no real detail to speak of. At least that is what most people think. If we go back to the cylinder seals, we will find that there is a great deal of information on this mythical beast.

In order to understand this scene, we must return to the ongoing war and the idea that there must have been ongoing meetings that took place between the different factions. As we can see here, after Behemoth is built a new meeting takes place between the Main-Group and the Fallen Watcher. We can see the completed Behemoth proudly displayed in the center.

I would also like to point out that this seal also shows the Pleiades star cluster in a different configuration than what we have seen before. Not only is the star configuration different, but for the first time we can clearly see which individual star is moving the most in relation to the other. Once again, I think this movement of the stars is the reason why I think that the seals show that Leviathan was built first and not Behemoth.

Cylinder seal from the Berlin Museum of Ancient Near East, Frankfort, Germany. Plate XXXIII, seal b (Fig.35) [36]

Looking at Behemoth in the middle. You can see there is not much detail outside of the fact that it looks like a dragon with two large objects on its back much like the experts say. But when we think of this as a great-war machine that had the military capacity of one of the towers in order to bring the fight to the enemy. It completely changes what we are looking for. Remarkably, I think I have found a more detailed image of this monster and what it may have actually looked like.

While looking at Behemoth on this cylinder seal. I noticed that there were only a few things that seem to provide any information about it. One was the two objects on its back. The second was that it appeared to be a large mobile war machine with the third being that it was connected to the gods. With these observations in mind, I went looking for anything in the cylinder seals and other artifact that might have these features. To my shock, I quickly found two seals that show the very same scene with all three of these features that give a much more realistic idea of what this thing might have looked like in real life.

Both of these cylinder seals show a large tower-like structure on a set of wheels with a god standing upon it. As you can see, this tower looks very similar in basic design when compared to the ones showing Behemoth. It is clearly a large mobile weapon of war and has the same animal figures and symbols as the other cylinder seals. I think the following cylinder seals will speak for themselves and you will quickly understand that they are very likely showing us a more realistic version of Behemoth. It is also easy to imagine how something like this thing could be interpreted as great monster by our ancestors.

Cylinder seal impression from Kultepe depicts the god Pirwa standing on a four-wheeled chariot drawn by four horses. A human figure lies prostrate under the chariot. 1,450BC -1,180 BC (Fig.36) [37]

Cylinder seal impression from old Assyrian period – 1,920BC-1,740BC (Fig.37) [38]

If these last eight-cylinder seals are actually showing us the legendary monsters remembered as Leviathan and Behemoth. Then logic dictates that the Fallen-Watchers and their allies must have had their own similar war machines. The Biblical tradition does speak of a number of monsters or beasts that are associated with the Fallen-Watchers. The two most famous are the Great Red Dragon and the Seven-Headed Beast with ten horns that are spoken of in the Book of Revelations. Additionally, both of these mythical creatures seem to be and remembered in some fashion by every single ancient tradition from around the world.

There is a cylinder seal that shows the Great Red Dragon of the Fallen-Watchers that is spoken of in the Book of Revelations. But you can only understand this seal if you understand that Crescent Moon symbol is connected to the Fallen-Watchers along with all the other ideas we have explored up to this point

Late Babylonian - 7thC BC-6thC BC - A bearded god (probably the moon god Sin) in a tall, horizontally-ridged, crescent-topped, cylindrical head-dress, holding a staff in one hand and raising the other, rises from a crescent and hovers facing right, before a bearded worshipper, who wears a round, narrow-brimmed hat and raises one hand. Back-to-back with this worshipper stands another identical figure, who raises one hand before a couchant 'mushhushshu' dragon (a composite creature) with the spade of Marduk on a stand on its back. (Fig.38) [39]

The next cylinder seal has a similar vague design as we saw earlier with the cylinder seal showing the great beast Behemoth. But, on this seal, we do not see Behemoth, we instead see a representation of the legendary Seven-Headed-Beast of mythology and religion. Although it might be lacking in some details. This seal does contain the Star symbol which clearly shows us that the Main-Group is attacking this terrifying Seven-Headed Beast.

Remarkably, it appears that every single ancient culture and tradition across the entire world remembers this monster in some fashion. In all of them the Seven-Headed-Beast was a thing of unbelievable horror that brought death to anyone that stood in its way. It is also universally believed that this great beast was defeated in an epic battle. Most commonly this was accomplished by single hero with some aid from the gods. In a few of the stories, it is the gods themselves who fight with a great hero that destroy this beast once and for all.

Although this beast is remembered around the world, there are in fact, very few artifacts showing it. But, as you can see on this cylinder seal, the Seven-Headed-Beast locked in battle with both the gods and the great human hero. Just like the ancient stories and myths. We can also see that four of the seven heads appear to be 'dead' while the three remaining ones are still engaged in battle.

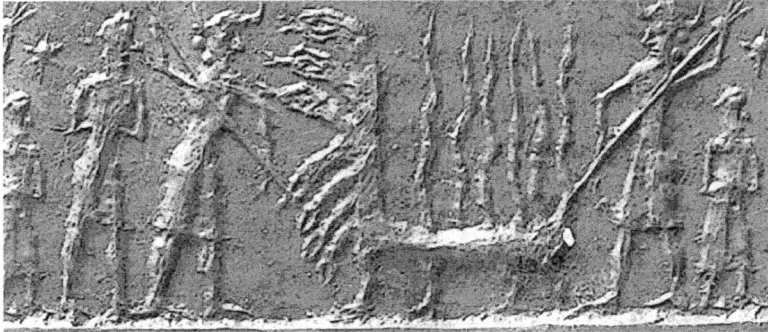

Oriental Institute, University of Chicago (Fig.39) [40]

Unfortunately, there does not appear to any other ancient artifacts that give us a better idea of what the dreaded Seven-Headed-Beast may have looked like in real life as we saw with Behemoth. Returning to Behemoth and the previous cylinder seals showing that it was most likely a great mobile platform with a tower-like structure upon it. Along with a god that controlled it, which could be represented by the second tower we saw that was placed upon the great beast's back

If we take these ideas that we have learned about Behemoth and use them to try and find artifacts that might show this great beast in a more realistic manner. I think you might be surprised that there are in fact artifacts showing us how this great Behemoth possibly looked like in real life. I have found what this monster might have looked like.

This artifact is not a cylinder seal, but scene from a relief that was found in the ancient city of Nimrud. As you can see, it has all the same characteristics we have seen on the cylinder seals. But at the same time, you can also see that this relief is clearly showing us a large siege tower like machine that is on wheels, with a single large battering ram sticking out of it. We can also see the great gods upon it fighting against the city walls. Additionally, we can also see that it has one single tower like structure that is very similar to the earlier cylinder seals we saw.

It is also important at this moment to point out that there are a number of other reliefs and artifacts that show this or a very similar siege-like tower on wheels. The main difference that is found upon these artifacts is that some of them show two battering rams instead of one we see here. At a later point we will see some additional items that will explain why this little detail is important and connects them back to the Great Red Dragon of the Book of Revelations.

Relief of Ashurnasirpal and his Army Attacking an Unnamed City with a Battering Ram, Northwest Palace, Nimrud (Fig.40) [41]

As you have seen, all of these legendary monsters of the ancient world appear to be great-war machines that were based on the basic design of the original towers that gods once stood upon. This may be one of the most important of missing factors of this ancient and largely forgotten war. These great machines appear to be a primary way for the gods to attack each other and to terrorize humans in general. Now that we have this new idea along this new information, we need to return back to the story of the towers and their destruction.

Within all the known ancient myths, stories, and legends about the towers. They all have one fact in common that never changes and that is fact that the tower or towers were destroyed by the gods. This destruction of the towers takes many forms and for many reasons, but the idea of the destruction of the tower by the gods never changes. This destruction of the towers is one the last things will we look at in this chapter before moving back to the rest of the Dream Vision of Enoch and this story.

Unfortunately, and much like the Seven-Headed-Beast, there does not appear to be any ancient artifacts showing us this destruction of the towers by the gods. With that being said, I have found a possible cylinder seal that could be related to the destruction of the tower.

The reason I possible, is because I do not believe this cylinder seal to be authentic and think it is a hoax. Not necessarily a hoax to deceive people but I think it is more likely that it based on someone's idea of this event happening. There are two reasons for this conclusion.

The first reason is because I can only find this image on the internet and cannot find the original source of the image. Outside of some vague technical information found on Wikipedia about the image itself, there does not appear to any information on where this cylinder seal comes from. It does not appear to come from any museum, university, or private collection.

The second reason is because as I have examined this image. I have found that although as first glance it seems lite its symbolism is right, there are small little differences that are not quite right when compared to other authentic cylinder seals. One of the primary problems is the Winged-Sun-Disk, the Star, and the Pleiades star cluster.

As you can see, the Star and the Winged-Sun-Disk are shown in a much different manner than any of the other cylinder seals we have seen or that I have ever found. This is the first clue that this is not a real cylinder seal. The next problem is the configuration of the Pleiades star cluster. As we saw, the great Behemoth, which can be seen on the left-hand side, was built after the Pleiades star cluster appeared in this configuration.

These two items alone show us beyond doubt this cylinder seal must be a fake. But, at the same time it seems to be showing us that the tower is being attacked in some manner. I think it is safe to say that it rather clear that whoever made this cylinder seal had a very good working knowledge of this story but made simple mistakes on how exactly the symbols really shown on the artifacts. This gives me the impression that someone hired and told an artist to make this image. But the artist had no actual knowledge of how the symbols are actually shown on ancient artifacts.

Even with all these problems I am still including it here. This is because it raises many important questions about who could know this story. It also begs the question of why somebody would go through all the trouble to make something like this. These questions along with some others will be looked at a later point.

A possible 1st Millennium BC seal showing a worshipper and a fish-garbed sage before a stylized tree with a crescent moon and a winged disk set above it. (Fig.41) [42]

As you have seen, when taken as a whole, these ancient cylinder seals appear to be telling the story of the towers. Not only are they showing the story of the tower, they also appear to be telling the same story found in the Dream Vision of Enoch. Especially when you remember within the Dream Vison that animals represent people and groups of people and men represent Angels or a Higher-State of being. Based upon what we have seen on the cylinder seals, that not only do men symbolically represent Angels or a Higher-State of being but they can also symbolically represent the gods.

When we also realize the importance of the Pleiades star cluster and that the movement of its stars over time is recorded on the cylinder seals. We can understand that this provides us with a way to put the series of events that led up to the destruction of the tower into their proper order. Not only that, the Pleiades star cluster also provides undeniable evidence that these events took place over thousands of years and tens of thousands of years ago. In the next chapter we will return to rest of the Dream Vision of Enoch so we can address many of the questions and the various ideas this all brings to mind.

But before we return to the Dream Vision of Enoch and this thought experiment. I would like to present a series of images that I have created showing the configurations of the Pleiades star cluster as we saw them on the cylinder seals. These images only show the visible stars as seen on the cylinder seals and provide a realistic movement of the stars over time. They also provide us with a starting point for actually dating these events.

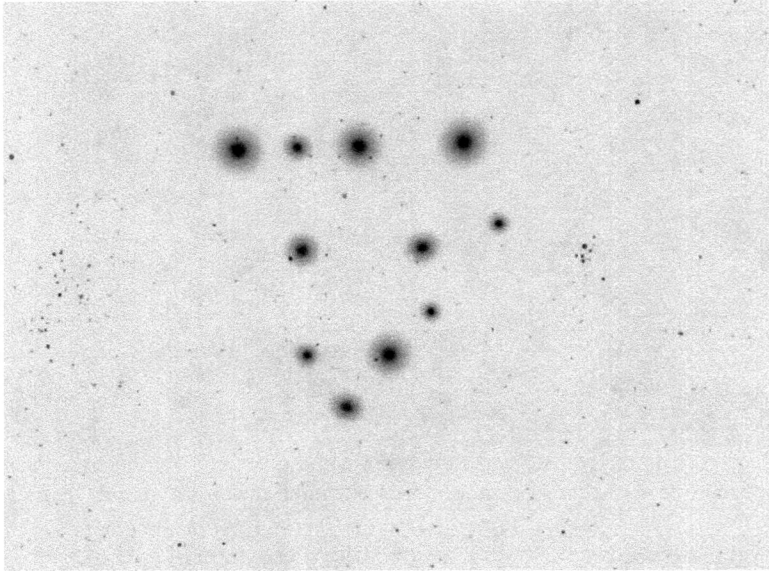

(Fig.42) [43] - This is the time of the events shown on the first cylinder seal and could be related to the actual founding and layout of the house that will be great and broad.

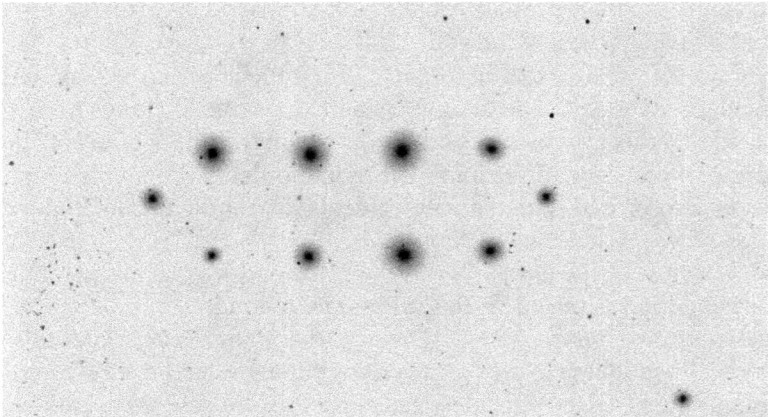

(Fig.43) [44] - This configuration of ten stars is when the first lofty tower was constructed upon the house.

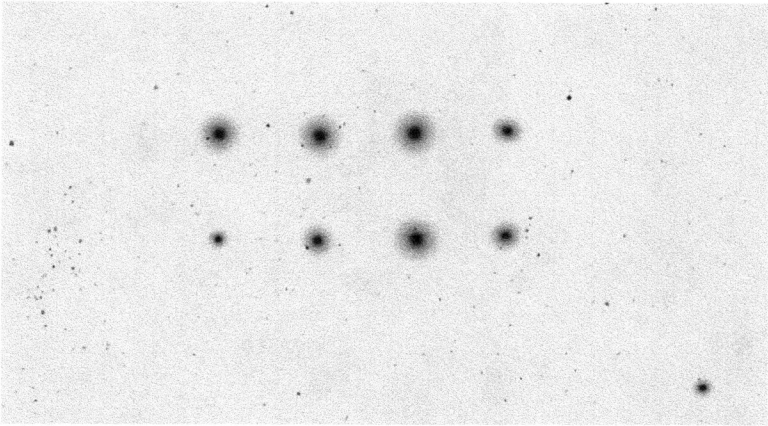

(Fig.44) [45] - This configuration of only eight stars in two parallel lines of four stars. Is when the one we know as Enoch was saved and taken up to heaven away from the generations of the earth to be with God. This also marks the time of the beginning of the war and the time when many symbols gained much of their hidden meaning.

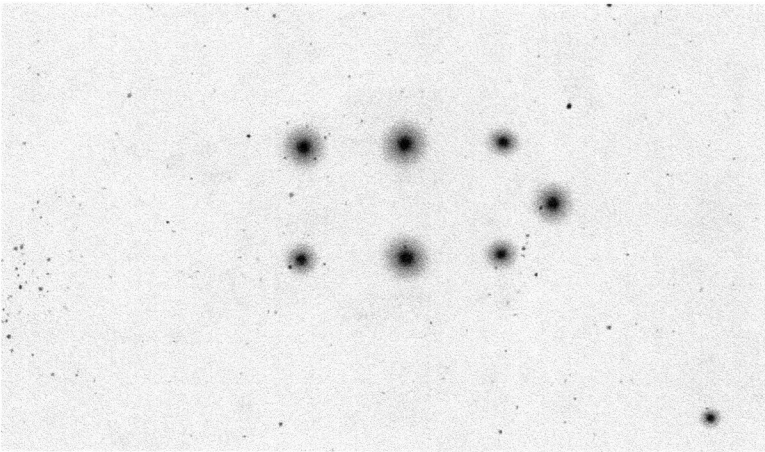

(Fig.45) [46] - This is the time of meetings between the different parties and great battles involving Leviathan.

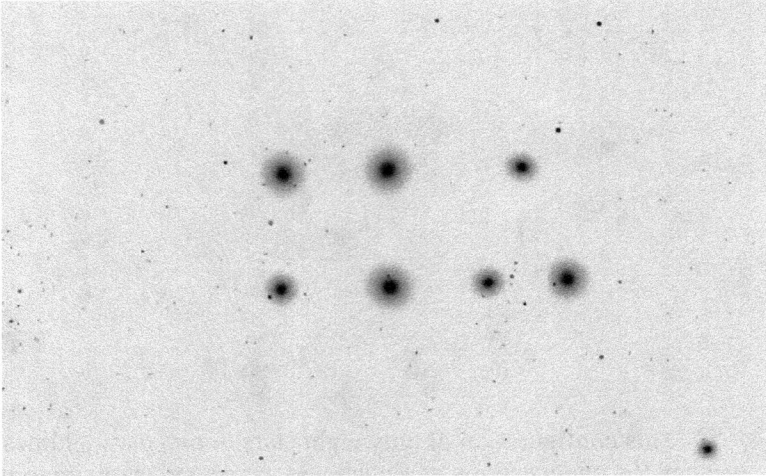

(Fig.46) [47] - This is when the great and terrible land monster Behemoth was created by the Main-Group. It is also possible that many of the legendry ancient monsters of the Fallen-Watchers like the Dragon and the Seven-Headed-Beast are built at this time.

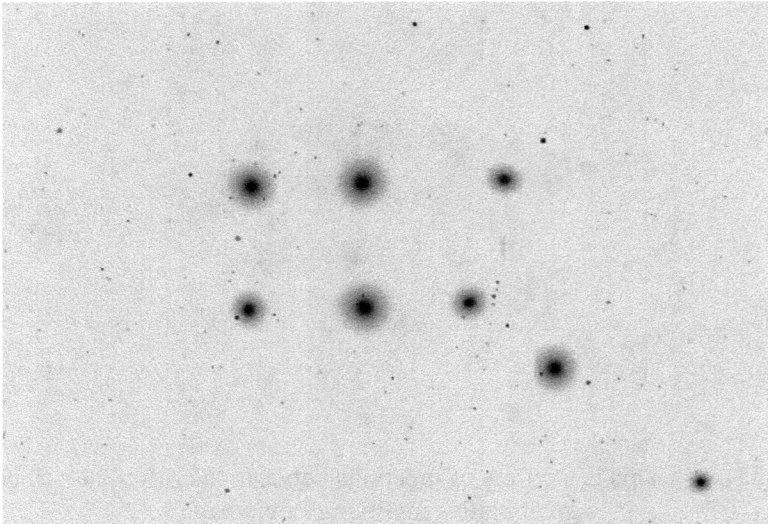

(Fig.47) [48] - This configuration is based on the cylinder seals that show another meeting between the two different parties and is highly likely to be just before the destruction of the first tower.

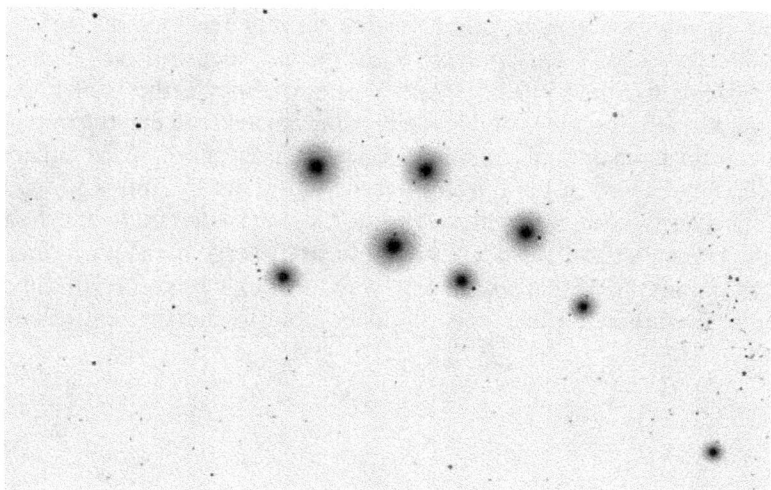

(Fig.48) [49] - This image is based on a few items you have not seen yet but will shortly. It shows seven stars in a configuration that is very close to the one we have today with only six stars. I present it because it could be recording the event of the towers actually being destroyed or another very important event that we have not explored yet.

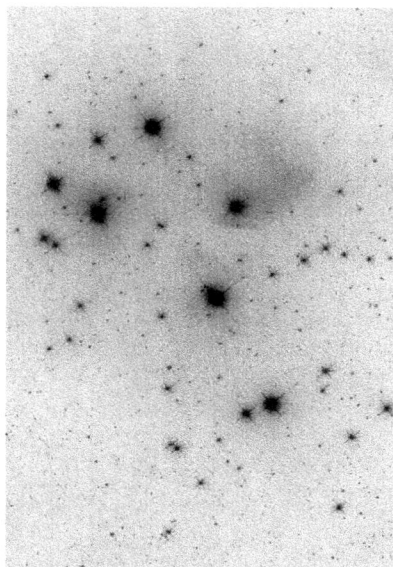

(Fig.49) [50] – The Pleiades star cluster as it appears today in the night sky.

There is one last item to point out concerning the cylinder seals and the images that they show. As you have seen, the cylinder seals are clearly telling the same story as found in the Dream Vision of Enoch, the Bible, along with numerous other mythologies and legends. You can also see that the cylinder seals show the exact same animal characters as stated in the story of the Dream Vision of Enoch. This is one of the missing pieces to the puzzle and why we have all missed the fact that the story that is told on the cylinder seals is the same one told in the Dream Vision of Enoch, the Bible, and a large number of other ancient traditions and myths. If there was some way to be able to gather all the different cylinder seals into one place, we might be able to put this entire story back together.

Chapter 9

The Destruction

And I looked, and behold a pale horse: and his name that sat on him was Death,
and Hell followed with him.
~Revelation 6:8~

eturning to the story of the Dream Vision of Enoch the next set of verses
right after we are told of the destruction of the second tower that was
built by the three sheep that turned back that we read about in chapter
seven.

The Dream Vision speaks of how these actions do not appear to have had the
desired effect. We are told that Lord of the sheep touches all the eyes of the sheep
and the shepherds so they were "*blinded and saw not*" and then they delivered
the sheep in large numbers for destruction

With a better understanding of the towers and a rough idea that a great war
going on. This great number that was delivered for destruction could have been
the result of a counter attack by the Main-Group. All of this gives the impression
that Lord of the sheep is causing the vast majority of this death and destruction.
It makes me wonder if the Main-Group was starting to really lose this war and
that this was a direct attack on the followers and allies of the Fallen-Watchers.
This may have been done in the hope to reduce their numbers to a point that they
could not continue the war.

Even without all the details, it is clear the story speaks of great destruction
and death on an epic scale, a biblical scale. A scale that most likely can only be
compared to our own modern world and the wars of the last couple of centuries
that have killed hundreds of millions of people. It truly makes one wonder if

there was the use of airpower, heavy artillery, and weapons of mass destruction in this large-scale war being fought over an almost unbelievable amount of time between two different ideological groups.

"And as touching all this the eyes of those sheep were blinded so that they saw not, and [the eyes of] their shepherds likewise; and they delivered them in large numbers to their shepherds for destruction, and they trampled the sheep with their feet and devoured them. And the Lord of the sheep remained unmoved till all the sheep were dispersed over the field and mingled with them [i.e. the beasts], and they [i.e. the shepherds] did not save them out of the hand of the beasts."
(Book of Enoch 89: 75-76)

This death and destruction of this war, is recorded and reported to the Main-Group on what is starting to appear to be a rather regular basis. The individual that is tasked with recording these events in what is now called an *"actual book"* that is then given to the Lord of the sheep who then *"laid it down beside Him."* This same individual begins to give a testimony against the all the shepherds and their doings. This could be the origin of the idea of a Book of Life or book that is used to judge you at the end of time that is spoken of in the Book of Revelations and referred to by other traditions.

"And this one who wrote the book carried it up, and showed it and read it before the Lord of the sheep, and implored Him on their account, and besought Him on their account as he showed Him all the doings of the shepherds, and gave testimony before Him against all the shepherds. And he took the actual book and laid it down beside Him and departed."
(Book of Enoch 89: 76-77)

The text then goes on to explain how thirty-five of these shepherds undertook the pasturing of the sheep and that they completed their periods as the first ones had done before. It also says that each shepherd received the sheep from the one that came before in order to pasture them for a period time. It is unknown how long each one of these time periods of the shepherds where, but when thought of with the cylinder seals. I think it is reasonable to estimate that these events took place over a very long period of time.

It also appears to mean that only one shepherd (Watcher) was in charge at any one period of time. They took turns in this genocide, with each one picking up where the last one left off.

"And I saw till that in this manner thirty-five shepherds undertook the pasturing (of the sheep), and they severally completed their periods as did the first; and others received them into their hands, to pasture them for their period, each shepherd in his own period."
(Book of Enoch 90: 1-2)

The next part speaks of a new battle being undertaken by the *"birds of heaven"* coming to devour the flesh of the sheep. This is the reason why I chose to include the cylinder seal showing the birds of heaven and beasts of the field attacking the tower in the last chapter.

The cylinder seal along with the text of the Dream Vision, this appears to be referring to the use of some type of air power. It also seems that each type of bird is referring to a different type of aircraft. Much like we do today with our own modern air-forces.

It is easy to imagine how these birds could be a symbolic representation of different aircraft like bombers, fighters, gun-ships, or attack helicopters. Especially when the verses speak of how the all the skins and flesh of the sheep was torn from their skeletons leaving nothing but their *"bones"* standing there until they *"fell to the Earth."*

This description sounds strangely familiar to death and destruction that heavy weapon systems being delivered by aircraft bring to the enemy. Modern weapons like Napalm or a chemical-like weapon comes to mind when reading these verses. These types of weapons can and do *"devour"* the flesh, leaving only *"bones"* behind. It is also possible that some type of advanced energy-based weapon that quickly destroyed soft tissue was deployed. It is possible that a laser-based system that produced high heat would only leave the skeleton behind. We could go on forever wondering what type of weapon systems were being used by the birds of heaven against the sheep. But, based on the mythology, it is clear that whatever they were using it was devastating to their enemies. It is also very probable that these weapon systems were meant to terrify our ancient ancestors as much as possible too.

This ongoing war and these battles seem to go very badly for the Cro-Magnon-Man humans. We are told in the text that their numbers become few with next to nothing remaining. The new shepherds appear to do nothing to aid or stop this attack in any manner.

These events just add to the great amount of confusion about what is exactly going on between the different parties and how this war is unfolding. Without more details it is almost impossible to say with any confidence on what the actual motivations and reasons behind all this chaos. I think the birds or heaven are showing us that there is possibly other party involved in all of this, which again adds to the ongoing confusion. It is also possible they are working with the Fallen-Watchers and their allies. It is even possible that they have been corrupted in some way by the Fallen-Watchers.

> *"And after that I saw in my vision all the birds of heaven coming, the eagles, the vultures, the kites, the ravens; but the eagles led all the birds; and they began to devour those sheep, and to pick out their eyes and to devour their flesh. And the sheep cried out because their flesh was being devoured by the birds, and as for me I looked and lamented in my sleep over that shepherd who pastured the sheep. And I saw until those sheep were devoured by the dogs and eagles and kites, and they left neither flesh nor skin nor sinew remaining on them till only their bones stood there: and their bones too fell to the earth and the sheep became few."*
> (Book of Enoch 90: 2-5)

After losing this battle, the war goes on for an unknown period of time. The Dream Vision only says that *"until twenty-three had undertaken the pasturing and completed in their several periods fifty-eight times."* All we know is that fifty-eight shepherds had each taken their turns and these events took place when these fifty-eight shepherds were in charge.

During this unknown period of time while this great and horrible death and destruction is going on. We are told that *"lambs"* are born to those white sheep and their eyes begin to *"open and to see"* and they began to cry to the other sheep but that the other sheep did not listen or see.

This reference to the *"white sheep"* does not seem to be speaking of the possible racial features as we saw with the Bulls from earlier. The traditional interpretation is that this reference is referring to the idea of being a "pure" or "righteous" follower of the Lord of the sheep. I think this interpretation is correct, but it also raises the question of why the gods stopped using the racial features as some type of identification for our ancestors. Unfortunately, neither the Book of Enoch nor the Bible gives any information to why this change occurred.

The lambs that are born among the sheep appear to be a turning point in this ongoing war. The Dream Vision speaks of how they *"cry to the sheep,"* but for some reason the sheep do not listen. This gives the impression that these "lambs" had a different way of thinking. This could be a clue to who these lambs where.

If the bulls in the story are symbolic represent Neanderthal humans and the sheep symbolically represent Cro-Magnon-Man humans. Then it is perfectly reasonable to speculate that the lambs are us, Homo sapiens, sapiens. This could be why these lambs are seeing and understanding things much differently from the sheep. It also seems to match our modern understanding of human evolution. It is well known that one of the major things that make us different from earlier forms of humans is our unique way of thinking. Once again, the text does not indicate if these lambs were the product of the Main-Group or that it just some fluke of nature that happened on its own.

"And I saw until that twenty-three had undertaken the pasturing and completed in their several periods fifty-eight times. But behold lambs were borne by those white sheep, and they began to open their eyes and to see, and to cry to the sheep. Yea, they cried to them, but they did not hearken to what they said to them, but were exceedingly deaf, and their eyes were very exceedingly blinded."
(Book of Enoch 90: 5-8)

This introduction of the lambs being born among the sheep at first does not seem have much of effect on the war. The text does speak of how the "ravens" take one of the lambs and then dashed the other sheep in pieces and devoured them. Exactly which lamb was taken or why is unknown. The Dream Vision doesn't appear to ever speak of this individual again. I have also been unable to find any other reference to this individual within the Judeo-Christian tradition.

Shu-ilishu, cylinder seal. Department des Antiquities Orientales at Musee du Lavue Paris. (Fig.1) [1]

The only idea that I have about this individual that is taken by the Fallen-Watchers. Is that this person eventually comes back as a false prophet or maybe even the one that is remembered as the Antichrist in Christian tradition. There are many other possibilities on who this lamb actually was, but the hard truth is, there is not much else to go on. I have found a cylinder seal that could be showing a scene that might be related to this event. As you can see, it shows a smaller figure sitting upon the lap of one of the gods, who is apparently speaking with him. The symbolism of the crescent moon clearly shows this is a scene about the Fallen-Watchers. When compared with the other cylinder seals we have seen, it is difficult not to think this scene is related somehow to this story.

The text then tells of how these lambs grew "*horns*" that were "*cast-down*" down by the ravens until one of the sheep sprouted a "*great horn*" and that the eyes of all that saw it were opened. This great horn had a great impact on all the remaining sheep and rams causing them to run to that sheep. This gives the impression that the great horn had something to do with a great leader that arose who thought and fought differently. This may be a clue to our unique way of military thinking when compared to Neanderthal or Cro-Magnon societies.

"And I saw in the vision how the ravens flew upon those lambs and took one of those lambs, and dashed the sheep in pieces and devoured them. And I saw till horns grew upon those lambs, and the ravens cast down their horns; and I saw till there sprouted a great horn of one of those sheep, and their eyes were opened."
(Book of Enoch 90: 8-9)

We are told that this sprouting of a "*great horn*" takes place under battle in what appears to be a constant air attack from the birds of heaven. Although the ravens were able to cast down the horns of the lambs, we are told in the next set of verses that they were unable to cast-down the great horn on one of those sheep. We are also told the ravens had "*no power over it.*"

This seems to imply and make me think that this great horn could be also be related to a weapon system of some type. Possibly one that was very effective against airpower like a surface-to-air missile defense system or maybe even an energy-based system that was easily seen over a wide area. It could also be referring to one of mobile tower platforms we saw on the cylinder seals. It is easy to imagine how the missiles of a modern-day missile system could be viewed as having horns like an animal after looking the cylinder seals. Once again, it could be even simpler with it all just being a new way of thinking that involved changing the military tactics and techniques and that the other side could not compensate for.

To me, all of this is starting to appear to be some type of lead up to a great and final battle with the "great horn" being a major turning point in this ongoing war. It is clearly something that tipped the balance of power and changed everything.

"And it looked at them [and their eyes opened], and it cried to the sheep, and the rams saw it and all ran to it. And notwithstanding all this those eagles and vultures and ravens and kites still kept tearing the sheep and swooping down upon them and devouring them: still the sheep remained silent, but the rams lamented and cried out. And those ravens fought and battled with it and sought to lay low its horn, but they had no power over it."
(Book of Enoch 90: 10-12)

The Cro-Magnon-Man humans, the sheep and the rams under the leadership of the sheep with the great horn appear to go on the offensive and start fighting back on a large scale. This results in shepherds joining forces with the birds of heaven. After this alliance is formed, they launch some type of large counterattack trying to destroy this great horn. This event could be what we saw on the cylinder seal from earlier showing the birds of heaven and the beasts of the field attacking a tower. Which then gives us the idea that the great horn might actually be speaking of one of the towers.

The next verse seems to indicate that the battle grew so intense that this new ram with the great horn cried that "its help might come." This seem to imply that some part of the Main-Group was secretly allied and supplying this group of Cro-Magnon-Man humans.

"And I saw till the shepherds and eagles and those vultures and kites came, and they cried to the ravens that they should break the horn of that ram, and they battled and fought with it, and it battled with them and cried that its help might come."
Book of Enoch 90: 13)

The next part of the story speaks of how the one that was ordered to write down everything the shepherds did. Then carried up this mysterious book to the presence of the Lord of the sheep. It also tells of how the individual recording these events for the Lord of the sheep is the one that was helping the ram with the great horn and not the Lord of the sheep. I think this is another clue that the Main-Group did not have complete control of these events. It is also a clue that there must have been a number of different groups were working against the Lord of the sheep, including his own people.

These events lead to the Lord of the sheep to openly intervening with his "*wrath.*" We are told that all who saw "*Him*" fled and they all fell into "*His shadow from before His face.*" Although the description is vague, this could be describing a large ship that dominated the sky casting a great shadow upon the ground. It also brings to mind that it must have been some type of very powerful weapons platform that had superior fire power and possibly even technology when compared to the other groups. This could be a describing the Winged-Sun-Disk we have seen on the cylinder seals. This event and this ship appear to be the beginning of the final battle of this ongoing war.

> "*And I saw till that man, who wrote down the names of the shepherds [and] carried up into the presence of the Lord of the sheep [came and helped it and showed it everything: he had come down for the help of that ram]. And I saw till the Lord of the sheep came unto them in wrath, and all who saw Him fled, and they all fell into His shadow from before His face.*"
> (Book of Enoch 90: 14-15)

This arrival of the Lord of the sheep which is most likely a large ship of some type. Results in the birds of heaven rallying all of their remaining forces along with what is called the "*wild sheep.*" We are told this was done so they could "*dash that horn of the ram into pieces.*" These wild sheep are most likely any remaining Cro-Magnon-Man humans that had not allied themselves or were in service with either group.

> "*All the eagles and vultures and ravens and kites, gathered together and brought with them all the wild sheep, and they all came together and helped one another in order to dash that horn of the ram into pieces.*"
> (Book of Enoch 90: 16)

The next verse of the text then jumps back to the one that was recording everything. We are told that this individual presented the book that recorded the destruction to the Lord of the sheep. We are also told that these last twelve shepherds caused even more destruction than the other fifty-eight that had come before them.

> "*And I looked at that man, who wrote the book at the command of the Lord, until he opened that book of the destruction that those last twelve shepherds*"

had wrought. And he showed, in front of the Lord of the sheep, that they had
destroyed even more than those before them had."
(Book of Enoch 90: 17)

All of this leads up to one of the most important parts of this entire story. It is also critical to understanding what we have missed about our past and why we have missed it. I think we can accurately date the next set of events that happen much so than most of the other parts of this thought experiment. Additionally, it will also give you a much better idea of what may have really happened all those thousands of years ago. It will also provide some possible explanations to number of questions that do not seem to fit into our understanding of the past.

This mysterious event that I am speaking of. Is the one that leads to the final climatic battle of this war. This event caused a great destruction that was unbelievably vast and impacted the entire globe. This destruction was very similar to how a full-scale nuclear war of today would wipe out almost every trace of our modern civilization. In the end, this massive event wiped almost every major and minor population center off the map. It also ended up destroying entire cities, people, cultures, and a way of life around the planet. We will look at this event in just a few moments and what could have caused so much to be lost as if it never existed. But before we do that, we must take a look at second part of the verses and the "great sword" that it speaks of.

This great sword that was given to the sheep allowed them to *"proceeded against all the wild beasts of the field to slay them."* This great sword is clearly a great weapon of some type. When viewed with the knowledge of the cylinder seals from the last chapter. I think it is rather apparent that this great sword must be the Behemoth-like animal we saw being built on the seals. This understanding then provides an idea of the proper order of the unfolding events. More importantly, it will also allow us to use the Pleiades star cluster to help date these events. In order to get a better understanding of these events we need to return to the destruction I just touched upon before the great sword.

This destruction is described in a rather vague way and may not be apparent at first on how this could be speaking of a great global catastrophe that leads to an epic final battle. We will first have to expand on the idea that this destruction can be dated.

"And I looked until the Lord of the sheep came to them and took the Staff of
His Anger and struck the Earth. And the Earth was split. And all the animals,
and the birds of the sky, fell from those sheep and sank in the earth; and it
closed over them. And I saw till a great sword was given to the sheep, and

the sheep proceeded against all the wild beasts of the field to slay them, and all the beasts and the birds of the heaven fled before their face."
(Book of Enoch 90: 18-19)

The idea I wish to present to you may seem a little out of place at first, but it will provide a greater understanding of the whole story. It will also provide a starting point for when the Pleiades star cluster had the configurations we have seen on the cylinder seals. I also believe it will provide undeniable evidence and support that all of these events actually took place.

The idea that is in my mind is this. When I think of this final battle with all its death, destruction, and misery wiping cities and entire groups of people off the map. I can only think of one thing that happened thousands of years ago that could fit this idea. It is what we call the Holocene extinction that began around 11,000 BC.

This is a very well know historical event that resulted in large numbers of animals, plants, and human cultures going extinct all around the planet. It is also most likely the mysterious event that led to a time known as the Younger Dryas. The Younger Dryas, also commonly known as the Big Freeze, was a rather geologically brief period of time spanning about 1,300 years between approximately 10,800 BC to 9,500 BC. During this time, harsh Ice Age conditions returned to the world causing a mass extinction.

There have been a number of rival theories proposed over the years trying to explain what happened around 11,000 BC that led to such an extreme change in the climate in such a short amount of time. It has been difficult for experts to come up with something that could explain why Ice Age conditions of cold and drought returned for about 1,300 years. Especially given the fact that this event was abrupt enough to cause the extinction of most pre-historic animals and plants in the process.

One of the more interesting theories that have been proposed during the late 1990s and early 2000s is the idea that some type of large impact event caused the Younger Dryas event. It has been hypothesized that a large air burst or possible earth impact of a comet or similar object initiated the Younger Dryas climate change around 10,900 BC. This has come to be known as the Younger Dryas impact hypothesis or the Clovis comet hypothesis.

The scenario proposes that an air burst similar to the Tunguska event of 1908 in Siberia, but many orders of magnitude greater occurred over the North American continent north of the Great Lakes over the Laurentide Ice sheet. This massive air burst could have been the cause of the extinction of most of the large animals in North American and the reason for the demise of the Clovis culture among many others. This burst was so large that it resulted in coast-to-coast wildfires across North America that would have destroyed most of the plant and animal life. Any survivors would have starved on the burnt surface of the continent.

The evidence for this impact hypothesis includes a charred carbon-rich layer of soil that has been found at some 50 different Clovis-age sites across North America. This layer has been found to contain unusual materials that seem to indicate an impact event. These include nano-diamonds, metallic micro-spherules, carbon spherules, magnetic spherules, iridium, charcoal, soot and fullerenes enriched in helium-3.[2] This is very similar to the evidence that is found in the K-T boundary layer and presented for the Chicxulub impact that killed the dinosaurs 65 million years ago.

This scenario has been the subject of much criticism and doubts. There are been a number of specialists that have studied the claim and they concluded in a 2010 paper [3] that there never was such an impact event. The main reason given for this conclusion is that physical signs of such an impact cannot be found outside of the Clovis sites. They claim there does not appear to be any evidence of an impact event of any type in the ice cores that date from this time. In addition, they also claim there is not any other supporting evidence of a worldwide event outside of the climate change and the extinctions of many large animals 12,000 years ago. Many have dismissed this hypothesis and claim that it is no longer a viable scientific hypothesis that requires any further study.

This is clearly a cop out on the part of the experts. Because if do any serious research on 10,000 BC you will find that there is a large body of scientific research and data that it supports the idea of a large impact event or even a nuclear event occurred around 10,800 BC.

The authors of the papers trying to debunk the Younger Dryas impact hypothesis do not even attempt to try and explain the evidence that has been found at the Clovis sites. Nor do they explain how this evidence does not point to some type of impact or even a nuclear-like event. But, even if they do take this evidence into account, they normally present some rather crazy ideas to explain it.

If these papers trying to debunk the idea are true. Then this raises the question of where did this unusual material come from? If it was not a large impact or air burst that produced this material it then raises the next question of what could? Is there anything else that could do this and leave this type of evidence behind? What could cause worldwide extinction and climate change that only leaves local evidence of the type found but also cause worldwide extinctions?

One of the major problems confronting the experts is the fact that there is a large body of research and evidence that clearly supports that whatever happened about 13,000 years ago was a nuclear event of some type. There is clear evidence of uranium-235 and of plutonium-239 along with the radioactive isotopes they decay into found in the carbon-rich mat of material at the Clovis sites.

This evidence has led a number of people to claim that this supports the idea of a large scale thermo-nuclear war happening around 13,000 years ago. Although this idea might sound a little crazy at first. It does provide a possible solution with answers to many questions surrounding this extinction event and the evidence that has been found. There are countless websites that claim that only a nuclear war could leave behind the local evidence of the blast that would be very similar to what has been found in the carbon rich mat of material.

Although this idea might be a bit hard to believe. It is possible that most of the dust and radioactive fall-out would settle out of the atmosphere in just a few days over a few hundred miles of area depending on the wind. It would not have much chance to reach the polar areas to leave much evidence in the ice. Nuclear blasts would also create a large number of aerosols that would have been suspended in the upper atmosphere for a very long period of time and would only slowly settle out over time. This would likely leave little trace in the ice by spreading it out over a rather long period of time and could easily be missed unless you knew what to look for. Additionally, these aerosols would have reflected sunlight back into space thereby cooling the planet to the point that the climate changed into the period we now call the Younger Dryas. It all makes for a nice story, but again, the evidence is lacking for a large-scale nuclear war and there are other possibilities that do a better job explaining what has been found.

The radioactive isotopes and other material found at the Clovis sites seem to the "smoking gun" so to speak, of a nuclear event happening 13,000 years ago. This is the reason why we can date this material so accurately. A nuclear event would also explain why iridium has been found and why the soot and fullerenes are enriched with helium-3. The primary problem is that all of this evidence, outside of the evidence for uranium-235 and of plutonium-239, can be explained by some type of impact event. This alone makes it difficult to imagine how this evidence could not have come from an impact event from outer space. It is also very difficult to say it is not evidence that an unknown ancient civilization used nuclear weapons on a large enough scale that it resulted in them being literally bombed back to the stone-age.

I must admit, I do like this idea. While I like this idea, I do not think it is correct simply because there is no evidence of a number of ancient nuclear blast sites found around the world. There are a lot of claims that have been made to

THE FORBIDDEN KNOWLEDGE OF ENOCH

explain this possible ancient nuclear war with some even appearing to fit the evidence rather well. Unfortunately, in the end, they all fall short of the mark. The truth is that all we really know is that we have evidence that something horrible happened 13,000 years ago on this planet and it left evidence behind that it was nuclear in nature.

There has been some serious research into this idea of a nuclear like event causing all of this death and destruction 13,000 years ago. The nuclear event that has been proposed is not an ancient nuclear war but a supernova that is theorized to have occurred approximately 41,000 years ago and about 250 light years away.

This theory that a supernova could be the cause all of the destruction was first proposed by the nuclear scientist Richard Firestone of the U.S. Department of Energy's Lawrence Berkeley National Laboratory (Berkeley Lab) and Arizona geologist Allen West in 2005 at the 2nd International Conference titled "The World of Elephants" in Hot Springs, South Dakota. They proposed that they had found evidence to support the idea that the supernova explosion's initial shockwave in 34,000-year-old mammoth tusks that are peppered with tiny impact craters apparently produced by iron-rich grains traveling at an estimated 10,000 kilometers per second. They believe that these grains may have been emitted and accelerated by a supernova that exploded roughly 7,000 years earlier and about 250 light years from Earth.[4]

They propose that this event was then followed by a 10-kilometer-wide comet that may have been composed from the remnants of this supernova explosion that hit North America 13,000 years ago.[5] In support of their theory Firestone and West found the same magnetic metal spherules and other evidence in the Clovis sites as stated before and excess radioactivity was also found at these sites. Analysis of the magnetic particles by Prompt Gamma Activation Analysis at the Budapest Reactor and by Neutron Activation Analysis at Canada's Becquerel Laboratories revealed that they are rich in titanium, iron, manganese, vanadium, rare earth elements, thorium, and uranium. This composition is very similar to lunar igneous rocks, called KREEP, which were discovered on the moon by the Apollo astronauts, and have also been found in lunar meteorites that fell to Earth in the Middle East an estimated 10,000 years ago.[6]

In addition, Berkeley Lab's Al Smith used the Lab's Low-Background Counting Facility to detect the radioactive isotope potassium-40 in several Clovis arrowhead fragments. Researchers at Becquerel Laboratories also found that some Clovis layer sediment samples are significantly enriched with this isotope. The potassium-40 in the Clovis layer is much more abundant than potassium-40 in the solar system. This isotope is formed in considerable excess in an exploding supernova and is a major factor in the idea of whatever hit the Earth 13,000 years ago originated from a recently exploded supernova.[7]

This theory is also corroborated by other radiocarbon measurements. The timeline of physical evidence discovered at the Clovis sites and in the mammoth tusk mirrors the radiocarbon peaks found in Icelandic marine sediment samples that are 41,000, 34,000 and 13,000 years old. Richard Firestone contends that these peaks, which represent radiocarbon spikes that are 150 percent, 175 percent, and 40 percent above modern levels, respectively, can only be caused by a cosmic ray-producing event such as a supernova.[8]

This is a very intriguing and interesting theory that I personally believe to be false and absolutely beyond belief. For no other reason that it is physical impossible for an iron-rich grain traveling at 10,000 kilometers per second to survive contact with the atmosphere and make it to the ground. This is very easily proved by a quick mathematical calculation of the kinetic energy of one of these grains and the observation and understanding of a common meteor.

The typical meteor or shooting star that most of us have seen over the years are actually very small in size, normally about the size of a grain of sand up to the about the size of a pea. The reason why we see a falling star is because these small grains are moving at a large velocity when they hit the upper atmosphere of Earth, this velocity is typically around 40 to 60 kilometers per second but it is not unusual for many to be up to 70 or 80 kilometers per second. This speed is what causes the friction between the meteor and the atmosphere which then generates a large amount of heat that then burns up the object making the shooting star we are all so familiar with.

The idea that a similar sized iron-rich grain moving at velocity of almost 165 times that of the typical falling star could survive hitting the atmosphere and not burn up and make it all the way the surface of the Earth and make impact craters and become lodged in the Tusks of mammoths 34,000 years ago is utterly beyond the realm of belief and common sense. Especially if you do the mathematical calculation for the kinetic energy based on the velocity that is given by Richard Firestone of 10,000 kilometers per second which is about 5% the speed of light and the mass of the typical grain of material that hits our atmosphere of about .1 gram using the formula: Kinetic energy = ½ mv2 (m = mass in kilograms, v = velocity in meters per second). If you do this you will get the answer of 5,000,000,000 joules of energy, which is equal to about 1.195 tons of TNT [9] compared to the 180,000 joules of energy produced from the typical meteor moving at a velocity of 60 kilometers per second, which is equal to about 0.000043021 tons (0.086 lbs.) of TNT.

This is a huge difference in energy and clearly shows that the iron-rich grains should have blown apart in the upper atmosphere never reaching the ground, much less make small impact craters on and then become lodged in the tusks of mammoths. In fact, if by some miracle they did manage to make it to the ground the force of the impact would have destroyed the tusks and killed the mammoths on the spot. In light of this simple little examination of the theory I think you can say with great confidence that his idea of supernova being the ultimate cause behind the extinction event of 13,000 years ago and of it being the cause of the iron-rich grains in the mammoth tusks of 34,000 years ago is clearly false and is not supported by any real science or the actual evidence. If simple physics can prove that it could not be a supernova that caused this evidence, then what could?

This brings us right back to the idea of nuclear like weapons being used by some advanced civilization thousands of years ago. Thermo-nuclear weapons can and do produce the exact same type of evidence that has been found at the Clovis sites and in the tusks of the mammoths. There are many who do not understand why the so-called experts and scientists are so resistant to this idea when the evidence so clearly supports that some type of nuclear event happened in the past that led to unbelievable change on the planet 13,000 years ago.

It is hard not to believe some of the claims when it appears that the experts are so against it that they will concoct some of the greatest fantasies that do not even follow the basic laws of physics or science. Not only do they make up some great stories, they then present them as a scientific theory and fact while the rest of the scientific community accepts it all without question. The supernova example clearly provides more than enough evidence to support this conclusion.

This leads me to believe that there might be something more going on here than just bad science and a lack of creativity. I will return to this idea a little later, but for now, we need to return to the Dream Vision before we get to far off track. We will return to this subject later and explore it in greater detail that will provide a totally new idea on what could have caused all the destruction 13,000 years ago. But, before we do that, there is one other idea we must touch upon concerning this event and the climate change that happened.

There are many that have noticed that many of the climatic events that happened during the Younger Dryas appear to be what the native people of the Americas are speaking of in their stories of the different worlds that have come before our own. The Hopi Indians of Northern Arizona and their myths of different worlds along with a great destruction and rebirth is a good match and a perfect example of this. There are many similar stories from many other tribes speaking of different worlds all across the Americas and I think they are all talking about the same set of events.

"The first world was destroyed, as a punishment for human misdemeanors, by an all-consuming fire that came from above and below. The second world ended when the terrestrial globe toppled from its axis and everything was covered in ice. The third world ended in a universal flood. The present world is the fourth. Its fate will depend on whether or not its inhabitants behave in accordance with the Creator's plans."
World Mythology. (1993, Henry Holt and Company, LLC. Duncan Baird Publishers)

This myth from the Hopi Indians appears to speaking of the same event of a final battle with the destruction of the first world by an all-consuming fire that came from above and below. This is very similar to the last set of verses above, of the Lord of the sheep took his *"Staff of His Anger and struck the Earth. And the Earth was split."* It is difficult not think this is speaking of the same thing as the Hopi myth with fire coming from above and below the earth.

I think the rest of the Hopi myth is describing the climate events that happen over the next 1,300 years. The second world would be the Younger Dryas period and the return of ice sheets that had been retreating for some time. The third is the flooding that occurred when the Younger Dryas came to an end and the ice melted resulting in large local flooding around the world. With the fourth being our current world. It is very likely that the ancient Native America stories are firsthand accounts of these largely forgotten events and are actual history.

Chapter 10

The Judgment

And whosoever was not found written in the book of life was cast into the lake of fire.
~Revelation 20:15~

K eeping all the ideas I have presented so far in our minds. I will now return to the final parts of the Dream Vision of Enoch. With this ever-growing idea that is looking less and less like a hypothetical scenario and thought experiment and more like an actual scientific hypothesis and dare I say a possible theory?

The Dream Vision, along with so many other ancient texts, indicates that there was a great destruction and then a final battle of this grand war. The last remaining parts of the Dream Vision that we will look at appear to indicate that the Cro-Magnon-Man humans along with a few of us and the Main-Group are victorious over all the other groups. The text speaks that a "*throne was erected in the pleasant land*" and that the "Lord of the sheep" sat upon it and that another one unsealed the books and opened them before the Lord.

> "*And I saw till a throne was erected in the pleasant land, and the Lord of the sheep sat Himself thereon, and the other took the sealed books and opened those books before the Lord of the sheep.*"
> (Book of Enoch 90: 20)

After the opening of these mysterious books. The next set of verses speaks of a judgment that takes place. This judgment is the reason I originally said I did

167

not think the judgment spoken of after the Great Flood was correct. This again is just one of the many examples of how all these stories have become mixed-up with each other over time. It should give you an idea about what I meant when I said that the genesis story about the creation of the world is actually speaking of many different stories all crammed together. This is how it is speaking of the Fall of the Angels and the creation of the world and humanity all at the same time. We will see that this Judgment is very similar.

This judgment also includes the seventy shepherds besides the Fallen Stars or Watchers. The shepherds seem to be included due to the fact that they did not follow the command of the Lord of the sheep and killed more than they were commanded too. In an earlier part of the Book of Enoch it speaks of how these Fallen Stars were bound with great chains holding them in a large cage of fire. We will take a closer look at this in a few moments, but first the judgment of those that were bought before the Lord.

"And the Lord called those men the seven first white ones, and commanded that they should bring before Him, beginning with the first star which led the way, all the stars whose privy members and were like those of horses, and they brought them all before Him. And He said to that man who wrote before Him, being one of those seven white ones, and said unto him: 'Take those seventy shepherds to whom I delivered the sheep, and who taking them on their own authority slew more than I commanded them.' And behold they were all bound, I saw, and they all stood before Him."
(Book of Enoch 90: 21-23)

There are two more ancient cylinder seals that are related to the slaughter of the sheep and the judgment of the shepherds. I will be starting with a cylinder seal that we have already seen before to help complete this part of the story.

I will start with the cylinder seal from earlier showing the possible extermination and destruction of the sheep by the shepherds. With our new and greater understanding of what and who the symbols of the Star, Crescent Moon, and the Solar-Disk actually represent. You will now see that this scene from earlier has much more meaning than before.

Starting on the left-hand side with the Star and the moving to the right-hand side with the Crescent Moon and Solar-Disk symbols. We can now be able to understand what each symbol in this image is telling us. As we have learned, the Star represents the Main-Group or the Lord of the sheep high up in the sky. The floating head to the right of the Star is the one that has been watching and recording everything the shepherds do and all that they destroy. The bull, the

168

sheep, and the human head that is clearly being chopped off on an altar are the groups being delivered to the shepherds for destruction. The last symbol in the sky is the Solar-Disk over the Crescent Moon represents that the Heaven was under control or at least being heavily influenced by the Fallen-Watchers. The smaller figures between the shepherds are humans that have been raised up to a higher state of being and represent some of the groups that were associated and helping with the destruction. As you now see and understand that the symbolism of these ancient cylinder seals is not some mystery that cannot be understood by the common person as the experts claim.

Goddess, Suppliant Goddess, Priest, and Worshiper Carrying Kid Before Sun God with Goddess and Goat Behind; in the field: Star Demonic Mask, Bull, Human Head, Star and Crescent Cylinder seal and impression. Mesopotamia, First Dynasty of Babylon: (ca. 1894–1595 B.C.) (Fig.1) [1]

The next cylinder seal appears to show us a moment sometime around the final battle. This seal clearly shows a monster or dragon in the center with the Crescent Moon symbol directly above it. It also shows two larger monster-like creatures attacking one another. We can also the shepherd having one hand up possibly representing that they are dealing in good faith while the other hand is behind his back touching the creature or beast. This appears to show us that this group, the Fallen-Watchers did not deal in good faith with the Main-Group which is represented by the figure holding the knife his hand and the small fish looking figure behind it. It also appears that the larger creature behind this individual might be holding hands or something jointly, but unfortunately, the seal is damaged and it is difficult to see what it actually is.

Old Assyrian – 1,920 BC – 1,740 BC (Fig.2) [2]

The last cylinder seal in this series is clearly related to the judgment of the Fallen Stars, the shepherds, and their associates. This scene is so similar to the story of the Dream Vision we have been exploring. As you can see, it shows many of the same animals found in the Dream Vision. Once you understand the Dream Vision and is connection to the symbolism. This seal alone it makes it almost impossible to deny that all of the cylinder seals are showing some version of the story found in the Dream Vision of Enoch.

Cylinder seal Date: ca. 20th–19th century B.C. (Fig.3) [3]

As you can also see, this seal shows the heads of dead animals and dead human bodies. We can now understand that the heads represent the groups of humans that made war against the sheep or allied with the Fallen Stars. We can also understand that the dead human bodies are actually symbolically representing the shepherds. We can also clearly see the Lord of the sheep sitting upon his throne passing judgment upon those Fallen Stars and shepherd that were bought before him.

As with the other cylinder seals, we can see one of the monsters of legend in the back ground. This also gives us a clue to what great sword that was given to the sheep before the final battle may have been. When looked at as a whole with all the other cylinder seals. It is quite possible that the great sword was in fact the great and mythical beast remembered in the Biblical tradition as Behemoth. One last interesting observation that I have noticed about this ancient cylinder seal from the Middle East. Is that style of the artwork on this cylinder seal seems to have a very similar to the art style of ancient Central and South America cultures. It could be a clue that cultures on both sides of the world were in fact in contact with each other and influencing each other long ago. It also makes one wonder this story might actually be real history and not legend and mythology like we have been taught to believe.

This judgment is very similar to the one spoken of in Chapter 88; verse one though three of the Book of Enoch way back at the beginning of our little journey through the Dream Vision. The main difference between the two stories is that in this later one, the shepherds and their blinded sheep are also judged and punished. Just as we have seen on the last cylinder seal. We are told that the shepherds meet the same fate as the Fallen Stars. Based upon the Book Enoch, this would mean they were also cast into an abyss that was full of fire and pillars of fire. This could be where the idea of eternal punishment by fire in hell may come from. It could be based upon this judgment and imprisonment of the Fallen-Watchers, the shepherds, and their followers.

The Fallen-Group and the shepherds are cast into the abyss and imprisoned. But the Cro-Magnon-Man humans that were allied with them suffered a different fate. We are told that they were cast into another pit that was "*alike abyss was opened in the midst of the earth, full of fire*" that was opened to the right of that house. They were then found guilty and executed by being cast into this pit that was full of fire. The story implies that these wayward Cro-Magnon-Man humans were burned alive. I cannot help but think this punishment must be tied in some way to the practice of the ritual of "passing through the fire" that is spoken of in the Bible. Because I do have to admit, based upon the ancient traditions, I think this would be viewed as a fitting punishment for anyone that practice the ritual of burning your children alive for material gain in this life.

"And the judgement was held first over the stars, and they were judged and found guilty, and went to the place of condemnation, and they were cast into an abyss, full of fire and flaming, and full of pillars of fire. And those seventy

shepherds were judged and found guilty, and they were cast into that fiery abyss, And I saw at that time how alike abyss was opened in the midst of the earth, full of fire, and they brought those blinded sheep, and they were all judged and found guilty and cast into this fiery abyss, and they burned; now this abyss was to the right of that house. And I saw those sheep burning and their bones burning."
(Book of Enoch 90: 24-27)

The text speaks of how after this punishment of the Fallen Stars, the shepherds, and the wayward sheep the *"old house"* was *"folded up."* We are also told that the pillars, ornaments, and beams where also folded up with the house and *"carried it off"* to a place *"south of the land."* The Lord of the sheep then brings a *"new house"* that is greater than the first and *"set it up"* in place of the first with all the sheep within it.

"And I stood up to see till they folded up that old house; and carried off all the pillars, and all the beams and ornaments of the house were at the same time folded up with it, and they carried it off and laid it in a place in the south of the land. And I saw till the Lord of the sheep brought a new house greater and loftier than that first, and set it up in the place of the first which had been folded up: all its pillars were new, and its ornaments were new and larger than those of the first, the old one which He had taken away, and all the sheep were within it."
(Book of Enoch 90: 28-29)

The Cro-Magnon-Man humans that were left or survived this final battle and judgment where then elevated to a much higher position than before. The next set of verses speak of how all the *"beasts on the earth"* and all the *"birds of the heaven"* fall down and do homage to the sheep. They also obeyed and made petition to them for everything.

The surviving humans seem to become the new heroes or even the new rulers over all the other groups. This could this be where we get a number of the hero or old men of renown stories from. With understanding that there are multiple stories speaking of the same events in similar but slightly different viewpoints that was broken into at least two main-camps. It is a little bit easier to understand how they could fit together and how they do not fit together all at the same time.

"And I saw all the sheep which had been left, and all the beasts on the earth, and all the birds of the heaven, falling down and doing homage to those sheep and making petition to and obeying them in everything."
(Book of Enoch 90: 30-31)

All of this allows us to finally understand that the individual that is witnessing all of these events is the one we call Enoch. The one that was seized by his hand and brought him above a tower and then back to the sheep before the judgement took place. This might help explain why this story places the imprisonment events of the Fallen Stars at the beginning and at the end with the shepherds. This individual would have only witnessed the last parts of the story and was only told about the first part. Additionally, we know that according the Biblical tradition there was some type of judgment against the Watchers around the time of the Great Flood. So, I think it is very possible that the author of this story superimposed the judgment and punishment he witnessed upon both events.

By realizing where Enoch himself fits into this story. It also gives us a greater understanding of what the rest of the Book of Enoch is speaking of. It is speaking of the time between when this individual was saved and brought up to heaven and his return before the judgment. This means that the other chapters that are contained within the Book of Enoch are talking about the events that were witnessed by this individual during his time in Heaven before returned just before this final judgement took place. If you go back and read the rest of the Book of Enoch with this knowledge in hand. The book will make much more sense and will give you the order of some of these events and how they unfolded.

"And thereafter those three who were clothed in white and had seized me by my hand [who had taken me up before], and the hand of that ram also seizing hold of me, they took me up and set me down in the midst of those sheep before the judgement took place."
(Book of Enoch 90: 31-32)

Once the victory is complete with all unwanted elements of the Cro-Magnon-Man humans having been eliminated. We are told that the wool of the sheep became white and abundant and clean. Again, this is not a racial reference but a symbolic reference to purity and righteousness of the remaining Cro-Magnon-Man humans. It is curious as to why the gods stopped using the racial component to classify humans. I think it is possibly due to the fact that human society had become to complex for such a simple system that also clearly causes problems among humans themselves by breaking people into different groups.

The text then speaks of how all the beasts of the field and the birds of heaven also assembled in that house and the Lord of the sheep was filled with great joy and rejoiced because all were good and had returned to His house. Again, this sounds like complete victory with the full reestablishment of power by the Main-Group over earth and its remaining population. It is also very similar to the story that is contained within the Book of Revelations. So similar in fact, that I can find no expert, scholar, theologian, or layman that does not agree that the story contained within the Dream Vision of Enoch and the Bible's Book of Revelations are speaking of and telling the exact same story. The only difference between the two in the amount of detail given. With the greater amount of detail being contained within the Book of Revelations.

> *"And those sheep were all white, and their wool was abundant and clean. And all that had been destroyed and dispersed, and all the beasts of the field, and all the birds of the heaven, assembled in that house, and the Lord of the sheep rejoiced with great joy because they were all good and had returned to His house."*
> (Book of Enoch 90: 33)

We are then told that the great sword is then returned to the Lord of the sheep and sealed before Him. The returning of this mighty weapon appears to be important enough that it led to all the sheep being invited into that house and they all had their eyes opened and they could see the good.

> *"And I saw till they laid down that sword, which had been given to the sheep, and they brought it back into the house, and it was sealed before the presence of the Lord, and all the sheep were invited into that house, but it held them not. And the eyes of them all were opened, and they saw the good, and there was not one among them that did not see. And I saw that that house was large and broad and very full."*
> (Book of Enoch 90: 34-36)

174

Chapter 11

Transformation

And the Lord said, My spirit shall not always strive with man, for that he also
is flesh: yet his days shall be an hundred and twenty years.
~Genesis 6:3~

After all the events that have taken place. A great change takes place that
will possibly help explain the mystery behind Genesis six and its first
six verses that speak of the sons of God. It will also give a greater
understanding on how all these stories tie together in one way or another.

In the next series of verses in the Dream Vision of Enoch we are told that that
a "*white bull was born, with large horns.*" We are also told that all the beasts and
birds feared him and made petition to him all the time. This white bull, whoever
he is, is clearly very powerful in all the ways that where important to ones around
him. He also appears to very special in some other way too.

Not only is he important to the other animals, he also appears to be the catalyst
that changes everybody back into white bulls that includes all the beasts of the
field and the birds of the heaven. This implies that all these different animals
may not have been so different as normally believed. How this was done is not
really known, but I suspect, as you have no doubt already figured, that some form
of large-scale genetic engineering or breeding program was under taken. This
results in "*all their generations were transformed*" and them all becoming white
bulls. This is most likely the same transformation that is spoken of in Genesis
six in verse three "*yet his days shall be a hundred and twenty years.*" This
transformation would help in explaining where this idea may have come from
and why it is an important piece to understand.

This would also explain what happened to all the other animals and closely related humans from 13,000 years ago and why we have not found much evidence for them. It was simply because they were transformed back into a type of Neanderthal. Which we can understand was the original genetic matrix to begin with. Which then raises even more questions than before while providing possible solutions at the same time. Because it would mean that the evidence of this happening could be in our genetic code. This would explain why we appear to have genes in our DNA that do not seem to do anything. Both of which could prove this idea one way or another. All of this is testable by our current science and could be confirmed or falsified with the proper research.

After this grand transformation, we are told that the Neanderthals give birth to a "*lamb*" and that lamb becomes a "*great animal.*" Not only was it a great animal it had "*great black horns on its head*" and that the Lord of the sheep rejoiced over it and all the oxen.

Like before, I think this is us, Homo sapiens, sapiens or modern humanity. We are the lamb that was born among them and became a great animal with great black horns. As before, this is symbolically speaking of how we have superior mental prowess of any of our predecessors. The "*great black horns*" are most likely speaking of our brain and our unique way of thinking when compared to earlier humans. I think this makes perfect sense while also providing an explanation to some of the mysteries contained within our own genetic code.

"And I saw that a white bull was born, with large horns, and all the beasts of the field and all the birds of the air feared him and made petition to him all the time. And I saw till all their generations were transformed, and they all became white bulls; and the first among them became a lamb, and that lamb became a great animal and had great black horns on its head; and the Lord of the sheep rejoiced over it and over all the oxen. And I slept in their midst: and I awoke and saw everything."
(Book of Enoch 90: 37-39)

The last part of the text speaks of Enoch awaking from his dream vision and that he blessed the Lord of righteousness and gave Him glory and then he wept for all that he had seen. He speaks "*for everything shall come and be fulfilled*" and that he was shown the future in the sense that he was told all the "*deeds of men in their order.*" As you can now understand, I do not think Enoch is speaking of our future as is commonly believed, but is instead speaking of his own future which is our ancient past.

176

Not only does the movement of Pleiades star cluster on the cylinder seal prove this, but the other reason I say this is because the story speaks of Enoch being taken up from the generations of the earth. Which, again, is how Enoch is able to witnesses all of this and then write it all down. As we have seen, these events seem to take place over a much longer period of time than even Enoch's long-life of 362 years that is spoken of in the Bible. Common sense tells us that he would have had to been shown or was told about many of these events. Given that it seems pretty clear that some type of advanced technology was available to at least the gods, Enoch could have very well watched these events on a monitor or TV screen. It would also help explain why the confusion of some of these events. Additionally, the story in the Dream Vision clearly states that the destruction, judgment, and grand transformation has already happened thousands of years ago. This is speaking of our ancient and largely forgotten past. A past that is only remembered within the mythology and legends of the ancient world.

"This is the vision which I saw while I slept, and I awoke and blessed the Lord of righteousness and gave Him glory. Then I wept with a great weeping and my tears stayed not till I could no longer endure it: when I saw, they flowed on account of what I had seen; for everything shall come and be fulfilled, and all the deeds of men in their order were shown to me. On that night I remembered the first dream, and because of it I wept and was troubled because I had seen that vision."
(Book of Enoch 90: 40-42)

Before moving on the next chapter where we look at understanding of all of this. I would like to take a few moments and examine the rest of the Book of Enoch with the idea that it is speaking of the time period between when the sheep or Enoch was saved and brought up to heaven and then later returned to earth before the final judgment.

With this idea in mind and using the story of the Dream Vision as a general outline you can understand exactly what the first eighty-four chapters of Enoch are talking about. It also allows one to realize why so many people over the years have misunderstood what this book is actually talking about. I will only be summarizing a few points and the general sequence of events that are contained within the first eighty-four chapters to give you an idea of what I trying to say. I highly recommend that you go and read the rest of the Book of Enoch after reading this summary to fully understand the point I am trying to get across here.

If you begin with the Dream Vision in the Book of Enoch that starts on chapter eighty-five and use it as a general outline of events. You will discover that chapters one to eighty-four in the Book of Enoch start at the point where the sheep or Enoch is saved and taken from the generations of the earth in Chapter eighty-nine, verses fifty to fifty-four and taken up into what is traditional thought of as heaven. As you will remember, in Chapter eighty-seven we are told that Enoch was "*grasped me by my hand and took me up, away from the generations of the earth, raised me up to a lofty place, and showed me a tower raised high above the earth.*" This is the event that allows to understand how the Book of Enoch is laid out and how this story is kind of mixed up because the book is not laid out in what we typically think of as the normal order of a book.

It is at this point in reading the Dream Vision that you should go back and start reading the first eighty-four chapters of the Book of Enoch. Not will the story begin to make more sense, but you will also notice that these chapters appear to be a firsthand account of the events and things that Enoch was spoken about or shown.

After Enoch was raised up to a lofty place. He begins describing how he was shown the creation of man and the general events leading up the Fall of the Watchers. This begins with the deal that was made on Mt. Hermon by the individuals that Enoch calls the Angels and the Watchers at different points in the book. He is then shown the heavenly knowledge that the Fallen-Watchers brought to humanity and all the trouble that came with it.

After the Fall of the Watchers, he is then shown the events leading up to the Great Flood and the reconquest of earth by the Lord and his Arch-Angels. In this part of the story we learn that the ones that looked like white men were Arch-Angels named Michael, Uriel, Raphael, and Gabriel. After the reconquest of earth there is some additional detail given about Noah, the Great Flood, along with information of the events surrounding this part of the story.

The next part of the Book of Enoch is one that can be confusing and help leads to some of the misunderstanding about this book. Enoch goes on to describe what can only be described as a very advanced ship with high-technology that embarks on some type of journey to another place that is not earth. I agree that Enoch is describing some type of high-technology that he himself did not understand. I will let you make up your own mind on this part of the Book of Enoch. What I think is more important here is not the journey itself, but the fact that Enoch is shown some very specific locations and told some very specific information that helps to give an understanding of what he is seeing.

In this journey, Enoch is taken to a location that he describes in some detail. He gives enough detail that it may provide an actual location if you could figure out if the mountains and the other landmarks that he describes really exist in any form today. I am unsure as to a real location that exists today that could be the place he is describing. But he describes a place that burns day and night with seven mountains made of different stone. This seems to indicate that this was a large area that was volcanically active.

> *"And I proceeded and saw a place which burns day and night, where there are seven mountains of magnificent stones, three towards the east, and three towards the south. And as for those towards the east, (one) was of coloured stone, and one of pearl, and one of jacinth, and those towards the south of red stone. But the middle one reached to heaven like the throne of God, of alabaster, and the summit of the...(Verse nine missing)...throne was of sapphire. And I saw a flaming fire. And beyond these mountains is a region the end of the great earth: there the heavens were completed."*
> (Book of Enoch 18: 6-11)

In the next couple of verses, Enoch describes what he saw at this location and what was going on.

> *"And I saw a deep abyss, with columns of heavenly fire, and among them I saw columns of fire fall, which were beyond measure alike towards the height and towards the depth. And beyond that abyss I saw a place which had no firmament of the heaven above, and no firmly founded earth beneath it: there was no water upon it, and no birds, but it was a waste and horrible place. I saw there seven stars like great burning mountains, and to me, when I inquired regarding them, The angel said: 'This place is the end of heaven and earth: this has become a prison for the stars and the host of heaven. And the stars which roll over the fire are they which have transgressed the commandment of the Lord in the beginning of their rising, because they did not come forth at their appointed times."*
> (Book of Enoch 18: 12-16)

This is clearly the prison or abyss of the shepherds and fallen stars that is spoken of before. This gives us another clue as to the proper sequence of events.

This would mean that at this point in the Book of Enoch the shepherds and the fallen stars are already imprisoned. This would also mean that Enoch is seeing them just before the final judgement that is spoken of in the Dream Vision and the Book of Revelations. This would also mean that by this point the final battle has already taken place. It also means that the rest of the Book of Enoch is speaking of the events leading up to his return and seeing the judgment take place. This also allows us to place the odd story of Enoch returning briefly to tell his son Methuselah of what he has seen and to warn him about the impending destruction and final judgment of humanity. This meeting must have happened some time before the great destruction and the final battles.

This would mean that the proper order of these events would be that after Enoch was taken from the generations of the earth. Then a war began shortly after this event. During the course of this war, the great ship known as the Heaven was destroyed causing great destruction. After this great destruction both sides gear up for one last grand battle to decide the winner once and for all. It is during this final battle that the Fallen-Watchers and their allies are defeated. This leads to the capture of the Fallen-Watchers, the shepherds, their allies, and the final judgment along with their punishment. After this punishment we are told that new house comes down and the great transformation gets underway. We can realize now that Enoch first return to his son to warn his family and others of the final events that will lead to everybody's death accept a chosen few was before the great destruction. His second return is just before the final judgment but after the Fallen-Watchers and shepherds had already been captured awaiting judgment. If you return to the Book of Enoch with this understanding in mind. You will quickly realize why everybody has mistaken what the Book of Enoch is speaking about.

The final piece that is missing is understanding that the final destruction of everything by the Lord using *"Staff of His Anger and struck the Earth. And the Earth was split."* Was in fact the great Heaven, symbolically remembered as the All-Seeing-Eye came crashing to earth causing widespread destruction. We also have to realize that everything that happened after this point was dealing with the after effects of this destruction with a final attempt to save something of their world.

This allows us to understand why Enoch was temporarily sent back. It was so he could tell his family and other righteous ones of the death of the old sinful world that was coming after the events of the upcoming judgment of the shepherds and fallen stars. This is where the parts of the Book of Enoch that speak of Enoch talking to the fallen angels. As with his family, he is speaking to all the Fallen-Watchers and their allies before the great destruction, the final battle, and the judgment to come.

This also means that I was incorrect with my original idea that Chapter eighty-three was talking about the rebellion of the Fall of the Watchers. But what it is really talking about is Enoch warning his son Methuselah and others of why the final judgment and destruction was coming, but that there was hope. This was because some were going to be saved, transformed, and live with the Lord forever.

180

"And now, my son Methuselah, I will show thee all my visions which I have seen, recounting them before thee. Two visions I saw before I took a wife, and the one was quite unlike the other: the first when I was learning to write: the second before I took thy mother, (when) I saw a terrible vision. And regarding them I prayed to the Lord. I had laid me down in the house of my grandfather Mahalalel, (when) I saw in a vision how the heaven collapsed and was borne off and fell to the earth. And when it fell to the earth, I saw how the earth was swallowed up in a great abyss, and mountains were suspended on mountains, and hills sank down on hills, and high trees were rent from their stems, and hurled down and sunk in the abyss. And thereupon a word fell into my mouth, and I lifted up (my voice) to cry aloud, and said: 'The earth is destroyed.' And my grandfather Mahalalel waked me as I lay near him, and said unto me: 'Why dost thou cry so, my son, and why dost thou make such lamentation? And I recounted to him the whole vision which I had seen, and he said unto me: 'A terrible thing hast thou seen, my son, and of grave moment is thy dream-vision as to the secrets of all the sin of the earth: it must sink into the abyss and be destroyed with a great destruction. And now, my son, arise and make petition to the Lord of glory, since thou art a believer, that a remnant may remain on the earth, and that He may not destroy the whole earth. My son, from heaven all this will come upon the earth, and upon the earth there will be great destruction. After that I arose and prayed and implored and besought, and wrote down my prayer for the generations of the world, and I will show everything to thee, my son Methuselah. And when I had gone forth below and seen the heaven, and the sun rising in the east, and the moon setting in the west, and a few stars, and the whole earth, and everything as He had known it in the beginning, then I blessed the Lord of judgement and extolled Him because He had made the sun to go forth from the windows of the east, and he ascended and rose on the face of the heaven, and set out and kept traversing the path shown unto him."
(Book of Enoch 83: 1-11)

Now that we understand that is speaking of the destruction of a great shop. This would mean that it is possible to find the location of where this "Heaven" crashed to earth based on the idea of the final destruction happening about 13,000 years ago.

Using the description given by Enoch. We can see that Enoch talks about how the Heaven collapsed and fell to earth and how it created a "*great abyss*" and that the "*mountains were suspended on mountains.*" This description makes it next to impossible to deny that Enoch is speaking of massively large explosion that created an equally large crater. I think logic dictates that if this story is true and this event was large enough to create a crater. Then you should be able to find it because it should have a higher-than-normal metal content if it was a large ship that would date from around this time.

Remarkably, there is a large crater that fits the above idea perfectly. It is known as the Sithylemenkat meteor crater that was discovered in 1972 by the Landsat 1 satellite in a mountainous and desert region in the north central area of Alaska and dates to approximately 12,000 years ago. This crater is about 12.4 kilometers (7.705 miles) in diameter and has a depth of 500 meters (1,640.42 ft.) and there is a small 3-kilometer (1.86 mile) diameter lake at the bottom of the depression formed by the crater.

Samples taken from inside the crater revealed an abnormal high proportion of nickel and other heavy metals, which stunned the researchers. The researchers were even more stunned to find that the same strong nickel and high metal concentrations were also found in the peripheral soil samples of the depression. It is estimated that it would take a solid iron-nickel metal object about 600 meters across (1,968.50 ft.) to create this crater and leave the high metal concentrations we find today. A magnetic study of the area also indicated a strange negative magnetic anomaly associated with this crater. It is evidence pointing to an intense fracturing of the crater bed below the impact zone and an unusually deep cracking of the bedrock not seen in other craters. It has been estimated the total kinetic energy that was liberated at the time of the impact was of the order of 1.1 x 1020 Joules. [1] This translates into about 26,290 megatons of force. [2]

The fact that this crater dates from the about the right time. It has an unusually high metal content and that the object that made this crater also released a very large amount of energy. Makes this site a good candidate for the possible location of where this Heaven could have crashed to earth if the ancient story in the Book of Enoch is correct. It also provides us with the idea that the final destruction may not have been the use of large scale thermo-nuclear weapons or a super-nova 250 light years away. But it was in fact this Heaven crashing to Earth that resulted in a 26,000+ megaton blast is the real reason behind the destruction.

This would provide an explanation to the many ancient ideas, stories, myths, and legends that the great and final destruction could not be stopped, even by the gods themselves. This would also explain why the same ancient stories state it was going to happen at a certain time and only a select chosen few would be saved. If this was a large ship in orbit around earth with a slowly decaying orbit that was going to impact the earth for some reason. This would explain why this final destruction could not be stopped by anyone, including the gods.

Expanding on this combined with our early ideas. We can speculate that the large eight-pointed star commonly shown up in the sky is most likely a symbolic representation of the mighty Heaven. It is also the origin of the ever famous All-Seeing-Eye of God looking upon humanity. For something to be seen from the ground by the naked eye and looking like a giant eye looking down. implies that this Heaven was truly a massive ship in low earth orbit.

When added to our understanding that a great war was going on. It is easy to understand that somehow this great and magnificent ship that our ancestors called the Heaven was damaged before the final battle. This damage was so great that it caused the Heaven's orbit to begin slowly decaying. This decaying orbit is what eventually caused it to impact the earth.

This impact and the resulting 26,000+ megaton explosion from this impact was so huge that the ones I have been calling the Main-Group really did not have much of a choice in the whole matter. I think they were only doing what they could to minimize the incredible damage that was coming in the hope something would survive. This would answer many questions about why these gods who appear to have spent so much time, effort, and resources here on earth into whatever they were actually doing, to only turn around and destroy everything they created and then also leave. As you can now begin to realize that it most likely did not happen the way most believe. Not only is all of this an intriguing idea. But it does explain a great number of questions that have been asked over the years.

This would mean that everything up to the grand transformation had taken place except the final death of everybody that was not saved at the end of time due to the climatic weather changes that were coming from this great destruction. This also means this was the reason for many of the things that the Main-Group did. They really did not have much choice in the matter after a certain point. It is also clear that the great destruction changed the environment so much they had to create and dispersed the new animal over much of the world. As we have already learned, this new animal was us, Homo sapiens sapiens or modern man. This would explain why the transformation had to take place. It was so some remnant of humanity could survive the coming worldwide death and destruction. This was done by making us more adaptable than the humans that came before so we could survive the great changes to the climate that were going to happen from this impact and massive explosion of the Heaven.

This would explain how and why we all have the same basic stories about some ancient worldwide catastrophe that all seem to be based upon the same horrible event. This also helps provide an answer to why our ancient ancestors went underground around 12,000 years ago. They were the small remnant of humanity that was saved at the end of days and also managed to survive the final destruction itself.

This brings us to the end of the story in the Book of Enoch and how far I am going to go looking at this story in the Book of Enoch. The primary reason for is simply because it is the end of the Dream Vision and the Book of Enoch. Although it may be the end of the story and the Book of Enoch it is not the end of the story by any means. The next few chapters, I will now try to provide some additional creditably to this entire idea by showing you a few different connections that reach from this ancient time of myth, legend, and folklore into our own modern world of today.

Chapter 12

Understanding

He who controls others may be powerful, but he who has mastered himself is
mightier still.
~Lao Tzu~

How nothing was hidden, And the truth is so clear.
~The Mirror, R.J. von Bruening~

Y ou have no doubt noticed that almost every single thing I have presented
up to this point is not new or even that original. Outside of the ideas the
alignments between the pyramids and the four stars mentioned before,
the Pleiades cluster, and the connection of the symbols to the Dream Vison of
Enoch everything else has general familiarity to it all. As you have also noticed
that are many different elements, aspects, and parts of this story that you are very
aware of for some odd reason. There are others elements that you might never
have heard about before, but they are still vaguely familiar in some strange way.
All of which might seem a bit out of place to you.

Now, to be completely honest, I know much of this seems little bit 'out-there'
to say the least. But at the same time, you have to admit to yourself that there is
a certain type of logic and symmetry to it all. The other rather strange thing is
that something about it all feels like it could be the truth or if not the truth, then
it is at least seemingly pointed in the right direction. All of which should make
you ask the question of why does it seem like you already know so much of this
story and much of what I have said?

There is actually a very important reason for this. It is because whether or not you are personally aware of it you already know this story very well. It is the story you have been told all your life. For it is the story that told through all the symbols that surround you.

This is the story that is told by the 13 symbols of mystery I started with. This is the core belief behind all the esoteric schools of thought, occult knowledge, the mystery religions we all have heard about over the years. This is a major part of the actual "forbidden knowledge" that is spoken of only in whispers and rumors. This is hidden story of creation is the real "secret" that is at the heart of the mystery that we have all wondered about. This is what has been hidden from all of us. This is the core story of the belief system of the different esoteric schools of thought. It is also the story that much of the occult knowledge is speaking of, the knowledge of the gods.

This is the core story that you must understand in order to understand anything else about this belief system. If you do not know this story or how it is hidden within the symbolism, nothing will ever make any sense when you try and study it. The hard truth is that it really makes no difference if you personally believe it to be true or not. The undeniable fact is; there are a number of individuals and their families, that tend to hold some of the most powerful positions of government, religion, economics, military, and education all around the world in every single nation that do believe it. Not only do they "believe it," but they believe it to be fact beyond all doubt.

This is the core story behind all the conspiracy theories we hear about some small shadow group that controls everything on the planet trying to bring about a New World Order. This story is why the elites of world use the governments, religion, education, economic systems and spend so much time, resources and material trying so hard to confuse everyone. They truly do not want you to know that any of this could actually be true. They do not want you to understand that all the ancient stories about the "gods" coming to earth with advanced technology and mating with us, could all be true. Not only be true, but the real fact of the matter is that this hidden story of creation is at the heart of their belief system and what they are trying so hard to hide from us all.

They do not want you to know that all the ancient myths and religious stories that speak of magical artifacts, relics, legendary weapons, or the items that possessed great mythical divine power are really highly advanced technology from an ancient lost civilization. This is one of the greatest secrets of the forbidden knowledge and is what they have also been hiding from everybody else. Not have they been hiding it but they have also been using it for at least the last thousand years. This is the real source of their worldly power. It is also why certain families, clans, bloodlines, and members of certain groups are always the ones in power and ruling no matter which nation they are in.

This largely forgotten story is the missing piece that ties it all together. This symbolic story of creation along with its hidden history is the story that gives the entire idea its life and form. This is a vastly ancient belief system that is just as fully developed, highly structured, and institutionalized as the Catholic Church or any other large ancient traditional religion. The main difference is that this belief system is not really a 'religion' in the traditional sense although it has many of the same elements. This is because it is really what is known as a 'mystery religion.' As many are aware, Christianity had its origin as a mystery religion, but unlike Christianity, esoteric schools of thought do not wish to convert the masses into their belief. They only want people who can figure it out on their own or start asking the right questions.

I know this might seem rather confusing at the moment. Because what do I mean that this story is the basis of all the conspiracy theories while also being part of some big ancient mystery religion? In order to help you understand the point I am trying to make here; I will return to the thirteen symbols of mystery and how the story is contained within them. This will allow you to see with your own eyes and remove a large amount of doubt you must have at this point. It will also begin to show you how much of this has be done and that it has always been right in front of our faces the entire time.

As I stated way back at the beginning of our journey each individual symbol has many different meanings and concepts that can change and do change as they are used. These meanings and concepts are not normally very important in and by themselves to the average person. But when you put them together with the other symbols their true meaning comes to light. This is one of the major secrets of the symbols and is a key piece to understanding the group that is ultimately behind them. Only when looked at as a whole and understanding the story contained within the Dream Vision of Enoch that you can truly begin to really understand. As we saw with the cylinder seals, the easiest way to explain this is to show it to you.

I will begin with a 400-year-old print that can be easily found on the internet. This print comes from secret society of Rosicrucianism. This secret society is said to have been founded in late medieval Germany by a man named Christian Rosenkreuz. He claimed that Rosicrucianism was "built on esoteric truths of the ancient past that have been concealed from the average man." [1] It is agreed by researchers that Rosicrucianism was an actual 17th century philosophical secret society and mystery religion. It is also well known that it is the foundation for many of the elements of modern Freemasonry and heavily influenced the rites of the Lodge as a whole.

Rosicrucianism has always been shrouded in great mystery and is normally spoken of only in whispers and rumors. It is normally with outlandish claims that everything about this group is nothing more than a conspiracy theory or a hoax. It is believed and claimed by many researchers, to also be the foundation of almost all the modern-day esoteric groups that came about in late 1800s and early 1900s. Helena Petrovna Blavatsky and her Theosophical movement, Aleister Crowley and the Hermetic Order of the Golden Dawn, are just two examples of the different groups that came out of this time. Both Helena Blavatsky and Aleister Crowley made claims about the Rosicrucians but little if any of it is rooted in actually truth.

Although there is a great deal of mystery to this group, this idea and claim that the philosophical secret society known as Rosicrucianism might be or at least heavily influence the foundation of modern-day Freemasonry appears to be true and beyond all doubt. This can be seen in the symbols and the story they tell.

The Temple of the Rosy Cross, Teophilus Schweighardt Constantiens, 1618 (Fig.1) [2]

188

This 400-year-old drawing has an almost unbelievable amount of information in it hidden within its symbolism. If you keep in mind everything I presented, you can very easily understand what I am trying to say about this story. This drawing contains many of the elements that I spoke of earlier pertaining to a great ancient war being fought. It also contains the all the elements that the horrible monsters of legend were actually large weapons platforms based upon the design of the towers. When you combine this drawing with the Dream Vision of Enoch and the Book of Revelation you can see that it provides even more information than we already have. It also shows you beyond doubt that somebody knows this story very well.

I will start with a quick general overview beginning in the background on the left-hand side and then expand out from there. You will notice Noah's ark sitting on a mountain. Then moving to the right side of the image, you will see a small tower located in a city, many think this is the first tower located in the capital city of Jerusalem. That is incorrect, this is actually the tower located at the center of the capital city of the Main-Group remembered as the legendary lost city of Atlantis. This will make a bit more sense as go through this drawing.

The tower in the foreground and the focus of the drawing may at first be a little confusing to you, but it will quickly make perfect sense when you realize what you are looking at. It is actually a symbolic representation of one of the legendary mythical monsters of under control of the Fallen-Watchers. When examined carefully we can figure out which one. When we compare this to the images on the cylinder seals along with knowing that the Fallen-Watchers had at least two grand war machines of similar design based on the story in the Book of Revelations. Which were the great Seven-Headed-Beast and the Great-Red-Dragon that could fly. This will become clearer to you as we look closer at this drawing.

The next part to examine is at the top-center and a hand coming down from a cloud in the heavens, under the Winged-Sun-Disk, as if holding the tower by a line. If you look closely at the shape of the cloud under the winged-sun-disk, you will notice it is in the same exact shape of the Crescent Moon symbol we have seen on the cylinder seals. These symbols tell us that this is when the Fallen-Watchers were in control of the Heaven and that this tower was directly under their control. This is also a clue to one of the primary reasons for the ongoing conflict between the different groups; they were fighting for control of this great ship that is remembered as the Heaven in low earth orbit.

This is a perfect example of how the story is hidden right in front of everyone and how most are misled. This is also why there are always at least two stories, but sometimes more, associated with each symbol and image. One is use for distraction and confusion for the general public, normally something related to the dominate religion, which in this case is seventeenth century European Christianity. This is the answer given if anybody happens to notice the symbolism and makes it easy to dismiss. The other holds the real meaning and true story, but only for the ones that know and understand the forbidden knowledge that is never spoken of.

Returning to the drawing and looking at the upper right and left sides, you can see two six-pointed stars, looking like they are being shot into the sky. With now knowing that the six-pointed Star represent the Main-Group this part of the drawing can truly be understood. When combined with the story in the Book of Revelations you can see that the six-pointed Stars are not being shot into the sky, but rather they are attacking the tower in the center. This then brings to light what the man with the serpent on the left and the swan on the right represent. The man and serpent represent the Arch-Angels of the Lord fighting the old serpent known as Satan as in the Book of Revelation. The swan represents the idea of purity and beauty, but it also represents the one remembered as the Son of the Lord who was like the son of man. These taken together are showing us the great battles that took place in the sky that are recorded in the Book of Revelation.

The bird-like winged letters, directly under the man and the swan, represent the birds of the heaven attacking the tower. The lower ones flying away from the tower have a line drawn connecting them to the tower are ones that allied with the people in the tower. As you can see they are flying messages to their allies, but also defending the tower. The others represent the birds that Enoch speaks of in Chapter ninety of the Dream Vision; "*And after that I saw in my vision all the birds of heaven coming, the eagles, the vultures, the kites, the ravens; and they began to devour those sheep, and to pick out their eyes and to devour their flesh.*" You will also notice this scene is very similar to the cylinder seals shown earlier with the birds of heaven attacking a tower.

Staying on the right of the drawing just under the bird-like images you will notice a man falling off a cliff. This represents the final judgment that is spoken of in the Book of Revelation and the Dream Vision of Enoch where we are told "*And I saw at that time how alike abyss was opened in the midst of the earth, full of fire, and they brought those blinded sheep, and they were all judged and found guilty and cast into this fiery abyss, and they burned; now this abyss was to the right of that house*".

Moving in a clock-wise direction to the lower right-hand side. You will see that there is a man kneeling and sighting the Winged-Sun-Disk though a boat anchor. It is traditional believed that this represents Noah and is related to his

Ark. Only when you begin to understand this story that you can see that this Man and Anchor really are related to the great and terrible sea monster know as Leviathan. Once you realize this is related to Leviathan, you can understand that this indicates, just we are told in the myths, that part of this war and quite possibly a large part of the final battle was fought over and on the oceans of the world.

To the left of the man keeling, there are four other individuals that are dressed in 17th century military uniforms carrying weapons with one on a horse. These represent the armies of the Fallen-Watchers marching to battle against the Main-Group.

On the far left of individual on the horse, you can see a man climbing out of a well up a rope attached to the tower. This is some rather intriguing symbolism that indicates a type of underground base or city. This would be a really good fit for all the ancient stories related to some type of Underworld. It could also be something like the ancient underground city of Derinkuyu, located in the Cappadocia region of modern-day Turkey.

Remarkably, there is an ancient cylinder seal that appear to be directly related to this part of story and this part of the drawing. It gives the impression of an underground base or that similar events took place in ancient underground cities, like the one found at Derinkuyu.

A seal impression of a cylinder seal of the Scribe Adda 2,200 BC (Fig.2) [3]

If we take a closer look at the tower. You will see three individuals holding shields and large feathers. All three appear to fighting off the bird-like attackers. These men are clearly defending the tower for some form of aerial attack. The feathers appear to be representing a type of anti-aircraft weapon system that could not be understood in the seventeenth century or any other time until our own.

You will also see a Sword and what at first appears to be a large gun sticking out of the tower. These are pretty self-explanatory; in that they represent the major weapon systems of the tower in this battle. The fact that there are two weapons sticking out of the tower brings to mind the cylinder seals showing the two tower-like structures on the back of the beast or dragon. I think this may provide a much better idea of and a clue to how this ancient war-machine may have actually looked like in real life. This image is so very similar to the Assyria reliefs shown earlier with a large battering ram-like object coming out of it.

Although at the first look at the tower, the second object looks like a seventeenth century gun. But upon a closer look you will notice it is actually a trumpet. This gives us the idea that this is some type of sound weapon or what we would call a sonic weapon. Surprisingly enough, there are numerous ancient and modern myths and stories about sound being used as either a weapon or tool by the gods. This, along with all the other the similarities between this drawing and the other artifacts we have seen, you can now understand that it is much more than mere coincidence or blind chance that this drawing is showing the same story.

Additionally, although it may be difficult for you to see in this copy of the drawing. There is a small window on the right of the center of the tower. When examined closely it clearly shows two small towers of the exact same spear-like design as we saw on the ancient cylinder seals, sitting on a table. This is absolutely amazing and almost unbelievable, because there is no doubt and no way to argue that this drawing that was made a little over two hundred years before any of the ancient artifacts or cylinder seals were found. This then raises the all-important question of how could this group the seventeenth century could have known this before any of the ancient artifacts where found? I think the answer is a rather easy one, it is because this is part of the forbidden knowledge of the forbidden story they have always known.

The last item I will talk about for this drawing is the fact that the tower is on wheels and has wings on the upper section that is held by a rope from the hand of the Winged-Sun-Disk. When viewed as a whole and combined together with all the ancient stories, you can begin to see and understand that this tower symbolically represents the Great-Red-Dragon spoken of in the Book of Revelation.

This all allows you to figure out what this whole scene is really showing you. It is showing us the part of the great and final battle of Armageddon as recorded in the Book of Revelation. This is the time when the Fallen-Watchers and their allies were launching one final desperate battle against the Main-Group just after the great destruction and just before the final judgment where many of the followers of the Fallen-Group were cast into a pit of fire.

As you can now plainly see with your own eyes that someone already knows this story with much more detail and information than I have presented. The fact that this drawing is almost 400 years old and it is directly connected to what is known as modern-day Freemasonry and the controversy surrounding them. It makes it next to impossible to deny that this is part of the core story of the esoteric belief. Additionally, this drawing is also clearly is telling the exact same story as the Dream Vision in the Book of Enoch and as we saw on the cylinder seals. This should make you wonder what is really and truly going on. It should make you realize that this entire idea is not as strange or racial as when we started. In order to get a better understanding of this story we will have to examine a couple more images that are also related to the esoteric belief system.

I will now move on to a very well-known painting that contains many of the same elements that will help provide for a clearer understanding of the story and the symbols. This is famous painting is from 1784 and is of the initiation ceremony of Wolfgang Amadeus Mozart into a Viennese Masonic Lodge. As you will see, it contains a large amount of symbolic meaning and tells different parts of the same story as before.

Initiation ceremony in a Viennese Masonic Lodge during the reign of Joseph II, with Mozart seated on the extreme left. 1784 by Ignaz Unterberger (Fig.3) [5]

One piece that does not seem to be present in this painting is the towers themselves. But, if you look closely, you will see the columns in the background that appear to be part of the building itself. Normally within Freemasonry, these are the columns that stood on the grand porch in front of the entrance into King Solomon's Temple and Citadel. But now, we can understand these columns also symbolically represent the towers that the gods stood up. This allows you to begin understanding that we can also have multiple meanings held within the same symbolism. You will also see that there is additional information and clues about the towers contained within this painting once you understand what you are looking at and what part of the story it pertains too.

We will begin in the very back and center of the painting. Here you will see another painting hanging on the wall. This is an image of the Lost Paradise that is spoken of in the Biblical tradition. It shows a pleasant land next to a sea. This is very similar to what is described in the book of Enoch when *"And I saw till the sheep came to a goodly place, and a pleasant and glorious land and I saw till those sheep were satisfied..."* This is the idea and meaning behind this part of image.

There are two other important elements in this painting-within-a-painting I would like to bring to your attention. The first is the sun and the surrounding light it gives off. This represents the Bringer of Light-and the divine knowledge he brought to humanity. It is also related to the symbols that represent the sun and divinity in their many forms. In addition to those meanings, it has another meaning that may not be easily seen at first. This additional meaning can only be understood it you know most of the story that I have presented so far. That meaning is that this also represents the Heaven and is a major focus of the belief.

The second element to examine is the rainbow to the right of the sun. This symbolically represents Iris the divine messenger of goddess Hera, wife of Zeus. The rainbow is the personification of this divine messenger of the goddess. These elements are a good example of how many different traditions, myths, and legends are all tied directly back to the same general story.

The next item to look at are the two columns on each side of the background painting. These represent the two large brass pillars of King Solomon's Temple that stood in the grand entrance known as the porch. They were named Boaz, which stood to the north, and Jachin, to the south. As we have already touched upon, these columns have a number of different meanings for both the Freemasons and esoteric thought as a whole.

In this setting they have a rather special meaning with the serpents coiling around them. This represents the corruption of not only of mankind in the Garden of Eden, but more importantly, it also represents the corruption of the Temple

194

and Citadel of King Solomon. Additionally, it provides a clue too and is related to the whole idea of some grand conspiracy that started long ago that is bent on taking over the world that is very popular in our culture today.

I find this is to a rather curious and intriguing connection to our modern world from over two-hundred years ago. This gives the impression that the idea of some grand evil conspiracy to take over the world from within, starting with the Temple or Lodge that is contained within this painting. This appears to lend creditable to the claim that ultimately some form of esoteric or possibly occult worship may lie at the center of this group. The next element in the painting seems to support this idea.

There are two stones that are in front of the corrupted columns. They may be difficult to make out on this copy of the painting, but the one the left is an uncut stone and the one on the right is a cut or "hewn" stone. These stones have a very specific meaning and come directly from the Bible and Deuteronomy 27:5 and more specially the story of Exodus 20: 25, "*And if thou wilt make me an altar of stone, thou shalt not build it of hewn stone: for if thou lift up thy tool upon it, thou hast polluted it.*" The meaning of these stones is rather clear and next to impossible to deny, even for a non-believer. This is a direct insult to the Lord and His altar by mocking his commands on how to build it. It gives a very blunt visual representation of this insult by openly polluting it. With our new understanding, we can also realize it also a symbolic representation of the act of rebellion against an unjust Lord.

The next items in the painting to point out are the two figures or statues that are on each side of the scene on the walls. They both have a special meaning and have a very important story to tell. I will start with the male figure on the right. You will see that he is holding a Caduceus in his left hand. This once again represents all the different mythologies and meanings related to this Herald's Staff, but primarily the Greek and Roman versions. You will also notice that this is very similar to the representation of the staff seen earlier on the cylinder seals. This is clearly an important item of the gods has a special meaning to the believers and followers of the esoteric mystery religion.

This figure is basically a statute of Apollo, Mercury, or Hermes with all the meanings and stories that surround these individuals, just like the Caduceus. The one thing to keep in mind is this is also the representation of the Bringer of Light that is remembered as coming to earth and imparting humanity with divine knowledge all those many of thousands of years ago. This is the event that is spoken of in the Book of Enoch, the Biblical tradition, and every other religion on the planet.

With realizing this is figure is also a symbolic representation of the Bringer of Light you can begin to understand why he is shown with a blindfold covering his eyes. The blindfold has three main symbolic meanings that are directly related to the final battle and their loss of the war, the judgment, and the imprisonment of Lucifer and his Fallen Watchers. All three of these events are all symbolically represented by the blindfold. The first is the shame of losing the war, the second is being captured, as prisoner eyes are normally covered, and the third is their punishment and imprisonment. It also has one other meaning that is related to the female figure on the opposite side of the painting and we will look at this in a few moments, but we need to examine the female figure first.

The figure on the left is a statue of a woman holding her head down. To understand what this statue represents you must understand the story of what happened to human women that were taken as wives by the Fallen Watchers. This is not the story you heard in Sunday school or in Church. In fact, the only way I know how to learn this story is by learning the various esoteric schools of thought and the different occult knowledge they hold, along with careful reading of the ancient mythologies and legends.

Within these esoteric beliefs and traditions, it is believed and claimed by many that when the Fallen Watchers or Sons of God came to earth and took human women as wives. It was a violent and brutal encounter for the human women involved. It is believed that these Sons of God brutally raped and forcibly took the human women and kept them as prisoners to be their sexual playthings. This is one of the reasons behind the general belief in much of the religious world, regardless of tradition, that women have a lower place in society. It is because it is how the Fallen-Watchers themselves treated women. In turn, for many, these Sons of God were gods themselves, so who could or can go against the will of the gods?

This is the primary reason for the female figure in the painting has her head down, it represents her shame, her fear, and her place based solely on how the Fallen-Watchers imposed themselves upon human women when they took them as wives. It cannot be seen in this painting but this woman is leaning on a broken stone column. I will be giving another example shortly showing this. But this broken column symbolically represents the seduction and rape of the first woman by the leader of the Fallen-Watcher came into contact with. It also represents the breaking of the blood line of man with the birth of the bastard offspring of these Sons of God and human women, the Nephilim. All traditions, cultures, religions and beliefs agree that this sexual lust for human women was the reason the Fall of the Angels and why the gods came to earth. This is a major component to this story and can never be overlooked. Once again, shortly, we will examine more of this, but we need to return to painting before we get to far off track.

You notice that all the individuals that are seated around the room are all carrying swords. These swords represent the idea and the meaning that the people holding them are part of an ancient religious military order of legendary Armies and lost knowledge. They are the hidden Lords of Battle, the secret Captains and Princes of a new army. Many believe they are the vanguard that will one day restore the Lost Paradise and Empire of the Fallen-Watchers and reclaim their glory that was lost so long ago in that ancient final battle. That could be true, but normally it is viewed as remembrance of these ancient deeds and past events.

One of the last items I wish to focus on is the small triangle with three candles hanging from the ceiling in almost the center of the painting. There is no doubt that this represents the triangle that was seen in the sky at the time of the coming of the Bringer of Light and is forever recorded in the Great Pyramid. You can now understand that the three candles on the corners of the triangle represent the stars Betelgeuse, Aldebaran and Rigel as they looked in the night sky all those eons ago.

As you will remember, this is the symbol I started looking for in the very beginning of our journey. It is something that is very simple and easy to make just like the cross of Christianity. Also, as you can now understand this simple symbol is the vital connection that ties many different elements, aspects, ideas, concepts, and mythologies together in a way that can only be seen once know the story behind it. The other understanding is how this is all told though the symbols along with their different meanings. Which you can now see how this simple symbol of a triangle has stretched across time from almost the very beginnings of humanity to our own familiar modern-day world.

The last item to look at in this painting before moving on is the candlesticks that are grouped together around the room. At first, these candles may seem unimportant and nothing more than eighteenth century indoor lighting, but they actually hold a special meaning and provide another clue about the towers.

You will notice that the candles that are grouped together in threes. You will also notice that these candles are arranged in the exact same way as the symbol of Three-Columns is normally shown. Because of the cylinder seals we now know that the Three-Column symbol is directly related to the towers and the building of the great and terrible war-machines of an ancient war. The Three-Columns have an additional meaning that we touched upon earlier, in that they are also related to the Temple and Citadel of King Solomon. Again, we will look at this in more detail very shortly, but for now, you only need to understand that what each of the columns represent by themselves and together.

The two shorter outer columns represent the pillars known as Boaz and Jachin that stood at the entrance of the Temple. With knowing this, it is very easy to understand that he third and larger column in the center represents the Citadel or Tower that sat upon the Temple. This means that the three-column symbol has a dual meaning both of which are related to the towers. The first one is for the building of the great war-machines to fight the war. The second one is for the very towers themselves. I think the fact that this is being represented by candles or candlesticks is an important clue to part of the story.

By understanding that the candlesticks are connected to the towers. We can take the next step and realize the number of these groupings of candlesticks refer Biblical passages related to candlesticks, normally golden candlesticks. There are two different references in the Bible about candlesticks that are perfect examples of what I mean.

The first is in the Book of Zechariah in the Old Testament of the Bible. In Chapter four of the Book of Zechariah, he speaks of seeing a golden candlestick with a bowl and seven lamps upon it. He says that he also sees seven golden pipes running from the seven lamps. He then speaks of seeing two olive trees on each side of the golden candlestick with seven golden pipes connecting into two pipes and then each one of these empties out their golden oil to each tree.

Without going into much more detail, it has always seemed to me that Zechariah is talking about seeing a large tower like structure with the references to lamps, pipes, golden oil, appearing to be describing a large refueling depot or supply point which would fit into this general idea of the towers and a war.

The other reference in the Bible is in the first chapter of the Book of Revelation where John speaks of seeing seven golden candlesticks and one that was like the Son of Man standing among them. When compared to this information, it rather hard to deny that the candlesticks shown in the painting are connected to these references in the Bible.

As you can see, the story we have been exploring is the story that is clearly being told to us through the symbols. It is also the story that is remembered in Christianity as the fall from grace for Lucifer and his Angels and the events that came after. There is no doubt that the 400-year-old drawing and the 200-year-old painting we have just looked at are clearly and undeniably telling major parts of this story.

This story as it is told through the symbols is more fully developed in the final image we will examine. This final image will leave absolutely no doubt in anyone's mind as to who is directly related to and using these symbols. This image comes from the Library of Congress and was donated to the Library by Freemasonry itself. It also clearly states that this is the "Symbolical History of

Free and Accepted Masons" and as you will see, it clearly tells a large part of the Dream Vision of Enoch.

(Fig.4) [6]

Before I begin going through the symbolism, I would like to point out that there are a few small symbols that are directly related to this whole story. Although these symbols originate and are used by Freemasonry, I will not be providing much in the way of commentary on these symbols. There are two reasons for this, the first being the fact that there has already a large amount of material written on the subject of Freemasonry symbology and the meanings related to the black-and-white checkered tiles on the floor or the stair-case on the lower-right for two quick examples. Since there is such a large amount of existing information available, anyone can quickly research the subject on the internet and make up your own mind on this symbolism.

The second reason is because in "Appendix – B" I provide you with many of the actual Biblical verses that are referred to by Freemasonry themselves. This information is not secret or hidden in any way, but it helps provide an example of how the Biblical text contains more information than is commonly believed, but only if you know what you are look for. I will go into more detail about this shortly after we take a closer look at the latest image. If you take the time to go through these numerous Bible verses. You will discover that many are directly related to the different images and symbols we have seen up to this point.

We will now begin with a closer examination of the latest image. The first item to bring to your attention that ties back to the previous painting is the female figure and the "Angel" standing behind her on the bottom center of the image. As you can see, the female figure is in a similar head-down position as before. This scene shows us what we could not see in the painting from before and that she is standing next to a Broken Column. This Broken Column has a very special symbolic meaning and is important to understand what it represents.

To understand this Broken Column, you must realize that the Column shape has another meaning in the ancient world that is not normally talked about in history class or in most of the text books in any real detail. That meaning is that it is also a phallus or phallic symbol which is a stylized image of the male sexual organ. It was central to ancient cultures and has its origin in the fertility rituals and rites that surrounded and came from the Middle Eastern and the Mediterranean Sea areas.

Once you understand that the column is a phallic symbol. You can easily understand what the meaning is of a Broken Column. It represents the original pure human bloodline that was broken or corrupted by the Fallen Watchers as they violently raped human women and took them as wives in an unholy union. It was not uncommon in most of the ancient world that a woman that had be raped, regardless of the reason, is traditionally viewed as being unclean or polluted somehow. This way of thinking typical results in the victim being blamed for the rape with the idea that the woman must have done something to make or allow it happen.

This ancient viewpoint has traditionally led to the rape victim as being looked upon as bringing shame or dishonor to her family or community. This shame or dishonor normally led to the woman being exiled or killed by her family or community. In light of this, it is now easy to understand that this female figure with her head down leaning on a broken column symbolically represents the traditional reason for why the Fallen Watcher who is standing behind her came to earth. This is symbolically showing us the reason why the Fallen Watchers or Sons of God came to earth. It was their sexual lust that the Watchers had for the beautiful daughters of man as recorded in Genesis six.

This then provides the clue to the identity of male Angel or Watcher standing behind her. As if you have any doubt about who this figure is. It is the one traditionally remembered by his Latin name as Lucifer, the morning star, who is remembered as the great god of light or the Bringer of the Light, that freed humanity from a long and horrible slavery. It should be noted that this is a very good image of how this individual is believed to have looked. Remarkably, in almost every single culture on the planet that remembers this individual, remember him as a bearded middle-aged white man that had a grandfatherly appearance. He is also remembered and as the bringer of great knowledge to humanity.

One final item to address is that fact that there is always this consistent theme and idea of the gods in some form coming to earth and breeding with humans. This event of the Watchers lusting after the fair daughters of man is what that leads to everything changing. This is the one part of the story that is one of the major factors in this entire story. I will address this subject in greater detail in a later chapter. But, at the moment, it is important to understand that traditionally this is the primary reason why this Lord of Light rebelled and came to earth. Additionally, it is commonly believed that this rebellion led to a great war in heaven between the gods.

This first war of the gods leads to the meaning behind the crypt that the woman and the Fallen Watcher are standing upon. This crypt is an empty tomb that symbolically represents the unknown and largely forgotten death of the all ones that fell fighting in is ancient war. It is to honor all those that never received a proper burial fighting on that long-forgotten battlefield. It is in essence a 'Tomb of the Unknown Soldier' that is used to remember the fallen dead of this ancient time. It is also the origin of the modern idea for a Tomb of the Unknown Soldier.

The next part of the image we will examine begins in the upper left-hand side, just above the Column known as Boaz with the small picture of the failing star and the Pleiades cluster of stars. From here we will take a clockwise circular path around the image moving left to right and will return back to our starting point. You must follow the proper right circular pattern while also understanding the symbolism of the Dream Vision of Enoch to understand the story that is shown on this image. I first will point out the pattern of these small pictures then I will comment on them.

Starting on the upper left-hand side above the column known as Boaz and located directly above the globe of the Earth and right above the Pleiades star cluster, there is a 'Falling Star.' Although it might be difficult to see in this image, this Falling Star this is the beginning of the story and symbolically represents the monumental event of the Light Bearer coming to earth.

We must then move to the right-hand side of the image above the column known as Jachin where we can see the sun shining through the clouds. From here we will move to the right-hand side of image next to the small picture of a rather idyllic scene of the Lost Paradise with a beautiful waterfall coming down a mountain surrounded by trees. The next part is told by the glowing 'G' with rays of light radiating from a 5-pointed star or pentagram in the center. The last part of the story before returning to the starting point is located to at the bottom of the left column Boaz. As you can see, it is directly across from the symbolism of the Lost Paradise. This little scene shows us Noah's ark and a tower surrounded by Three Columns. The final scene is the Pleiades star cluster under the Falling Star we started with. As you can see these little symbolic pictures a very large part of the story that is contained within the Dream Vison in the Book of Enoch and the Bible is told on this image. But, if, and only if, you understand this esoteric story that is told through the symbolism.

Returning to and beginning with the Falling Star. As we have already touched upon this symbolically represents the Lord of Light coming to earth. Not only is the beginning of the story, but it is also an event that the that followers of the esoteric believe is important. Although the monotheistic religions remember this event as evil and try to downplay it, it is important from an esoteric point of view because this actually the beginning of human history. This is the time that the great Lord of Light came to earth to free humanity from slavery and impart heavenly knowledge upon humanity. This is also perfect symbolic representation of the line from Enoch where he says *and behold a star fell from heaven.*"

The next scene in this story above the column known as Jachin and the sun to radiating beams of light from behind the clouds. This is a symbolic representation of the light of knowledge that broke through the darkness of the storm of ignorance and oppression that existed before the coming of the Light-Bearer where he delivered freedom and enlightenment to an enslaved humanity.

This then leads to the next part of the story with the founding of the Lost Paradise of the Fallen-Watchers. This is the time that many within the esoteric long to return too. This is when the "gods" themselves walked among mankind. It is also the time when the followers and believers of the Fallen Watchers ruled as kings and could do anything they wished. For many, they wish to restore this Lost Paradise of eons ago.

The next item is the glowing 'G' and the pentagram directly above the two figures on the crypt. If you pay attention at this grouping of symbols along with their placement in relation to the Lost Paradise and the Flood of Noah. You can understand what it represents the second war of the between the gods where the Main-Group or Lord-God reestablishes their power and control over the world. That is why the 'G' is superimposed on the pentagram it is showing us who won this war between the gods.

This war then leads to the next part of the story and the Great Flood of Noah and the building of the towers. You can see that Noah's Ark and the great storm that is associated with the Great Flood. To the right of the Ark upon a little hill you will see an altar with a Bible sitting upon it. This represents the first tower built, the Temple and Citadel of King Solomon. The three towers surrounding this symbolic tower are the Three Columns along with the shape of a triangle.

The other and much more hidden meaning and lay-out of these three columns surrounding the main tower can only be understood if you know of the placing of the towers onto a mobile weapons platform. This is a symbolic representation of the crane system that we saw on the cylinder seals. It also allows you to understand the meaning behind the symbolism of the Three Columns and why they represent strength, beauty and wisdom. These Three Columns also represent the three stars in the original shape of the pyramid at the time of the Fall of the Watchers. This is why they are normally also shown in a triangle configuration as we saw the earlier painting with the small triangle with three candles at each corner.

As you can see and understand, this is the story of the Fall of the Watchers up to the Great Flood of Noah. It also has elements of the events surrounding the tower that I have been speaking of. It also shows that these events are all related symbolism that allows one to understand how these symbols hold a hidden story. It also supports the idea that this story covers a large amount of time that are actually speaking of time periods that span tens of thousands of years.

This also allows one to realize and understand that the vast majority of people within the professional that are Freemasons or belong to one of many esoteric organizations that try so very hard to debunk and mock this entire idea actually know all of this information. Not only do they know this information but it actually the core story of the esoteric. Which then raises the question of why would anyone try and debunk the very thing they believe in? This is a very good question that I will address a little later, but for now, let us return to the image.

This brings us back to our starting point and the Pleiades star cluster. Again, it might be difficult for you to see on this image, but you will notice that the Pleiades star cluster is a similar pattern to the nest to last picture we saw showing the changes in the Pleiades start cluster shown on the cylinder seals. Based on what we already know, we can understand that this is the pattern of the Pleiades star cluster at the time of the great and terrible destruction that was followed by the great final battle between the forces of Light and Darkness.

When combined together as a whole, these small images tell us the time period and the major events that are believed to be important to the different branches of esoteric thought, but especially Freemasonry. The other symbols and images found in the picture provide additional information about the story. The symbols can only be understood if you realize that the Dream Vision in the Book of Enoch is the outline of the story with the Bible and the cylinder seals filling the little the details.

As we have seen, the cylinder seals provide many missing details related to the towers and a great war of the gods. They also show a number of the same animals as spoken of in the Dream Vision. Additionally, they show us that most of the symbols have their origin in the story as told by the cylinder seals.

What we have not really looked at in any real detail is the fact that the Dream Vision of Enoch closely parallels the Biblical story. The images we have seen help provides the clue at which point the Dream Vision and the stories in the Bible come together at one point. This point provides a greater understanding of how the stories in Bible are giving many of the details of the individuals or groups that are in the Dream Vision. Again, the easiest way to explain this is to show you.

In the last image, you will see two small images located at the base of each of the columns Boaz and Jachin. The one on the right column, Jachin, shows the scene of Jacobs's ladder as told in the Bible. The column on the left, Boaz, shows the next part of the story with Jacob anointing the rock that he used as pillow with oil and he called the place Beth-el. It is the story of Jacob's ancestry that is important here and not the details of his dream about a ladder to heaven.

If you go and read the whole story in the Book of Genesis about Jacob's ancestry back to his grandfather Abraham and then compare it to Chapter eighty-nine, verse ten through twelve in the Book of Enoch which speaks of how the "sheep" came to be. You will quickly realize that Jacob is the first sheep that was born. With this understanding, you can now superimpose the Biblical stories onto the Dream Vision of Enoch. If you do that, you can begin to truly understand how all of this ties together into one complete story and forgotten history. We will take a much closer look at this in the next chapter, but we need to return to the image with this new knowledge in hand.

With understanding that Jacob of the Bible was the first sheep spoken of in the Dream Vison. This knowledge provides us with the starting point for the next series images and symbols and the story they tell. As with before, the images and symbols follow a pattern in order to tell the story. This one is rather straight forward and easy to see once it is pointed out. It starts with the pictures of Jacob and moves straight up to the two small images in the center of the picture right next to the columns Boaz, Jachin. It then finishes with the lambs at the top of the image.

Starting with the center image on the right, you will see that this the scene of when the sheep crossed a steam of water and came to a pleasant and glorious land as told by Enoch in the Dream Vision. It is also the same scene from the Biblical the story of Exodus when the Israelites came to the Promised Land. Once again, this is giving us the time period that these events are taking place. This then allows us a greater understanding of the small symbols that can be seen in the next part in the image on the left side directly across from the pleasant land.

One of the first things you should notice about these symbols is the fact they are almost exactly the same ones seen on the cylinder seals from earlier. The only one that is really different is the scythe that the Fallen Watcher is holding is not found on the cylinder seals. Although it might sound confusing at the moment, but this scythe is related to the ever-famous Caduceus. This is because if you improperly used the Caduceus to contact the gods, but especially the Fallen Watchers, you were unlikely to make it out alive. Outside of that one small difference, all the other symbolism is the same as seen on seals. This makes next to impossible to deny that these modern images and the ancient cylinders are evidence that they are connected together. As we have seen, every symbol seen on the cylinder seals are connected directly to the gods and the story of the Dream Vison of Enoch.

This then leads us to the final part and the images of the lambs at the top on the left-hand and the right-hand sides. These are now easy to understand what this lamb symbolism represents us, modern humans.

There are only few more elements and symbols we need to examine before moving on that will help provide an understanding of what the reason for the war was. These last elements are found at the top of the picture and include the All-Seeing-Eye, the two small globes on top of the columns, the handshake, and the large golden disk at the very center.

We will start with the All-Seeing-Eye and then move out from there. You will quickly notice that the All-Seeing-Eye and the two globes setting atop the columns make a triangle shape. This pyramid shape and the three corners represent a number of different things if you know how to read them. This is another example of how different story elements are hidden within itself.

The two corners of the base of the triangle are also associated with the first set of images we examined and need be included in with this set of symbols. Just as before there is a pattern to how you read the symbols. In this case, you start with the All-Seeing-Eye and then move to the left column with the globe of the earth. You then move to the right-side column with the globe of the universe. You then return to the All-Seeing-Eye.

We will be starting with the old eyeball in the sky. As we now know this is not the 'eye' of anything, but it actually symbolically represents the Heaven that is remembered in every tradition as the abode of the gods. This gives a good idea of how this thing might have looked to the people on the ground and how it was thought to be an All-Seeing, All-Knowing, All-Powerful, and Radiating His divine light by looking down upon all of humanity. We then move to the left and where you see the globe of the earth. When combined with the Falling Star this symbolically represents the Light-Bearer coming to earth from the heavens. Just as it is described in the Book of Enoch and remembered in the Biblical tradition.

Even though it is very difficult to see in this copy of the picture, the globe of the earth is different than a normal modern-day globe of the earth. In fact, it clearly shows the North and South America land masses as they would have looked during the last ice age when the ocean level was hundreds of feet lower than it is today.

It also shows two large islands in the area of the Gulf of Mexico. This is amazing to see a picture from 1874 showing a late 20th to early 21st Century understanding of the last few ice ages and how ocean level would have been affected. This is something that is undeniably years ahead of its time. It also clearly shows once again, that the esoteric religion is based on fact and not myth. This also gives another clue that the followers of the esoteric may have even more detailed information on the past than ever thought before.

We now need to move to the right column with the globe of the universe in order to understand what the Light-Bearer brought and gave to humanity. He enlightened humanity with the knowledge of the of the divine or universe. It is this knowledge or heavenly enlightenment that is the basis of the idea of him being the Bringer of Light or the Light-Bearer that is still remembered today. This divine knowledge is always represented as a form of 'Light' with the understanding that it symbolically means the knowledge that was given to mankind by this Lord of Light. This understanding of the Light will lead you right back to the All-Seeing-Eye and the realization that it truly represents the Heaven because that was where all the power, knowledge, and resources of the gods actually came from.

This is one of the most important secrets within the esoteric and why the All-Seeing-Eye along with the pyramid or triangle shape is so important. As you can now begin to understand that it has multiple meanings. You will also realize that none of the modern ideas about this symbolism we have been taught or hear about are not true.

It is this understanding of what the All-Seeing-Eye and the pyramid represents that provides us with one of the final pieces on how this all goes together. It will also help explain the meaning to the last couple of symbols on this image.

Starting with a short recap. The pyramid or triangle shape is a symbol to the monumental event of the Fall of Lucifer and his fellow Watchers along with the knowledge they bought to humanity. The All-Seeing-Eye actually represents the Heaven. This is the one thing that both the Main-Group and the Fallen-Watchers were fighting over. When we put all this together, we can understand that they represent the beginning of the last great war that led to the destruction of everything. They symbolize the event that started it. Which was Enoch, the righteous scribe of God escaping from being killed and then being saved and taken away from the generations of the earth by the Lord-God. This is why nothing you have ever heard about these symbols has ever made any sense or is so vague and lacking in details that it does not make much sense to the average person. This is because they do not understand or know this hidden story within the symbolism. As for the people that do know, they cannot speak of it without telling you the whole story. Which is something they really do not want to do. It also helps you understand why the symbols are not really hidden from anybody, it is just that most everyone has forgotten this story or were never taught it in the first place.

This then leads to one of the last symbols we will examine, the handshake that is under the All-Seeing-Eye. This handshake represents the deal or agreement that the Fallen Watchers made between themselves before launching their rebellion and coming to earth to take human wives. In chapter six of the Book of Enoch in verses three through five, Enoch speaks of this deal between the Watchers. Enoch says the deal was stuck on Mount Hermon. It should be noted that this is very similar to the ancient Greek mythology with the deal that was made between Zeus and his fellow Olympiads before going to war with the Titans.

"And Semjaza, who was their leader, said unto them: 'I fear ye will not indeed agree to do this deed, and I alone shall have to pay the penalty of a great sin.' And they all answered him and said: 'Let us all swear an oath, and all bind ourselves by mutual imprecations not to abandon this plan but to do this thing.' Then sware they all together and bound themselves by mutual imprecations upon it."
(Book of Enoch 6: 3-5)

The last two symbols I would like to point out before moving on the final item are the Crescent Moon that can be seen just to the right of the Pleiades star cluster, The second is the large golden disk in the very center of the picture.

As we have seen on the cylinder seals. We already know the Crescent Moon symbol represents the Fallen-Watchers. It is rather interesting that this symbol is on this picture but the six or eight-pointed Star that represents the Main-Group is not found anywhere on this print. Since the members of Freemasonry all publicly claim to believe and follow the teachings of the great architect of the universe. Freemasonry claims this is just continuing a long tradition of using an allegorical name for the Deity. Which is one of two most common ways Enoch commonly refers to the God of the Bible in the Book of Enoch, the other is the Most-High. But as you can see with your own eyes and now understand that there really is not any symbolism on this image that is directly related to Lord-God of the Bible. Which based upon the symbolism more or less proves that Freemasonry is not being truthful about who or what they worship. I will allow you to make up your own mind on that question and the possible answers to it.

The next to last symbol we will look at is the large golden disk in the center. This may not at first seem like much of a symbol in this setting but it is important. You will only notice its importance once you remember the cylinder seals and the symbol of the Solar-Disk. This is an image of the Solar-Disk or the Heaven. The reason it is in the center of the picture is because this Heaven was the main focus of and the primary reason for everything that happened including the destruction of it all. This is what the wars were really over, the control of this grand ship of the gods which is remembered as the Heaven.

The last item that we will examine are the Two-Columns that lie on each side of the picture. The columns known as Boaz and Jachin which were placed in front of the porch leading to the great and beautiful Sanctuary of King Solomon's Temple and Citadel that is spoken of in the Bible in 2 Chronicles 3: 15; 1 Kings 7: 15-22; and 2 Chronicles 4: 12-13.

It is well known that these passages from the Bible represent the connection of modern-day Freemasonry to the original ancient craftsmen and builders of King Solomon's Temple and Citadel. This connection to the builders of the Temple of Solomon is one of the primary claims and beliefs of the Masons. They claim that the organization known as Freemasonry can trace its historical roots all the way back to the original builders of King Solomon's Temple. It is also claimed that this knowledge has been passed down from that time until our own through the mystery schools and religions that were the foundations of modern-day Freemasonry.

This is one of the final pieces of the puzzle that ties all of this back into the Bible. It will also give a clearer understanding of the story. The secret is having access to a Masonic Bible. In my case, I come from a Masonic family and I was the one that inherited all of my family's Masonic items. The Masonic Bible I have come from my grandfather and was his initiation, Bible.

This Bible is not unusual or any different than any other Authorized King James' Version of the Bible, outside of a small 14-page Masonic study guide at the end and a 79 page forward written by a Dr. John Wesley Kelchner. Who is said to have been an Archaeologist, Bible Student, Lecturer, and Mason that spent a large part of his own personal fortune and life into a world-wide search for archaeological data and period decorative technique, from which he rendered the most accurate, down to the minutest detail, the ornamental scheme revealed by the Biblical story of the Temple and Citadel of King Solomon". [7]

This forward section and the information that it contains is the only thing that is different about this Bible than any other King James Version. This forward section contains an astonishing amount of information about Freemasonry and its history, but more importantly it has the actual Scripture references that hide this story inside the Bible, and a number of cryptic references to the Light and its meaning. There is a good possibility that this is the origin of the idea of a Bible code, just not in the way most think.

This is where the Masonic Bible comes into play. If you do not have access to this information, you will have great difficulty in trying to understanding anything about what the Freemasons truly believe and how this story has been hidden in plain sight. If you go and get yourself one of these Masonic Bibles, please keep in mind that there are numerous small differences in the available versions. This is mainly due to individual beliefs and traditions of each Lodge that produced each Bible for their members. Although there are small differences, but as a whole there are very few differences between the Lodges, their Bibles, and when it comes to this particular story we have been exploring.

Remarkably, almost all the information contained within these Bibles is actually readily available online. In fact, the Wikipedia webpage on Freemasonry contains almost all of the same historical information found within the Masonic Bibles, with some of it appearing to be almost word for word. The only parts that are not on the Wikipedia page are the on the Light and the Scripture verses that describe King Solomon's Temple and Citadel in great detail. Additionally, the Masonic Bible also has a listing of each set of Scripture verses that are related to each symbol and its place within Freemasonry. But even this information is available if you want to look for it. Freemasonry do not actually hide it in any way from anybody. In fact, the Masons will even tell you why the symbolism is important and how it was derived and taught in the Middle-Ages.

"The religious instruction and inspiration which the Bible supplies nowadays was then derived from three sources: (1) ecclesiastical symbolism and ceremony; (2) mystery plays or Biblical entertainments; and (3) architecture. Masons may have participated in the second; they were of primary importance in the third. When people could not read books, the lessons of religion had to be taught in other ways. They were taught by sermons of the priests and by the ritual of the sacraments. They were also taught dramatically through mystery plays, performed often by the craft guilds. The Masons may possibly have used a mystery play whose story survives in the third degree. Above all, the lessons of religion were taught during the Middle Ages through architecture and sculpture. Every village church was a message from God, and the cathedral was an entire Bible. The Masons part in telling this story was a most important one, and this as well as other circumstances set the Masons apart from other crafts"
The Bible and King Solomon's Temple in Masonry, p.23, Dr. John Wesley Kelchner

This tells you why, you always see the same symbols in the architecture of many large stone buildings from the Middle Ages. They are telling you a religious story that is hidden within the symbols. Which should start giving you an idea of why you see the symbols on everything. They are trying to tell you this hidden story of creation and forgotten history Although the meaning of the symbol may not be known to the average person. It does not change the importance of the symbols or how they are used. The reason the meaning has faded is because of printing and it has become much easier to transmit knowledge and information though letters than ever before.

Printing and a growing population of literate people basically put the whole reason behind the symbols out of business so to speak for the general public. It also radically changed society as it became easier to teach somebody how to read and write than it was to teach them the symbols, the allegory, and the stories related to them. The forward section written by Dr. Kelchner in the Bible I have does comment on this fact about the symbols and how there meaning was lost to many people.

"The medieval period, which saw such a growth of Masonry, was essentially an age of symbolism. Everything in architecture, in ceremonial, in heraldry,

in religion, had it symbolic meaning. Interpretation of the symbolism was left almost entirely to one division of the community, the Church, and to a few thinking people it must've seemed that as time went on the symbols grew in importance and the meaning faded. The letter became dominant, and the word was lost."
The Bible and King Solomon's Temple in Masonry, p.23, Dr. John Wesley Kelchner

This Word that was lost to the general public was preserved and passed on by the followers of Freemasonry and a few other esoteric groups. This Word is actually the religion of Freemasonry and the story I have presented to you. This Word is in the esoteric belief is combined with the Bible and that is how it has been transmitted and hidden from the general public. If you do not know the 'Word' or 'symbols' along with the verses in the Bible or 'letter' that are related to the 'Word,' you will not be able to figure it out. This is another one of the pieces that have been missing for most people. It is also why there has been so much confusion over the years.

This Word or symbolism is how you are able to put this story together. It is through this Word that the last piece of the story is told. This should allow you to understand that this is actually a religion and not a conspiracy.

The key point in understanding is that the Freemasons believe that the Temple and Citadel of King Solomon spoken of in the Bible is the "house" that is spoken of in the Book of Enoch that "became great and broad … and a tower lofty and great was built on the house".

Dr. John Kelchner speaks of this in the forward section and is a vital part that is easily missed if you do not know the rest of the story. Dr. Kelchner states very clearly which Temple and Citadel that he is recreating and that is spoken of in the Bible.

"Its actual life was short, but its influence has been incalculable. Built to endure for centuries, only a few years elapsed before it was desecrated and then completely destroyed by invading armies. Yet its fame did not die. The children of Israel, with fervid determination, rebuilt it twice, and twice more it was destroyed."
The Bible and King Solomon's Temple in Masonry, p.21, Dr. John Wesley Kelchner

You will notice that Dr. Kelchner states that the Temple of King Solomon was rebuilt twice and twice more it was destroyed. According to current belief and tradition there was no second rebuilding of the Temple of King Solomon nor was this second rebuilding destroyed. In fact, it is currently believed by both the people of the Jewish faith along with many Christians that the third rebuilding of the Temple of King Solomon will usher in the End of Days and the final battle of Armageddon. This supports the idea I have presented that the great destruction, the End of Days, and Armageddon has already happened. Not only has it already happened, but it happened almost 13,000 years ago.

This allows us to understand that the recreations of the Temple and Citadel of King Solomon that were made by Dr. Kelchner are showing us what the house and tower that Enoch speaks of actually looked like. As you can see, this recreation of the Temple of King Solomon by Dr. Kelchner shows us a lofty tower upon a broad house.

Elevated view of the Temple and Citadel of King Solomon; by Dr. John Wesley Kelchner (1924). (Fig.5) [8]

This all leads right back to the symbols which almost of which can be seen in the last painting of the series that Dr. Kelchner created of the Temple and Citadel of King Solomon. Almost every single symbol I have spoken of can be found in the painting called "Miscellaneous Details of King Solomon's Temple, Plate 19."

If you move on tracing these symbols and images from this painting and the earlier one dated from 1874, and follow them to our present time. They will lead you right back to what I said at almost the very beginning and started with the subjects of Gnosticism, Rosicrucianism and the Hermetic Order of the Golden

Dawn and the esoteric and occult belief of a Bringer of Light in the form of knowledge and was an enlightenment for mankind and the connection to the symbols.

The above painting is claimed by Dr. Kelchner to be "first and only accurate interpretation of the Scriptural description of that famous edifice of Masonic symbolism" (Fig.6) [9]

This then leads right back to all the conspiracy theories that surround all the symbols that we have examined and many others that I have not. It is also related to the questions of why these symbols are on every single item and product you see. It also leads to why the pyramid and the All-Seeing-Eye is on the back of every dollar bill. It is because it is commemorating the event of Enoch being taken away from the generations of the earth. It is also the beginning of what will become the last final war of the gods.

This should allow you to understand this is where everybody has made their mistake about all these symbols and the groups tied to them. Because this is not

213

some type of grand conspiracy to take over the world by some mysterious unknown evil group of power-hungry men that call themselves the Illuminati or some New World Order through Freemasonry with the idea of everybody on the planet living in some type of super fascist state like the one described in George Orwell's book 1984. But this is in fact a religious belief and an organized religion. A religion that is just as developed, structured, powerful, and well organized with many followers that are deeply devoted to their belief and very willing to defend it with as much passion as any other follower of any other mainstream religion. Once you understand that it is a religion and not some conspiracy, you can truly begin to really understand what is going on in the world. It is not a conspiracy to take over the world in the traditional sense, it is a religious movement to covert everybody to one religion and belief by any means necessary.

As with any religion or belief system, if you want to really understand anything about it in any meaningful way, you must know what the original story is and what it is based on. Once you know the original story it will provide the understanding of the basis for the entire belief and the motivation behind it. Because if you do not understand this, then nothing about will ever make any sense no matter how you look at it. This was the point of the earlier example of Christianity and the symbol of the cross, that you need to know the story about Jesus Christ before you can understand anything else that is related to the whole idea of the cross or of Christianity with all its history over the last 2000 years. If you do not know the story you cannot understand anything about the motivation behind it.

Once you understand it is a religious belief that we are all dealing with. Then you can really begin to understand how this has all been done through the centuries. It also allows you to realize how it has been passed from one generation to the next. It has been done in the exact same way as the Catholic Church and the way they train their priests in the teachings and message of the Church. This is how they and other believers pass on this information to others over the generations. Additionally, they are just like the Catholic Church or other similar groups that try very hard to recruit the sons and daughters of the wealthiest and most powerful families that exist in each nation into their priesthood in order to establish influence and control they normally would not have in society. They also are active in recruiting other individuals that may aid their cause through talent and intelligence, normally though the University System of higher learning, the miliary, or Government.

The easiest way to explain how this works is to look at the economic side of this influence. This group only gives the illusion that there are really different types of economic models at work in the world, like Communism, Capitalism, and Socialism. These different systems of economic thought are not really put into practice in the real world and that is why I say illusion.

This is very easily proved. All you have to do is look at the actual ownership of the different companies and corporations that make up most of the world's economy. If you do this, you will quickly learn that vast majority of the world's total economic output is from a network of approximately 43,000 major multinational corporations.

In a recent University of Zurich study that examined these 43,000 major multinational corporations gives a clear description of how this works. This study discovered an almost unbelievable world wide web of interlocking ownerships of these 43,000 corporations that is controlled by a "core" of 1,318 giant corporations. In addition to that, the study also found that those 1,318 giant corporations are themselves controlled by a "super-entity" of 147 monolithic corporations that are very tightly knit together through Board Members of each company. Adding to that, a recent article in NewScientist noted these 147-corporations directly control approximately 40% of all the wealth in the entire network.

"When the team further untangled the web of ownership, it found much of it tracked back to a "super-entity" of 147 even more tightly knit companies - all of their ownership was held by other members of the super-entity - that controlled 40 percent of the total wealth in the network. "In effect, less than 1 percent of the companies were able to control 40 percent of the entire network," says Glattfelder. Most were financial institutions. The top 20 included Barclays Bank, JPMorgan Chase & Co, and The Goldman Sachs Group." [10]

Unsurprisingly, this "super-entity" is dominated by international banks and large financial institutions with Goldman-Sachs, Morgan Stanley, Bank of America, etc... these are all in the top 25. This allows this "super-entity" complete control of almost every single aspect of society by the simple fact that they own every piece of it in one way or another. This is how all the symbols end up on every single product and item that you can buy or see and gives you an idea of who is really behind of this. These are the symbols of the esoteric religion of Freemasonry. It also means that this is the religion of the owners of these companies.

This basic plan of economic control has also been applied to most of the governments of the world, the major religions, many militaries, and almost all of the educational system. This can be easily seen and understood, if you follow the symbols, you follow this group and their beliefs.

If you do this, you will quickly understand, and this is very important, we are not dealing with a handful of very wealthy families that control everything. No, we are really dealing with a very small and powerful priesthood which is made up of many different members of the very wealthiest families that control the world's economy through this network of companies.

This is the same system that was used during the Middle-Ages when the local Catholic bishops had loyalties to both the local lord or king and the Pope in Rome. The history books are full of the power struggles over this group and the influence they had over the world's political and economic systems and how they broke up into different groups in each nation to hide their influence and blend into the local population. This understanding gives you an idea of when and where to start looking, in order to trace this group through history. This is the basic idea of how this story and idea is controlled and passed through the generations. This also shows which organization is at its very core of this and truly makes up the "church" that these individuals work within.

Chapter 13

The Forbidden Knowledge

Pull a thread here and you'll find it's attached to the rest of the world.
~Nadeem Aslam, The Wasted Vigil~

W e have finally reached the point where we can put all these ideas, possibilities, and information together into one complete story. We can also now understand that this story is told through the symbols that are used by the followers of the different esoteric schools of thought. Which is the same one that is told in the Dream Vision of Enoch and possibly more important, it is also the story told on the ancient cylinder seals. This knowledge then allows us to put together not only the story but also a timeline with an idea of possible dates for many of the major events contained within it.

This is the forbidden knowledge that is taught within the various mystery schools and within the deepest regions of the religions of the world. It is the core story of esoteric belief system known as Freemasonry. As you can now understand that all the other stories, legends, myths, rumors of occult belief, and practice that many of us were raised with or see online are in fact false. As you can now understand that it is only by understanding the esoteric symbolism and its connection to the Dream Vision of Enoch that you can actually put it all together in one coherent systematic story that has a logical chain of events that has a timeline that you can understand.

I will now reconstruct this story from the beginning to the present time based upon the hidden story of creation that is held within the esoteric belief system of Freemasonry. Please keep in mind that I will only be summarizing many parts in this retelling since we have already covered them in more detail. Additionally, there are few different factors that just cannot be avoided by anyone.

The first and probable the most important one is due to the fact that the members of the various esoteric schools of thought, but especially Freemasonry, are forbidden to speak to any non-member about the symbolism or the story it holds. This in and by itself can make it next to impossible for the average person to actually understand the symbolism in meaningful manner. This is why it is so important to understand the connection between the symbols, the Dream Vision of Enoch, the Bible, and the ancient cylinder seals in order to understand this hidden story.

The second factor is due to the fact that these same members of the various esoteric schools of thought, and once again, especially Freemasonry, go to great lengths to hide, confuse, and lie about this subject to everybody who is not a member of their school of thought. This again makes it very difficult to do any meaningful research into the subject. In the next chapter we will explore the how and some of the why this is done.

The third and final factor is by far the most important of any reason. It is due to the fact that it appears that nobody, including the members of these different esoteric schools of thought, that nobody really knows for sure what exactly happened all those thousands upon thousands of years ago. The followers themselves give the impression that the primary reason for this is rather simple. It is because almost everything was destroyed in the great destruction and the final battles that are spoken of in the Book of Revelation. Additionally, as we have seen, there is the added factor that these events took place many thousands of years ago than we have been led to believe. The simple truth is that a huge amount of the information about this time was truly lost to history and we may never know exactly what happened.

Because of these factors, it is easy to understand that the sequence of some of these events are educated guesses. It is because of this uncertainty that some things will just sound crazy or outrageous as we go along. Although some of this will sound crazy, but do not forget that the general idea here is correct even if some of the details are missing. This is still the story that contains the forbidden knowledge of the hidden story of creation as told by the symbols.

This story begins long ago in the deep dark misty past within the mystery of our origins. It was a time when the most advanced form of hominid that is thought to have walked the earth was our ancient ancestor known as Homo erectus at approximately 250,000 years ago.

It is at this point when it is believed and claimed that a technologically advanced species came to earth in a massive circular or possibly spherical ship that our ancestors came to know as the Heaven or the abode of the gods. It is claimed that this species possessed such great knowledge and were so technologically powerful when compared to our ancient ancestors. Our ancestors believed these creatures were the gods themselves.

Any of the ancient stories that speak of this Heaven are in fact speaking of this great ship of the gods. This Heaven becomes the basis of the All-Seeing-Eye and also the great Solar-Disk symbols. This is why these symbols have always been connected to the Sky Gods. This massive ship was placed in low orbit and used as main base of operations by this advance species as they established a colony or outpost on the earth. It appears that this colony's main propose was natural resource extraction of raw materials in order to support and supply the Heaven and this new colony.

At some point around 200,000 years ago it is said that there was a great rebellion among the gods and open warfare broke out between them. The events of this rebellion resulted in the creation a slave race called Man. This Man is the one we know as Homo neanderthalensis or Neanderthal. This is the time from which the stories about the Garden of Eden, Adam and Eve, Cain and Able, along with similar stories come from. None seem to know for sure if the ones we remember as Adam, Eve, Cain and Able were single people or actually different small groups of people. The Dream Vision of Enoch tells us that they were single people that basis which became the different groups of people that were broken along racial lines for some long-forgotten reason. This seems to imply that over time the names Adam, Eve, Cain, and Able become names of families and then of clans. This is classic example of how this story can be so easily confused and misinterpreted.

This is also from this ancient time that another symbol originates, the shape of Two-Triangles. This symbolism of Two-Triangles will slowly change through time to become the symbol that most know today as the Star of David. As we have learned, the original shape or pattern of these Two-Triangles was originally made by the stars Betelgeuse, Rigel, Aldebaran, and Pollux. This symbol represents the time of when all the gods are working together and ruling an enslaved mankind.

It is believed that this slave society of humans serving the gods went on for tens of thousands of years. It is also believed that the Leader of these gods was oppressive in his rule and was rather uncaring to their creation Man as is so often reflected in myths of the oldest gods. There are whispers within esoteric circles that it was this original Leader of the gods was the one that decided that they would portray themselves as gods to early man and demand worship from them. These same whispers speak that all of gods agreed with him at first with him, but later came to regret it. It is hinted that this was what started the whole problem which led to the original group of gods to braking into two or possibly more warring factions.

This is why the ones that will later be remembered as the Watchers started getting closer to the humans. They were trying to lessen the oppression and treatment of this brutal slavery. If this is true, then it would help to explain how the personal relationships started to develop between the Watchers and some of the early human females. Regardless of the reason, it is agreed by the all traditions that these personal relationships were the major reason for the event that is remembered in the monotheistic religions as the Fall of Lucifer and his Angels. This is also the event that is remember in all the other ancient traditions of when a great Lord of Light came to earth as a falling star bringing the light of divine knowledge and freedom to an enslaved humanity.

This event brings us to the next symbol and its true meaning, the Five-Sided-Star or Pentagram. This is the origin of the Pentagram and one of the meanings behind it. It is how this Bringer of Light looked to ones that witnessed it as he came to earth. There are a great number of ancient and modern stories, myths, and legends that remember and speak of this monumental event.

One of the most remarkable ones is the ancient Mesoamerican belief of the Feathered Serpent or Plumed Serpent god. What makes this belief so amazing is if you have ever seen an object reenter the atmosphere, like a meteor, the space shuttle, or any other man-made object you will observe that the object will glow brighter than the sun and will leave a trail of very hot ionized gas in its wake. If this happens before sunrise or just after sunset, when the sun is not above the horizon, the sunlight will make the gas glow like a huge neon light. When this gas is pushed around by the winds in the upper atmosphere, it moves around much like a great glowing serpent in the sky.

This is where the idea of the Serpent or Snake comes in. It is just another type of symbolic representation of this event of the Lord of Light coming to earth. With knowing that, you can easily understand that every single thing you have ever heard about the serpent and its relationship to being evil in some way or even Reptilian-like aliens of modern day is most likely incorrect. They are just corrupted stories that come much later trying to remember this event. This allows to realize that much of the modern lore about serpents and reptilian aliens should be viewed with skepticism.

This event leads to the legendary time that all the ancient stories, myths, including the Biblical agree upon, the time of the Giants and the Great Men of Renown. These are the bastard offspring of the gods and their human wives.

These are the mythical Nephilim that the Biblical tradition vaguely remembers. This is the time of the legendary heroes that were half-man and half-god.

It is also the time from which the idea of a Lost Paradise originates from. This is the time the Fallen-Watchers and their followers all wish to return too. This is the time when they were worshiped as gods and ruled all of earth and humanity. This is the time from which the symbol and meaning of the Triangle and its origin. As we learned, the triangle shape is based on just three of the four original stars we started with and forever frozen in time by the shape of the Great Pyramid. This allows us to estimate when this event of the Fall of Lucifer and his Angels could have happened in time and as we learned in an earlier chapter this was approximately 155,000 BC.

This then provides us with the real reason why the Great Pyramid was built. It was a monument to the monumental and almost unbelievable event of when the one remembered as the great Bringer of Light came to earth with the divine knowledge of the gods and freedom for humanity. This is also why the Great Pyramid has all the mathematical information encoded in it. Because it is some of the knowledge that this Bringer of Light or Light-Bearer brought to early humans. This is the great secret of the Great Pyramid and all the information that it holds. Not only is it a monument to the event that is known in the Biblical tradition as the Fall of Lucifer and his Angels, but it also encodes much of the mathematical knowledge that given to humanity.

This mathematical knowledge is not only hidden within great monuments like the Great Pyramid, but it is also hidden in many of the symbols themselves. I will only give one quick example of this to provide you with a better idea of how this is done so we do not stray too far from the story. The Five-Pointed-Star or Pentagram is the best example of encoded mathematical knowledge in a symbol and provides you with the idea of how easily it is done. Below is a pentagram with one of the main lines labeled A, B, C, and D.

You will notice that the line (A, D,) is bisected at the two points B and C. This breaks the original line of A and D into three-line segments; line (A, B,); line (B, C,); line (C, D,). We now have 4 lines of different length when counting the original line we started with. When these line segments are put in the proper order of left to right starting shortest to longest, you will get the "golden ratio" of geometry. When combined with basic factions and very simple algebra, you can figure out almost everything about natural geometry. It also provides the mathematical framework for art, engineering, harmonics, and many other aspects of physics and the natural world. This is one of the most important secrets of the symbols. That they also hold much of the actual divine knowledge that was given to humanity by the Lord of Light.

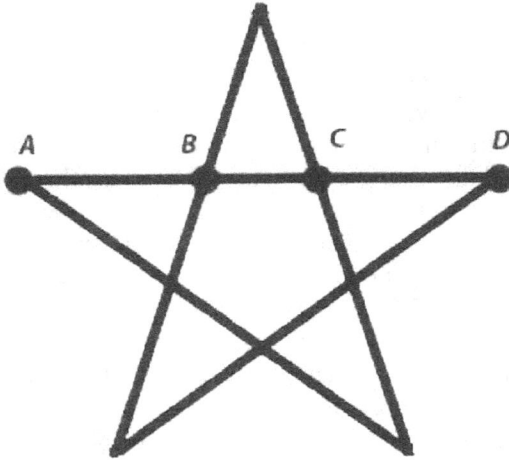

(Fig.1) [2]

As you can now understand that the Great Pyramid and the symbol of the Pentagram are vastly older and have much greater meaning than most have ever guessed or even imagined. Not only are these symbols of the event of the Bringer of Light coming to earth, but it helps remind the followers of the esoteric religion of the Lost Paradise that the Fallen-Watchers believed they created at this time. This is why this symbol is on so many different products and items that surround us today. It is showing you the monument built to the Bringer of Light and helps their followers to remember the Lost Paradise that many seen too long to return to.

This Lost Paradise of the Watchers lasted for tens of thousands of years until the ones that the Fallen-Watchers rebelled against came back into power. It is believed that this return to power and the war that followed caused the loss of this Paradise and its final destruction. This is thought to have happened at some time around 74,000 years ago and resulted in the event that is recorded in all ancient traditions as the Great Flood. Within modern science this event is remembered as the Toba super volcano event. As we can now understand, the Great Flood and possibly the Toba event itself were the final events of this original group of gods returning to power and their reestablishment of control over the planet.

All of the destruction that occurred at this time is believed by both of the followers of the esoteric belief and the monotheistic tradition to have resulted in killing many of the Fallen-Watchers and almost all of their half-human, half-god children. Both the Biblical tradition and the esoteric belief agree that many of these individuals become the ones known as, or are the basis of, the stories of demons, devils, and lost souls that were dammed to walk the earth by the Lord-God.

The ones that were not killed were captured and punished for their crimes and sins against man and beast. It is traditional thought that the Fallen-Watchers were stripped of their power and exiled to earth. It is also said that their punishment included them being physical changed in order to prevent anything like this from happening again. This is the origin of the ideas and stories of the Fallen Angels being turned into devils with their demon offspring and dammed to walk the earth for all time. With only the power of temptation, the temptation of the forbidden knowledge.

These events of the original group or Main-Group reestablishing their power over earth, also results in the changes in the monuments on the Giza plateau and the Great Pyramid. As we saw, there was the addition of two new pyramids at this time. It also results in new buildings at new sites like Teotihuacan, Mexico, among many others around the world. These changes and the new monuments are aligned to the original four stars as they were seen at that ancient time.

This reestablishment of power and control also resulted in great changes to the population. It appears that the Main-Group began to create a number of different sub-groups of humans. These sub-groups all appear to be based on Neanderthal DNA. These sub-groups then slowly moved around world and established many of the mythical kingdoms of legend after the Great Flood. By understanding the animals brought upon the Ark actually represent people and groups of people. We can then combine this knowledge with the Biblical account which then allows us to understand for the first time how the some of the Giants, the Nephilim, and others survived the Great Flood. They are the 'unclean' animals that were taken aboard the Ark. I think the only reason they were allowed to live is because they allied themselves with Main-Group during this reconquest of earth from the Fallen-Watchers.

This understanding that the animals symbolically represent people and groups of people. It is then rather easy to understand how people have always mistaken this animal symbolism as actually representing animals and not people. This animal symbolism is why different sub-groups or their leaders become confused as some type of animal god.

223

Over time as the original story and the real meaning of the symbolism was forgotten. People naturally started remembering these people or their leaders as a special type of half-human half-animal. As more time passed, the stories began to include elements that these animals could talk to humans and sometimes helping while at other times not. As even more time passed and more was forgotten. These half-human, half-animal creatures turn into monsters that would terrorize their ancestors and would do horrible things to the humans that crossed their path. These mistaken half-human, half-animals are also the origin of many of the idols that look like humans with animal heads. Many of which are still worshipped today by many esoteric, pagan, and occult followers.

Many of these sub-groups are said to have followed or where at least allied with one of the two primary groups of the Lord-God or the Light-Bearer along with his Fallen-Watchers. There are others that were said to be independent and whose loyalties could not be trusted. The overall information about this time and the way these different groups interacted with each other is so vague that next to nothing can be said with much confidence. The Dream Vision speaks of how these groups in time go to war with each other when we are told *"And they began to bite and gore one another."*

During this war, we are told of how a *white bull* was born among them. This white bull then begat a *wild ass* and another *white bull*. The asses multiplied but that white bull then begat a *black wild boar* and a *white sheep*. That sheep then begat *twelve sheep* and those twelve sheep gave *"one of them to the wild asses."* Who in turn gave that sheep to the wolves.

These events spoken of in the Dream Vision are some of the most important to understanding how all the different stories and traditions come together at one point in time. These events of a war and changes of the bulls to sheep is the point when you can really begin to truly understand that this is not all myth and legend but is rooted in actual history. This is beginning to the true understanding of the forbidden knowledge of Enoch and is a key to unlocking everything else.

The first thing to realize is who the first white bull was at this point it the story. This white bull is remembered as Abraham in the Book of Genesis. In the Book of Genesis, he has two sons, Ishamel and Isaac. His first son Ishmael is the wild ass, and his second son is Isaac who is the second white bull in this part of the story.

The Book of Genesis goes into great detail about Isaac's two sons, Esau and Jacob. If you go back and read the Esau and Jacob story in chapters twenty-five through thirty-six in the Book of Genesis. You will clearly see and understand that Esau is the *"black wild boar"* spoken of in the Dream Vision, which is also the wild man known as Enkidu of the Epic of Gilgamesh. You will also quickly realize that Jacob is the white sheep and could be one of individuals that story of Gilgamesh is based on. This is another example of where many of the ancient myths and legends come together at one point in time, but only if you understand the symbolism and its connection to the Dream Vision of Enoch.

This is the point where you can clearly see and understand that the Bible is actually giving us a great amount of detail on these individuals and the events going on around them. While the Dream Vision gives us the overall outline of the story. You will also realize that the destruction of the cities of the plains, remembered as Sodom and Gomorrah, is speaking of the war of the kings that was going on at the time. Using the description given in the Book of Genesis about this destruction and everything else I have presented up to this point, you can begin to understand that this is also where modern day science comes into play with solid evidence to help support it all.

It has been noticed by many over the years that this destruction of the cities of the plains as described in the Bible eerily sounds much like the effects of a nuclear weapon being detonated. The use of this nuclear weaponry actually allows us to date these events. It also allows us to get a really good idea of what was going on all those thousands of years ago.

Returning to the radioactive isotopes that are found in the Icelandic marine sediment samples, the mammoth tusks, and numerous Clovis sites. We can now theorize with high confidence that the first radioactive peak seen at 39,000 BC is evidence of this destruction of the cities of the plains and this war of the kings. The next two major peaks seen at 32,000 BC and 13,000 BC; will be examined as we move forward with this story. This is also the approximate time that first evidence for Cro-Magnon-Man starts to enter the fossil record.

All of this allows us to say with some confidence that it is highly likely that the individual remembered as Abraham and the events surrounding the destruction of the cities of the plains took place at about 39,000 BC. This is why we have never found any direct physical archaeological evidence for most of these events and any of these people. It is because we are not looking far enough back in time; in fact, we are not even close.

It should also be noted that there are a large number of ancient cultures and traditions from around the world that believe and argue that their original civilizations all began at this same time of about 39,000 BC with ancient Egypt and ancient India being two of the best-known examples. As you can see, religion, myth, legend, history, and science all come together at this one point in time at approximately 39,000 years ago.

With knowing that the next radioactive peak happens at about 32,000 BC and that the next major event in the story is the Exodus. We now have a clue to the reasons for this radioactive peak. We are told within the Dream Vision and the Biblical story of the Exodus of how the Lord-God openly attacking the wolves or Egyptians as his people leave the land of Egypt.

The Dream Vision speaks of how the wolves were blinded and "*His face was dazzling and glorious and terrible to behold*." As with the Bible, it speaks of one of the most famous events of all time, the parting of the waters of a sea and the destruction of the army that pursued them by the Lord-God. These are the events that caused the mammoths to have iron-rich particles imbedded into their tusks at this time. This again appears to be evidence that whenever these gods came into conflict with each other they used some type of nuclear weapon against one another. It also shows that these conflicts of the gods were much larger events that took place in many different areas around the planet than is traditionally believed.

The next important events after the parting of the waters described in both the Dream Vision and the Bible is the detailed wanderings in the wilderness by these people. In time they come to the Promised Land. Once they settled this land, they eventually establish a great and powerful empire that had built a "*house that became great and broad....and a tower lofty and great was built on the house for the Lord*." This broad house and lofty tower are the origin of many of the ancient myths, legends, and stories of a tower or great building that was connected to and then later destroyed by the gods or God. This brings us to the point where the cylinder seals pick-up up the story with the aid of the Pleiades star cluster along with the fossil record help guide us through this forgotten time.

The fossil record shows us that Cro-Magnon Man began to slowly move out of the European and Middle Eastern areas after 32,000 BC. This is also the time that any available astronomy software can show anybody that the original triangle shape in that part of the night sky can no longer be seen. This is the point in time that the Pleiades star cluster becomes associated with the gods. As we have already learned this gives us an estimation of when the Pleiades star cluster contained eleven stars as seen on the cylinder seal made famous by Mr. Zecharia Sitchin. This then allows us to fill in many of the missing pieces of the forbidden knowledge of Enoch and ties in a number of the other symbols we have examined.

In Freemasonry and many other closely related esoteric belief systems. It is believed that this house and tower that Enoch is speaking of is actually the Temple and Citadel of King Solomon that is described in the Bible. It is also believed that this was the first of a series of towers that were built across the world as Cro-Magnon-Man immigrated around the world. These towers are based on the design of the Temple and Citadel of King Solomon. They are also

226

some of the High Places that so common with ancient myths. It appears that these towers were to become the foundation of power for the one remembered as the Lord-God. This is the next point where esoteric belief, mythology, legend, and the Biblical story come together. It is also why I spoke of Atlantis as I did earlier with the idea of seven towers.

It is believed in some esoteric circles that the legendary lost city of Atlantis was in fact the capital city of this network of towers. That the Lord-God of the Biblical tradition and the ancient Greek god of the sea Poseidon; are in fact, one and the same. They also claim that any ancient story, myth, or legend that speaks of a "god" that is connected to the sea or ocean is talking about this individual with an empire built around seven towers that were centered on the one the stood in the capital city of Atlantis.

The Temple and Citadel of King Solomon is very important to this story for a number of reasons. One it was the first tower built outside of the city of Atlantis. Two it was where all the problems started. Three it was destroyed and then rebuilt. Interestingly enough, there a few esoteric groups that claim it has was rebuilt twice. Four, it is the one we have the most detail on and five, many of the upcoming events happen in and around this grand building. This building and tower are also where the symbols of Two and Three-Columns originate from, in addition to all the other symbols, artifacts and legends connected to this building.

This next part gets a little hazy and can be confusing as to the proper order of events that unfold. It also heavily relies on our new understand of the connection between the cylinder seals and the Dream Vision of Enoch. Additionally, there are many details that are just plain missing and appear lost to history for this part of the story. As far as I can tell from my research of the followers of the esoteric; they themselves do not seem to know what may have exactly happened once this war began.

It is thought by some within the different esoteric schools of thought is that this network of towers was completed sometime between 20,000 to maybe around 16,000 BC. Once this network of towers was completed is when the real problems began. It is said that for a few thousand years, the Main-Group primarily focused on his network of towers and the control they gave him over his Cro-Magnon humans. He left all the other groups alone and honored all treaties that were made with them. But over time his power and control began to grow as the number of humans grew larger.

It was at this point in time that some unknown event happened and it is said that he possibly began to go a little mad with power. He began to claim that he was the one and only "God" above all the others and started demanding to be worshiped as such, not only by his followers, but by all the other groups too. It is said that for any that did not agree to this were then attacked by his armies of humans. The Bible is full of stories of the Lord-God commanding great armies of humans against all those that would not submit to his will. This is said to be the real reason of why the war started and why the Fallen-Watchers and their allies fought back was because the others ones, the one that were like the Lord-God, knew he was not what he claimed to be and they would not submit.

This led to the Fallen-Watchers infiltrating and corrupting the Temple and Citadel. This was done so they could steal the technology and resources that they needed in order to fight this tyranny of the Main-Group. As we saw on the cylinder seals, we know that the Fallen-Watchers was able to build their own tower with the knowledge and resources they took.

It is because of this falling away of the followers of the Temple and Citadel, the Main-Group goes too and then sends a number of people to the Fallen-Watchers. This is in order to speak to them and show them the errors of their ways. This resulted in these new fallen humans killing all but one of the individuals sent by the Main-Group. The one that was not killed, escaped somehow and was later saved and *"taken away from the generations of the earth."* This one that escaped was the one we call Enoch. This event could be where the idea of being saved in some way and taken up to heaven may have originally comes from.

This is one of the single most important events that happen and brings us to the final meaning of the All-Seeing-Eye and Triangle symbol. This is the event that begins the great and final war that will lead to the destruction of everything. As we saw on the cylinder seals and the other artifacts, Enoch escapes from the Temple and Citadel in Jerusalem to the Great Pyramid in Egypt and uses the Caduceus to summon the Lord-God. Who then arrives in his all his Glory which is seen as the Solar-Disk which then saves Enoch at the last second just before the Fallen Ones and their allies can reach him. This event and the location that it takes place in is the final meaning behind the symbol of the All-Seeing-Eye and Pyramid seen on the back of every single dollar bill on the planet.

To many followers within the esoteric this event is the first-time people openly fought back against the "Main-Group and to them they won. I think this is event is very similar to the first battle of the America Civil War at Bull Run. Where the south very easily routed the north and was hailed as a great victory to be remembered and that the war was going to be short lived and in their favor. The symbol of Enoch being taken from the generations of the earth comes to represent this idea while also becoming a banner under which they fight and remember. This combined with the other meanings for this symbol will give you a very good idea of why this All-Seeing-Eye and what becomes the unfinished Pyramid is important to the followers of esoteric and on just about everything you see.

It appears to be the esoteric version of the Christian cross. It has just as much meaning to its believers as the cross does for the followers of Christianity. Also, just like Christians or any other religious like group for that matter, the followers of the esoteric enjoy displaying their most powerful and favorite symbol that has come to represent their whole belief. This also done to show everybody how they are truly a devoted follower and believer of the esoteric. It is also done to rub it in the faces of the unbeliever or the one that does not know the truth held within the symbolism.

This event is what gives the final meaning to the All-Seeing-Eye and the unfinished Pyramid. It is also the event that launched this final war. This event can be estimated based on the Pleiades cluster seen on the cylinder seals showing Enoch being saved and the fossil record. The cylinder seals show that eight stars, in two lines of four, were visible in the night sky when this event took place. When combined with the knowledge that at the end of the last Ice-Age at around 15,000 BC that there was a small extinction event. We can for the first time give a possible reason for the last Ice-Age coming to an end after 50,000 years of ice. Because in all honestly, the reason why the last Ice-Age started to come to an end 17,000 years ago is a complete mystery to modern science. Based on this story, the reason could be the beginning of this final war.

This brings us to the next part of forbidden knowledge and the events that happened after Enoch was saved and taken up to Heaven. The clue is given on the Masonic Register we saw in the last chapter.

On the lower right-hand side of the Masonic Register, there are five small columns connected together on the black-and-white checker floor. These represent the five towers that fell to the Fallen and their allies. This should allow you to now realize that the two columns of Boaz and Jachin also represent the two towers of the Lord-God or Main Group that did not fall. This should then allow you to also realize that those two columns look like the 'golden candlesticks' spoken of in the Bible. This is an important part of the forbidden knowledge that begins to fill in a large missing piece of the story. That the 'candlesticks' spoken of in the Bible are actually symbolically talking about the network of towers spread around the world. This understanding is a great aid in tracing many parts of this story and how some of this war unfolded. It also allows us some understanding of a few of the other references in the Bible related to candlesticks with their references to the 'glory of the Lord' or 'spirit of the Lord' that came and sat upon them are speaking of the towers. Are in fact referring to a similar event when the Lord-God came and stood upon the Temple and Citadel of King Solomon. Which by this time as we are told in the Book of Revelation that there seven of them.

It is now easy to imagine and finally realize that the 'Glory of the Lord' that came with all kinds of smoke, fire, lightning, and thundering sat upon the tower was actually some type of highly advanced ship. It also makes sense that there may have been one of these ships per tower. We can now understand that as these craft were approaching a tower, they would perform a vast light show to dazzle our ancient ancestors and make them think a god was coming to stand upon the tower. I think this would have been an impressive sight to anyone who witnessed it. Using the cylinder seals as a guide, I found a clipart image that explains all of this much better than I could in words.

(Fig.2) [3]

With a bit of imagination. One can easily see how such an event would be very impressive visual sight to the eye. This image also gives you the best idea of what the cylinder seals are actually showing us and how the towers might have really have functioned as a type of landing pad for the gods. This should allow you to begin to realize that this is reason why there are so many towers around you in the world. They all symbolically representing these ancient towers that gods once stood upon. They also symbolically represent the power that these ancient buildings held. These towers were one of the primary components of this war and one of the things they were fighting over.

As these towers fell, one-by-one to the Fallen and their allies, the "Lord" and his allies appear to have begun a two-front counter-attack. The first part of this counter-attack is well known and rather detailed in the Bible. The Dream Vision tells us that the "Lord" sent many others to "testify unto them and lament over them". In the esoteric religion, it is believed that these others sent to testify, are actually all the great prophets, teachers and holy men from history. These "others" are the foundation of most all ancient, and many modern-day religions belief systems.

It is thought by some and believed by others that almost all the stories of the ones we call Jesus Christ, Buddha, Confucius, Zoroaster, Mithras, and many others, are actually the ones sent from the Lord of the sheep as spoken of by Enoch in the Dream Vision. They were sent to humanity in the hope that they could turn them from the corruption of the Fallen Ones and their allies. It seems to be unknown in which order these individuals were sent. But, within some esoteric schools of thought it is believed that the one remembered as Jesus Christ was the last one sent before the end. This is another part of the secret; that many, if not all, of these great and holy men of history, actually existed, it is just that they lived from about 13,000 to maybe 15,000 years ago or possibly more.

You should start realizing that everybody on the planet has different pieces, parts, and fragments of this story. That should also allow you to understand that we should not be arguing with each other about who has the true story or belief. But we should be working together to see who has which part and how it all really goes together. You can also begin to see and understand how this knowledge can and has been used against us all. Again, this is why we have never found any historical or archaeological evidence for these individuals and many others from history. It is because we are not looking far enough back in time.

The second part of this counter-attack appears to have two phases. The first phase involves the mysterious 'seventy shepherds' and their slaughter of the Cro-Magnon-Man humans. The second phase involves the building of the great and legendary monsters.

It is unknown on who these seventy shepherds actually where and what their ultimate part in all of this was. The esoteric religion and the symbols are of little help in this matter. These seventy shepherds appear to be unknown to them. Outside of the idea of them providing the basis and origin for human sacrifice and that they took part in this war, nothing else is really known about them.

I have to wonder if these mysterious seventy shepherds could be the basis of many of the ancient stories and myths that speak of the number seventy in some manner. There have been a large number of people over the years that have noticed that the number seventy or a number very close to seventy is used in many ancient texts and traditions. This number is normally related to the gods but at other times it is related to kings or rulers. There are other times the number is hidden within the stories themselves referring to the number itself. For example, the numbers that the ancient Egyptians used on a regular basis in many of their ancient writings have the number seventy or seventy-two in them. Many writers of the ancient astronaut theory and lost civilizations call them the Osiris Numbers.

A great number of these researchers have related this number seventy or seventy-two to processional motion or some type of long-term time keeping. In light of everything, I think when this number seventy is seen in the ancient stories and texts; they are actually referring to these seventy shepherds in some way. This could be a way to trace these individuals through the different cultures and stories. Although these seventy shepherds may be a mystery, we are told they unleashed great death upon humanity at the command of the Lord of the sheep.

For the second phase of this counter attack we must return the cylinder seals. The seals show us that the Main-Group then began building the great and terrible sea monster remembered as Leviathan. The seals give the impression that Leviathan was actually a large ocean-going machine that was of a similar design of modern-day nuclear submarines. When combined with the information given in the Book of Job in the Bible. It is clear that this sea-going ship was also designed to look like a terrible monster to any that saw it. It also appears that one of the primary features of this Leviathan was that its head or front-section could rise up like a great animal. The stories tell us that all the power and most of the weaponry of Leviathan, was contained within its head.

This understanding that Leviathan is directly connected to the Lord-God and the ocean is another clue that the one shown on the cylinder seals must be the Lord-God remembered in the Bible. When this is added to our understanding of the symbols. We can now begin to truly understand what many of the ancient artifacts from around world are actually showing us. That the individual god that is known as the Lord of the waters or oceans, or referring to the mighty sea monsters like Leviathan are in fact speaking of the Lord-God that is remembered in the Bible.

There is an image that clearly shows all the elements of what I am trying to explain. This image has been traditional interpreted as the Mesopotamian god 'Marduk' and the dragon is known as 'Mushhushshu.' You can now understand what you are looking at with this picture. It is not only the god Marduk or the dragon Mushhushshu", but it is also showing us the one that is remembered as the Lord-God and the great beast Leviathan.

You can easily see the Eight-Pointed-Star that we now know is a symbol for the one known as the Lord-God. You can also see Leviathan with rather good detail. Enough detail to get a very good idea of how the front section could have been raised and lowered as needed. When this picture is compared with the description given in chapter forty-one of the Book of Job. After reading that chapter of the Book of Job you will realize that Job is describing this picture of Leviathan. You should then realize that all the references in the Bible about a large fish, including the ever-famous Jonah being swallowed by a large fish, are actually speaking of this great ocean-going machine.

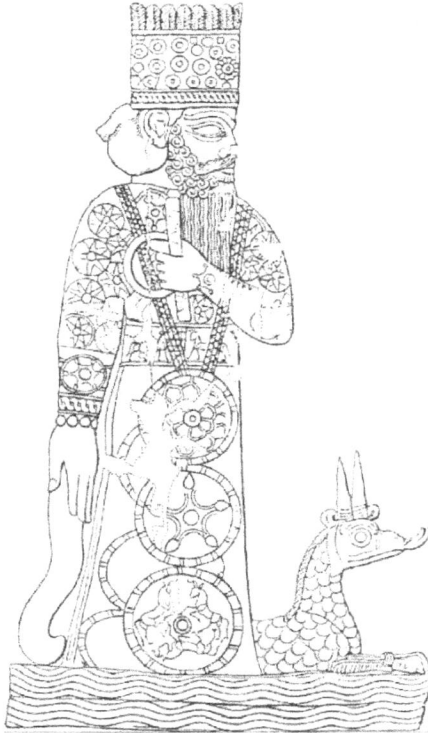

Drawing of an ancient relief of the god Marduk and the dragon Mushhushshu (Fig.3) [4]

Legend tells us and the cylinder seals show us. As this war progressed the Main-Group began to lose control of more towers. We are also shown that the Main-Group constructed a similar war machine as Leviathan but for the land remembered as Behemoth. As we saw on the cylinder seals, this was done by using a large two-tower crane system to lift structure based on the original design of the tower onto a mobile platform. Both of these great-war machines were then used to attack the Fallen and their allies.

The seals show us that the Fallen responded by constructing their own great and terrible war machine. This one becomes the legendary "Great Red Dragon" that is remembered all around the world. The construction of this Dragon is represented by the Three-Column symbol and is another one of the meanings behind this symbol. The Masons give the impression that this two-tower-crane was also used in the construction of the original towers which then adds an additional layer of meaning. This is represented in the earlier painting of Mozart in the Lodge with the seven grouping of three candles seen on the walls of the Lodge. This is another tie in point on understanding the symbols and the story they tell.

The next series of events that unfold after these great machines are built are clouded in mystery. As we know by the movement of the stars of the Pleiades cluster as shown on the cylinder seals. The events of the great monsters being built and their use in this war took place over a very long period of time. The seals indicate that it was over thousands of years. The few myths and legends about this war that I am aware of, give me the impression that both sides were evenly matched. Without going off on some tangent about this, mainly due to the fact that most of this is unknown and you will understand some of my reasoning about what I will say in just a few pages. I think over time as this war went on, both sides were unable to deliver a knock-out blow or victory over the other leading them to a stalemate. Just like our own wars where each side was trying to develop a new weapon system that would give them the advantage in this war and lead to victory for their side. I this this is the reason why each war machine was built.

These great war machines were unable to turn the tide of war for either side and much like World War I, the slaughter just went on and on for years on end. This led to the piece of the story that the followers of the esoteric have tried so hard to erase from time. Luckily for us they missed a small piece that is located in the arid expanse of southwest Texas. This piece provides the greatest understandings of the forbidden knowledge and will lead you to the realization of what has really been going on.

The piece I speak of is located in the area of the confluence of the Pecos River and the Rio Grande. It is the famous rock paintings and artwork of the "White Shaman" at the White Shaman rock shelter above the Devils River located in Panther Cave. These rock paintings have been a total mystery to all that have seen them, expert and lay alike. It has been argued since their discovery that the true meaning of these paintings would never be understood by anybody. I will now show you that everybody has been incorrect in thinking that and these ancient rock-paintings are actually providing us with the missing piece of this story.

Before we get to the rock paintings, I must provide a little more back story for you to understand what you are looking at and how it will all become very clear to you in a way you never imagined.

With the war becoming stalemated and likely turning into a war of attrition. The Fallen Group was beginning to run out of resources and becoming desperate for an end of the war. This led them to formulate a daring and dangerous plan that would end the war in one fell swoop and bring victory to their side once and for all. The plan was to directly attack the Heaven and the two remaining towers of the Main-Group. This attack was the one that led to the Heaven being heavily damaged and then leading to its total destruction with its lost to both sides. This is what the rock paintings of the White Shaman in Texas show us. They are showing us this attack on the Heaven and most of the battle or battles surrounding the attack on one of the towers which may have been located here in the Americas.

Ancient rock painting from the lower Pecos River, Texas, USA. (Fig.4) [5]

The first painting clearly shows the Heaven being attacked with arrows and a number of large god-like figures involved in the attack. You will notice that the characters are similar in style and give a similar impression as the ones seen on the cylinder seals and spoken of in the Dream Vision.

Within this first painting you can see a large cat figure, this figure has been traditional viewed as a panther, but in light of this story, you can see and realize this is very similar to the beast that looked like a leopard described in the Bible's Book of Revelation. This beast has two bird figures that appear to be attacking it and there is a line of animals headed toward it also possibly attacking it. This is similar to what is described in the Dream Vision with the "birds of heaven" and the "beasts of the field" and their attacks on the sheep. The second painting shows a similar scene as the first, but without the attack on the panther.

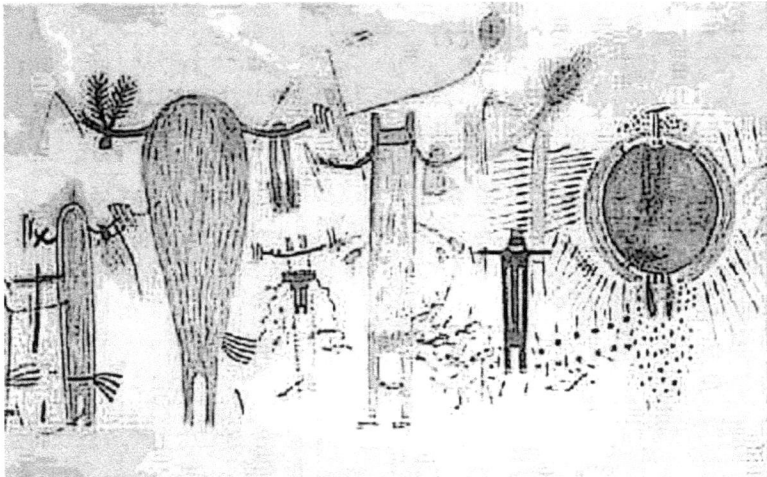

Ancient rock painting from the lower Pecos River, Texas, USA. (Fig.5) [6]

When these two-rock paintings are looked at in the context of the esoteric belief and the symbolism we have explored. What can I say? They speak for themselves and it is almost impossible to say that they do not show this attack on the Heaven.

The next rock painting is very famous and is the legendary White Shaman panel that gives the site its name. One of the most amazing things about this rock painting is the fact that we have already seen the scene that it shows from before. In fact, shows the exact same scene as shown on the print of "The Temple of the Rosy Cross". If this does not provide proof that this story is the correct one, then I don't what will. You will clearly see a great monster in the center attacking a tower on the right-hand side. On the left-hand side, you can see a similar scene of something underground as on the Temple of the Rosy Cross. It also has the same similar "birds of heaven" attacking the monster in the center. This monster has the same similar design as the tower seen on the drawing and is clearly showing us the same thing

White Shaman rock painting from the lower Pecos River, Texas. USA. (Fig.6) [7]

Again, what can I say about the fact that a drawing from 1618 Germany shows the exact same scene as a 4,000-year-old rock painting in southwest Texas. This is proof that this story and all the information I have been presenting is the story at the heart of the esoteric symbolism and the many groups that hide this knowledge.

As you can now understand that these mysterious rock paintings are not a mystery at all. They are in fact telling us one of the most important parts of this story and the reason for the destruction of everything. It was this attack on the Heaven that led to its destruction. This destruction of the Heaven is what caused the end of everything that they knew. It also appears to have been the fault of the Fallen and their allies that it happened. I think this is also the origin of the idea of a great betrayal that led to the destruction of the towers that is remembered in the story of the legendary tower of Babel.

Before moving on, I would like to present one additional rock painting related to this battle and attack on the Heaven and one of the towers. I am unsure as to where this scene exactly fits into the battle. But when viewed with our new understanding of these rock paintings and the symbolism, it is clear this is showing us a modern-like battle with flying craft and modern weapons. It is also clear that our ancient ancestors did not understand what they were seeing or the technology involved.

The next set of events that happen after the Heaven is attacked and damaged are now rather easy to follow. This is because this is the point where the Bible's Book of Revelation picks up the rest of story at. I highly recommend you read or have a copy of the Book of Revelation for this next part. It is written with the idea that you the reader are rather familiar with the Book of Revelation along with most of the confusion that surrounds it.

Ancient rock painting from the lower Pecos River, Texas, USA. (Fig.7) [8]

This attack on the Heaven by the Fallen Ones led to it being heavily damaged. This damage was the reason the Heaven's orbit began to decay. It was at this point that the Main-Group realized what was going to happen. That the mighty Heaven was going to impact the earth and be destroyed. They also realized that this impact would lead to great changes in the climate that next nobody would survive in their current state. This coming destruction of the Heaven and all the death that was sure to follow provides us with the reason for the actions of the gods and why so many were killed.

The Main-Group came up with a plan to save a remnant of the world from the oncoming destruction. This plan to save a remnant is the reason for rest of the events that unfold in the Book of Revelation and provides a background for what many of the prophets of the Bible are truly speaking of. This will provide you with the first true understanding of the Book of Revelations and the story it contains. Again, much of this will become clearer to you as we go along with the story.

Within the Book of Revelation, we are told that the fateful servant of the Lord, a man named John, sees *"seven golden candlesticks"* along with a being that he says is *"one like the Son of man"* standing among them with *"seven stars in his right hand.*" This individual then tells John that the seven candlesticks and the seven stars that he sees are the seven churches and the seven angels that rule them. Now with our understanding that the seven golden candlesticks are actually symbolically representing the seven towers. Additionally, we can also understand that the seven Angels or Shepherds are the ones that stood upon them as spoken of in the Bible and see on the cylinder seals. It is only after you understand the symbolism can truly begin to understand this story.

John is then commanded to write seven letters to each church and Angel. These seven letters speak of the five towers that have fallen and the two that have not by this time. They tell the Angels that only a true follower of the Lord-God is going to be saved from the coming destruction. They also give the warning that the Main-Group was going to begin a campaign of death and destruction against those the felt caused this destruction of the Heaven.

John is then taken to see the throne of God in heaven and the wonders of those that serve Him. He describes seeing the seven "Sprits of God" and "*four beasts that were full of eyes before and behind*" around the throne on a great floor like a "*sea of glass.*" He speaks of how lightnings and thundering proceeded out of the throne. He also talks of how the four beasts have six wings that never rested and each beast was different from the others. What John is being shown some of the hardware and weapon systems that are going to be used in the upcoming battles.

This brings us to chapter five in the Book of Revelations and the "*sealed book*" that no man in heaven or on earth could open. The only person that could open that book was the "lamb" which is traditionally thought of as the one remembered as Jesus Christ the son of the Lord. I think this book is the same one spoken of in the Dream Vision that recorded the deeds of the shepherds. The information contained within this book is then used to identify those who were guilty of helping the Fallen Ones. It is also reasonable to think that this book may have also contained important military information about the Fallen. That could be why only one special person could open it.

The next chapter in Revelation is one of the most famous and the part everybody remembers. It contains the Four Horsemen of the Apocalypse and the opening of the seven great seals in order. The first four-seals symbolically represent the Four Horsemen. Each one represents one aspect of the attack. The first two Horsemen represent the allies of the Main-Group attacking the Fallen and their allies. The third one clearly represents attacking the food supply and the economy. With the last one Death, represents exactly what it says, Death. The text says that these actions resulted in the deaths of about one quarter of the human population.

The next seal, the fifth one, is confusing and I have no good answer on what it could be describing. It speaks of the souls under the altar that died in the name of the Lord and that they were crying out to be avenged. This could be some type of technology or something completely different. But like I said; I have no good answer to what this is speaking about. I will leave it to you to decide what the symbolism of the fifth seal could mean.

The opening of the sixth seal and seventh seals and what they represent has always been a mystery to those who study the Book of Revelation. Just as before with the rock paintings, the mystery disappears as soon as you know the background story. It can only be understood if you realize that the Heaven is in a decaying orbit and the Main-Group is getting desperate to minimize the damage from the impact. The opening of the sixth seal is describing the Main-Group trying to move the Heaven, most likely using its main propulsion system. This is what verses twelve through seventeen in chapter six of the Book of Revelation is describing.

> *"And I beheld when he had opened the sixth seal, and, lo, there was a great earthquake; and the sun became black as sackcloth of hair, and the moon became as blood; And the stars of heaven fell unto the earth, even as a fig tree casteth her untimely figs, when she is shaken of a mighty wind. And the heaven departed as a scroll when it is rolled together; and every mountain and island were moved out of their places. And the kings of the earth, and the great men, and the rich men and the chief captains, and the mighty men, and every bondman, and every free man, hid themselves in the dens and in the rocks of the mountains; And said to the mountains and rocks, Fall on us, and hide us from the face of him that sitteth on the throne, and from the wrath of the Lamb; For the great day of his wrath is come; and who shall be able to stand?"*
> (Book of Revelation 6: 12-17.KJV)

This movement of the mighty Heaven appears to have cause wide spread damage across the globe and left a number of smaller objects in its wake that quickly rained down upon earth. This movement also appears to have generated a large cloud of gas that temporally blocked out the sun and moon. I will let you decide what type of exotic high-tech propulsion system could have this effect and how much energy it would take. But I will leave you with the idea that some of this effect could be due just to the shear mass of the Heaven.

This movement of the Heaven appears to have been done for two reasons. The first is rather simple and straight forward in that they were just trying to buy a more time and delay the impact. The second reason may not be apparent at first, but it will make sense shortly as we go deeper into this story. This other reason was so they could remove or separate a section of the ship and keep it in a higher and possibly a more stable orbit. They were trying to save some of their technology from the coming destruction and it was necessary for their plan to save a remnant. Again, we will see the reasoning for this shortly.

Before the opening of the seventh-seal, we are told that the remnant that is going to be saved from the destruction is marked or "*sealed... in their foreheads.*" We are also told that this remnant numbered 144,000 individuals, with 12,000 being chosen from each of the 12 tribes of the children of Israel. Who we can now understand was Cro-Magnon-Man and not us.

After this marking of the remnant to be saved. We are told that the seventh-seal is opened. The description of this opening of the seventh-seal is actually the Heaven entering the atmosphere. Chapter eight of the Book of Revelation gives us a surprisingly amount of good detail of this massive ship braking up into at least two main pieces. With one piece impacting the ocean "*as it were a great mountain burning with fire.*" We are also told that this impact turned one-third of the sea to blood along with killing one-third of all the creatures of the sea. This was said to have also destroyed one-third of all the ships too. We are then told that the second piece impacts land. This is "*the great star that fell from heaven, burning as a lamp, and it fell upon the third part of the rivers, and upon the fountains of waters: And the name of the star was Wormwood*" in Revelation 8: 10, 11, KJV.

This is describing the great and final destruction of fire that comes from the sky. This is the beginning of the end for this civilization and starts the process that wipes almost every single trace of it from existence, as if it never was. This second impact over land, by the great star remembered as "*Wormwood,*" is the impact that released around 26,000 megatons of force, creating the Sithylemenkat crater in Alaska. This is why this crater has such a high metal content; it was created by this fragment of the Heaven as it was vaporized in one massively huge explosion. This is the event that began the Younger Dryas and caused all the death around the globe at about 10,800 BC (±70 yrs.).

With this information, we can actually figure out how this fragment came in across the planet as it entered the atmosphere of earth. Knowing that the final impact site is in Alaska and that all the evidence from 13,000 years ago points to the North America landmass as being at the center of this destruction. It is highly probable that this thing came across North America landmass moving from the southeast to the northwest impacting in Alaska. This would mean that this fragment entered the atmosphere somewhere over the Atlantic and began breaking up over the eastern United States. This would explain the mystery of the Carolina bays, which are 500,000 small depressions spread over an area of 100,000 square miles on the Atlantic coast from North Carolina to Florida.[9] These depressions could be the evidence that many have been seeking all of these years. This is the first area that was impacted by fragments of the Heaven as it began to break up as it entered the atmosphere.

This clue gives us the possible path of this fragment across North America and an idea to the wake of devastation and death it left. When combined with the material found at the Clovis sites. We can get an idea that this fragment of the Heaven must have been massive enough to leave so much material behind as it entered the atmosphere. We can begin to imagine the horror that the witnesses must have felt as this huge object started to burn up with large flaming sections and pieces breaking off and exploding when they impacted the ground or blowing up in the air. It would have literally been raining fire and death from the skies all over North America. This fire from sky is would have started great forest fires all across the continent creating even more damage than before. These fires would then destroy the food supply for any that might have survived this horrific event. There is a good chance that if there were any survivors they would be shocked, stunned, and probably injured. The loss of the food supply would be a death sentence for these people and would explain what happened to the Clovis people.

Then a short time later, after these pieces had done their damage and started the continent on fire. A massive shock wave that was created by a 26,000-megaton explosion from the impact would do the rest. The evidence clearly shows that it killed just about everything in about two thousand miles in every direction from ground zero. This is why we find the fossil remains of millions of pre-historic animals all thrown together as if they were all picked up as one group and killed at one time while being slammed into the mud and ice of the North.

It is easy to imagine how a single large blast of this size would change everything on the planet. The shockwave alone, would change every-single weather and wind pattern on the planet, possibly for hundreds of years. If the Younger Dryas is anything to go off of, then this type energy release in one single large explosion changed the weather and the climate for about 1,300 years.

This then moves us back to the story and the rest of the Book of Revelation. Everything from this point on is because of the effects of this impact. This is also where the Dream Vision comes back into play and fits into the Book of Revelation with both telling us the next set of events to unfold in this ongoing saga. Both stories tell us that after this destruction the Main-Group unleashes a great war against all those who were not chosen to be saved.

The Book of Revelation tells us that up a third of the men were killed in this phase of the war. When you begin to add up the amounts we are told are killed by this point, you can quickly realize that as much as 75% to 80% of the population may have been destroyed by this time. This explains the reason why the sheep in the Dream Vision become so few in number. This could be when the mysterious Shepherds play their part in this war with their orgy of death.

The next chapter in the Book of Revelation, chapter ten is speaking of when John is given the information of what the Main-Group is planning to do and is told to *"prophesy again before many people and nations, and tongues, and kings."* [10]

This then leads us to the next two mysterious chapters of the Book of Revelation and their meaning. In chapter eleven, verse three, we are told of two witnesses that prophesy for *"a thousand, two hundred and three score days, clothed in sackcloth."* We are then told in verse four that these two witnesses are *"the two olive trees, and the two candlesticks standing before the God of the earth."* With knowing that the symbolism of the candlesticks represents the towers. While combining this with the cylinder seals that show us that some of these towers had outer covering. We can finally understand what this is describing.

These *"two witnesses"* are in fact the last two-towers in last city that is still loyal to the Main-Group. The next two verses give an indication of some of the capabilities and power of these towers. Verse five tells us that they could shoot fire from them against their enemies. While verse six states that they had control of the weather and *"that it rain not in the days of their prophecy."* Verse six also tells us that they could unleash all manner of plagues as often as they wished.

We are also told that these two towers were being use to blast out a never-ending stream of propaganda for their followers and against the other side for twelve-hundred and sixty days. This event is still remembered and practiced to this very day in every single Muslim country, when the minarets call the faithful to prayer five times a day. The modern-day minarets represent the last two ancient towers of the Lord-God and their call to the faithful to prayer and the unbeliever to be saved. This is also the meaning behind the two towers or bell-towers you see on all the different Christian churches around the world. They represent the last two-towers of the Lord-God just before the final battle and judgment. The symbolism of the churches gives the impression that these last two towers fell one at a time. While the Book of Revelation indicates that both fell more or less at the same time.

In verse seven we are told that after the twelve hundred and sixty days had come to an end *"the beast that ascendeth out of the bottomless pit shall make war against them, and shall overcome them, and kill them.*" You should now be able to realize that this is speaking of the very scene we saw earlier with the White Shaman rock painting and The Temple of the Rosy Cross drawing. They are both showing us the "beast" or "dragon" attacking one of the towers. When combined with the Bible and the Dream Vision, we know the outcome of this battle and what happened to the last two-towers. The Book of Revelation tells us that both were destroyed. We are then told they were both salvaged by the Main-Group after three and half days. After this salvage operation took place, the towers were said to have *"ascended up to heaven in a cloud."* [11]

Soon after these events we are told in the next unassuming verse thirteen that there was *"a great earthquake, and the tenth part of the city fell, and in the earthquake were slain of men seven thousand: and the remnant were affrighted."* This is the beginning of the end for the legendary city of Atlantis.

Chapter eleven ends with a verse that provides us with a final clue for some of the symbolic language used in rest of the Book of Revelation. It tells us that *"the temple of God was opened in heaven and there was seen in his temple the ark of his testament."* This is an indication that the Main-Group still has a major base of operations in low earth orbit.

This is also a clue that this temple is the throne that was erected in the *"pleasant land"* that Enoch speaks of just before the judgment. This is the same throne that is referred to in the rest of the Book of Revelations. It is highly likely this throne is also the Winged-Sun-Disk seen on the cylinder seals and other ancient artifacts. This throne also appears to have a very large military capability and is what gave the Main-Group the upper hand in all of this. In the next chapter we will see some things to help support this idea.

The meaning of chapter twelve of the Book of Revelation has been debated about since the 2nd century AD. With our new understanding of this ongoing war. We can begin to understand what this chapter is describing and get a rough idea of what John was actually seeing. The chapter starts with:

"And there appeared a great wonder in heaven: a woman clothed with the sun, and the moon under her feet, and upon her head a crown of twelve stars: And she being with child cried, travailing in birth, and pained to be delivered. And there appeared another wonder in heaven: and behold a great red dragon, having seven heads and ten horns, and seven crowns upon his heads. And his tail drew the third part of the stars of heaven, and did cast them to the earth: and the dragon stood before the woman, which was ready to be delivered, for to devour her child as soon as it was born. And, she brought

forth a man child, who was to rule all nations with a rod of iron: and her child was caught up unto God, and to his throne."
(Book of Revelation 12: 1-5. KJV)

This is describing the section of the Heaven that was removed earlier. It also tells us that was some type of manufacturing section. This manufacturing section is being used to construct what will soon be referred to as the New Jerusalem or Temple that comes down from the heavens in Revelation. Which is also the *"new house, greater and loftier than the first"* that Enoch speaks of in the Dream Vision. We are also told of the attempt by the Fallen-Group who is using the *"Great Red Dragon"* to try and capture both the manufacturing section and what it is building. The last line of verse five supports the earlier idea that the throne has a great military capability. This military capability was great enough that the Great Red Dragon was no match for it. We are then told that *"her child was caught up unto God, and to his throne."* This event then leads to a great battle in heaven between the Arch-Angel Michael and his fellow Angels and the Great Red Dragon.

The Great Red Dragon of Revelation is the same dragon or great beast we saw in the rock paintings. It is also the Tower on the Temple of the Rosy Cross drawing is symbolically representing. It is also the same dragon we saw on the cylinder seal where the god Sin was standing on the Crescent Moon symbol. All of these are describing the same great and terrifying war-machine of the Fallen Ones and the battles it fought in, against the Main-Group.

The rest of chapter twelve goes on to describe the remainder of this failed attempt by the Fallen Ones trying to capture any of the remaining resources in low orbit. Even though the Fallen Ones failed in their attempt, but it came at a high cost to the Main-Group Verses eight and nine tells us that it the Arch-Angel Michael and his fellow Angels were destroyed *"And prevailed not: neither was their place found any more in heaven. And the great dragon was cast out…"*

The text is rather vague on what exactly happening to this woman or manufacturing section outside that she escaped from the dragon and came to the earth somewhere. Based on the text, I think it is fair to speculate that this manufacturing section of the Heaven may have survived and could still be somewhere on the planet. The text is so vague it is next to impossible to even guess where this might be, but it is an interesting mystery to wonder about.

This failed attempt by the Fallen One to capture this mysterious woman and the child she birthed leads to a desperate situation for the Fallen Ones and their allies. There is a good chance that many of the after effects of the impact and explosion of the Heaven are now being felt across the world. Food, water, and resources in general must be running low. Adding in the burden of fighting a losing war are all starting to take their toll. This leads to the chapter thirteen of the Book of Revelation and the Beast and his number of 666. It will also be the last chapter of the Book of Revelation we will look at with any real detail or comment on.

This desperate situation leads the Fallen Ones to make one last ditch attempt to take what they needed from the Main-Group in order for them to survive the slowly unfolding death from the impact event. Chapter thirteen of Revelation tells us that they construct a new powerful Beast. This is the mythical Seven-Headed-Beast of legend that is remembered around the world. This is the Seven-Headed-Beast we saw on the cylinder seal fighting the Main-Group.

By understanding that this Seven-Headed-Beast is similar to the Great-Red-Dragon in design. Which means it is in essence just another large war-machine. Once you can understand that, the rest of this chapter speaks for itself. You can realize that if one of the seven heads was destroyed or heavily damaged is could somehow repair itself or replace the head very quickly which was unlike any of the other war-machines. Over time, this gives rise to the legendary stories of a multi-headed monster that could re-grow its heads after it was destroyed or cut off. The myths tell us that the destruction of this war-machine was an absolutely epic battle with one individual making the last and final blow to destroy this great beast.

In verse eleven of chapter thirteen we seem to be told of what happened to the lamb that was taken by the Fallen Ones as spoken of in the Dream Vision of Enoch. He appears to become the second Beast that comes *"up out of the earth and had two horns like a lamb and he spake as a dragon."* This lamb then becomes the one remembered as the Antichrist that deceives all of mankind but a small group of true believers. The rest of the chapter tells us the Fallen Ones use the Great-Red-Dragon, the Seven-Headed-Beast, and the one remembered as the Antichrist to convince all that remain to help them launch one last great desperate battle against the Main-Group and their allies. It seems that they used the hope that they could defeat the Main-Group and capture the remaining resources to survive the unfolding death of them all. It is easy to understand how the ones that were not saved would not be hard to convince to go to war against the ones that were going to be saved.

These events lead up to the destruction of what is called the great city of Babylon which is then followed by the great final Battle of Armageddon. With understanding that these events are set against a backdrop of a slow-moving death from the after effects of the impact of the Heaven. It is not hard to imagine how society must be coming apart and creating its own chaos.

At some point before this city of Babylon falls and is destroyed. We are told the Main-Group comes and takes any remaining people to be saved. Soon after this, we are told of how this city of Babylon is destroyed along with all that lived in it. The description given in chapter eighteen and nineteen of the Book of Revelation gives great detail on this destruction and how it happened. In verses seventeen and eighteen in chapter nineteen. They talk of how *"For in one hour so great riches is come to nought. And every shipmaster, and all the company in ships, and sailors, and as many as trade by sea, stood afar off. And cried, when they saw the smoke of her burning, saying, What city is like unto this great city."* In verse twenty-one in the same chapter tells us *"And a mighty angel took up a stone like a great millstone, and cast it into the sea, saying, Thus with violence shall that great city Babylon be thrown down, and shall be found no more at all."*

This is the next piece of the forbidden knowledge. That this great city of Babylon in the Book of Revelation is actually speaking of the destruction of the legendary city of Atlantis. This destruction appears to be the result of the Fallen Ones taking over the city after the Towers or Two-witnesses had been removed. That is why it is remembered as Babylon and not Atlantis. It is because this great city had become corrupted by the Fallen Ones. It is also possible that this city had become their last capital after the Main-Group had left along with the ones that had been saved.

In order to understand this better. It is necessary to realize that word Babylon is not only the name of an ancient city but it also means any society or group in a society considered as corrupt or as a place of exile by another society or group. Once you realize that meaning of the of the word Babylon it is easy to understand why there has been so much confusion about this part of the Book of Revelation. This is not the ancient city of Babylon located in the Middle East. But it is really talking about how the ancient city of Atlantis located in the Americas had become corrupted by the exiled Fallen Ones after the Towers were destroyed and then removed. This is speaking of what happen to the city and not as the city itself. This is why it is remembered as corrupted or Babylon and not as Atlantis.

This then leads to the final Battle of Armageddon and the destruction of the Fallen and their allies. The details to the events surrounding this battle are told in chapter nineteen of the Book of Revelation. This is also the final battle spoken of in the Dream Vision and the '*great sword*' that was given to the "sheep". We now know that this great sword was most likely the great war-machine and monster remembered as Behemoth. Verses eleven though sixteen in chapter nineteen give us a very symbolic description of this great sword and a rather anti-climactic finish to the battle leading to the final judgment.

The Book of Revelation and the Dream Vision of Enoch have the same basic story of the Fallen Ones and their allies being captured and put on trial for their crimes and sins. They are all judged guilty of their crimes against the Lord-God and their crimes against man and beast. The Fallen Stars or Watchers are the first to judged and punished. Their punishment is eternal damnation and punishment in a prison of fire and brimstone. The shepherds and their companions suffer the same fate of imprisonment and damnation as the Fallen Stars. The human followers of the Fallen Ones suffer a slightly different fate where they are just burnt alive in a large pit and not imprisoned. This punishment and imprisonment of the Fallen Angels is recorded in the Book of Enoch and the Biblical tradition. It is highly probable this is the origin of the idea of an eternal punishment for the dammed in a realm of fire or more famously as Hell, Hades, or sometimes as Tartarus.

Enoch and the Bible tell us that after this final judgment and punishment a *"New Jerusalem"* or *"new grand house came down from the heavens"* to be among mankind. The main difference between the two stories is when the New Jerusalem comes down from heavens. Enoch states that it happens before the transformation begins and the Bible seems to say it is after this transformation. Within esoteric circles it is believed that the order of events in the Dream Vision of Enoch is the more correct of the two stories. This is another good example of how the esoteric uses these two books together in order to hide and tell this story.

This then leads into another and possibly more important secret of the forbidden knowledge and greater understanding of this knowledge. Which is that all the ancient stories, myths, and legends that speak about or refer to a great and final battle at the end of time between the forces of good and evil that leads to the destruction of earth and a final judgment for all of humanity. Are in fact actually speaking of events that have already taken place. It is not prophecy of what is yet to come but real ancient history of what was. We have forgotten that we have forgotten. This allows us to understand one of the greatest secrets hidden within the symbolism. That we have stories hidden within stories hidden within the ancient symbols that are all telling the same story of this incredibly destructive war.

This then leads us to the logical question about where this New Jerusalem that came down from the heavens could be located? I think logic dictates that they would have located it as far as possible from the impact side. An area that would suffer the least amount due to the climate change from this massive explosion. The best possible location for this would be the Antarctica landmass. This would explain why so much time, money, resources and manpower has been and is still currently spent in Antarctica. I have to wonder what they are looking for or may have found. Could it be related to this New Jerusalem that the Bible speaks of? Although that idea may rely more on faith than science at this point, but you have to admit it would explain a lot of strange stuff that has been claimed over the years about Antarctica.

This then brings us to the time of the great transformation of everybody that had been saved by the Main-Group. This is the remnant that is remembered and becomes the basis for all of us alive today. The Dream Vision tells us that this begins with a single individual human that was transformed back into the original genetic matrix of Neanderthal Man. This individual appears to be a rather special Neanderthal for we are told he had "*large horns*" and that all the others "*feared him and made petition to him all the time.*" I think this is a clue that this Neanderthal Man had a different type of brain. Possibly one designed much like ours This would provide him with greater intellect than the others. Which who help explain why the feared him and petitioned him all the time.

The next step in this phase was to transform the rest of the human-like beings back into this type of Neanderthal. We have to assume this was done by their offspring and not the original beings themselves. The offspring of these new Neanderthals where then genetically modified to only give birth to us, Homo-sapiens-sapiens or modern man. A human being with a large complex brain combined with a lighter much more adaptable body. This was done so we could survive the unfolding destruction and climate change from the impact. I think this great transformation the reason why we have so much junk DNA that does not appear to do anything in our cell. It could be the leftovers of this transformation.

If we return to the Book of Revelation for a moment with this idea in mind. We can realize that the first and second resurrection spoken of in chapter twenty of Revelation is speaking of this transformation that is in the Dream Vision of Enoch. In the Bible we are told that this whole process took one thousand years to complete. This indicates that this was not a quick and easy process to complete as many have traditionally believed. In fact, this one-thousand-year period appears to be more in line with our modern day understanding of genetics and how long it would really take to accomplish something like this. Using this information and the approximate date of 10,800 BC for the destruction. Combined with our knowledge of the 1,300-year Younger Dryas time period. We can estimate that this grand transformation was completed just before the end of the Younger Dryas at around 9,500 BC.

It was at this point that the newly transformed humans were moved around the globe broken into the different groups we are all so familiar with today. This is why we just seem to pop-up out of nowhere approximately 10,000 years ago all over the planet with little to no development. It is also why sites like the Göbekli-Tepe temple site near Sanliurfa, Turkey just seems to be there with nothing known about the people who built it. These were the first of the descendants of the remnant that was saved as they were moved around the world. It also seems to be some of the last signs that the gods were still active in our development.

Then something new happens and all the traditions appear to go silent on these on these gods and their servants. They just seem to just disappear from the story and all contact between them and us comes to an end. Additionally, the ancient traditions also go silent and are of little help in guiding us at this point. Since we have no other sources, we must rely on what we know about the end of the Younger Dryas to give us a possible idea of what may have happened during this dark time.

I think the reason the gods seem to disappear is because of all the ice melting as the Younger Dryas came to an end. As the ice melted there was corresponding rise in sea levels all around the world. According to modern science this rise of sea levels was upwards of 420 feet or 128 meters. This alone makes it highly probable that this sea level rise just cut them off from us. When this is combined with the changes in the weather patterns around the planet it just made it next to impossible for them to interact with our ancestors. Additionally, if the New Jerusalem is located somewhere on the Antarctica landmass. Then we can speculate that as the climate changed and sea levels started rising this New Jerusalem was slowly covered in the ice. It is also possible that they were forced to move their operations underground to avoid the ice or the sea leave rise. This could be the origin of the many stories about a Hollow Earth with a beautiful city at its center or some vast underground Lost World at the ends of the earth.

We know that the Younger Dryas coming to an end was over around 7,500 BC. It is believed that it took around 500 years for all the ice to melt causing the sea level rise and the general chaos of the large local flooding that occurred during this time. This knowledge gives us a clue that our ancestors were on their own for possibly the very first time in all of human history. These events of the destruction, the coming of cold and ice, and then the large local flooding when the ice melted are where the stories of the different worlds being destroyed and then being reborn that are remembered by many native cultures and traditions around the world most likely come from. This is our first clue that the Mesoamerican cultures and traditions pick up the next part of the story.

There are a number of Mesoamerican traditions that speak of the time after the ice melted for the last time and the world settle into the form we see and know so well today. These traditions provide us with a possible clue to what might have happened to these advanced beings once the ice had melted. Most of the traditions that have survived speak of a great man coming from the sea after the last round of flooding and trying to teach mankind about civilization.

One of the stranger facts about this great man is how he is normally described as an older white man with grey hair looking like a grandfatherly type figure. He is also said to have had great knowledge and divine powers at his command. Many traditions say that when this man was threatened, he could call down fire from the sky that would shield him. At other times it was used as a weapon against those who threatened him.

It has been argued by many other researchers that this mysterious individual could be a survivor of a lost civilization, normally Atlantis. Which, based on what we have learned, this idea is basically correct. But, as we can now realize, it is highly probable that this individual was not just any old survivor of the Main-Group. I think it is more likely this individual was the leader of the Main-Group, the one recorded and remember as the Lord-God in the Bible or the Lord of the sheep in the Dream Vision. The many references to this individual always coming and going by sea are another clue to his identity. All around the world we have very similar ancient stories of a great individual coming from the sea to teach mankind about civilization. Surprisingly enough, a great number of them describe him using a great sea going beast that seem so similar to the great monster of the sea like Leviathan.

These same traditions tell us that this individual found our ancestors at such a low level of understanding and technology that he spent vast majority of his time just trying to provide them with most basic education while trying to lift them up out such a primitive state. What exactly his motives were and what his true goal was at this time appears to be lost to history. But it is possible that this individual was making one last ditch attempt to make sure they were not totally forgotten. He could have also been trying to reestablish a new civilization where we would worship them as gods once again. According the accounts, this was not to be, because it appears that the grand transformation had worked to well and our ancestors no longer perceive him as a god but only a man with great god-like power.

Based upon the ancient accounts, it appears that this individual slowly moved his way around the globe teaching mankind the knowledge of civilization. Remarkably, once he had educated the people, he then disappears from the stories and from history. It seems that when he left, he would say the same words of how he would one day return. But, alas, it appears that he never returned. This also appears to the last bit of open contact that our ancestors had with gods.

This disappearance raises a couple of different possibilities on what many happened to this mysterious individual and the gods in general. The first one is rather straight forward and that he just returned to their hiding spot at the bottom of the world and have never publicly made themselves known ever since. This could be due to the fact that we would not perceive them as gods or angels, but only as highly advance human-like creatures like ourselves. Additionally, based upon our history, it is possible that we might be a great danger to them.

The second possibility is that legendary Leviathan had catastrophic failure and is sitting on the bottom of the ocean somewhere. This possible failure could have killed everybody on board and the simple fact is that they could all be dead. It is also possible that they could have survived such a failure and made their way back home. The key point is that they just do not have the means to move out like before. I also do not think it is likely they left the planet simply because they do not have the means to leave since the destruction of the Heaven.

As we say, the events surrounding this mysterious individual happened sometime around 7,500 BC. It is hinted at in the writings by many followers of the different schools of esoteric thought that the time period between the great destruction at about 10,800 BC to the founding of what we are taught are the first civilizations at around 3,500 to 3,000 BC was a great dark-age of ignorance for humanity.

Modern history gives us the reason on the rediscovery of the ancient world and the founding of the first civilizations of first Ancient Sumer and then a little later Egypt came to be. They teach that when the climate started to change around 5,000 to 4,000 BC and people started to move out of the areas that they were living in. These people in time found and entered into the river valleys of the Tigris and Euphrates in the Middle East along with the Nile River in Egypt. This also happened at other important places around the world at about the same time. The final push of this migration due to climate change appears to have happened around 4,000 to 3,500 BC.

As our ancestors began to be forced to move into the river valleys, they found the ruins, remnants and fragments of these ancient civilizations. As people started to explore the ruins, they found books filled with knowledge and items of ancient technology that had survived the destruction so long ago. It is not hard to imagine how books and pieces of technology could survive such a great destruction only to found hundreds if not thousands of years later by others that had completely forgotten about it all.

It is also not very hard to imagine how the use of this ancient knowledge and possible lost technology would allow certain individuals and their families to come to power and influence so much of society. This also explains the mystery of how a simple tribal people went from a such a primitive way of life to building massive monuments reaching such a high level of civilization in less than a hundred years. This explains why our own modern priesthoods have always had so much power and influence on society and governments. It is most likely because they were the people who found this knowledge and technology along with the stories about all the ancient civilizations.

It is easy to understand that the individuals that found this knowledge used it to become the founders and leaders of modern-day priesthoods. The secret of this knowledge has been passed down through their families for the last few thousand years, right until our own day. These 'ancient' families that become the foundation of the priesthoods are the origin of the different esoteric schools of thought and holders of occult knowledge. In time, these become the mystery schools and religions that so many of us have heard and read about. These mystery religions have survived into our own time with Freemasonry and their Lodges being the best known to the general public.

Once again, it is easy to understand how the use of this knowledge and ancient technology that the early priesthoods where able to control or heavily influence most governments of the world over the last thousand or so years. It also makes it easy to understand why religion and government are so closely related and dependent on each other over the years. It is because the governments needed the knowledge and the technology that only the priesthoods possessed. These priesthoods would only grant use of if it, if and only if, the king or government did what they said. This is the origin of all the stories about holy relics or artifacts or any item that had magical qualities associated with it. These were not actually magical or holy artifacts and relics, but it is most likely advanced technology that had somehow survived the destruction and the many thousands of years of time since then.

This is one of most important conflicts that has been going on for the last few thousand years behind the scenes between governments, religions, and secret societies. They are in essence all fighting over this ancient knowledge, technology, and the mythology that hides the truth from the general public. It is this knowledge and the conflict over it that ultimately gives it life and power.

It is this conflict over this ancient knowledge, technology, and the mythology is the reason for all the weird and strange stories you have ever heard in your life. Every single story, artifact, relic, powerful weapon, legend, myth, rumor, whisper and general concept or idea that has mystical, magical, divine or alien powers associated with it. Has something to do with this ancient knowledge and technology along with the never-ending conflict over it. Additionally, the ones that have been and are currently fighting over this knowledge go to great lengths to keep this information from the general population.

All of this allows us to finally understand how these ancient stories and mythology are modified to fit into our modern timeline. A timeline that is built around the Middle Age religious idea that our world is only six to ten thousand years old. Not only has the timeline been built into this idea but many of the stories have been selectively edited to present mystery when none actually exists.

I will use the Exodus story to show how this was done. Within our modern timeline we are told much of the early stories in the Bible are said to have their historical starting point at around 2,000 BC to 1,800 BC after the fall of city state of Ur. Based on our new understanding of when the Exodus most likely happened around 32,000 BC, we can get a rough idea of how the ancient timeline has been shorted. Remarkably, we know who these new nomadic people were and what they were called, the Hyksos. The ancient Egyptians called these people 'Apiru' which meant 'wanderer.' These are the forerunners of the ancient people who are remembered as the Hebrew people. In time they will become known as the Jews.

Interesting enough, both the Bible and the history tell us that these Apiru people found something in the vast area of the Middle East they wandered through. It has been debated on what exactly they found, but there is no doubt that it was powerful enough that allowed a number of simple nomadic and semi-nomadic tribes that were politically, economically and militarily powerless, to unite. Soon after they had united into one group then quickly conquered the world's only real super power at the time, Ancient Egypt around 1,785 BC on the modern timeline.

Not only did these people conquer Egypt, but they took over all of the existing social systems and bureaucracy. All while maintaining everything with little to no change to society as a whole for almost 200 years. It was not until the Eighteenth Dynasty that the Egyptians evicted the Hyksos in a war of peoples. This was the start of the Kew Kingdom, whose first great success was to follow up the victory over the Hyksos in Egypt in the years after 1,570 BC by pursuing the Hyksos out their strongholds in south Canaan. In the end, the Egyptians occupied much of Syria and Palestine for the next couple of centuries. [1]

It was because of this occupation that what is now remembered to be the 13 tribes of the Apiru could not return to the land of Canaan until the 12th Century BC. This is also the origin of the occult idea of the original 13 bloodlines that many believe are the real power behind everything. This is also one of the first changes made to the story and an example of how it has been done.

The original story had 13 tribes of the Apiru. Over time, one tribe is removed, but not removed. This is the first change with one tribe being changed into a tribe of priests that would own no land or have title. Two of the other tribes eventually settle in the Land of Canaan and tend to be forgotten about. Although we know the other ten tribes settled their lots of land, we are always told these tribes somehow become lost. With the much later event of the Kingship of these tribes collapsing and opening them up to invasion as being the primary reason for them being lost. But the truth is they were never lost or missing, it is just a poor retelling of the story to help confuse people. Much like how the story of Noah confuses the true meaning of the animal symbolism.

The next part of the story is where the real confusion begins. Modern scholars claim that First Temple of Solomon was built in the time period around the 10th Century BC. They also claim that its destruction was during the 6th Century BC. They then claim its rebuilding occurred sometime during the 5th and 4th Centuries BC. Within the esoteric, we have seen on the cylinder seals that it is more likely these events happen between 20,000 BC to around 14,000 BC. Remarkably, modern science also places the founding of most all other traditions like Buddhism, Confucianism, and even Hindu belief at around the same time as the rebuilding of King Solomon's Temple.

The next step in recovering this lost history was when Christianity was rediscovered. It is thought within some schools of the esoteric that about 2,300 or so years ago or around 300 to 200 BC based on our modern calendar. A number of ancient stories and documents were found in and around the areas of Jerusalem, Alexandra, and most importantly Rome.

These ancient stories and documents are rumored to be the original sources for all the books that make up Western Christianity and much of modern Jewish belief. This is also when the Book of Enoch was found with many other texts that was later rejected by the Catholic Church. These documents and possibly even technology become the basis for a large number of different mystery religions that begin at this time in addition to Christianity. This should also allow you to begin to understand why these cities has always been so important to everybody over the two thousand years. It is because these are the places where the documents, holy books, and knowledge were found.

Remarkably, some of these mysterious ancient documents and books were not rediscovered until the twentieth century. These were of course the famous Dead Sea Scrolls written by the equally mysterious people known as the Essene that lived at Qumran in Israel. It is believed by many in the esoteric religion that the Essene were trying to preserve this knowledge. This is one of the reasons why the majority of the Dead Sea Scrolls have been off limits to the lay person, that is until very recently. But even then, you need to be versed in ancient languages to properly interpret them.

This allow us to understand why there are small differences between the New Testament stories and the ones contained in the Dead Sea Scrolls. It also allows us to understand why religious scholars have been so protective of them. It is because they can show people many of the changes that have been made to not just to text but in many cases the meaning of the stories changes too. This could be why the Essene went to such lengths to hide these scrolls in caves. Lucky for us they did, because as we all know the early Fathers of the Catholic Church most likely would have destroyed or hidden them away from the public if they had been the ones to find them. The heretics that became known as the Gnostics and their writings are the most famous example of the early Catholic Church going out of its way to destroy competing ideas.

The next important series of events we need to look at is the Crusades. The Crusades started around 1095 and lasted until 1270 AD. It was during this time that the Catholic Church was able to raise large armies of the faithful and launch a total of eight Crusades to retake the Holy Land from the unbelievers. There are many different reasons given for the cause of the Crusades and why it was so important to retake the Holy Land from the Muslims. The only one you have most likely not heard of before is the esoteric reason for the Crusades. It will give you a much greater understanding of how all of this relates to our own world of today.

The esoteric reason for the Crusades is a rather simple one in light of everything else. It was because the Church thought that there might be more hidden knowledge or possibly even technology or as they would likely call 'holy relics' in the ancient city of Jerusalem. It is likely that the Church Fathers of the time realized that the Muslims or followers of Islam were also based on the same stories as their own. Historically, Islam is believed to have been founded by a man named Mohammed in the seventh century. Which, based upon what we have learned, this modern idea of Islam being founded only fourteen-hundred years ago must be incorrect. But, the Church Fathers of this time must have realized that when the Muslims took over Jerusalem they might find more of this knowledge or relics and use it against them. It does not take much imagination that this would be completely unacceptable to the Fathers of the Catholic Church. The result was almost two centuries of warfare and countless deaths based on a lie to save the holy land and sites from the unbelievers. Not to mention they would also have their sins forgiven by killing the infidels.

It was during this time that the ever-famous Knights Templar enter the story. It is also claimed that that during their time at the Temple Mount in Jerusalem they did many excavations under the site. Supposedly they unearthed treasures that have fueled speculation and conspiracy theories for centuries. It is claimed that whatever they found under the Temple Mount was of such great importance that it allowed these Poor Knights of King Solomon's Temple to quickly grow from a small handful of nine older men to one of the largest and most powerful sects of warrior monks the world has ever seen. It has also given rise to hundreds of tales, stories, myths, and legends that surround these mysterious Knights.

What exactly the Knights Templar found under the Temple Mount has been debated for centuries. It has been rumored to be any number of different holy artifacts with the Holy Grail, the Ark of the Covenant, the True Cross, or the Spear of Destiny being some of the more popular items proposed. In the last few decades, it has been put forward that they found documents about Jesus Christ and his possible children. It does seem like that about every Christian or Jewish religious artifact that you can think of has been claimed to have been found by this group.

I think based upon the available evidence of the last 800 years and all stories, legends, myths and claims made about the founding members of the Knights Templar. It is fair to day that they must have found something under the Temple Mount. Although it is highly probable that they actually found something of great importance, nobody seems to know exactly what it was. But there is no denying that whatever it was, it was important enough that it gave rise to all numerous myths, legends, and conspiracies that are still being told and talked about to this very day.

Like everybody else who has ever thought about the Knights Templers. I have wondered what they could have found under the Temple Mount all those years ago. What could have they found that would give nine middle aged men so much power in such a short amount of time?

If this esoteric story of creation we have been exploring is correct. Then I think it would be a fair guess to say that they most probably found some type of technology that still worked. Not only did it still work but somehow, they were able to figure out how to operate it and use it for their gain. Although it is a mystery to what they might have found, but if it was some type of high technology, I think we might be able to figure out what it was based on a clue that might answer one of biggest questions about the Knights Templar.

As I have researched the Knights Templar over the years reading the many stories, myths, legends, and conspiracies that surround them. I have always tried to keep an eye out for anything that sounded like it could actually be technology. What I mean is, real technology, technology that we ourselves could design, engineer, and build. I do not mean something like the Ark of the Covent, the

Holy Grail, or similar items that seem to only have strange stories about weird powers and abilities that sound magical or God-like that could or could not be based in science. At the moment, these types of objects lie in that hazy realm between fact and legend. A place where your own personal faith and beliefs rule on what is real and not real.

While reading all the stories I could find about the Knights Templars, I found one that at least to me seemed to stand out from all the others. This little story I will shorty recount to you, probably should not really be called a legend or even a myth. In fact, this story could be much more modern and only loosely based on history. The reason I say this, is because I have not been able to find out where this story originally came from. It is possible that this story may have originated in only the last few decades. It appears to be pieced together from a number of different stories and claims about the Knights Templar. Some of which are old while others are clearly more recent. Some parts are based in fact while other parts do not seem to be real at all. Additionally, there does not appear any actual evidence to back much of it up, just like any good story.

This story of what the Knights Templar might have found goes something like this: It is said that the original founding members of the Knights Templar were digging under the Temple Mount and that they did find something. It is just not what everybody else thinks. It is said that they did not find any ancient holy relics, religious artifacts, and certainly no documents about Jesus Christ. It is said they only actually found one thing in all their nine or so years of digging.

This one thing they found was a said to be a human head that had magical or divine powers associated with it. Many have claimed that this head was the head of John the Baptist and the highest parts of the leadership of the Templers worshiped this head. It is also claimed that the worship of this head was one of the blasphemies that was used against the Templers that led to their almost total destruction and forced them deep underground and hiding. This claim of blasphemy of the Templars worshipping a Head of some type is the only part that appears to be based on any fact. Even if the claim seems made up by the Templars accusers, it has always remained a mystery to researchers over the years if it was true or not.

I have often wondered if there could be anything to this claim about a mysterious Head that was worshipped by the highest parts of the Templar leadership. One of the reasons it has stood out to me is because worshipping a Head is rather odd and rare practice, especially in Western Christianity. Although body parts of Saints are commonly found in Churches where they are placed in a reliquary for veneration, which is not a form of worship. What is a reliquary? It is a container designed to hold and display the relics of a saint. Since the very idea of worship of a body part, especially a Head, is out of the question, it naturally raises the question of where did this idea come from? As I researched this over the years, I found another legend that could answer what this Head was or is. It could also answer why it could give the ones that had found it so much power.

This other legend of a mysterious Head is none other than the myths about the almost legendary Bronze or Brazen Head of the ancient world. The Bronze Head is said to be a prophetic device that was used by almost all the great prophets and seers of the ancient world. It has been attributed to many Medieval scholars who were believed by many to be wizard-like or great wise men that were able to answer any question.

In all the different stories of the Bronze Head, both ancient and modern, it is always in the form of a man's head like a bust made out of a bronze-like metal. It is also always said that this Bronze Head could answer any question that was asked of it. Depending on the story, the Head is sometimes describe as being mechanical in nature, although descriptions of it being more magical-like are more common.

All the stories agree it would answer questions that were presented to it. Although there seems to be a great difference of opinion in the stories of how it would answer. In a few stories it would answer freely of any question asked of it. In other stories it is restricted to a simple yes or no answer. While in other stories it is claimed that you had to give something, like an offering, or the individual would have to perform some type of task for the Head before it would answer the question. There are a few modern ones in which the Head could or would decide whether or not to answer your question. It should also be noted that there are a few comical versions that portray the Head as having quite the attitude problem with it auguring with everybody it comes into contact with. In these, if the Head did not care for you, it would not answer questions or would just give you the wrong answer to run you in circles.

Although these stories, myths, and even legends about a Bronze Head that could answer any question posed to it might be a bit unfamiliar and even a little on the strange side of things to many. But when added to the claim that the upper leadership of the Knights Templers were possibly worshipping a Head of some type. All of a sudden you can realize that the legendary Bronze Head might be what the Knights Templar may have found under the Temple Mount. Additionally, it would help explain so much about this group and how it turned into such a powerhouse so quickly.

Because, if the founding members of the Knights Templar did in fact find a legendary Bronze Head and it could answer any question. Then it is rather easy to realize they were not 'worshipping it' but it is more likely they were using it and asking it questions. This of course would take place in secret from prying eye as not to let the cat out of the bag as the old saying goes. Over time this alone would explain where the claim of them worshipping a Head could have come from. This secret ceremony would be their main source of knowledge and information which in turn gave the Templers their power. It was having access to this Bronze Head that could answer any question that allowed them to acquire so much wealth and influence is such a short amount of time after returning from Jerusalem. This would also help provide a reason why they were eventually destroyed.

It is not hard to understand that if the King of France, Phillip IV and Pope Clement of Rome had discovered that the Templars had a Bronze Head through their network of spies and paid informants. That both of these greedy power-hungry men would go out of their way to destroy the Knights Templar by any means necessary to gain control of such an item. Since neither of men were stupid and both wanted the same thing, they worked together to destroy the Templers and retrieve the Bronze Head for themselves.

We know from history, neither man was successful in retrieving anything of real value from the Templers. There was no treasure, no documents, with only a small handful of questionable religious artifacts being found and certainly no Bronze Head. The whole affair only seems to have succeeded in destroying most of the banking system Knights Templars had established and much of the economic structure of Europe that depended on it while driving the rest of the Templars into hiding. Only the Knights Templar that survived and escaped this destruction know what really happened to any of their treasure or other items if they really had them at all.

I cannot help but wonder that if something like this was is true. Then both the King Phillip IV and Pope Clement would have been plotting and planning to destroy the other one as soon as they could once they had their hands on this object. I think it would have made the last eight hundred years of history play out much differently than it has.

It is out of the ashes of this destruction of the Knights Templar with a bit of modern conspiracy theory thrown in that the rest of this idea comes from. It is said that through the twists and turns of history with the help of unseen hands that this Bronze Head finds its way into the possession of Sir Francis Bacon (1561-1629). The English philosopher, statesman, scientist, lawyer, author and pioneer of the scientific method. The conspiracy theory says that the Bronze Head is how Sir Francis Bacon was able to accomplish so much in his life. The story points to his 1623 book New Atlantis (released in 1627) with all the aspirations, ideals and possibilities of an ideal land and society on an island it held.

This idea is clearly open to debate on many levels, but the idea that Sir Francis Bacon may have had access to advanced technology like the Bronze Head does make a certain type of sense and has a strange logic to it all. There is no doubt that he would have been intelligent enough to have been able to figure out how to use something like a Bronze Head. In fact, in everything I have ever read on the man, I think he would have been smart enough to actually figure out that it was a piece of technology and possibly even some of the basic science behind it. Unfortunately, all the current evidence supports the idea that Sir Francis Bacon was quite able to do everything he did without any outside help from a legendary Bronze Head.

The conspiracy theory then goes to say that after the death of Sir Francis Bacon in 1629 this Bronze Head somehow makes its way into what will become the first Lodges of Freemasonry. It is also believed that the Freemasons still have it today hidden someplace. Outside of the Bronze Head, this part of the story is true. It is well known and documented that Sir Francis Bacon was either a member or had close ties to many secret societies, including, but not limited to Rosicrucianism and the Temple of the Rosy Cross, the Royal Society, and the many different groups that would become Freemasonry in 1717.

As you can see, this story or even conspiracy theory has very little to back it up. Never the less, this idea of a Bronze Head and the legend that surrounds it is very intriguing. So much so, that this is the reason I said this could be a clue to real technology that could be at the heart of this mystery and so many more.

Although this story has very little to back it up, every single aspect of the Bronze Head from ancient, medieval, and modern sources describes it as being very mechanical like when it answering questions. Even the more magical descriptions of this Head also sound mechanical or technological in origin. Much like if you were talking to or interfacing with a highly sophisticated intelligent computer system that could respond to verbal commands. This is why I think this might be a clue that we might be dealing with real technology. Because we could actually build a computer system with all the exact same capabilities that the legends and stories describe about a Bronze Head.

There are only three questions about building something like a Bronze Head. One would be the amount of processing power that would be needed. Two, would be how large the storage medium would need to be. With number three being what type of long-lived stable power source would you use to power it. The only real problem would be the power source. Unless the power source it nuclear, I find it hard to envision what type of power source could actually be stable and long lasting enough to survive for thousands of years. Especially if it still had power after almost 12,000 years of sitting in the dirt.

This problem of a power source may finally have a solution and may provide a solution to many other ancient stories about magical or holy objects and how they could have been powered. In the early twenty first century it has been discovered that particular metal alloys that can produce electricity when heated. There has been ongoing research and development to try and understand if this can be developed into a practical power source for small electronics and a possible future replacement for batteries.

This discovery of metal alloys that can produce electrical energy when heated could be the answer to the power source for the Bronze Head. It could also be a clue that is how some of this ancient lost technology was powered. If this Bronze Head along with other similar magical artifacts are actually technology based on electricity being generated by heating metal. Then it is very easy to understand how everybody up until our own time could and would most likely view these items as magical or powerful in some strange way.

It would also help provide an explanation for why somebody went to all the trouble to invent and then make a number of Bagdad Batteries thousands of years before the discovery of electricity. Not to mention the mathematical understanding that is needed to use it properly. We can speculate they might have learned how to create batteries from the technology itself. They might have been forced to make them when the primary power source failed. It would provide an ingenious solution to the problem if true.

Simple electricity would look like magic to anyone who does not understand what it is. Even in our modern age that is completely dependent upon electricity terrifies many people. It is not uncommon for people to view electricity in a kind of mystical or magical way. Over the years I have met and talked to many people, many who have higher education that truly believe that electricity is some type of magic and that we really do not understand how it works. This idea has always blown my mind and could not be farther from the truth. If for no other reason than it is the basis of our whole modern world of technology. If people of our own day and age do not or cannot understand the basic ideas and principles behind the most widely used technology, they themselves use every single day. How could we think anybody who lived before our modern time would have any idea or understanding of what they were experiencing and not think it was not magic or divine power in some way?

Because the hard truth is that only advanced electrical based technology, like our own, looks and acts like magic, nothing else does. Only electro-magnetic fields can move stuff around without touching it and only releases of electrical energy could produce many of the effects that are recorded in many ancient stories. It is only things like video technology like TV's and computer screens that can look and act like 'sprits' or 'demons' in magical mirrors. Common sense and logic dictate that it is highly probable that all the ancient stories, myths and legends are actually speaking of technology that appears too much like our own. This realization gives us a possible idea of the level of technology we could be dealing with and give us an insight into the Bronze Head.

If this way of thinking is correct, then it would mean that the Bronze Head would have a large data base of information of general knowledge. If this technology is very close to our level of technology or just a little bit ahead. I think it would be in a simple to use format and very user friendly. If this was technology that was left by the gods. Then it would be easy to understand how and why something like the Bronze Head this would be so easy to use. I would think that it would have to rather strong and well-built to survive the day-to-day use of people handling it while asking questions or advice from it. It would make sense that a bronze like metal would be used given the level of human metal technology so it could be patched up as needed. It is also easy to imagine how this technology would be given to certain people and become the basis for many stories about oracles or wise men that could answer your questions to the gods.

Could this idea of a Bronze Head be true? Is there any possible evidence that could back up this crazy little story in any way or does it have to stay firmly in the realm of fantasy and conspiracy? There are many that would say that there is not any evidence at all to support this idea in any way shape or form. But as we have seen throughout our journey the true story is hidden within the esoteric symbols. With knowing how the followers of the esoteric like to present all the little pieces of the story in their symbolic artwork. Remarkably, there does appear to an old drawing that could be showing us this Bronze Head. There is Masonic print from 1741 that appears to clearly show this Bronze or Brazen Head of legend. When compared with everything else we have learned about the esoteric symbolism, it is very difficult to not think this is a picture of the ever-mysterious Bronze Head of legend.

The next important fact related to the Knights Templar that cannot be forgotten. Is that out of the destruction and ashes of the Knights Templar. The beginnings of modern-day esoteric thought including Freemasonry can trance their origin. This link is also claimed by the Freemasons and all the esoteric groups that I am aware of. This then brings us back to the symbols and the story that they tell and a possible greater understanding of the ideas behind them.

It is only when you begin to understand the story that is at the core of the esoteric symbolism. That you can begin to understand the belief that surrounds it. This story of creation is one of the big secrets of the esoteric and occult belief systems. This is the story the followers both hide and tell you at the same time. This is the story that both major religions of the world and the secret societies have been using to confuse and frighten everybody over the centuries.

Frontispiece of The Builder Jewel with masonic symbols. (1741) (Fig.8) [12]

Although this version of the forbidden knowledge is lacking some details and has its fair share of speciation and problems. It should give you a good if rather rough idea of the story that makes up much of the forbidden knowledge as a whole. It should also give you a very good idea of how this story is told through the esoteric symbolism and hidden in plain sight.

This new understand should also help provide a new context for almost all the stories in the Biblical tradition among others. This fact alone brings new meaning to the stories in the Old and New Testaments of the Bible. It helps by providing some context of the world these people lived in. If nothing else, it is fascinating and thought provoking just to ponder the possibilities.

This new understanding also allows us to fill in many of the strange gaps and the vague reasons given for much of our own history. For example, with knowing which parts of the story is missing. We can quickly realize why the Catholic Church and the Western governments were so destructive to the Mesoamerica cultures and people when they came into contact with them. The Catholic Church quickly realized that the cultures of Mesoamerica remembered the time of the shepherds and more importantly, the great destruction. Two of the most important parts of the story that they have being hiding from everybody. This is why these people and more importantly their culture had to be destroyed without mercy. They had the part of the story that would take away all the power away for the leaders of the Catholic Church and much of the Western world. This is why the books were burned, the buildings and temples destroyed, and the hundreds of thousands of people that were slaughtered in the name of God and his Son. Every piece of it was and is a threat to the powers that be and the lie they all tell.

This brings us to one of the biggest questions of all; is any of this really true? Ultimately that is up to you to decide, based on your own personal knowledge, ideas, questions, ideals, feelings, beliefs and probably the most important, your own faith. But as you wonder about this forbidden knowledge and ponder all its possible implications. There are few things to always keeping the back of your mind when thinking about this subject matter.

The first is the fact that given enough time the stars themselves slowly move and change position in the night-sky. This means that the night-sky we see today is not the same night-sky our ancestors looked upon. I think I have presented a solid idea and argument for the shapes of the Great Pyramid of the Giza Plateau and the Pyramid of the Sun in Mexico are based on the positions of the stars Betelgeuse, Rigel, Aldebaran, Pollux and possibly even the star Bellatrix in the night-sky. At a time far beyond what anybody else has ever thought or even proposed over the years. I also think I have provided a good argument that the Great Pyramid was originally built to be a monument to the enormous event of the great Lord of Light coming to earth after he had freed mankind from slavery.

This Lord of Light and his fellow gods not only brought freedom but they also brought enlightenment to humanity with the knowledge of civilization. Much of the mathematical knowledge is actually built into the Great Pyramid itself while also being a monument to the unbelievable event of the Lord of Light coming to earth. After thousands of years, this grand event slowly changes into and remembered in the Biblical tradition as the fall of Lucifer and his fellow Watchers which began the corruption of man and his fall from grace.

The next fact is that the ancient cylinder seals of the many different cultures from the Middle East clearly show the story of the Dream Vision as told in the Book of Enoch. This is one thing that everyone has missed, that this entire story appears to be told in little symbolic pictures on the ancient cylinder seals. As you have seen, these scenes show the same animals as spoken of in the Dream Vision of Enoch doing the very things as described in the stories. I think there is much more information and detail about this story contained on the cylinder seals. This would also be one of the best places to start looking for more ideas and information.

The next fact is that these same said cylinder seals also show the Pleiades cluster of stars in many different configurations and with different numbers of stars shown. It is clear that these cylinder seal are actually showing the changes of the Pleiades cluster of stars as they moved over time. They also give us a good idea of which stars could be seen with the naked-eye allowing us to use this as a method to date these events. Given the long amount of time that is needed for the stars move as much as shown on the cylinder seals. This is clearly evidence that the events spoken of in the Dream Vision and the Bible took place tens of thousands of years ago and not in the last five or six thousand years as claimed by main stream science. This raises a number of questions about the dates and the dating that modern science claims for all these events. I will let you wonder about that part and why they might be lying to us.

The next to last fact to keep mind is the one of the almost unbelievable and catastrophic destruction that occurred approximately 13,000 years ago on this planet. The evidence of this destruction and the path of death that it left are well documented. An event that is hotly debated by many scholars and experts, right down to the everyday person on the street on what could have caused all this death destruction and climate changes on the earth? Was it an impact? Was it a volcano or earthquakes? Was it Pole shift? Was it nuclear war? Was it a war between the gods? Was it aliens? Was it something else? We may never really know what exactly happened all those years ago. But the ancient stories appear to tells us that once long ago it was as if hell itself came to earth. A time of war and destruction on a level unseen until our modern age.

The next fact is always important to remember and should never be left out. It is the simple fact that this whole story is told through the esoteric symbols that everyone is bombarded with in a never ending twenty-four hour seven days a week cycle. It is beyond all doubt that these esoteric symbols and the story they tell can be traced directly to Freemasonry among a few other secret societies. These symbols in our modern world originate from, are used by, lead to, and are about the story that is at the heart of, the esoteric and occult belief system all seem to lead back Freemasonry and their Lodges.

This raises the next question of why are they doing this? Why are they bombarding us day and night with these symbols and this story and at the exact same time they are denying, debunking, and lying about it all while trying to confuse everybody at the same time? I mean I can truly understand why something like this could and would need to be kept secret from the general public. But that does not explain why anyone would go through the trouble to you tell this story through the symbolism while denying it at the same time. What is the propose in doing this? We will look at these and many other things in the next chapter.

Chapter 14

The Gates of Tomorrow

None are more helplessly enslaved than those who falsely believe they are free
~Johann W. Von Goethe~

The true mystery of the world is the visible, not the invisible
~Oscar Wilde~

I n order to understand why we are bombarded every single day with all the esoteric symbolism and the story it tells. We must explore one last piece to this this strange puzzle. This last piece we will explore is like all the others we have examined with the fact that it appears to have been overlooked by the vast majority of people. I think the best way to explain this part to you is to explain how I stumbled upon it.

This part begins approximately a year or so before I started writing this book. I was half-heartedly doing a little research on the internet about the occult and Freemasonry. I was not really looking for anything special. But I was having a rather good laugh at some of the claims made by a number of conspiracy websites. As I was surfing around the net and not really finding anything new or insightful. I came across a rather obscure conspiracy website that made all the same old claims about the New-World-Order, UFOs, and grand conspiracies that contained all the same old far-out claims with the same pictures as dozens of other sites on the subject.

As I poked around the site, I quickly found that there was nothing different about this site than the hundreds, if not thousands I have seen over the years. Before I left the site, I thought I would take a moment and read a few of the comments that other people had left about the site. Even the comments were the same similar comments seen on so many other conspiracy sites. Some people praised it while others hated it, with the rest being all over the place not saying much of anything. But remarkably, it was in this comment section of a website I cannot even remember its name that I found a comment that claimed that some obscure book that I had never heard of before was somehow connected to the whole idea of a grand worldwide conspiracy to take over the world by secret societies. The obscure book and author that was mentioned in the comment was "The Politics of Experience" by Dr. Ronald D. Laing.

Since I had never heard of the book or the author before. I did what anybody else would do in our modern age, I begin looking for it on the internet. In the course of my quest, I found a large amount of people talking about Dr. Ronald D. Laing and a great number of websites selling the book. But I could not really find any information about the book itself or much of anything about the author. I found a few pictures of the cover art on the book that contained many esoteric symbols like the All-Seeing-Eye within a triangle shape along with others. Outside of a bit of esoteric symbolism, I could not find much of anything that would lead me to believe this book was important to anybody, much less have anything to do with a grand conspiracy to take over the world.

As I about to give up my search I came across the website for "The International R.D. Laing Institute" that was founded in two-thousand-and-four, fifteen years after his death. Although the website provided general information about the Institute in provided little on Dr. Laing. The only bit of real information I could gleam from the website about Dr. Laing was that he was seen as an important figure of the anti-psychiatry moment that started in the early nineteen sixties. It also appears that he had some very strange ideas about schizophrenia and he basically rejected most of the modern medical models of mental illness of the time and how to treat it. As for the website for the Institute itself, it does have all the normal esoteric symbolism we have explored, but it does not seem to be related in any manner to any grand conspiracy.

As a whole, my internet search did not turn up much of anything of value. I just could not see how this rather obscure psychiatrist that died in nineteen-eighty-nine could be related too much of anything outside of the world of psychiatry. Except for some esoteric symbolism on a website created by group fifteen years after his death and the cover art of his book. It all appeared to be little more than a dead end with little chance of finding anything of importance.

Although it all appeared to a dead end in the conspiracy department, I did want to read the book. Over the next few weeks, I tried to find the book in my local library, which they did not have. All the local book stores in the area also did not have it. Even online, I found it difficult to find a complete copy of the book in print with only used copies seemly available in the United States at the time.

Remarkably, the next day I discovered my wife actually had a copy of this book that she picked up while she was attending college for her degree. Not only did she have the book, but it was a copy of the third printing from nineteen-sixty-nine. Which was before any changes were made to the book as new information and data about schizophrenia came to light during the seventies and nineteen-eighties. It was quite the stroke of luck on my part that my wife had this book. Because it turned out this book was the key to a greater understand of how these different ideas fit together.

As I read this book, I begin to find that it was one of the most interesting books I have ever read. It basically provides the whole psychological aspect and purpose behind all of this symbolism. It also provides the reason why we are bombarded with this symbolism in a never-ending cycle. The book does not come right out a say it, but it does give the psychological reasoning that is behind it all. In many ways it is a textbook of the what, when, where, why, and how to psychologically manipulate and exploit people in order to control their behavior.

The book was put together from a series of lectures that Dr. Laing gave through the nineteen sixties. In many ways it has the aspect of a textbook when you look at the concepts and ideas that are presented in the text. I think this could be one of the primary books that are given to many of the people that will become politicians, media personalities, or other similar individuals that deal with the public through the university system clearly influenced by the esoteric knowledge. The reason I say this is because this book appears to contain a number of ideas and concepts that allow you to learn how to say something, without saying anything. These ideas and concepts are all very familiar sounding when looked at from the perspective of what the vast majority of politicians and spoke-people of many different governments have said since the nineteen seventies.

The trick seems to be the old subject-verb-object argument that most all professions use to justify their positions. A quick example of this is the infamous testimony of former President of the United States Bill Clinton about the sexual scandal that he was involved with during his time in office. During his testimony he argues and questions the word "*is*." Many at the time believed his answer was brilliant. Unfortunately, Mr. Bill Clinton was not brilliant but he in fact took his answer from this book which basically gives the same argument that he used. It is almost word for word straight out of The Politics of Experience. It is so close that it I believe that the former President must have taken it directly from this

271

book and then presented as his own. There are other examples in the book that politicians have used time and time again over the years. But that should be enough to give you an idea that many politicians are using the ideas and concepts contained within this book.

There are many other elements to this book. The first of the two primary elements focus on the argument that humanity as a whole is basically insane with the idea that all of our behavior is directly based on our experiences. The second main focus of the book is an argument that all individual experience is valid and real no matter how mentally ill or brain damaged the individual is.

This is the part of the book that makes Dr. Laing a member of the anti-psychiatry movement with a very flower-power hippy way of thinking. I find this part of the book to very dated in its ideas and understanding of schizophrenia. Especially the physical damage it does to the brain as the disease progresses. Although this part of the book is rather dated in its thinking, it is an interesting read that gives many good ideas for circular arguments using the subject-verb-object argument. The more important aspects of the book are the first few chapters on experience and behavior.

Within the first four chapters of the book Dr. Laing argues that within our modern-day society and our civilization as a whole all of humanity is basically alienated and fragmented from itself. That every single human on this planet is actually living in a world of "pseudo-events" in which we create a false consciousness that is adapted to see these pseudo-events as true and real. [1]

He argues that the reason we do this is because if the average person looks at the social realities that surround them in a very truthful and meaningful manner, they are quickly overwhelmed by the fact that it is so ugly, violent, brutal, and heartbreaking. It is so overwhelming that the average person just goes into a kind of shock that shuts it all out of their minds by not dealing with it in any meaningful manner.

What this means is that within our modern world that everybody is suffering from Post-Traumatic Stress Disorder or PTSD due to the trauma that they have seen or experience over the course of their normal everyday life. Dr. Laing also argues that we all are basically alienated from each other because of this trauma and that our society reflects this alienation. This alienation then causes us to become disassociated with ourselves and the world around us. He then claims this disassociation from the trauma has the long-term effect of driving all of us insane.

According to Dr. Laing all of humanity is basically insane with our civilization and society reflecting this fact. This insanity is then considered to be normal with society trying hard to enforce this insanity on everyone else no matter the cost. This madness can be best seen when large numbers of humans come together, almost all violence, especially the most brutal, cruel and destructive, is normally only committed by groups of people working together. He argues that the evidence is the historical fact of how the typically normal people that make up the bulk of society have willingly and many times very happily murdered over one-hundred million innocent people in insane brutally violent and incredibly wasteful wars during the twentieth century.

He then argues that if that is not enough proof of this madness and insanity of humanity. He then points out how we also cerebrate with great pomp and ritual all this death and destruction of humanity. Not only do we cerebrate it, but we go to great lengths to turn the killers of their fellow humans into great heroes. The reason we do this so we can all live with this insanity of endless death while allowing us the luxury of not having to think about what we are really doing. Which is killing each other in an insane orgy of self-destruction with unbelievable levels of violence with a mindless brutal madness of blood and gore.

Dr. Laing then argues that this condition of trauma, disassociation, alienation, and the insanity that comes from it creates two separate parts in each person. He calls these parts the "inner" and "outer" parts of our being. Both of them are based on our experience and that these experiences are the primary reason for our behavior. This is the basic idea of understanding how to control the behavior of people by controlling their experiences. That might seem a bit confusing, please let me explain.

The "inner" part of ourselves according to Dr. Laing is rather easy to understand and explain. It is what you actually think, feel, and personally experience in your day-to-day life. It is what makes you, you. It is everything that you think about in terms of right and wrong or what you use to make choices. In short, it is your values and ethics which are normally based upon how you were raised by your family and the values of the community you grew up in. He argues that this inner experience is the basis of all our behavior and that we only really believe something if, and only if, we experience the evidence personally. If we do not experience the evidence first hand, we will never really believe it or will always have some type of doubt about it.

This leads to his concept of the "outer" that is spoken of in the book. This is the rest of the world that we observe but do not personally experience. This is where it starts to get a little confusing and hard to follow. He says *"We can see other people's behavior, but not their experience. We only experience others by observing their behavior and they only experience us by observing our behavior."* [2] To keep this idea easy to understand, what he is saying is that we can't not, and will not, now or ever, be able to "experience" what somebody else is "experiencing" or "feel" what they "feel" and because of this we never really know or believe what is going on around us when it comes to other people we interact with on a daily basis.

It is through this understanding that our behavior is a product of our experience of dealing with the separate outer world and our own personally inner world that Dr. Laing argues that you can control the behavior of a person by controlling their experience. This is accomplished by destroying your experience. Which is simply done by separating the inner and outer parts of yourself by getting you to focus on the outer behavior you observe.

This separation of the inner and the outer has the effect of causing you to have doubt about everything making you always question your experience. This is why the "group" is always put over individual. This helps force you look at and focus only on the outer world and not your personal inner world. This simple act has the effect of destroying your life experience by separating you from your inner personal feelings by making you doubt them in the first place. By destroying your life experience or feelings your behavior will also become destructive or as Dr. Laing says his own words.

"Our behavior is a function of our experience. We act according to the way we see things. If our experience is destroyed, our behavior will be destructive. If our experience is destroyed, we have lost our own selves."
R.D. Lang – The Politics of Experience, pp. 28

It through this understanding that *"our behavior is a function of our experience"* that we can begin to realize why we always see the same violent themes and esoteric symbols in all forms of media. It is all designed to keep everybody focused on the outer world and never on their own personal inner world. This is accomplished by simply sending a never-ending stream of conflicting ideas and mixed messages about every level of society that surrounds us all.

A perfect example of how this is done. Is how the average person is shown an endless stream of TV programs, movies, videos, and video games along with millions of pictures showing brutal violence and oppression as the only and best means to solve every single problem in life, especially by the authorities. But if that same person who has been shown their entire lives nothing but the idea that all problems are solved by violence actually uses violence to solve a problem. Well, we all know that person will be punished beyond belief and treated as a monster by the very people that have done nothing but show this same person the never-ending message that violence solves problems.

This has the effect of causing not only that person to think, but the vast majority of people will also think that everybody else can use violence to solve their problems but they cannot. This then causes people to become alienated from each other. This is because they think other people are getting away with something they cannot. It causes a type "negation" which will lead the individual to become destructive to themselves and the world around them. My personal favorite example of this term and happens to someone who has been negated is from the renowned psychologist Erik Erikson with his famous study of Adolf Hitler's childhood where he states that "A person or child that is negated will likely develop the desire to destroy."

This alienation along with the negation it feeds into will keep most people in a permanent state of agitation with a constant feeling that nothing good ever happens in the world or more importantly that nothing good happens to them personally. This makes the person very easy to aggravate and easily pushed in certain directions, normally with only the threat of violence. One of the primary goals of this is to make people easier to exploit without them realizing that they are being exploited or as Dr. Lang puts it.

"It is not enough to destroy one's own and other people's experience. One must overlay this devastation by a false consciousness inured, as Marcuse puts it, to its own falsity. Exploitation must not be seen as such. It must be seen as benevolence. Persecution preferably should not need to be invalidated as the figment of a paranoid imagination; it should be experienced as kindness."
R.D. Lang – The Politics of Experience, pp. 57

This devastation is then exploited by either one of two methods; one is described in the book. The other is based on the technique of what is known in modern popular media as MK-Ultra or Monarch mind control and manipulation. Although these project names are far out of date with any current projects being called something else, I will use these terms because so many are familiar with them.

The first example of this devastation in the book is the classic Us-vs-Them method. The book has an entire chapter exploring the subject. This is the one most everybody familiar with. The book uses the Big Lie from Nazi Germany as an example of this Us-vs-Them method. It is also the same method used today telling us who to hate and go to war with.

The other method is based on the modern MK-Ultra mind control and Monarch mind manipulation systems that were first researched and developed by the Nazis during World War Two. Much of this work was done by the SS and their infamous Death Head units. These individuals, many who were known war criminals, were brought to America under a Project Paperclip after the war. By the late nineteen fifties the mind control aspects were taken over by the CIA. By the late nineteen sixties it was developed into the MK-Ultra mind control project that was exposed by the Church Hearings in the nineteen seventies. After the Church Hearings, MK-Ultra more or less disappeared into the world of Black Projects and Special Access Projects far from the public eye. But, many of the mind manipulation aspects were further developed into what is commonly known in modern pop-culture as Monarch Mind Manipulation that is widely used in entertainment. A system that relies heavily on esoteric symbolism and the hidden story it tells.

For those who might be unfamiliar with these ideas. The entire concept and the techniques of this system of mind control known as MK-Ultra are based around the systematic and ritualized use of trauma. This is usually done some type of audio and visual stimulation to invoke an emotional response. The ever-common music and major Hollywood movies are a perfect example of how this is done. It is ideal if you can get the subject to use drugs or alcohol to help stimulate the mind into an altered state.

This is one of the primary reasons why alcohol and drug use are the major themes shown in entertainment all the time, it helps in the trauma. Additionally, the showing of same images of drug and alcohol use over and over while also telling everyone it is wrong to do it is the easiest way to make you do it. This is the ever-famous peer-pressure technique that tries to make you think it is cool and that everybody else is doing it because you are breaking the rules. This type of Group Think is important in helping to get people to do things they normally would not do on their own. Dr. Laing also points out that the group is fantastic at using trauma in all its different forms. This trauma is the key to this control and manipulation with it taking almost any form.

This is the basic technique that is currently being used in mainstream media and the entertainment industry as a whole. This never-ending theme of sex, drugs, violence, with some type of state oppression is always built into similar story lines. Which if you take a few minutes and think about all the story lines you have seen over the course of your life, you will notice that they are all basically the same. The reason is because you are being told the exact same story over-and-over in every single movie, video game, TV program, and in entertainment as a general rule. The piece of the puzzle that has always been missing is this story that I have presented to you. The story that is told within the Dream Vision of Enoch and all the ancient artifacts. It is a hidden story of creation that is told through the esoteric symbols that surround us. It is the forbidden knowledge.

This of course raises the question of why anyone would go to the trouble to do all of this? This question actually has a remarkably simple answer. It is because this forbidden knowledge goes against everything that Western Christianity and the civilization that was built upon it over the last fifteen-hundred-years. It is a direct challenge to the history we have been presented along with the timeline we have all been taught. It also allows one to realize the great destruction and the End of Days that Christianity welds like sword to scare people into believing and behaving has already happened. It also proves much of what we think we know is most likely false or lacking numerous details. It is in essence a threat to everything that gives much of the power to the major institutions that make up the backbone of modern civilization. History has also shown that these institutions will go to great lengths to destroy any that challenge their version of history, especially the six-thousand-year timeline of human history.

It was at this point that I understood why we are bombarded every single day with all these symbols and being told this story without us knowing it. It is not because they are trying to convert you to their evil religion as so many Christians would like you to believe. But it is more of a conflict between the old guard that makes ups the traditional institutions that Western Civilization is built upon and those who know this non-traditional version of history. It is a conflict that has its origin in the many different schools of thought that came into being starting in the early sixteenth century. This includes the many schools of religious thought that is now known as Protestant Christianity. This time also gave rise to the various groups that would become modern Freemasonry along with other esoteric groups. Both of these extremes were viewed as a threat to the Catholic Church and the governments that were dependent upon it. This is why the esoteric symbolism was used. It has traditionally been the only way to comminate this knowledge to each individual that is aware of this forbidden knowledge and the threat it presents to the established institutions of society and Western Civilization. Until recently, this knowledge could get one put to death for trying to share this type of knowledge.

With idea in mind, I went back and very carefully re-read the whole book of The Politics of Experience taking great care to look for anything that seemed out of place or strange in some way. Overall, the whole book is a little strange in its own way and seemed out dated for its viewpoint on schizophrenia. With an overall idea that all experiences no matter how strange or fantasy based were as real as this world. Not only are these types of experiences real Dr. Laing argued that there was something to be learned from studying these experiences.

This idea of strange experiences is the other main argument in the book. This focus on strange experiences made more sense when I learned that Dr. Laing experimented with LSD and had an alcohol problem. It is also claimed that he had suffered from depression and possibly had some other mental health issues most of his adult life. Looking at this book with the idea that Dr. Laing might have been under the influence some type of drug like LSD or was heavily using alcohol during the time of him putting this book together would go a long way to explain some of the stranger ideas he puts forward.

Dr. Laing using some type of mind-altering drug would go a long way to explain a very odd section of the book that seems so out of place when compared to the rest of the book. In fact, the first time I read it I was completely confused as to why it was included. This section is contained in the very last part of the book and is called "The Bird of Paradise."

When you read this section of the book the whole thing appears to be little more than a possible LSD trip that the good Doctor went on and just happened to write down his experience. Which given his idea that all experiences are real, there is a logic to why it would be included, although the lack of explanation to put it into context only adds to the mystery. It is only nineteen pages long in the paperback copy I have. It is rather short with it being easily over looked and discounted. What little information I could find on this part of the book was not very helpful in explaining any of it. So, I decided to look at it from a different viewpoint than I had before. I decided to look for the story that is told through the esoteric symbolism and the Dream Vision of Enoch.

I also first made the assumption that Dr. Ronald D. Laing was connected to this esoteric knowledge. I also thought it would be highly probable that he would take the same approach as any other person that knew this knowledge by hiding things in plain sight while allowing others to think it is something else. I did this based on the fact of the similar esoteric religious symbolism on the cover art of his book along with what I could find for the International R.D. Laing Institute.

The symbolism is how you can trace and follow the various esoteric groups. But you also have to remember that the esoteric is much like Christianity. All the different groups have the same story and basic beliefs but they do not agree with each other's interpretation of that information. Additionally, the symbolism is also used from more than telling a story. Again, as with Christianity, the symbols are also used for commutation between followers of each group and between the various groups. They are also used to mark territory and used to show rank and standing within the membership of the various esoteric groups. This is the perfect example of a sleeper cell system and how they commutate with each other without ever having to meet each other once certain level of knowledge has been reached.

The reason why I say this is because contained within this section called The Bird of Paradise is a very intriguing part that basically contains the entire esoteric story I have presented to you. It is clearly speaking of the same story as the Dream Vision of Enoch. It also contains the idea of a great and ancient war along with the battles that destroyed everything approximately thirteen-thousand years ago. It also contains a number of elements that I have not discussed. Many of which will hopefully provide you with a few answers to a number of questions you must have by now.

This section of The Bird of Paradise seems to be more of a vision than a drug induced hallucination when looked at with the esoteric story in hand. Unfortunately, I was unable to secure copyright permission to reprint this section in its entirety. This has forced me to summarize the vast majority of it. I highly recommend you find an older copy of The Politics of Experience that contain The Bird of Paradise and read this section this book for yourself.

He begins with speaking of a grand primeval forest that has majestic trees that reach from the earth up to the heavens. A great virgin forest as when the earth was young long before the coming of man. He then talks of mysterious woodcutters that come and chop all the great trees down with great saws that no tree can escape or endure. The great trees are felled and then processed in great sawmills that grind them down into sawdust. Then this sawdust is ground down finer and finer until nothing is left of the once magnificent trees or the forest they made. He is speaking of the Main-Group coming to earth and extracting resources.

The vision then moves on to what I can only describe as moving beyond reality into ultimate reality. It is very similar to what is described by a Native American Shaman when they participate in a vision quest. He speaks of moving beyond all form of being and non-being. He speaks of how the vastest of space and the tiny center of the atom are one. He then describes that this ultimate reality is nothing more than a cosmic froth of bubbles moving in a perpetual movement of life, death, and rebirth. He says this releases an inner light of understanding that blazes like ten thousand suns within him that threatens to consume him.

He speaks of how this fills him with fear and how he is terrified of being blinded and destroyed by the light of understanding. He clutches at himself as he falls away from the light into the darkness. He speaks of falling from heaven to earth and then into exile. He speaks of demigods, heroes, and mortal men all with their carnage and butchery as they come into the final horror of incarnation. In short, he is symbolically describing The Fall of the Watchers as if he is experiencing this himself as one of the fallen ones. He speaks that it was time of blood and agony with a struggle between death and rebirth that *"exhausted the spirit as if fell away though eternity into time."*

The vision then comes to an end and he says he begins to dream once again. He talks of a dream that allows him to begin grasping at the loss of the world that once was and how so much has been forgotten. He speaks of how so many through the centuries have been searching and re-searching for lost knowledge. He also speaks of all the false signposts and dead ends with the terrible danger posed by forgetting that one has forgotten or at least remembering that you have forgotten. He also states that we must never forget again because that ancient war still rages on to this very day in all of us. He describes this war as a grand cosmic conflict between great powers and principalities that we cannot comprehend or have any hope of identifying with.

This leads to an interesting piece of information that has been missing and how many people who study the esoteric view themselves along with idea of their relationship to it all. He goes on to describe how they are the lost and shattered fragments of a once glorious Army. An army that has the Captains, Princes, along with the great Lords of War counted among their ranks. With them all longing to recall the long forgotten final battle with the hope of trying to make contact with headquarters and the rest of the Army. He claims they believe that they are the lone soldiers standing on the frontier of the empire out of contact with their comrades in arms praying that the call from the Capital will come in good time.

He then speaks of how they have found fragments and crumbs of information. Small bits and pieces of the jigsaw puzzle that may help them in the reconstruction of a lost message from long ago. A message that allows them to slowly begin to regain the lost memory with the realization of all that was lost, including themselves. He talks of déja-vu and faint sounds of old familiar music from a time forgotten long ago with an agony of realization that it was all a debacle. Of how greed, lust, betrayal, cowardice, and horror led to the loss of the grand Kingdom along with all the power and the glory of a Paradise Lost. It was their endless lust for power that ultimately led to the loss and destruction of all that was.

He then speaks of how they are lost and are nothing more than derelicts with no time for dignity or heroics. Their best bet for survival is treachery and cowardice. To hide in the shadows and take their time until they have rebuilt their army. Once that grand task is done, they will be ready to move again and make the world theirs. This then leads to the most important part of this vision, the aftermath of the great final battle from that almost forgotten war at the end of time. He describes a mid-ocean shipwreck after a great battle where the survivors are being picked up by a rescue ship as if he is flying above the scene. He says that the crew is saved but the Captain is nowhere to been seen and left for dead as the ship moves away from the wreck. He talks of slowing tracking over the surface of the ocean like a bird where he swoops down when he spots the Captain.

"Suddenly, like a bird, I swoop down. There is the Captain. Is he dead? A sodden doll just afloat and no more. If he is not already dead, it seems he will certainly drown soon. Suddenly he is washed up at a fishing village. The fishermen don't know whether he is alive or dead, a captain or a doll or a queer fish. A doctor comes along, guts him open like a fish, or rips him open like a doll. There is sodden, grey little man inside. Artificial respiration. He moves. He reddens with blood. Maybe he will make it. How careful I must be! What a near thing! If only this really is the King coming back again. The Captain come to take command. Now I can start up again. Putting things in order. Repairs, reconstructions, projects. Plans. Campaigns. O Yes."
R.D. Laing - Politics of Experience. The Bird of Paradise: pp. 185 (1967)

I was astonished when I re-read this part of the Bird of Paradise. It appears that Dr. Laing was saying a whole lot more than what you would expect from your average young psychiatrist of the late nineteen-sixties. It is also something more than your everyday LSD hallucination. Because you now understand that this is the esoteric story that is told through the symbolism and contained within the Dream Vision of Enoch. This little bit of strange writing seems to contain a number of elements that complete the story that I started with in the beginning.

This idea of the Capitan and how he is described as a *"sodden, grey little man"* that looked like a *"queer fish"* just grabs my attention. The first thing that leaps into my mind is all the ancient stories that are related in some way with a fish-like figure, as we saw on the cylinder seals from earlier, that came from the ocean for one reason or another. There are many different stories associated with and a number of reliefs of a fish-garbed figure from all over the world. Could these two figures be related? Could this be similar looking technology?

The other idea that jumps into my head is that there were survivors from the losing side of the Fallen-Watchers. These survivors either escaped and were rescued by a ship of some type. It is clear that their leader was left behind and believed to be dead. This raises the question of where did these survivors go?

281

Because if any other part of this idea is correct, then it is highly probable that they could not return to the Heaven since it had been destroyed. This would mean that they would had to have gone someplace close by to hide. It is also probable that if the leader had survived the final battle he would find and go into hiding with other followers that survived.

This also raises the third possibility of what might have happened to the Main-Group and the great monster Leviathan. It is possible that when the Main-Group was moving around the world using Leviathan trying to bring civilization back to our ancestors after the last of the ice melted. The surviving remnant of the Fallen-Watchers saw them and Leviathan moving around the world. At some point they attacked Leviathan sending it to the bottom of the ocean. If true, it is possible that one remembered as the Lord-God and the mighty vessel known as Leviathan are long gone, laying somewhere on the bottom of the ocean.

It should be noted that it is also possible that the Lord-God figure and Leviathan were attacked but made it back to the New Jerusalem. Without the support of the Heaven, they could not repair the mighty Leviathan and have not been able to leave their hiding place since them. These ideas and the couple from the last chapter are only a few of the possibilities on what could have happen or why we have not seen the Main-Group or their allies for such a long time.

I have to speculate that this could explain a great number of the stories, myths, legends and ideas about the modern UFO phenomenon. This little vision of a *"sodden, grey little man"* seems so close to the whole idea of the typical Grey Alien of our modern age.

I also like to speculate about where the rescue ships may have gone if the Heaven was unavailable. I think these survivors could not have gone very far because the just do not have the means too. I think it would fair to say that the Heaven was their primary source of their technology, resources, and manufacturing capability. When this was lost, they all lost the ability to manufacture any new ships or technology. This means they all became trapped here on earth or somewhere in the nearby solar-system with only the resources, equipment, and technology they each had at that time.

If you take a few minutes and think about it, this could provide an explanation to almost every single strange rumor and story about the Grey Aliens. Especially the claims that they are working with different governments here on earth. It would also explain the story in UFO lore of why some type of deal was made years ago between them and us. A deal that is said to have involved trading people and resources for technology.

I have always wondered about stories like these. Because in my mind I always think that if these Aliens and their ships are so technologically advanced that they could do just about anything they want, without having to worry about us or our primitive technology. Why would they go through the trouble of making a deal or even contacting us If any of the UFO stories can be believed, it is clear that our technology is a total joke when compared to theirs. Not only is their technology far beyond ours, there does not appear to be anything we can do about it. Even if we have captured one or more of their craft, it is possible that much of their technology is too far ahead of us. With it taking decades or possibly hundreds of years just to figure out what it does and the science behind it.

This idea has always made me a little skeptical about the whole secret deal between Aliens and certain governments of earth. But with this story in hand, it all has a strange and weird kind of logic of why some technologically advanced alien group would go to any trouble at all in making a "deal" with some of us in secret and not make formal contact.

It is because they do not have the numbers, resources, or ships, to really do anything at all. In fact, based on the UFO reports, their also do not appear to have much in the way of weapon systems or any meaningful military capacity that is any real threat to us either. I think that it would be a fair guess to say that there is a good chance that these UFOs could be up to thirteen-thousand plus years old. It is a fair guess to say that some of them could be the rescue ships spoken of earlier. It is all due to the simple fact that they cannot build new ships to replace the existing ones. In short, they just cannot do much of anything but what they are doing, because they really cannot do anything else.

This would mean that these Aliens have to be really close to earth to account for the number of good sightings it they are only using a small number of ships. The most logical place I can think of is earth's Moon. It would also provide an explanation to all the strange sightings and reports about UFOs around the moon reported over the centuries. There are other possibilities besides this one, but it should give you enough of an idea of how this whole esoteric religious story fits into so many different places and provides a frame work that gives context to many weird things you have heard or read about over the years.

This vision also appears to provide a clue to the identity of the individual that is rumored and whispered about in certain religious circles that is claimed to be at the center of all of this. Many Christians believe that followers of the occult and the esoteric ultimately worship and serve this individual. The whispers and rumors that I have heard over the years about this individual is that he is referred to as a living god that is the bringer of light or sometimes as the living god of light. This vision seems to be giving the idea that this leader was the one that was left for dead, but somehow survived might be at the center of much of this.

This little vision or hallucination or whatever you wish to call it, also appears to give an idea of the ultimate goal of the followers of the esoteric and the reason behind all the symbols being bombarded at you every day. They wish to reestablish this ancient and long forgotten Empire or Lost Paradise they lost so long ago. This also provides the meaning behind the last symbol we have yet to look at, the Phoenix. This symbolizes the resurrection of the Lost Paradise and the forgotten empire of the Fallen-Watchers. The main thing to remember here is that this time around they do not wish to make the same mistakes as before and destroy everything process.

There is one last part in the Bird of Paradise that I would like to point out before I leave this part of the idea and move on. It also appears to be speaking of the conspiracy behind all of this. It also seems to be giving a small window into the attitude that is behind it.

"Watch it. Care. Calm. Caution. Don't try it on too much, don't exploit it. Just keep your place, just don't ask for trouble. Remember your hands have blood on them, just don't be too cheeky or greedy. Don't health yourself up too much. Remember your place in the hierarchy, don't try to come it, don't shout about, don't posture, don't give yourself airs, don't think you're going to get away with it, you've had a bit of the piss taken out of you, don't make excuses. Don't kick it around. Who are you trying to kid. A little humility, a fraction of love, a grain of trust, you've been told as much as you need to know, you've had quite sure fair share, don't try the patience of the gods. Shut up and get on with it. Remember. There's not much time left. The flood in the fire is upon us."

R.D. Laing - Politics of Experience. The Bird of Paradise: pp. 187 (1967)

This last small piece of the puzzle provides the last clue that is needed to fully understand the depths of the motivations behind the followers of the esoteric school of thought that believes this. That clue is the seven little words of *"don't try the patience of the gods."* This gives us the final piece that allows us to speculate that the very top of the hierarchy structure of the esoteric you will most likely find one the Dr. Laing refers to as the Capitan, but he also clearly states that there are still gods in the plural and not the singular God. This is the same individual that many religious people believe is the Devil or Satan, the Fallen-One. But as we have learned, the story is much more complex than these simple ideas could ever convey.

With this final understanding in hand, we can then realize one of the greatest secrets of the forbidden knowledge. That we have all been very wrong in our assumption that these Aliens, either in the past or currently in the present, have been traveling back-and-forth from our solar-system to another solar-system. All with the support of a highly advanced civilization providing the necessary resources for such an undertaking. But now, we can understand that the story that is told through the esoteric symbolism tells us that entire idea is incorrect. Instead, it tells us that these Aliens never left once they arrived here on earth all those hundreds of thousands of years ago. This understanding changes everything about this entire subject. It should also allow you to finally began to understand just how huge this whole story is and how it really does tie everything together.

Chapter 15

Back to the Beginning

Live a good life. If there are gods and they are just, then they will not care how devout you have been, but will welcome you based on the virtues you have lived by. If there are gods, but unjust, then you should not want to worship them. If there are no gods, then you will be gone, but will have lived a noble life that will live on in the memories of your loved ones. I am not afraid.
~Marcus Aurelius~

Heaven wheels above you displaying to you her eternal glories and still your eyes are on the ground.
~Dante~

W e have now come full circle and have returned to the original questions I posed at the very beginning of our journey into the riddle of the 'something.'

As we have learned, this 'something' is not easily summed up in a couple of pages or just a few words. It is in fact the piece that has been missing and allows us to actually begin to truly understand the world around you for the first time. It also gives you the tools on how to follow the group that is clearly using this esoteric symbolism. A group that many claim is behind all the many horrible and terrible things that happen in the world over the last thousand or so years. It is also claimed that these followers of the esoteric religion are guilty of the greatest of all crimes against humanity and should be brought to justice for the sake of us all. But, as will shortly learn, the entire situation is vastly more complex than some simple conspiracy theory.

Returning to original six questions that I asked at the beginning will help provide some answers to the many questions you doubt have at this point. The first question we began with was:

1) Is there really anything to this whole Ancient Astronaut Theory as currently presented by the popular media in books and TV shows?

For this first question, I would have to say that the answer is definitely a Yes, there is something to it all. Fundamental I am not sure they are actually Aliens, but it is something that appears to be fundamentally at the very core of the civilization we live in. I would have to argue that the "Ancient Astronaut Theory" and traditional religion are actually one and the same. I would even go as far as to propose that the Ancient Astronaut Theory and our traditional religions are actually speaking of the same thing. I would also argue that both ideas are correct that these 'Advanced Beings' are the creators of humanity. But that does not automatically make them the gods. I think it is only when we can realize this simple fact, we will be able to truly begin to understand all the mystery that surrounds us.

My second question was:

2) Are the ancient religious stories that we are all so familiar with, really talking about some type of advance extra-terrestrial alien civilization that came to earth thousands and thousands of years ago?

Again, as we have learned, I think it is possible that the answer to this question is Yes. I will present a possibly better answer to this question shortly. Which brings us to the third question.

3) Were our ancestors too primitive to understand who these individuals where? Thereby misinterpreted them as gods?

This one is slightly harder to answer compared to the first two. This is due to the fact that we now know and understand that these advanced beings appear to have presented themselves as the gods to our ancestors. Additionally, the ancient stories indicate that these individuals went to great lengths to keep our ancestors in a rather primitive state to help them to believe these advanced beings where the gods themselves.

It makes one wonder about any civilization that would so brutally exploit another sentient species. Even one they had a hand in creating. In our modern world it would be akin to genetically enhancing an ape to look, act, think, and behave much like ourselves. Then using them as a slave race to support our needs while presenting ourselves as their God and creator demanding to be worshiped as such. With all of this being done in order to subjugate, control, and exploit them.

In our modern age it is difficult to justify any slavery, especially a slavery that would create or modify an existing species to subjugate it. Some would argue that we do the same thing to animals to suit our needs. Which I would agree is correct in many ways. But I think the ethical and moral questions of creating a sentient species and then having it worship you as a God go far beyond our use of animals. Unless, they are using us in the same way. The reality is that the hard questions this all raises is far beyond the scope of this book. I will leave it to you to decide for yourself on how an intelligent species could justify doing something like this. Although, I will say that I think any species that would do something like this is about as far away from being God as you can get. In light of this information, we might want to rethink some of the things so man believe about them.

The next question on the list was:

4) Is this contact where all the ancient religious stories, legends, and myths come from?

Think this question answers itself now. Yes, all the ancient stories, no matter the tradition, the culture, the myths, or the religious belief are speaking of the same set of events.

The last two questions can be answered together:

5) Has modern science misinterpreted the evidence?
6) Is there evidence to support any side in this argument?

The answer to both of these questions is Yes. The evidence is all around us, but it has been purposely misinterpreted to hide the missing parts of the story. Once you are aware of the missing parts of the story. You can begin the realization that every ancient artifact, building, myth, and religious story is the evidence everyone has all been looking for. The primary piece that has been missing is the complete story and the timeline of events.

As you can now understand in a way you could not imagine at the beginning. That yes, there is something to all of it. Although this journey has presented you with numerous ideas, possibilities, and evidence to explain it all. It should also be noted that the oldest, wealthiest, most powerful families of the world, along with the most secretive groups the world is aware of believe all of this or a version of it to be fact beyond any doubt. So much so that they spend time, money, and resources to hide this story in plain sight while leaving false trails in the process. This alone should make one wonder if there is not more to this entire idea.

This brings me to my final closing thoughts about whom these individuals that our ancient ancestors worshipped as gods may be. As we have made our way through this story, I have tried to not say one way or another on who I think these individuals could be. The reason for this is because I think there are two important aspects that must be examined in order to postulate any type of idea on their identities. Both of them are directly related and I will explore them together.

These different aspects are both related to the entire idea of how the ancient stories speak of the gods, angels, or aliens if you will, breeding with humans and having viable offspring. Not only did these unions create a viable offspring, but these offspring could also breed among themselves. The first aspect will explore is this idea itself. The second will be looking at the behavior of these gods.

I have always found the entire idea of this interbreeding between humans and the gods to be the most intriguing idea of all the ancient myths. Especially since there is normally nothing in the stories to indicate that there was technology or magic involved in these encounters. Remarkably, most of the stories describe that these beings had actual sexual relationships with human beings and that nine months later a child was born of this union. Not just any child but a half-god and half-human child that are commonly known as a Demigod, heroes, or the Nephilim. These stories also tell us that these children of the gods could also breed with each, but they could also breed with humans or the gods themselves. Additionally, these stories also tell us that these heavenly beings typically had very strong feelings for the humans involved in these relationships and the children that were born from them.

These ancient stories raise many more questions than they answer. On one side we have the religious argument that it was God and God can do anything it wishes. On the other side we have the Ancient Astronaut Theory saying it was all done with advanced genetic engineering and technology by an advance race of extraterrestrial aliens. Then between these two extremes we have the scholars and scientists somewhere in the middle while not really giving a straight answer one way or another. Which leave the average person wondering if any of the them have any idea about what they are talking about.

It is within this confusion of these ancient myths that speak of the interbreeding between the gods and humanity that I think we can some possible answers to who these creatures our ancient ancestors worshipped as gods. Interestingly enough, this particular subject tends to be ignored by all parties. Both the religious and scientific sides look upon the subject as something so childish it is not worth their time to even think about, much less actually explore or ask questions about. I also think that the reason they ignore this subject is because it can provide an idea on who these individuals could possibly be while answering a few other questions in the process.

To begin with, I have a number of problems with the idea that some alien species came to earth from some distant planet and through the use of advance genetic engineering created us in their image. After this creation of humanity these aliens then mated with our ancestors thereby creating a hybrid race. I know that you might find that a little hard to believe at the moment. Since I have basically presented the idea that some type of genetic engineering must have occurred to humanity long ago and I need to clarify what I am saying.

The primary problem with this idea of aliens mating with ancient humans is a scientific one. Because for any two species to be able to mate with one other and produce a viable offspring, they must be very closely genetically related. Additionally, we are told these offspring could also mate with both humans and gods to produce their own offspring that could also produce viable offspring of these unions. In order for something like this to happen, these two species would have to be directly related to each other. In order for this to happen we would have had to have a very recent common genetic ancestor. An ancestor that could possibly be as close as Neanderthal or Cro-Magnon man is to us.

This is where the idea of us being the product of advanced genetic engineering by an alien species to the point that they could interbreed with our ancient ancestors really starts to break down. If such a thing actually happened then our genetic code would clearly show that type of evidence. Because if such an event had happened our genetic code that would be almost totally alien to everything else on earth. We would simply not match anything else on this planet genetically. This in and by itself is pretty much a death blow to the entire idea of ancient aliens coming to earth and genetically engineering us.

The next major problem with this idea is the fact that nobody has put any plausible idea forward on why an alien species that would go through all the trouble of genetically engineering a whole new species to use as a slave. Only to turn around and end up having deep, meaningful, loving emotions for some creature they created on a different planet. In my mind, I cannot come up with any situation where an intelligent species would do something like that.

Additionally, given the animal symbolism in the stories, I think it is fair to say these advanced beings viewed our ancient ancestors as little more than a beast of burden or as the Dream Vision states as cattle or lambs. This fact leads me to think that there are only a few possibilities as to who these beings that our ancestors called gods could actually be.

The first possibility is that the ancient astronaut theory is basically correct in the idea that an advanced alien species came to earth hundreds of thousands of years ago. If you think about it for a few minutes, keeping in mind the enormous engineering challenges and the problems of going from one star system to another one we can come to a possible solution that is within the realm of science.

One of the greatest problems of long distant space travel is the amount of time it will take to get from one star to the next. Unless you can figure out some type of short cut like a wormhole or warp drive which our physics says is possible but unlikely, the cosmic speed limit is the speed of light. This speed limit of light is what limits any journey to the stars. Even if you are able to got close to the speed of light, it will still take many years to reach to the closest stars, if not generations. This long amount of time for the journey is one of the major problems to interstellar space travel. This is because you need to take massive amounts of food and supplies just keep your crew alive for the trip. This is actually an argument against why ancient astronauts or any other alien species is not already here. It is just too difficult to accomplish in any meaningful manner.

In both scientific circles and science-fiction stories there have been many different ideas presented over the years by some of the very smartest people on the planet on how you could solve this problem of traveling to the stars. Within these ideas there is one from science-fiction that could provide a possible answer if the technology is available.

Long ago I read a science-fiction story that presented a unique idea of how to get round the whole supply problem of sending people to the stars. The basic idea was that you would not actually send the physical bodies of people to other solar-systems. This was simply because too many things could go wrong along with the fact that due to the amount of time involved in traveling no human would actually live long enough to make the trip. The solution to this problem was to create a computer that was powerful enough that you could make a copy of your mind and download it into the memory of the computer and then place it on a ship. You would send a copy of your mind instead of your body. Then when the ship arrived at a new solar-system after many decades, if not hundreds of years of travel. Your mind would then be downloaded into some type of body that would allow you to be able to interact with the environment. If you happen to find a planet with life on it. Then you would construct a body based on that life and download your mind into it. This way you would not need any type of life support systems or other means to move around in the environment.

Although this basic idea is from an old science fiction story. It does provide a very sound idea on how you could get around many problems for long distance space travel if you had the technology. It also provides a possible idea of how an alien species could be able to interbreed with our ancient ancestors. Additionally, it would provide an explanation to the myths of how these beings seem to be able to change their form or shape at will. This could simply be them downloading their minds into different bodies or types of technology

This is one possibility that could explain and solve most of the problems on the physical side of things. Although it still does not address the question of why these beings would have or developed any emotion or deep meaningful relationships with a species they had found and then modified to be a slave. This is the one thing most people forget about when talking about this subject. This question of why would they care about our ancient ancestors and why would they want to have sexual relationships with something little more than an animal they had a hand in creating?

As I think about this problem. I can only come up with two possible ideas to solve this problem. Both of which require that these beings are originally from here, earth.

The first idea has been explored in science-fiction and may even be familiar to you. This is the idea that these beings originally evolved and developed here on earth millions of years ago. At some point they developed the technology to leave the solar system, slowly moving out into the galaxy. Over an unknown amount of time, they create a great space going civilization that spans countless star systems. As this happens, earth is abandoned and forgotten about. After countless years of expanding and growth, something terrible happens to the grand civilization. Some great catastrophe, like an unstoppable plague or war, shatters the fabric of this civilization and it collapses in a fairly short amount of time.

This destruction of their civilization leaves only small pockets survivors that are scattered around the galaxy. These survivors use all their remaining resources and technology to construct an unknown number of very large space-faring vessels. These massive vessels are basically whole cities in space which allows them to leave the ruins of their once great civilization behind in search of a new home. Then about 300,000 years ago a group of these survivors make their way back to their original home, earth. This type of scenario would help explain why they would have an emotional attachment to everything on earth, because it is home. This would also explain why it would have been easy for them to alter the genetic code without leaving any alien DNA for us to find, it is simply because it is not alien, it is from earth.

This type of idea could explain a great number of questions about the motivations behind why these beings did what they did. I will not be going into any more detail on this idea or spend much more time on it. This simply because so many others have already presented a large number of different ideas and concepts on this subject in both the worlds of science-fiction and scientific thought. Although there is one idea that is related to this subject I would like to explore for a moment.

This idea comes from two known facts. The first being that the planets Venus and Mars figure so heavily in most of the ancient mythologies. The second is the fact that if we could look at our own solar-system, with our current technology from about 20 or 30 light-years away we would deduce that both of these planets lay right at the edges of the habitable zone. We would also expect them to support liquid water with the possibility to support life.

Interestingly enough, we know that both planets must have had water and possibly life in the ancient past. But both planets are currently barren wastelands with no known life on either. The planet Venus is a burning hell hole with a toxic atmosphere that would crush you in mere moments if you could stand on its surface. With Mars at the other end of scale, being a dry cold wasteland with a landscape frozen in time.

These two facts, when combined with the esoteric ideas we have explored makes me wonder if Mars and Venus were habitable when these beings arrived with them settling on both worlds. Based on the ancient mythology, I would guess that the ones that I have been calling the Main-Group may have settled on Venus. This is because so many of the mythologies relate the planet Venus to ideas and concepts like, peace, love, understanding, and parenthood. This would mean that the others that I have been calling the Fallen-Watcher may have settled on Mars.

This type of settlement could help explain why we see the planetary wastelands of today. This destruction may have occurred due to the ancient and largely forgotten war remembered in the Book of Revelation as Armageddon. A war of such total destruction that the gods laid waste to each of these worlds that left then as lifeless husks of their former glory. Although this only an idea that is heavily rooted in science-fiction, it would go a long way in explaining what we see today with Venus and Mars.

The last idea I will present is the much more recent concept that they are somehow us, either from the future or the past. The main problem with this idea is the fact that it typically includes some type of time travel. Which, at this point in time is only found the realm of science-fiction.

The first is that they are us from the future and are time travelers. There have been many ideas put forward over the years on why future humans would travel backwards through time. The most common idea is because of great collapse of the environment and they are trying to save their world.

The second possible idea is that they are us from the past, but not in the typical time traveler way. Much like the idea from before. They are just advanced humans from the past that are immoral either naturally or through science and technology. Over time they created our ancestors as a slave race to serve their needs, but in the end, they destroyed their world. The UFOs and aliens of today are the last few survivors of this long-lost advanced human civilization.

These are all nice ideas for a science-fiction story, but could any of them be real? The truth is that is up to you to decide. But, anyone of these would help explain the weird and strange things that have been reported over the centuries. They would also help explain the out-of-place artifacts that science cannot seem to explain. If they are from the future, it could explain all the strange stories about knowing the future and prophecy. Because their past is our future. But sadly, the truth is this idea is least likely to be true. It is something that is interesting to think about and has a large amount of potential to be a good science fiction story, but does not have much to back it up in real life.

With that, my friends, finally brings us to the end of the rabbit-hole and back into the light of the real world. It is also the end of this little "thought experiment" and our journey through the story told by the esoteric symbolism and the story contained within the Dream Vision of Enoch. As we come to the end of this journey, I cannot help but wonder, that you might not be quite the same as you were, before we started.

Before I go and leave you to your thoughts and let you ponder what you have read. I would like to leave you with one last idea to always keep in mind when thinking about all of this.

Let us say, just for a moment and for the sake of argument, that everything I have presented to you is one-hundred percent correct. That there really was an ancient civilization that was highly advanced that existed before thirteen thousand years ago. Also, this advanced civilization destroyed itself which gave rise to our own world of today. But this destruction was not complete and small-pieces of technology along with knowledge from that civilization had somehow survived until our own day, like the legendary Bronze Head we explored earlier. Let us also say that you happened to be the hapless individual that found one of these legendary Bronze Heads. Not only found one, but you also happened to be smart enough to get it to work and it begins to answer all your questions like legend says. This I think raises one of the most important questions that only you can answer: "What would you do with it?"

Jesus said to them:
"When you make the two one, and when you make the inner as the outer and the outer as the inner and the above as the below, and when you make the male and female into a single one, so that the male will not be male and the female not be female, when you make eyes in the place of an eye, and a hand in the place of a hand, and a foot in the place of a foot, and an image in the place of an image, then shall you enter the Kingdom."
The Gospel according to Thomas.

Appendix A

The Dream Visions of Enoch

Primary Source: Book of Enoch, from The Apocrypha and Pseudeipgrapha of the Old Testament, vol. II, by R. H. Charles, Oxford Press, London, England, Published 1913. Print

Other Sources: please see References & Bibliography

[ ] The use of these brackets means that the words so enclosed are interpolations.

( ). The use of these brackets means that the words so enclosed are supplied by the editor.

The use of thick type denotes that the words so printed are emended.

† † corruption in the text.

. . . = some words which have been lost.

Chapter 83

83.01   And now, my son Methuselah, I will show thee all my visions which I have seen, recounting them before thee.

83.02   Two visions I saw before I took a wife, and the one was quite unlike the other: the first when I was learning to write: the second before I took thy mother, (when) I saw a terrible vision.

83.03   And regarding them I prayed to the Lord. I had laid me down in the house of my grandfather Mahalalel, (when) I saw in a vision how the heaven collapsed and was borne off and fell to the earth.

83.04   And when it fell to the earth I saw how the earth was swallowed up in a great abyss, and mountains were suspended on mountains, and hills sank down on hills, and high trees were rent from their stems, and hurled down and sunk in the abyss.

83.05   And thereupon a word fell into my mouth, and I lifted up (my voice) to cry aloud, and said: 'The earth is destroyed.'

83.06   And my grandfather Mahalalel waked me as I lay near him, and said unto me: 'Why dost thou cry so, my son, and why dost thou make such lamentation?'

83.07   And I recounted to him the whole vision which I had seen, and he said unto me: 'A terrible thing hast thou seen, my son, and of grave moment is thy dream-vision as to the secrets of all the sin of the earth: it must sink into the abyss and be destroyed with a great destruction.

83.08   And now, my son, arise and make petition to the Lord of glory, since thou art a believer, that a remnant may remain on the earth, and that He may not destroy the whole earth.

83.09   My son, from heaven all this will come upon the earth, and upon the earth there will be great destruction.

83.10   After that I arose and prayed and implored and besought, and wrote down my prayer for the generations of the world, and I will show everything to thee, my son Methuselah.

83.11   And when I had gone forth below and seen the heaven, and the sun rising in the east, and the moon setting in the west, and a few stars, and the whole earth, and everything as He had known it in the beginning, then I blessed the Lord of judgement and extolled Him because He had made the sun to go forth from the windows of the east, and he ascended and rose on the face of the heaven, and set out and kept traversing the path shown unto him.

Chapter 84

84.01   And I lifted up my hands in righteousness and blessed the Holy and Great One, and spake [spoke] with the breath of my mouth, and with the tongue of flesh, which God has made for the children of the flesh of men, that they should speak therewith, and He gave them breath and a tongue and a mouth that they should speak therewith:

84.02   'Blessed be Thou, O Lord, King, Great and mighty in Thy greatness, Lord of the whole creation of the heaven, King of kings and God of the whole world. And Thy power and kingship and greatness abide for ever and ever, And throughout all generations Thy dominion; And all the heavens are Thy throne for ever, And the whole earth Thy footstool forever and ever.

84.03   For Thou hast made and Thou rulest all things, And nothing is too hard for Thee, Wisdom departs not from the place of Thy throne, Nor turns away from Thy presence. And Thou knowest and seest and hearest everything, And there is nothing hidden from Thee [for Thou seest everything].

84.04   And now the angels of Thy heavens are guilty of trespass, And upon the flesh of men abideth Thy wrath until the great day of judgement.

84.05   And now, O God and Lord and Great King, I implore and beseech Thee to fulfil my prayer, To leave me a posterity on earth, And not destroy all the flesh of man, And make the earth without inhabitant, So that there should be an eternal destruction.

84.06   And now, my Lord, destroy from the earth the flesh which has aroused Thy wrath, But the flesh of righteousness and uprightness establish as a plant of the eternal seed, And hide not Thy face from the prayer of Thy servant, O Lord.'

Chapter 85

85.01   And after this I saw another dream, and I will show the whole dream to thee, my son.

85.02 And Enoch lifted up (his voice) and spoke to his son Methuselah: 'To thee, my son, will I speak: hear my words -incline thine ear to the dream-vision of thy father.

85.03 Before I took thy mother Edna, I saw in a vision on my bed, and behold a bull came forth from the earth, and that bull was white; and after it came forth a heifer, and along with this (latter) came forth two bulls, one of them black and the other red.

85.04 And that black bull gored the red one and pursued him over the earth, and thereupon I could no longer see that red bull.

85.05 But that black bull grew and that heifer went with him, and I saw that many oxen proceeded from him which resembled and followed him.

85.06 And that cow, that first one, went from the presence of that first bull in order to seek that red one, but found him not, and lamented with a great lamentation over him and sought him.

85.07 And I looked till that first bull came to her and quieted her, and from that time onward she cried no more.

85.08 And after that she bore another white bull, and after him she bore many bulls and black cows.

85.09 And I saw in my sleep that white bull likewise grow and become a great white bull, and from him proceeded many white bulls, and they resembled him.

85.10 And they began to beget many white bulls, which resembled them, one following the other, (even) many.

Chapter 86

86.01 And again I saw with mine eyes as I slept, and I saw the heaven above, and behold a star fell from heaven, and it arose and eat and pastured amongst those oxen.

86.02   And after that I saw the large and the black oxen, and behold they all changed their stalls and pastures and their cattle, and began to live with each other.

86.03   And again I saw in the vision, and looked towards the heaven, and behold I saw many stars descend and cast themselves down from heaven to that first star, and they became bulls amongst those cattle and pastured with them [amongst them].

86.04   And I looked at them and saw, and behold they all let out their privy members, like horses, and began to cover the cows of the oxen, and they all became pregnant and bare elephants, camels, and asses.

86.05   And all the oxen feared them and were affrighted at them, and began to bite with their teeth and to devour, and to gore with their horns.

86.06   And they began, moreover, to devour those oxen; and behold all the children of the earth began to tremble and quake before them and to flee from them.'

Chapter 87

87.01   And again I saw how they began to gore each other and to devour each other, and the earth began to cry aloud.

87.02   And I raised mine eyes again to heaven, and I saw in the vision, and behold
there came forth from heaven beings who were like white men: and four went forth from that place and three with them.

87.03   And those three that had last come forth grasped me by my hand and took me up, away from the generations of the earth, and raised me up to a lofty place, and showed me a tower raised high above the earth, and all the hills were lower.

87.04   And one said unto me: 'Remain here till thou seest everything that befalls those elephants, camels, and asses, and the stars and the oxen, and all of them.'

301

Chapter 88

88.01   And I saw one of those four who had come forth first, and he seized that first star which had fallen from the heaven, and bound it hand and foot and cast it into an abyss: now that abyss was narrow and deep, and horrible and dark.

88.02   And one of them drew a sword, and gave it to those elephants and camels and asses: then they began to smite each other, and the whole earth quaked because of them.

88.03   And as I was beholding in the vision, lo, one of those four who had come forth stoned. (them) from heaven, and gathered and took all the great stars whose privy members were like those of horses, and bound them all hand and foot, and cast them in an abyss of the earth.

Chapter 89

89.01   And one of those four went to that white bull and instructed him in a secret, without his being terrified: he was born a bull and became a man, and built for himself a great vessel and dwelt thereon; and three bulls dwelt with him in that vessel and they were covered in.

89.02   And again I raised mine eyes towards heaven and saw a lofty roof, with seven water torrents thereon, and those torrents flowed with much water into an enclosure.

89.03   And I saw again, and behold fountains were opened on the surface of that great enclosure, and that water began to swell and rise upon the surface, and I saw that enclosure till all its surface was covered with water.

89.04   And the water, the darkness, and mist increased upon it; and as I looked at the height of that water, that water had risen above the height of that enclosure, and was streaming over that enclosure, and it stood upon the earth.

89.05   And all the cattle of that enclosure were gathered together until I saw how they sank and were swallowed up and perished in that water.

89.06   But that vessel floated on the water, while all the oxen and elephants and camels and asses sank to the bottom with all the animals, so that I could no longer see them, and they were not able to escape, (but) perished and sank into the depths.

89.07   And again I saw in the vision till those water torrents were removed from that high roof, and the chasms of the earth were leveled up and other abysses were opened.

89.08   Then the water began to run down into these, till the earth became visible; but that vessel settled on the earth, and the darkness retired and light appeared.

89.09   But that white bull which had become a man came out of that vessel, and the three bulls with him, and one of those three was white like that bull, and one of them was red as blood, and one black: and that white bull departed from them.

89.10   And they began to bring forth beasts of the field and birds, so that there arose different genera: lions, tigers, wolves, dogs, hyenas, wild boars, foxes, squirrels, swine, falcons, vultures, kites, eagles, and ravens; and among them was born a white bull.

89.11   And they began to bite one another; but that white bull which was born amongst them begat a wild ass and a white bull with it, and the wild asses multiplied.

89.12   But that bull which was born from him begat a black wild boar and a white sheep; and the former begat many boars, but that sheep begat twelve sheep.

89.13   And when those twelve sheep had grown, they gave up one of them to the asses, and those asses again gave up that sheep to the wolves, and that sheep grew up among the wolves.

89.14   And the Lord brought the eleven sheep to live with it and to pasture with it among the wolves: and they multiplied and became many flocks of sheep.

89.15   And the wolves began to fear them, and they oppressed them until they destroyed their little ones, and they cast their young into a river of much water:

but those sheep began to cry aloud on account of their little ones, and to complain unto their Lord.

89.16 And a sheep which had been saved from the wolves fled and escaped to the wild asses; and I saw the sheep how they lamented and cried, and besought their Lord with all their might, till that Lord of the sheep descended at the voice of the sheep from a lofty abode, and came to them and pastured them.

89.17 And He called that sheep which had escaped the wolves, and spake with it concerning the wolves that it should admonish them not to touch the sheep.

89.18 And the sheep went to the wolves according to the word of the Lord, and another sheep met it and went with it, and the two went and entered together into the assembly of those wolves, and spake with them and admonished them not to touch the sheep from henceforth.

89.19 And thereupon I saw the wolves, and how they oppressed the sheep exceedingly with all their power; and the sheep cried aloud.

89.20 And the Lord came to the sheep and they began to smite those wolves: and the wolves began to make lamentation; but the sheep became quiet and forthwith ceased to cry out.

89.21 And I saw the sheep till they departed from amongst the wolves; but the eyes of the wolves were blinded, and those wolves departed in pursuit of the sheep with all their power.

89.22 And the Lord of the sheep went with them, as their leader, and all His sheep followed Him: and His face was dazzling and glorious and terrible to behold.

89.23 But the wolves began to pursue those sheep till they reached a sea of water.

89.24 And that sea was divided, and the water stood on this side and on that before their face, and their Lord led them and placed Himself between them and the wolves.

89.25   And as those wolves did not yet see the sheep, they proceeded into the midst of that sea, and the wolves followed the sheep, and [those wolves] ran after them into that sea.

89. 26   And when they saw the Lord of the sheep, they turned to flee before His face, but that sea gathered itself together, and became as it had been created, and the water swelled and rose till it covered those wolves.

89.27   And I saw till all the wolves who pursued those sheep perished and were drowned.

89.28   But the sheep escaped from that water and went forth into a wilderness, where there was no water and no grass; and they began to open their eyes and to see; and I saw the Lord of the sheep pasturing them and giving them water and grass, and that sheep going and leading them.

89.29   And that sheep ascended to the summit of that lofty rock, and the Lord of the sheep sent it to them.

89.30   And after that I saw the Lord of the sheep who stood before them, and His appearance was great and terrible and majestic, and all those sheep saw Him and were afraid before His face.

89.31   And they all feared and trembled because of Him, and they cried to that sheep with them [which was amongst them]: 'We are not able to stand before our Lord or to behold Him.'

89.32   And that sheep which led them again ascended to the summit of that rock, but the sheep began to be blinded and to wander from the way which he had showed them, but that sheep did not know thereof.

89.33   And the Lord of the sheep was wrathful exceedingly against them, and that sheep discovered it, and went down from the summit of the rock, and came to the sheep, and found the greatest part of them blinded and fallen away.

89.34   And when they saw it they feared and trembled at its presence, and desired to return to their folds. And that sheep took other sheep with it, and came to those sheep which had fallen away, and began to slay them; and the sheep feared its presence.

89.35   And thus that sheep brought back those sheep that had fallen away, and they returned to their folds.

89.36   And I saw in this vision till that sheep became a man and built a house for the Lord of the sheep, and placed all the sheep in that house.

89.37   And I saw till this sheep which had met that sheep which led them fell asleep: and I saw till all the great sheep perished and little ones arose in their place, and they came to a pasture, and approached a stream of water.

89.38   Then that sheep, their leader which had become a man, withdrew from them and fell asleep, and all the sheep sought it and cried over it with a great crying.

89.39   And I saw till they left off crying for that sheep and crossed that stream of water, and there arose the two sheep as leaders in the place of those which had led them and fallen asleep [lit. 'had fallen asleep and led them'].

89.40   And I saw till the sheep came to a goodly place, and a pleasant and glorious land, and I saw till those sheep were satisfied; and that house stood amongst them in the pleasant land.

89.41   And sometimes their eyes were opened, and sometimes blinded, till another sheep arose and led them and brought them all back, and their eyes were opened.

89.42   And the dogs and the foxes and the wild boars began to devour those sheep till the Lord of the sheep raised up [another sheep] a ram from their midst, which led them.

89.43   And that ram began to butt on either side those dogs, foxes, and wild boars till he had destroyed them all.

89.44   And that sheep whose eyes were opened saw that ram, which was amongst the sheep, till it forsook its glory, and began to butt those sheep, and trampled upon them, and behaved itself unseemly.

89.45   And the Lord of the sheep sent the lamb to another lamb and raised it to being a ram and leader of the sheep instead of that ram which had forsaken its glory.

89.46   And it went to it and spoke [spake] to it alone, and raised it to being a ram, and made it the prince and leader of the sheep; but during all these things those dogs oppressed the sheep.

89.47   And the first ram pursued that second ram, and that second ram arose and fled before it; and I saw till those dogs pulled down the first ram.

89.48   And that second ram arose and led the [little] sheep.

89.49   And those sheep grew and multiplied; but all the dogs, and foxes, and wild boars feared and fled before it, and that ram butted and killed the wild beasts, and those wild beasts had no longer any power among the sheep and robbed them no more of ought. And that ram begat many sheep and fell asleep and

89.50   And that house became great and broad, and it was built for those sheep: and a tower lofty and great was built on the house for the Lord of the sheep, and that house was low but the tower was elevated and lofty, and the Lord of the sheep stood on that tower and they offered a full table before Him.

89.51   And again I saw those sheep that they again erred and went many ways, and forsook that their house, and the Lord of the sheep called some from amongst the sheep and sent them to the sheep, but the sheep began to slay them.

89.52   And one of them was saved and was not slain, and it sped away and cried aloud over the sheep; and they sought to slay it, but the Lord of the sheep saved it from the sheep, and brought it up to me, and caused it to dwell there.

89.53   And many other sheep He sent to those sheep to testify unto them and lament over them.

89.54   And after that I saw that when they forsook the house of the Lord and His tower they fell away entirely, and their eyes were blinded; and I saw the Lord of the sheep how He wrought much slaughter amongst them in their herds until those sheep invited that slaughter and betrayed His place.

89.55 And He gave them over into the hands of the lions and tigers, and wolves and hyenas, and into the hand of the foxes, and to all the wild beasts, and those wild beasts began to tear in pieces those sheep.

89.56 And I saw that He forsook that their house and their tower and gave them all into the hand of the lions, to tear and devour them, into the hand of all the wild beasts.

89.57 And I began to cry aloud with all my power, and to appeal to the Lord of the sheep, and to represent to Him in regard to the sheep that they were devoured by all the wild beasts.

89.58 But He remained unmoved, though He saw it, and rejoiced that they were devoured and swallowed and robbed, and left them to be devoured in the hand of all the beasts.

89.59 And He called seventy shepherds, and cast those sheep to them that they might pasture them, and He spoke [spake] to the shepherds and their companions: 'Let each individual of you pasture the sheep henceforward, and everything that I shall command you that do ye.

89.60 And I will deliver them over unto you duly numbered, and tell you which of them are to be destroyed and them destroy ye.' And He gave over unto them those sheep.

89.61 And He called another and spoke [spake] unto him: 'Observe and mark everything that the shepherds will do to those sheep; for they will destroy more of them than I have commanded them.

89.62 And every excess and the destruction which will be wrought through the shepherds, record (namely) how many they destroy according to my command, and how many according to their own caprice: record against every individual shepherd all the destruction he effects.

89.63 And read out before me by number how many they destroy, and how many they deliver over for destruction, that I may have this as a testimony against them, and know every deed of the shepherds, that I may comprehend and see what they do, whether or not they abide by my command which I have commanded them.

89.64   But they shall not know it, and thou shalt not declare it to them, nor admonish them, but only record against each individual all the destruction which the shepherds effect each in his time and lay it all before me.'

89.65   And I saw till those shepherds pastured in their season, and they began to slay and to destroy more than they were bidden, and they delivered those sheep into the hand of the lions.

89.66   And the lions and tigers eat and devoured the greater part of those sheep, and the wild boars eat along with them; and they burnt that tower and demolished that house.

89.67   And I became exceedingly sorrowful over that tower because that house of the sheep was demolished, and afterwards I was unable to see if those sheep entered that house.

89.68   And the shepherds and their associates delivered over those sheep to all the wild beasts, to devour them, and each one of them received in his time a definite number: it was written by the other in a book how many each one of them destroyed of them.

89.69   And each one slew and destroyed many more than was prescribed; and I began to weep and lament on account of those sheep.

89.70   And thus in the vision I saw that one who wrote, how he wrote down every one that was destroyed by those shepherds, day by day, and carried up and laid down and showed actually the whole book to the Lord of the sheep (even) everything that they had done, and all that each one of them had made away with, and all that they had given over to destruction.

89.71   And the book was read before the Lord of the sheep, and He took the book from his hand and read it and sealed it and laid it down.

89.72   And forthwith I saw how the shepherds pastured for twelve hours, and behold three of those sheep turned back and came and entered and began to build up all that had fallen down of that house; but the wild boars tried to hinder them, but they were not able.

89.73 And they began again to build as before, and they reared up that tower, and it was named the high tower; and they began again to place a table before the tower, but all the bread on it was polluted and not pure.

89.74 And as touching all this the eyes of those sheep were blinded so that they saw not, and [the eyes of] their shepherds likewise; and they delivered them in large numbers to their shepherds for destruction, and they trampled the sheep with their feet and devoured them.

89.75 And the Lord of the sheep remained unmoved till all the sheep were dispersed over the field and mingled with them [i.e. the beasts], and they [i.e. the shepherds] did not save them out of the hand of the beasts.

89.76 And this one who wrote the book carried it up, and showed it and read it before the Lord of the sheep, and implored Him on their account, and besought Him on their account as he showed Him all the doings of the shepherds, and gave testimony before Him against all the shepherds.

89.77 And he took the actual book and laid it down beside Him and departed.

Chapter 90

90.01 And I saw till that in this manner thirty-five shepherds undertook the pasturing [of the sheep], and they severally completed their periods as did the first; and others received them into their hands, to pasture them for their period, each shepherd in his own period.

90.02 And after that I saw in my vision all the birds of heaven coming, the eagles, the vultures, the kites, the ravens; but the eagles led all the birds; and they began to devour those sheep, and to pick out their eyes and to devour their flesh.

90.03 And the sheep cried out because their flesh was being devoured by the birds, and as for me I looked and lamented in my sleep over that shepherd who pastured the sheep.

90.04 And I saw until those sheep were devoured by the dogs and eagles and kites, and they left neither flesh nor skin nor sinew remaining on them till only their bones stood there: and their bones too fell to the earth and the sheep became few.

90.05   And I saw until that twenty-three had undertaken the pasturing and completed in their several periods fifty-eight times.

90.06   But behold lambs were borne by those white sheep, and they began to open their eyes and to see, and to cry to the sheep.

90.07   Yea, they cried to them, but they did not hearken to what they said to them, but were exceedingly deaf, and their eyes were very exceedingly blinded.

90.08   And I saw in the vision how the ravens flew upon those lambs and took one of those lambs, and dashed the sheep in pieces and devoured them.

90.09   And I saw till horns grew upon those lambs, and the ravens cast down their horns; and I saw till there sprouted a great horn of one of those sheep, and their eyes were opened.

90.10   And it looked at them [and their eyes opened], and it cried to the sheep, and the rams saw it and all ran to it.

90.11   And notwithstanding all this those eagles and vultures and ravens and kites still kept tearing the sheep and swooping down upon them and devouring them: still the sheep remained silent, but the rams lamented and cried out.

90.12   And those ravens fought and battled with it and sought to lay low its horn, but they had no power over it.

90.13   And I saw till the shepherds and eagles and those vultures and kites came, and they cried to the ravens that they should break the horn of that ram, and they battled and fought with it, and it battled with them and cried that its help might come.

90.14   And I saw till that man, who wrote down the names of the shepherds [and] carried up into the presence of the Lord of the sheep [came and helped it and showed it everything: he had come down for the help of that ram].

90.15   And I saw till the Lord of the sheep came unto them in wrath, and all who saw Him fled, and they all fell into His shadow from before His face.

90.16   All the eagles and vultures and ravens and kites, gathered together and brought with them all the wild sheep, and they all came together and helped one another in order to dash that horn of the ram in pieces.

90.17   And I looked at that man, who wrote the book at the command of the Lord, until he opened that book of the destruction that those last twelve shepherds had wrought. And he showed, in front of the Lord of the sheep, that they had destroyed even more than those before them had.

90.18   And I looked until the Lord of the sheep came to them and took the Staff of His Anger and struck the Earth. And the Earth was split. And all the animals, and the birds of the sky, fell from those sheep and sank in the earth; and it closed over them.

90.19   And I saw till a great sword was given to the sheep, and the sheep proceeded against all the wild beasts of the field to slay them, and all the beasts and the birds of the heaven fled before their face.

90.20   And I saw till a throne was erected in the pleasant land, and the Lord of the sheep sat Himself thereon, and the other took the sealed books and opened those books before the Lord of the sheep.

90.21   And the Lord called those men the seven first white ones, and commanded that they should bring before Him, beginning with the first star which led the way, all the stars whose privy members and were like those of horses, and they brought them all before Him.

90.22   And He said to that man who wrote before Him, being one of those seven white ones, and said unto him: 'Take those seventy shepherds to whom I delivered the sheep, and who taking them on their own authority slew more than I commanded them.'

90.23   And behold they were all bound, I saw, and they all stood before Him.

90.24   And the judgement was held first over the stars, and they were judged and found guilty, and went to the place of condemnation, and they were cast into an abyss, full of fire and flaming, and full of pillars of fire.

90.25   And those seventy shepherds were judged and found guilty, and they were cast into that fiery abyss.

90.26   And I saw at that time how a like abyss was opened in the midst of the earth, full of fire, and they brought those blinded sheep, and they were all judged and found guilty and cast into this fiery abyss, and they burned; now this abyss was to the right of that house.

90.27   And I saw those sheep burning and their bones burning.

90.28   And I stood up to see till they folded up that old house; and carried off all the pillars, and all the beams and ornaments of the house were at the same time folded up with it, and they carried it off and laid it in a place in the south of the land.

90.29   And I saw till the Lord of the sheep brought a new house greater and loftier than that first, and set it up in the place of the first which had been folded up: all its pillars were new, and its ornaments were new and larger than those of the first, the old one which He had taken away, and all the sheep were within it.

90.30   And I saw all the sheep which had been left, and all the beasts on the earth, and all the birds of the heaven, falling down and doing homage to those sheep and making petition to and obeying them in everything.

90.31   And thereafter those three who were clothed in white and had seized me by my hand [who had taken me up before], and the hand of that ram also seizing hold of me, they took me up and set me down in the midst of those sheep before the judgement took place.

90.32   And those sheep were all white, and their wool was abundant and clean.

90.33   And all that had been destroyed and dispersed, and all the beasts of the field, and all the birds of the heaven, assembled in that house, and the Lord of the sheep rejoiced with great joy because they were all good and had returned to His house.

90.34   And I saw till they laid down that sword, which had been given to the sheep, and they brought it back into the house, and it was sealed before the presence of the Lord, and all the sheep were invited into that house, but it held them not.

90.35   And the eyes of them all were opened, and they saw the good, and there was not one among them that did not see.

90.36   And I saw that that house was large and broad and very full.

90.37   And I saw that a white bull was born, with large horns, and all the beasts of the field and all the birds of the air feared him and made petition to him all the time.

90.38   And I saw till all their generations were transformed, and they all became white bulls; and the first among them became a lamb, and that lamb became a great animal and had great black horns on its head; and the Lord of the sheep rejoiced over it and over all the oxen.

90.39   And I slept in their midst: and I awoke and saw everything.

90.40   This is the vision which I saw while I slept, and I awoke and blessed the Lord of righteousness and gave Him glory.

90.41   Then I wept with a great weeping and my tears stayed not till I could no longer endure it: when I saw, they flowed on account of what I had seen; for everything shall come and be fulfilled, and all the deeds of men in their order were shown to me.

90.42   On that night I remembered the first dream, and because of it I wept and was troubled because I had seen that vision

Appendix B

This information is provided to help guide your understanding of how the esoteric symbolism is rooted in the Bible and persevered by various esoteric groups like the Freemasons. It should be noted that not all Freemasons nor their Lodges will agree with this selection of Bible verses for each title.

The regular work in any grand Jurisdiction offers ample evidence of the importance of the two dominant themes, the Bible and King Solomon's Temple, in present-day Freemasonry. Their intimate relationship is best illustrated by the selected Masonic scriptural references which follow.

The references are classified under appropriate headings which are thought to be sufficiently explanatory without being in violation of the Masonic obligation to secrecy. The topics are arranged for convenience of reference in the order of the ritual. (Dr. John Wesley Kelchner, 1924)

OPENING AND CLOSING THE LODGE
CEREMONY
Numbers 9: 3

THE TILER
Genesis 3: 24 - Numbers 22: 31 - Psalm 84; 9-10.
See also; Joshua 5: 13-15 - 1 Chronicles 21: 14-19 - Nehemiah 7: 1-3

CONSECRATION
Exodus 32: 29
See also; Exodus 28: 3 - Exodus 28: 29 - Numbers 8: 5-7 - Leviticus 8: 1-12

THE VISITOR
Leviticus 19: 33, 34 - Hebrews 13: 2

THE FIRST MASTER CRAFTSMAN
Genesis 4: 22

CONFUSION IN THE CRAFT
Job 1: 6-12 - Joshua 7: 13-15 - Matthew 22: 11-14
See also; Job 2: 1-6 - Leviticus 10: 8-11

SELF-SUPPORT
1 Timothy 5: 8

WIDOWS AND ORPHANS
Psalm 68: 5 - Isaiah 1: 16, 17 - Psalm 82; 3, 4
See also; James 1: 27 - Exodus 22: 22-24 - Leviticus 23: 22 - Deuteronomy 10:
18-19 - Deuteronomy 24: 17-22 - Psalm 146: 5-9

GLORY AND BEAUTY OF THE DAY
Psalm 19: 1-6

THE DAILY WAGE
Deuteronomy 24: 14, 15 - 1 Kings 5: 10-12
See also; Matthew 20: 1-16

THE LODGE
Matthew 18: 15-20

BEFORE THE THRONE
Isaiah 6: 1-4

DEW OF HERMON
Psalm 133: 1-4

LABOR AND REFRESHMENT
Isaiah 28: 12 - Proverbs 14: 23.
See also; Proverbs 13: 11 - Psalm 104: 23 - 1 Thessalonians 1: 3 - Deuteronomy
5: 13 - 1 Corinthians 3: 9 - Exodus 31: 17 - Acts 3: 19

THE PREPARATION ROOM FOR THE CANDIDATE
Leviticus 21: 16-24 - Leviticus 22: 19-25
See also; Deuteronomy 23: 1, 2

THE FORBIDDEN KNOWLEDGE OF ENOCH

CLOTHING
Leviticus 8: 1-11
See also; Exodus 28: 39 - Ruth 4: 7

FATHERHOOD OF GOD
Genesis 1: 26-28 - Genesis 2: 7 - Genesis 5: 1-2 - Genesis 9: 6-8
See also; Deuteronomy 32: 6 - Job 12: 9, 10 - Isaiah 64: 8 - Malachi 2: 10 -
Ephesians 4: 4-7

CABLE TOW
Hosea 11: 4

RACES OF MEN
Acts 10: 9-35

LEVEL OF EQUALITY
Exodus 30: 11-16 - Deuteronomy 1: 16, 17 - Proverbs 22: 2 - 1 Samuel 16: 7 -
Romans 2:11
See also; Deuteronomy 16: 18-20 - 1 Samuel 2: 8 - 2 Chronicles 19: 5-9 - Job 3:
11-19 - Job 13: 7-10 - Job 34: 17-19 - Proverbs 28: 21 - James 2: 1-9

CHILDLIKE ATTITUDE
Luke 18: 15-18 - Mark 10: 13-16
See also; Matthew 10: 40-42 - Matthew 19: 13-15 - Mark 3: 33-37

INITIATION: FIRST DEGREE
FIRST SECTION

FROM DARKNESS TO LIGHT
Revelation 3: 14-18 - Matthew 14: 10-20
See also; 2 Samuel 22: 29 - Matthew 12: 22 - Mark 10: 46-52 - Matthew 23: 13-
19 - John 8: 12 - 2 Peter 1: 1-9 - Mark 8: 22-26

THE AID OF THE DEITY
Genesis 32: 24-32 - 1 Chronicles 29: 19 - 1 Kings 3: 9 - Matthew 6: 5-16 -
Matthew 21: 22
See also; Mark 11: 22-26 - Revelation 8: 24

UNITY
Psalm 133: 1-3
See also; Exodus 30: 22-33

TRUST IN GOD
Psalm 56: 11-13 - Proverbs 3: 5, 6 - Isaiah 26: 3-5
See also; Deuteronomy 31: 6 - Deuteronomy 33: 27 - 2 Samuel 22: 2, 3 - Psalm 31: 1-3 - Psalm 28: 7 - Psalm 37: 1-5 - Psalm 91: 1-16 - Psalm 121: 1-8 - Jeremiah 17: 7, 8 - Psalm 23: 1-6

THE ALTAR
Genesis 8: 20-22 - Genesis 12: 7 - Genesis 22: 1, 2 - Genesis 23: 9 - Genesis 26: 24, 25 - Exodus 24: 4 - Exodus 30: 10 - 2 Samuel 24: 21 - 2 Chronicles 8: 12
See also; Genesis 4: 1-15 - Genesis 13: 18 - Genesis 26: 24, 25 - Exodus 27: 1-8 - Exodus 37: 25-28 - Exodus 30: 1-10 - Exodus 38: 1-7 - 1 Samuel 14: 35 - Judges 6: 24-27 - 1 Chronicles 6: 49, 50 - Ezra 3: 1-6

THE OBLIGATION
Genesis 24: 3 - Numbers 30: 2 - Deuteronomy 23: 21 - Isaiah 65: 16 - Hebrews 6: 13-16 - Leviticus 19: 12
See also; Matthew 5: 33-37 - James 5: 12 - Revelation 10: 5, 6 - Hebrews 5: 16

LIGHT
Genesis 1: 1-3 - Exodus 13: 20-22 - Isaiah 60: 19
See also; Isaiah 30: 26 - Luke 11: 34-36 - John 8: 12 - John 9: 4, 5

THE MASTER
Genesis 1: 14-18 - Jeremiah 31: 33-37 - Samuel 23: 3, 4
See also; Numbers 27: 15-17 - Ecclesiastes 1: 5 - 1 Corinthians 15: 40, 41 - Psalm 50: 1 - Psalm 136: 5-9 - Ezekiel 34: 1-10 - Matthew 20: 25-29

THE LIGHT OF LIFE
Psalm 119: 105

THE PEARLY GATES
Revelation 21: 21

THE CLODS OF THE VALLEY
Job 21: 33

THE GREAT WHITE THRONE
Revelation 20: 11-15

THE FAITHFUL SERVANT
Matthew 25: 14-30

UNTEMPERED MORTAR
Ezekiel 13: 10-16 - Ezekiel 22: 28

THE POOR
Psalm 41: 1-4 - Isaiah 58: 6, 7 - Matthew 25: 31-46 - James 2: 14-17
See also; Job 31: 13-22 - Psalm 72: 12-14 - Psalm 109: 31 - Proverbs 14: 31, 32
- Isaiah 3: 15 - Ezekiel 18: 4-9 - Ezekiel 18: 16, 17 - Mark 12: 41-44 - Luke 21:
1-4

THE HOUSE NOT MADE WITH HANDS
2 Corinthians 5: 1-4 - 2 Corinthians 6: 16-18 - 1 Peter 2: 1-8
See also; John 2: 18-22 - 1 Corinthians 3: 10-20

THE NORTHWEST CORNER
Isaiah 30: 18-21 - Matthew 7: 13, 14

ACCEPTED
1 Samuel 18: 5

THE NEW NAME
Revelation 2: 17 - Proverbs 10: 19 - Proverbs 11: 12
See also; Proverbs 17: 28

DISTRESSED WORTHY BROTHER
Genesis 4: 9, 10 - Ecclesiastes 4: 9-12 - Matthew 6: 1-4 - Galatians 6: 1, 2 -
Hebrews 13: 1-3

FIRST DEGREE: SECOND SECTION

FIRST PREPARATION
1 Samuel 16: 7 - Proverbs 16: 1 - Kings 8: 39, 40 - Kings 8: 61 - 2 Chronicles 30: 17-19
See also; Jeremiah 17: 9, 10 - Psalm 51: 5-7 - Matthew 12: 35, 36 - Matthew 15: 17-20 - Mark 7: 14, 15 - Psalm 141: 3, 4

TESTIMONY
Ruth 4: 1-12

THE INNER DOOR
Jeremiah 29: 10-14 - Matthew 7: 7, 8
See also; Luke 11: 9, 10 - Revelation 3: 20

THE ATHEIST
Psalm 53: 1 - Proverbs 1: 7

THE CORNERSTONE
Isaiah 28: 16, 17 - Psalm 118: 22-24
See also; Matthew 21: 42 - Mark 12: 10, 11 - Luke 20: 17, 18

EMBLEM OF INNOCENCE
Proverbs 27: 26 - Isaiah 53: 4-9 - John 1: 35, 36
See also; Isaiah 65: 25 - John 21: 15 - Luke 10: 1-12

HILLS AND VALLEYS
Ezekiel 43: 12 - 1 Kings 14: 22, 23
See also; 2 Kings 17: 9-12 (and many similar passages) - Luke 22: 7-18 - Acts 20: 7-12 - Mark 14: 12-17

UNIVERSAL CHARITY
Luke 10: 30-37

THE PILLAR OF WISDOM
Proverbs 9: 1-6 - Proverbs 8: 1-36 - Job 28: 12-28 - Ecclesiastes 12: 13, 14 - James 2: 5-8
See also; Proverbs 9: 9, 10 - Proverbs 4: 5-7

JACOB'S LADDER
Genesis 28: 10-22

CHARITY
1 Corinthians 13: 1-13

THE NORTH SIDE
Isaiah 14: 12-23
See also; Psalm 48: 1-3

THE TABERNACLE
Exodus 25: 1-9 - Exodus 26: 30 - Exodus 40: 1-38
See also; Exodus 31: 1-11 - Exodus 35: 30-35 - Numbers 9: 15-20 - Hebrews 9: 1-12

BROTHERLY LOVE
2 Thessalonians 3: 15 - 1 Samuel 20: 16, 17 - Proverbs 18: 23, 24 - Hebrews 13: 1 - 1 John 2: 9-11 - 1 John 4: 19-21

ST. JOHN THE BAPIST
Matthew 4: 1-10
See also; Matthew 3: 11-17 - Luke 1: 5-25 - Acts 13: 24, 25 - Luke 1: 57-80 - John 1: 15-18

ST. JOHN THE EVANGELIST
Revelation 1: 9-20
See also; Matthew 4: 18-22 - Acts 8: 14-17 - Galatians 2: 1-10 - Revelation 1: 1-3

FORTITUDE
Daniel 3: 1-30 - Daniel 6: 1-28

THE CHARGE
Numbers 27: 22, 23

COVERING
Job 22: 14

LIGHTS
Genesis 1: 16
See also; Psalm 89: 37 - Psalm 104: 19

THE GOLDEN RULE
Luke 6: 27-38
See also; Matthew 7: 9-12

THE GREAT AND SACRED NAME
Exodus 20: 7
See also; Matthew 5: 33-37 - Matthew 26: 68-75 - Matthew 15: 1-6 - Deuteronomy 5: 11

THE MASON AS CITIZEN
Matthew 22: 17-22 - Romans 13: 1-7
See also; Mark 12: 13-17 - Luke 20: 19-26 - Ephesians 6: 5-9

PASSING: SECOND DEGREE
FIRST SECTION

THE PLUMBLINE
Amos 7: 7-9
See also; Isaiah 28: 17

THE PRECIOUS JEWELS
Nehemiah 1: 6 - Proverbs 12: 18
See also; Job 37: 2 - Psalm 130: 2 - Luke 19: 48

THE VALLEY OF JEHOSHAPHAT
Joel 3: 2, 12

SECOND DEGREE: SECOND SECTION
MIDDLE CHAMBER LECTURE

WORKS OF CREATION
Psalm 19: 1-14 - Psalm 8: 1-9
See also; Job 38: 1-41 - Job 39: 1-30 - Psalm 33: 6, 7 - Psalm 104: 1-10 - Psalm 139: 7-12 - Isaiah 45: 12, 18

THE SABBATH
Genesis 1: 31 - Genesis 2: 1-3 - Exodus 20: 8-11 - Leviticus 23: 3 - Ezekiel 20: 19, 20
See also; Exodus 23: 12 - Exodus 35: 1-3 - Exodus 31: 12-17 - Numbers 28: 25 - Nehemiah 13: 15-19 - Isaiah 58: 13, 14 - Jeremiah 17: 21-27 - Ezekiel 20: 10-12

THE CRAFTSMEN
2 Chronicles 2: 1 - 2, Acts 18: 3, Acts 19: 25
See also; 2 Chronicles 2: 17, 18 - 1 Kings 5: 13-18

WAGES OF FELLOWCRAFT
2 Chronicles 2: 1-18
See also; Numbers 18: 12, 13 - Deuteronomy 7: 13 - Psalm 104: 15 - Jeremiah 31: 12 - Joel 2: 18-20, Micah 4: 3-7 - Matthew 20: 1-16

PEACE ON EARTH
Luke 2: 1-20

THE PORCH
1 Kings 6: 3, 4

THE THREE CHAMBERS
1 Kings 6: 5, 6

THE WINDING STAIRS
1 Kings 6: 8-10

THE PILLARS
1 Kings 7: 13-22 - 2 Chronicles 3: 15-17

See also; Exodus 38: 28 - Deuteronomy 27: 2, 3 - 2 Kings 23: 3 – Jeremiah 27: 19-22 – Jeremiah 52: 17-24

DESTRUCTION OF THE TEMPLE
1 Chronicles 22: 5 – 1 Kings 9: 7-9
See also; 2 Chronicles 7: 19-22 – Mark 13: 1, 2 – Luke 19: 41-44 – Luke 21: 5, 6

THE SPIRITUAL TEMPLE
Psalm 127: 1 – Hebrews 3: 3, 4 – Hebrews 11: 8-10 – Psalm 15: 1, 2 – Proverbs 24: 3-5 – Zechariah 6: 15 – Matthew 7: 24-25
See also; Psalm 24: 1-4 – Psalm 26: 8-12 – Psalm 27: 4

THE CLAY GROUND
1 Kings 7: 40-46 – 2 Chronicles 4: 1-22

THE HUMAN SENSE
Exodus 4: 11

THE FORDS OF THE JORDAN
Judges 10: 15-18 – Judges 11: 4-10 – Judges 12: 1-7
See also; 2 Chronicles 20:1 – 2 Chronicles 25: 7-10 – Judges 8: 1-3 – 2 Chronicles 20: 20-25

THE LETTER G
Exodus 3: 13-15 – Deuteronomy 4: 39 – Deuteronomy 6: 4, 5 – Revelation 1: 8
See also; Deuteronomy 32: 39, 40 – Psalm 90: 1, 2

REVERENCE TO GOD
Isaiah 45: 22, 23 – Romans 14: 11, 12

RAISING: THIRD DEGREE
FIRST SECTION

DUST TO DUST
Ecclesiastes 12: 1-7

CONTENTION AMONG BRETHERN
Matthew 5: 23, 24 – Matthew 18: 15-17 – Luke 17: 3, 4 – 1 Corinthians 12: 14-31 – Mark 3: 20-26
See also; Matthew 18: 21, 22 – 1 Corinthians 6: 1-8 – James 5: 13-16 – James 4: 11 – Proverbs 6: 16-19

THIRD DEGREE: SECOND SECTION

RUBISH OF THE TEMPLE
Nehemiah 4: 10
See also; Nehemiah 4: 2

TROUBLES OF LIFE
Job 5: 1-7 – Job 14: 1, 2 – Ecclesiastes 8: 22, 23

PRAYER
2 Samuel 22: 7 – Psalm 55: 16 – Psalm 86: 7 – Psalm 141: 1
See also; Isaiah 40: 28-31

EMBLEMS OF INNOCENCE
Isaiah 1: 16-18 – Mark 9: 1-9 – Revelation 7: 13-17

SPRIG OF ACACIA
Ezekiel 27: 19
See also; Exodus 30: 24 – Psalm 45: 8

FLIGHT TO JOPPA
Jonah 1: 1-3

THE CLEFTS OF THE ROCKS
Isaiah 2: 21 – Obadiah 3, 4

THE JEWEL
Exodus 28: 36-38 – Exodus 39: 30, 31

THE WORD
Deuteronomy 8: 3-6 – Deuteronomy 30: 11-14 – Isaiah 55: 8-11 – John 1: 1-5
See also; Hebrews 4: 12

THE INTERMENT
Luke 23: 50-56
See also; Mark 15: 42-47

THE HAILING SIGN
1 Kings 20: 31-34

THIRD DEGREE: THIRD SECTION
HISTORICAL LECTURE

DAVID'S PLANS FOR THE TEMPLE
1 Chronicles 14: 1, 2 – 1 Chronicles 22: 1-19 – 1 Kings 2: 10-12 – 2 Chronicles 6: 14-15
See also; 2 Chronicles 6: 16-42 – 1 Chronicles 28: 1-21 – 1 Chronicles 29: 1-5

GOD'S PROMISE TO DAVID
1 Chronicles 11: 4-9 – 2 Samuel 7: 1-29
See also: 1 Chronicles 17: 1-15

BEGINNING OF THE TEMPLE
2 Chronicles 3: 1-17

THE MASTER BUILDER
2 Chronicles 2: 3-18
See also; 1 Kings 5: 1-18 – 1 Kings 6: 1-22 – 2 Chronicles 5: 1-14 – 2 Chronicles 7: 1-3

BUILDING THE TEMPLE
1 Chronicles 22: 1, 2 – 1 Kings 5: 8, 9 – 2 Chronicles 2: 16
See also; Ezra 3: 6, 7

WISDOM OF SOLOMON
1 Chronicles 29: 16-23 – 2 Chronicles 1: 7-12 – 1 Kings 3: 5-15

METAL TOOLS
Deuteronomy 27: 5-8 – Exodus 20: 24, 25 – 1 Kings 5: 17, 18 – 1 Kings 6: 7

KING SOLOMON'S LEVY
1 Kings 5: 13-16

THIRD DEGREE: SYMBOLISM

THE GRAVE
Job 21: 23, 34 – Job 21: 13, 14 – Isaiah 14: 4-11
See also; Job 3: 11-26 – Job 7: 1-10 – Job 10: 1-22 – Job 16: 21, 22 – Job 34: 12-15 – Psalm 90: 9, 10 – Ecclesiastes 9: 10

THE SCYTHE
Job 14: 2 – Isaiah 38: 10

THE COMMANDMENTS
Exodus 20: 1-18
See also; Deuteronomy 5: 1-21

ALL-SEEING-EYE
2 Chronicles 16: 9 – Psalm 11: 4 – Psalm 33: 18-19
See also; Zechariah 4: 10 – Job 28: 10 – Psalm 34: 15 – 1 Peter 3: 12

ANCHOR AND ARK
Hebrews 6: 19 – Hebrews 11: 7
See also; 1 Peter 3: 20 – Genesis 6: 15

IMMORTALITY
Job 14: 13-15 – Job 19: 23-27 – Job 33: 23, 24 – Luke 20: 27-38 – 1 Corinthians 15: 1-58
See also; Job 32: 8, 9 – Ecclesiastes 3: 20-22 – John 5: 25 – Hebrews 11: 17-19 – 2 Timothy 1: 6-10 – 1 Timothy 6: 16

ETERNAL LIFE
Matthew 19: 16-22 – John 4: 31-38
See also; John 1: 1-10 – John 5: 1-21 – Romans 5: 21 – Romans 6: 1-23

THE ETERNAL REST
Revelation 11: 19 – Revelation 21: 1-27 – Revelation 22: 1-21

References & Bibliography

Sources for the Book of Enoch:

The Ethiopic Book of Enoch, by M. A. Knibb; Oxford University Press. 1974 - There are many footnotes on the details of the translation and detailed comparisons of the various known manuscripts and fragments of the book.

The Book of Enoch, by R H Charles, SPCK London Published in 1917.

The Book of Enoch the Prophet, by Richard Laurence, Wizards Bookshelf, Published 1821.

Book of Enoch, From The Apocrypha and Pseudepigrapha of the Old Testament by R. H. Charles, vol. II, Oxford Press, 1913. Print

Book of Enoch, New Revised Standard Version (NRSV) Bible: with Apocrypha. New York: Oxford UP, 1989. Print.

Sources for the Bible and Freemasonry:

The Holy Bible – Old and New Testaments, including the 1769 Oxford 'Authorized edition' of the King James Bible and the original 1611 King James Bible.

Masonic Edition Temple – Illustrated. The Holy Bible: The great light in Masonry; Containing the Old and New Testaments; According to the authorized or King James' Version together with Illuminated frontispiece. Presentation and record pages and helps to the Masonic student: Published by the A.J. Holman Co. of Philadelphia, USA, 1924, 1925, 1929, 1930, and 1940.

The Bible and King Solomon's Temple in Masonry, By John Wesley Kelchner, Published by the A.J. Holman Co. of Philadelphia, USA, 1924, 1925, 1929, 1930, and 1940.

All artwork created by, licensed to use, or owned by R.J. VON-BRUENING PUBLISHING, unless noted otherwise.

Chapter 2
http://www.pbs.org/wgbh/nova/neanderthals/mtdna.html

Chapter 5
1. Fig.1 – Created by Author in Microsoft Paint and Adobe Photoshop.
2. Fig.2 – Created by Author in Microsoft Paint and Adobe Photoshop.
3. Fig.3 – Created by Author in Microsoft Paint and Adobe Photoshop.
4. Fig.4 – Created by Author in Microsoft Paint and Adobe Photoshop.

Chapter 6
1. Fig.1 – Original image from the public domain. No known copyright. Unknown artist. Digital recreation, R.J. Von-Bruening Publishing.
2. Ambrose, Stanley H. (1998). "Late Pleistocene human population bottlenecks, volcanic winter, and differentiation of modern humans". Journal of Human Evolution 34 (6): 623–651. doi:10.1006/jhev.1998.0219. PMID 9650103.
3. USA (2002-10-17). "Atlas of the Human Journey - The Genographic Project". Genographic.nationalgeographic.com. Retrieved 2011-11-05 https://genographic.nationalgeographic.com/genographic/lan/en/atlas.html
4. "Cro-Magnon (anthropology) - Britannica Online Encyclopedia", http://www.britannica.com/EBchecked/topic/143532/Cro-Magnon. Britannica.com. Retrieved 2011-11-05
5. "Cro-Magnon", Encyclopedia Britannica.
6. "Cro-Magnon", Encyclopedia Britannica.
7. April 2007, Author: Utilisateur: 120, http://fr.wikipedia.org/wiki/Utilisateur:120, From Wikipedia, the free encyclopedia, http://en.wikipedia.org/wiki/File:Cro-Magnon.jpg, File: Cro-Magnon.jpg.

Chapter 7
1. Fig.1, Original cylinder seal found in Sunrise Magazine Online. The Epic of Gilgamesh: A Spiritual Biography, By W.T.S. Thachara. Digital recreation: R.J. Von-Bruening Publishing.
2. Genesis 10:8 - Authorized or King James' Version
3. Genesis 10:9 - Authorized or King James' Version
4. Genesis 11:4 – Authorized or King James' Version
   Ophiolatreia: Chapter 6, London, 1889
5. Fig.2, Original cylinder seal number AN58779001. The Trustees of the British Museum Department: MiddleEast. Registration number: N.1070. BM/Big number: 89089. Digital recreation: R.J. Von-Bruening Publishing.
6. Fig.3, Original cylinder seal number AN417635001. The Trustees of the British Museum. Department: Middle East. Registration number: 1888, 0310.1. BM/Big number: 89082. Digital recreation: R.J. Von-Bruening Publishing.
7. Fig.4, Original cylinder seal number AN43205200. The Trustees of the British Museum. Department: Middle East. Registration number: 1938,0108.118. BM/Big number: 126064. Additional IDs: MNN 1. Digital recreation: R.J. Von-Bruening Publishing.
8. Fig.5, Original cylinder is at The Morgan Library & Museum, 225 Madison Avenue, New York, NY 10016. Digital recreation: R.J. Von-Bruening Publishing.

Chapter 8
1. Fig.1, Original imprint, made from a cylinder seal found in Mesopotamia during the Akkad Period (circa. 2,334-2,154 BC) Oriental Institute, University of Chicago. Digital recreation by R.J. Von-Bruening Publishing, © 2024 All rights reserved.
2. See Jeremy Black, Gods, Demons, and Symbols of Ancient Mesopotamia: An Illustrated Dictionary, University of Texas Press, in conjunction with the British Museum, (1992): page 168. This is an excellent reference source. Dr. Black is a well-known Sumerian scholar. He was formerly the Director of the British School of Archaeology in Iraq and is now university lecturer in Akkadian and Sumerian at Wolfson College, Oxford.
3. Fig.2, Cylinder seal VA-243 in the Berlin Near Eastern Museum. Digital recreation by R.J. Von-Bruening Publishing, © 2024 All rights reserved.

4. Fig.3, An Akkadian green serpentine cylinder seal, circa. 2,334-2,154 BC. Digital recreation by R.J. Von-Bruening Publishing, © 2024 All rights reserved.
5. Fig.4, Original cylinder seal number AN193452001. The Trustees of the British Museum. Department: Middle East. Registration number: 1945, 1013.22. BM/Big number: 129478. Digital recreation by R.J. Von-Bruening Publishing, © 2024 All rights reserved.
6. Fig.5, The University of Chicago Chronicle, April 15, 2004, Vol. 23, No. 14. Archaeologists review loss of valuable artifacts one year after looting, By William Harms. This modern impression of a cylinder seal from Tell Billa, which shows two cultic scenes involving a boat ride and a procession toward a temple. This artifact is still missing from the Iraqi National Museum collection. The artifact dates to around 3,000 B.C. Digital recreation by R.J. Von-Bruening Publishing, © 2024 All rights reserved.
7. Fig.6, Cylinder seal showing the construction of the "tower." Berlin Museum of Ancient Near East, Frankford, Germany. Digital recreation by R.J. Von-Bruening Publishing, © 2024 All rights reserved.
8. Fig.7, Neo-Assyrian period, modeled style 1989.361.1. In Heilbrunn Timeline of Art History. New York: The Metropolitan Museum of Art, 2000. Digital recreation by R.J. Von-Bruening Publishing, © 2024 All rights reserved.
9. Fig.8, Original cylinder seal number AN432041001. The Trustees of the British Museum. Department: Middle East. Registration number: 1957, 1216.1. BM/Big number: 132257. Digital recreation by R.J. Von-Bruening Publishing, © 2024 All rights reserved.
10. Fig. 9, Original cylinder seal number AN128087001. The Trustees of the British Museum. Department: Middle East. Registration number: 1945,1013.24. BM/Big number: 129480. Additional IDs: Q 24: 81. Digital recreation by R.J. Von-Bruening Publishing, © 2024 All rights reserved.
11. Fig.10, Accession Number: 1991.368.2. The Metropolitan Museum of Art, 1000 Fifth Avenue, New York, New York 10028-0198. Digital recreation by R.J. Von-Bruening Publishing, © 2024 All rights reserved.
12. Fig.11, Seal of chalcedony. Mansell, Phot. 595, Br. Mus. No. 89135. See further Unger in Ebert, RLV XI, 181.; in Eckhard Unger's, Two Seals of the 9th Century BC From Shadikanni on the Habur in BASOR, No. 130, April 1953, p. 16. Digital recreation by R.J. Von-Bruening Publishing, © 2024 All rights reserved.

13. Fig.12, Original cylinder seal at The Morgan Library & Museum, 225 Madison Avenue, New York, NY 10016. Digital recreation by R.J. Von-Bruening Publishing, © 2024 All rights reserved.
14. Fig.13, The British Museum, Department: Middle East. Digital recreation by R.J. Von-Bruening Publishing, © 2024 All rights reserved.
15. Fig. 14, Cylinder seal imprint of a King Standing on Sphinxes and Holding a Lion in Each Hand: Palm Tree with Winged Sun Disk Above. Persia, Achaemenid period. ca.550–330 B.C. Public domain. Digital recreation by R.J. Von-Bruening Publishing, © 2024 All rights reserved.
16. Fig.15, Original cylinder seal at The Morgan Library & Museum, 225 Madison Avenue, New York, NY 10016. Digital recreation by R.J. Von-Bruening Publishing, © 2024 All rights reserved.
17. Fig.16, Accession Number: 1985.192.6. The Metropolitan Museum of Art, 1000 Fifth Avenue, New York, New York 10028-0198. Digital recreation by R.J. Von-Bruening Publishing, © 2024 All rights reserved.
18. Fig.17, Cylinder seal located in the Museum at the Hague. Public Domain. Digital recreation by R.J. Von-Bruening Publishing, © 2024 All rights reserved.
19. Fig.18, Accession Number: 1987.96.11. The Metropolitan Museum of Art, 1000 Fifth Avenue, New York, New York 10028-0198. Digital recreation by R.J. Von-Bruening Publishing, © 2024 All rights reserved.
20. Fig.19, Department of Oriental Antiquities, Richelieu. Ground floor, room 6, case 4Accession number: AO 913. Digital recreation by R.J. Von-Bruening Publishing, © 2024 All rights reserved.
21. Fig.20, Cylinder seal from the Public Domain. Digital recreation by R.J. Von-Bruening Publishing, © 2024 All rights reserved.
22. Fig.21, Frankford Museum of the Ancient Near East, Frankford, Germany. Digital recreation by R.J. Von-Bruening, © 2024 All rights reserved.
23. Fig.22 - First image: Francesca Rochberg: "Astronomy and Calendars in Ancient Mesopotamia, Civilizations of the Ancient Near East", vol. III, pp. 1925-1940, ed., Jack Sasson, 2000. Digital recreation by R.J. Von-Bruening Publishing, © 2024 All rights reserved.
24. Fig.23 – J.N. Tubb, Canaanites pp. 140. Fig. 98: London, The British Museum Press, (1998). Dedicated by Gaius Julius Arish, son of Adon-Baal. This stela comes from a religious precinct known as the tophet at Carthage. Digital recreation by R.J. Von-Bruening Publishing, © 2024 All rights reserved.

25. Fig.24, Accession Number: 1984.383.22. The Metropolitan Museum of Art, 1000 Fifth Avenue, New York, New York 10028-0198. Digital recreation by R.J. Von-Bruening Publishing, © 2024 All rights reserved.

26. Fig.25, Original cylinder seal number AN159750001. The Trustees of the British Museum. Department: Middle East. Registration number: 1825, 0503.135. BM/Big number: 89331. Additional IDs: R.135. Digital recreation by R.J. Von-Bruening Publishing, © 2024 All rights reserved.

27. Fig.26, Cylinder seal imprint showing antelopes attacked by birds, signs of Cypro-Minoan script, hematite, Late Bronze II, maybe 14th century BC. From tomb 1 at Sinda in Cyprus. Public domain. Digital recreation by R.J. Von-Bruening Publishing, © 2024 All rights reserved.

28. Fig.27, Accession Number: 1999.325.65. The Metropolitan Museum of Art, 1000 Fifth Avenue, New York, New York 10028-0198. Digital recreation by R.J. Von-Bruening Publishing, © 2024 All rights reserved.

29. Fig.28, Original cylinder seal number AN678783001. The Trustees of the British Museum. Department: Middle East. Registration number: 1945,1013.82. BM/Big number: 129538. Additional IDs: Qc. 1. Qy.1. Digital recreation by R.J. Von-Bruening Publishing, © 2024 All rights reserved.

30. Fig.29, Original cylinder seal number AN45418001. The Trustees of the British Museum. Department: Middle East. Registration number: 1873, 0723.1. BM/Big number: 89810. Digital recreation by R.J. Von-Bruening Publishing, © 2024 All rights reserved.

31. Fig.30, Original image found at The Myth of a 12th Planet: A Brief Analysis of Cylinder Seal VA 243: By Michael S. Heiser, Ph.D. candidate, Hebrew Bible and Ancient Semitic Languages, University of Wisconsin-Madison. Cylinder seal from the Berlin Museum of Ancient Near East in Frankfort, Germany. Plate XXXIII, seal d. Digital recreation by R.J. Von-Bruening Publishing, © 2024 All rights reserved.

32. Fig.31, Original cylinder seal number AN511538001. The Trustees of the British Museum. Department: Middle East. Registration number: 1925, 0110.20. BM/Big number: 116722. Digital recreation by R.J. Von-Bruening Publishing, © 2024 All rights reserved.

33. Fig.32, Original image found in Odenwald, Sten, Ph.D. (Contributing Author); Bernard Haisch (Topic Editor). 2009. "Sun: Ancient Civilizations." In: Encyclopedia of the Cosmos. Eds. Bernard Haisch and Joakim F. Lindblom (Redwood City, CA: Digital Universe Foundation). [First published November 26, 2007Source: University of Chicago,

Oriental Institute Museum, item A11396. Digital recreation by R.J. Von-Bruening Publishing, © 2024 All rights reserved.

34. Fig. 33, Original image found in Visual Midrash from the TALI Education Fund Collections. Article - Four ways of Creation Author: Jo Milgrom and Yoel Duman. Digital recreation by R.J. Von-Bruening Publishing, © 2024 All rights reserved.

35. Fig.34 – Public domain. Neo-Babylonian cylinder seal, c. 7th - 6th Century BC. Depicting two standing robed figures facing one another, one holding a trident, a reclining goat behind with another robed figure further to right. Digital recreation by R.J. Von-Bruening Publishing, © 2024 All rights reserved.

36. Fig.35 - The Myth of a 12th Planet: A Brief Analysis of Cylinder Seal VA 243: By Michael S. Heiser, Ph.D. candidate, Hebrew Bible and Ancient Semitic Languages, University of Wisconsin-Madison. Cylinder seal from the Berlin Museum of Ancient Near East, Frankfort, Germany. Plate XXXIII, seal b. Digital recreation by R.J. Von-Bruening Publishing, © 2024 All rights reserved.

37. Fig.36 - Art of the ancient world, Art 211, Hitties; General history. Digital recreation by R.J. Von-Bruening Publishing, © 2024 All rights reserved.

38. Fig.37, Original cylinder seal number AN603440001. The Trustees of the British Museum. Department: Middle East. Registration number: 1825, 0503.178. BM/Big number: 89774. Digital recreation by R.J. Von-Bruening Publishing, © 2024 All rights reserved.

39. Fig.38, Original cylinder seal number AN417387001. The Trustees of the British Museum. Department: Middle East. Registration number: 1983, 0101.305. BM/Big number: 89780. Digital recreation by R.J. Von-Bruening Publishing, © 2024 All rights reserved.

40. Fig.39, Original cylinder seal is located at the Oriental Institute, University of Chicago. Public domain. Digital recreation by R.J. Von-Bruening Publishing, © 2024 All rights reserved.

41. Fig.40, Relief of Ashurnasirpal and his Army Attacking an Unnamed City with a Battering Ram, Northwest Palace, Nimrud. The Trustees of the British Museum 2008: Imperialist Networks: Ancient Assyria and the United States. by Reinhard Bernbeck, Freie Universität Berlin and Binghamton University. Digital recreation by R.J. Von-Bruening Publishing, © 2024 All rights reserved.

42. Fig.41, A possible 1st Millennium BC seal showing a worshipper and a fish-garbed sage before a stylized tree with a crescent moon and a winged

disk set above it. Digital recreation by R.J. Von-Bruening Publishing, ©
2024 All rights reserved.

43. Fig.42, Cylinder seal Date: ca. 9th–8th century B.C. Oriental Institute,
University of Chicago. Public domain. Digital recreation by R.J. Von-
Bruening Publishing, © 2024 All rights reserved.
44. Fig.43 - Created by Author, Microsoft Paint and Adobe Photoshop.
45. Fig.44 - Created by Author, Microsoft Paint and Adobe Photoshop.
46. Fig.45 - Created by Author, Microsoft Paint and Adobe Photoshop.
47. Fig.46 - Created by Author, Microsoft Paint and Adobe Photoshop.
48. Fig.47 - Created by Author, Microsoft Paint and Adobe Photoshop.
49. Fig.48 - Created by Author, Microsoft Paint and Adobe Photoshop.
50. Fig.49 - Created by Author, Microsoft Paint and Adobe Photoshop.
51. Fig.50 – Image of the Pleiades star cluster taken by Author with a ten-
inch Meade LXD75 telescope.

Chapter 9

1. Fig.1, Shu-ilishu, cylinder seal. Department des Antiquities Orientales at
Musee du Lavue Paris. Public Domain. Digital recreation by R.J. Von-
Bruening Publishing, © 2024 All rights reserved.
2. Dalton, Rex (2007-05-17). "Archaeology: Blast in the past?" (PDF).
Nature 447 (7142): 256–7. Bibcode 2007Natur.447.256D.
doi:10.1038/447256a. PMID 17507957. News article in Nature.
3. Pinter, N.; Scott, A. C.; Daulton, T. L.; Podoll, A.; Koeberl, C.;
Anderson, R. S.; Ishman, S. E. (2011). "The Younger Dryas impact
hypothesis: A requiem". Earth-Science Reviews.
doi:10.1016/j.earscirev.2011.02.005.
4. Research News, Berkeley Lab; September 23, 2005, News release: by
Dan Krotz, 510-486-4019. Berkeley Lab is a U.S. Department of Energy
national laboratory located in Berkeley, California. It conducts
unclassified scientific research and is managed by the University of
California.
5. Research News, Berkeley Lab; September 23, 2005, News release: by
Dan Krotz
6. Research News, Berkeley Lab; September 23, 2005, News release: by
Dan Krotz
7. Research News, Berkeley Lab; September 23, 2005, News release: by
Dan Krotz
8. Research News, Berkeley Lab; September 23, 2005, News release: by
Dan Krotz

Chapter 10
1. Fig.1, Goddess, Suppliant Goddess, Priest, and Worshiper Carrying Kid Before Sun God with Goddess and Goat Behind; in the field: Star Demonic Mask, Bull, Human Head, Star and Crescent Cylinder seal and impression. Mesopotamia, First Dynasty of Babylon: (ca. 1894–1595 B.C.) The Morgan Library & Museum, 225 Madison Avenue, New York, NY 10016. Digital recreation by R.J. Von-Bruening Publishing, © 2024 All rights reserved.
2. Fig.2, Original cylinder seal number AN164200001. The Trustees of the British Museum. Department: Middle East. Registration number: 1892,1212.2. BM/Big number: 89354. Location: G54/ANAT/3. Digital recreation by R.J. Von-Bruening Publishing, © 2024 All rights reserved.
3. Fig.3, Cylinder seal Date: ca. 20th–19th century B.C. Accession Number: 1991.368.3. The Metropolitan Museum of Art, 1000 Fifth Avenue, New York, New York 10028-0198. Digital recreation by R.J. Von-Bruening Publishing, © 2024 All rights reserved.

Chapter 11
1. THE APOCALYPSE OF THE YEAR 10,000 BC: MYTH OR REALITY? By Dr. Michel-Alain Combes. The Center for Quantavolution was established in 2002 at the University of Bergamo. Dr. Michel-Alain Combes has a doctorate in astronomy from Université Pierre et Marie Curie (Paris VI). Since the early 1970s, he studies "geocruisers," terrestrial impactism and catastrophism of cosmic origins. In 1982, he published LA TERRE BOMBARDEE (version 1), a reference book in the French language. His aim is to effect a juncture between science, myth and history. Since 2001, he keeps up a specialized website: LA MENACE DU CIEL. Asteroid "3446 Combes" was named in his honor in 1992.

Chapter 12
1. Lindgren, Carl Edwin, The way of the Rose Cross; A Historical Perception, 1614–1620. Journal of Religion and Psychical Research: Volume18; Number 3:141-48. 1995.
2. Fig.1, The Temple of the Rosy Cross", Teophilus Schweighardt Constantiens, 1618. Public domain.
3. Fig.2 – A seal impression of a cylinder seal of the Scribe Adda 2,200 BC Public domain. Digital recreation by R.J. Von-Bruening Publishing, © 2024 All rights reserved.

4. Fig.3, Public domain. Painting by Ignaz Unterberger of the initiation ceremony in a Viennese Masonic Lodge during the reign of Joseph II, with Mozart seated on the extreme left. 1784.
5. Fig.4, United States Library of Congress's Prints and Photographs division under the digital ID pga.02812.
6. The Bible and King Solomon's Temple in Masonry, Foreword. by Dr. John Wesley Kelchner (1940)
7. Fig.5 - Temple and Citadel of King Solomon; by Dr. John Wesley Kelchner 1924 The Bible and King Solomon's Temple in Masonry (1940). Digital recreation by R.J. Von-Bruening Publishing, © 2024 All rights reserved.
8. Fig.6 - The Bible and King Solomon's Temple in Masonry, First page of forward, Dr. John Wesley Kelchner, 1924, Plate 19. Digital recreation by R.J. Von-Bruening Publishing, © 2024 All rights reserved.
9. 'Super-Entity' Of 147 Companies Controls 40 Per Cent of World's Economy, Study Claims The Huffington Post Canada, Daniel Tencer First Posted: 10/24/11 01:37 PM ET Updated: 10/24/11 01:50 PM ET.

Chapter 13
1. History of the World, by J.M. Roberts, New York, Oxford University Press, 1993. pp. 65
2. Fig.1 – Created by Author in Microsoft Paint.
3. Fig.2 – Clipart file from the Public Domain. Digital recreation by R.J. Von-Bruening Publishing, © 2024 All rights reserved.
4. Fig.3 - Drawing of an ancient relief of the god Marduk and the dragon mushhushshu, Retrieved from the Public Domain. Digital recreation by R.J. Von-Bruening Publishing, © 2024 All rights reserved.
5. Fig.4 – Original work at Texas Memorial Museum at the University of Texas at Austin, Artist Forrest Kirkland. Digital recreation and illustration by R.J. Von-Bruening Publishing, © 2024 All rights reserved.
6. Fig.5 – Original work at Texas Memorial Museum at the University of Texas at Austin, Artist Forrest Kirkland. Digital recreation and illustration by R.J. Von-Bruening Publishing, © 2024 All rights reserved.
7. Fig.6 –Public Domain. Digital recreation and illustration by R.J. Von-Bruening Publishing, © 2024 All rights reserved.
8. Fig.7 – Original work Texas Memorial Museum at the University of Texas at Austin, Artist Forrest Kirkland. Digital recreation and illustration by R.J. Von-Bruening Publishing, © 2024 All rights reserved.

9. The origin of the Carolina Bays; by Douglas Johnson. Columbia University Press: 1942.
10. Book of Revelations, Chapter 10: 11
11. Book of Revelations, Chapter 11: 12
12. Fig.8 - No known copyright, frontispiece of The Builder Jewel (1741) with Masonic symbols.

Chapter 14
1. The Politics of Experience, By Dr. R.D. Laing. Introduction, pp. 1: Ballantine Books, New York, NY (1967).
2. The Politics of Experience, By Dr. R.D. Laing. Ballantine Books, New York, NY (1967).

Appendix A

The Ethiopic Book of Enoch, by M. A. Knibb; Oxford University Press. 1974 - There are many footnotes on the details of the translation and detailed comparisons of the various known manuscripts and fragments of the book.

The Book of Enoch, by R H Charles, SPCK London Published in 1917.

The Book of Enoch the Prophet, by Richard Laurence, Wizards Bookshelf, Published 1821.

Book of Enoch, From The Apocrypha and Pseudepigrapha of the Old Testament, vol. II, by R. H. Charles, Oxford Press, London, England, Published 1913. Print

Book of Enoch, New Revised Standard Version (NRSV) Bible: with Apocrypha. New York: Oxford UP, 1989. Print.

Appendix B
Masonic Edition Temple – Illustrated. The Holy Bible: The great light in Masonry; Containing the Old and New Testaments; According to the authorized or King James' Version together with Illuminated frontispiece. Presentation and record pages and helps to the Masonic student: Published

by the A.J. Holman Co. of Philadelphia, USA, 1924, 1925, 1929, 1930, and 1940.

The Bible and King Solomon's Temple in Masonry, By John Wesley Kelchner, Published by the A.J. Holman Co. of Philadelphia, USA, 1924, 1925, 1929, 1930, and 1940.